WORLD REVOLUTION

THE PLOT AGAINST CIVILIZATION

BY

NESTA H. WEBSTER

(MRS. ARTHUR WEBSTER)

AUTHOR OF "THE FRENCH REVOLUTION: A STUDY IN DEMOCRACY"
"THE CHEVALIER DE BOUFFLERS," ETC.

SCIRE · QVOD
SCIENDVM

BOSTON
SMALL, MAYNARD & COMPANY
PUBLISHERS

"Si les hommes comprenaient la révolution aujourd'hui, elle finirait demain."

JOSEPH DE MAISTRE in 1811.

" Les personnes qui ignorent la véritable situation des choses, et le nombre en est grand, s'imaginent que les sociétés secrètes ont pour objet l'alliance des peuples contre les rois; c'est une erreur capitale. Les sociétés secrètes sont ennemies des uns et des autres; elles flattent les passions, elles excitent les divisions, les haines, les vengeances; mais c'est à leur profit, ou plutôt à celui de quelques ambitieux qui ne voudraient détrôner les rois que pour mieux opprimer les sujets."

LOMBARD DE LANGRES in 1819.

Printed in the United States of America

AUTHOR'S NOTE

IN reply to numerous enquiries as to whether the statements I made in *The French Revolution* have since been disproved, I take this opportunity to say that, as far as I am aware, no one has attempted to bring forward any contrary evidence. The Socialist press was completely silent, whilst hostile reviewers in the general press contented themselves with saying the work was " biassed," but without quoting chapter and verse in support of this assertion. My book was not intended to be the last word on the French Revolution, but the first attempt, in English, to tell the truth, and had my view on any essential point been shown to be erroneous, I should have been perfectly ready to readjust it in further editions. No such honest challenge was made, however; my opponents preferring the method of creating prejudice against my work by attributing to me views I never expressed. Thus, at the moment of this book going to press, it has been brought to my notice that I am represented as having attacked British Freemasonry. This can only have been said in malice, as I have always clearly differentiated between British and Continental masonry, showing the former to be an honourable association not only hostile to subversive doctrines but a strong supporter of law, order, and religion. (See *The French Revolution*, pp. 20 and 492.) I am in fact indebted to certain distinguished British masons for valuable help and advice in my work, which I here gratefully acknowledge.

FOREWORD

AMONGST all the books, pamphlets, and newspaper articles that are now devoted to the World Revolution through which we are passing, it is strange to notice how little scientific investigation is being brought to bear on the origins of the movement. A frequent explanation advanced, and, I believe, the most fallacious, is that the present unrest must be attributed to " war weariness." Human nature, we are told, exasperated by the protracted horror of the recent international conflict, has become the victim of a *crise de nerfs* which finds its expression in world-wide discontent. In support of this theory we are reminded that former wars have likewise been followed by periods of social disturbance, and that by a process of analogy the symptoms may be expected to subside as the strain of war is relieved, in the same manner as they have subsided hitherto. It is true that political conflicts between nations have frequently in the past been followed by social upheavals — the Napoleonic Wars by industrial troubles in England, the Franco-Prussian War by revolutionary agitation not only in the land of the conquered, but of the conquerors — but to regard these social manifestations as the direct outcome of the preceding international conflict is to mistake contributing for fundamental causes. Revolution is not the product of war, but a malady that a nation suffering from the after-effects of a war is most likely to develop, just as a man enfeebled by fatigue is more liable to contract disease than one who is in a state of perfect vigour.

Yet this predisposing cause is by no means essential to the outbreak of revolutionary fever. The great French Revolution was not immediately preceded by a war of any magnitude, and to the observant mind England in 1914 was as near to revolution as in 1919. The intervening World War, far from producing the explosion in this country, merely retarded it by rallying citizens of all classes around the standard of national defence.

vii

The truth is that for the last one hundred and forty-five years the fire of revolution has smouldered steadily beneath the ancient structure of civilization, and already at moments has burst out into flame threatening to destroy to its very foundations that social edifice which eighteen centuries have been spent in constructing. The crisis of today is then no development of modern times, but a mere continuation of the immense movement that began in the middle of the eighteenth century. In a word, it is all one and the same revolution — the revolution that found its first expression in France of 1789. Both in its nature and its aims it differs entirely from former revolutions which had for their origin some localized or temporary cause. The revolution through which we are now passing is not local but universal, it is not political but social, and its causes must be sought not in popular discontent, but in a deep-laid conspiracy that uses the people to their own undoing.

In order to follow its course we must realize the dual nature of the movement by studying concurrently the outward revolutionary forces of Socialism, Anarchism, etc., and the hidden power behind them as indicated in the chart accompanying this work. The present writer believes that hitherto no book has been written on precisely these lines; many valuable works have been devoted to secret societies, others to the surface history of revolution, but none so far has attempted to trace the connection between the two in the form of a continuous narrative. The object of this book is therefore to describe not only the evolution of Socialist and Anarchist ideas and their effects in succeeding revolutionary outbreaks, but at the same time to follow the workings of that occult force, terrible, unchanging, relentless, and wholly destructive, which constitutes the greatest menace that has ever confronted the human race.

Parts of Chapters I and III appeared in *The Nineteenth Century and After*, and certain later passages in *The Morning Post*.

CONTENTS

CHAPTER I

CHAPTER II

CHAPTER III

CHAPTER IV

ix

CHAPTER X

CHAPTER I

ILLUMINISM

The Philosophers — Rousseau — Secret Societies — Freemasonry — Adam Weishaupt — The Illuminati — Congress of Wilhelmsbad — Illuminati suppressed.

IT is a commonly accepted opinion that the great revolutionary movement which began at the end of the eighteenth century originated with the philosophers of France, particularly with Rousseau. This is only to state half the case; Rousseau was not the originator of his doctrines, and if we were to seek the cause of revolution in mere philosophy it would be necessary to go a great deal further back than Rousseau — to Mably, to the *Utopia* of Thomas More, and even to Pythagoras and Plato.

At the same time it is undoubtedly true that Rousseau was the principal medium through which the doctrines of these earlier philosophers were brought home to the intelligentzia of eighteenth century France, and that his *Contrat Social* and *Discours sur l'origine de l'inégalité parmi les hommes* contained the germs of modern Socialism in all its forms. The theory of Rousseau that has the most important bearing on the theme of this book might be expressed in the colloquial phrase that "Civilization is all wrong" and that salvation for the human race lies in a return to nature. According to Rousseau, civilization had proved the bane of humanity; in his primitive state Man was free and happy, only under the paralysing influence of social restraints had his liberty been curtailed, whilst to the laws of property alone was due the fact that a large proportion of mankind had fallen into servitude. "The first man who bethought himself of saying 'This is mine,' and found

1

people simple enough to believe him was the real founder of civil society. What crimes, what wars, what murders, what miseries and horrors would he have spared the human race who, snatching away the spades and filling in the ditches, had cried out to his fellows: 'Beware of listening to this impostor; you are lost if you forget that the fruits of the earth belong to all and the earth to no one.' "[1] In these words the whole principle of Communism is to be found.

There is a certain substratum of truth in Rousseau's indictment of civilization — a substratum common to all dangerous errors. For if there were no truth at the bottom of false philosophies they would obtain no credence, and thus could never constitute a menace to the world. Rousseau's gigantic error was to argue that because there are certain evils attendant on civilization therefore civilization is wrong from the beginning. As well might one point to a neglected patch in a garden and say: "See the results of cultivation!" In order to remedy the evils of the existing social system more civilization, not less, is needed. Civilization in its higher aspects, not in the mere acquisition of the physical amenities of life, or even of artistic and scientific knowledge, but in the sphere of *moral aspiration* is all that separates Man from the brute. Destroy civilization in its entirety and the human race sinks to the level of the jungle in which the only law is that of the strong over the weak, the only incentive the struggle for material needs. For although Rousseau's injunction, "Go back into the woods and become men!" may be excellent advice if interpreted as a temporary measure, "go back into the woods and remain there" is a counsel for anthropoid apes.

It would be idle, however, to refute the folly of Rousseau's theories, to show that in Nature Communism does not exist, that the first creature to establish the law of property was not man staking out his claim, but the first bird appropriating the branch of a tree whereon to build its nest, the first rabbit selecting the spot wherein to burrow out his hole — a right that no other bird or rabbit has ever dreamt of disputing.

[1] *Discours sur l'inégalité des conditions.*

As to the distribution of the "fruits of the earth" one has only to watch two thrushes on the lawn disputing over a worm to see how the question of food supply is settled in primitive society. Nothing could be more absurd than Rousseau's conception of ideal barbarians living together on the principle of "Do as you would be done by"; only a dreamer utterly unacquainted with the real conditions of primitive life — the life of rule by the strongest, of pitiless preying on the weak and helpless — could have conjured up such a vision.[1]

Even eighteenth-century France, with all its avidity for novelty and its dreams of "a return to Nature," never regarded the primitive Utopia of Rousseau in the light of an attainable ideal, and it is as inconceivable that the philosophy of the *Discours sur l'inégalité* should have led to the attempt to overthrow civilization in 1793 as that the mockeries of Voltaire should have led to the Feasts of Reason and the desecration of the churches. The teaching of Rousseau never reached the people to any appreciable extent, his influence was confined to the aristocracy and *bourgeoisie*, and it was certainly not the hyper-civilized *habitués* of the salons nor the prosperous *bourgeois* of the provinces, nor indeed was it Rousseau himself, living on the bounty of the most dissolute amongst the rich and sharing their vices, who would have welcomed a return to aboriginal conditions of life.

The salons toyed with the philosophy of Rousseau as they toyed with any new thing — Mesmerism, Martinism, Magic — whilst the disgruntled members of the middle class who took him seriously used his theories merely as a lever for stirring up hatred against the class by which they believed themselves to be slighted, and never dreamt of emulating the Caribbean savages held up to their admiration by the exponent of primitive equality.

[1] On the Indian frontier, where still to-day no laws exist, the inhabitants are obliged to resort to the plan of building towers reached only by ladders wherein to sleep at night, and by ascending into these refuges and pulling the ladders up after them they are able to slumber in comparative security from assassination. Equality of wealth is maintained by the same primitive methods. "How do you prevent any one getting too rich?" a British general inquired of an inhabitant of the Swat Valley, where a rudimentary form of Communism is carried out. "We cut his throat," was the brief reply.

It is not then to the philosophers, but to the source whence they drew many of their inspirations, that the great dynamic force of the Revolution must be attributed. Rousseau and Voltaire were Freemasons; the *Encyclopédie* was published under the auspices of the same order.[1] Without this powerful aid the drawing-room doctrinaires of the eighteenth century could no more have brought about the mighty cataclysm of 1789 than could the Fabian Society have produced the world revolution of to-day. The organization of the Secret Societies was needed to transform the theorizings of the philosophers into a concrete and formidable system for the destruction of civilization.

In order to trace the origins of these sects it would be necessary to go back quite six centuries before the first French Revolution. As early as 1185 an order had been formed, calling itself the " Confrérerie de la Paix," with the main object of putting an end to wars, but also with the idea of establishing community of land. In their attacks on the nobles and clergy, the Confrères thus expressed their belief in the system now known as nationalization: " By what right do they invade the goods that should be common to all such as the meadows, the woods, the game that runs about the fields and forests, the fish that people the rivers and the ponds, gifts that Nature destines equally to all her children? " Accordingly the Confrères set out to destroy the châteaux and monasteries, but the nobles arming themselves in self-defence ended by destroying the " Confrérerie." [2]

It will be seen, therefore, that Rousseau in attacking the rights of property was proclaiming a doctrine that had not only been preached but which it had actually been attempted to put into practice in France 600 years earlier.

The fact that the Confrères of the twelfth century had been thus summarily suppressed did not prevent the formation of further subversive sects; early in the following century came the Albigeois professing much the same

[1] *Martinès de Pasqually*, by Papus, President of the Supreme Council of the Martiniste Order (1895), p. 146.

[2] *Recherches politiques et historiques*, by the Chevalier de Malet (1817), p. 17.

doctrines; in 1250 a Hungarian ex-priest named Jacobi organized a crusade against the priests and nobles, and at about the same date the order of the Templars was founded in Jerusalem by certain *gentilshommes* of Picardy during the Crusades. On their return to France the Knights Templars instituted themselves as a power independent of the Monarchy, and under their Grand Master, Jacques du Molay, rose against the authority of the King, Philippe le Bel. In 1312 several of their number were arrested and accused, amongst other things, of spitting on the crucifix and of denying the Christ. In the course of their cross-examination they declared that they had not been fully initiated into the Statutes of the Order, and that they suspected " that there were two sorts, some that were shown to the public, others that were carefully hidden and were not even known to all the Knights." [1]

Jacques du Molay and several of the leaders were executed, and, according to the Chevalier de Malet, "those who had escaped the storm afterwards met in obscurity so as to re-knit the ties that had united them, and in order to avoid fresh denunciations they made use of allegorical methods which indicated the basis of their association in a manner unintelligible to the eyes of the vulgar: that is the origin of the Free Masons." [2]

This last assertion finds further confirmation from the Martiniste Papus, who explains that the " Grand Chapter " of French Freemasonry founded in the eighteenth century was constituted under the Templars, " that is to say that their most eminent members are animated by the desire to avenge Jacobus Burgundus Molay and his companions for the assassination of which they were the victims on the part of two tyrannical powers: Royalty and Papacy." [3]

Meanwhile Freemasonry in England had developed

---

[1] *Recherches politiques et historiques*, by the Chevalier de Malet (1817), p. 37.   [2] *Ibid.* p. 39.

[3] *Martinès de Pasqually*, by Papus, p. 140. In the above passages I have only touched very briefly on the origins of Continental masonry, as the subject was recently fully dealt with in the very interesting articles that appeared in the *Morning Post* during July 1920 under the title of *The Cause of World Unrest*, and republished in pamphlet form by Grant Richards.

along quite different lines. This is not the place to discuss its aims or origins; suffice it to say that although French Freemasonry of the Grande Loge Nationale derived from one of the same sources — the Confrérerie of the Rose Croix — and received its first charters from the Grand Lodge of London (founded in 1717), the two Orders must not be confounded. The craft masonry of Britain, which was largely a development of the real guild of working masons, has always retained the spirit of brotherly association and general benevolence which animated its founders, and has adhered throughout to the principle that " nothing touching religion or government shall ever be spoken of in the Lodge." [1]

In France, however, as in other Continental countries, the lodges speedily became centres of political intrigue. The *Grand Orient*, founded in 1772, with the Duc de Chartres (later Philippe Egalité) as its Grand Master, was an undeniably subversive body, and by a coalition with the Grand Chapter in 1786 acquired a far more dangerous character. For whilst " the spirit of the Grand Orient was frankly democratic (though not demagogic)," the spirit of the Grand Chapter was revolutionary, " but the Revolution was to be accomplished above all for the benefit of the upper class [2] (*la haute bourgeoisie*), *with the people as its instrument.*" The brothers of the Templar rite, that is to say, of the Grand Chapter, were thus " the real fomentors of revolutions, the others were only docile agents." [3] In the opinion of Papus and of contemporary masons themselves the Revolution of 1789 was the outcome of this combination. [4]

Indeed the influence of Freemasonry on the French Revolution cannot be denied by any honest inquirer into the causes of that great upheaval, and, as we shall see later, the French Freemasons themselves proudly claimed the Revolution as their work. It was thus that George Sand, herself a mason (for the Grand Orient from the beginning admitted women to the Order), wrote long afterwards: " Half a century before those days marked out by destiny

[1] Robison, *Proofs of a Conspiracy*, p. 10.   [2] Papus, *op. cit.* p. 139.
[3] *Ibid.* p. 144.   [4] *Ibid.* pp. 142, 144, 146.

... the French Revolution was fermenting in the dark and hatching below ground. It was maturing in the minds of believers to the point of fanaticism, in the form of a dream of universal revolution. . . ." [1]

The Socialist historian, Louis Blanc, also a Freemason, has thrown much light on the question of these occult forces.

We know, moreover, that George Sand was right in attributing to the Secret Societies the origin of the revolutionary war-cry, " Liberty, Equality, Fraternity." Long before the Revolution broke out the formula " Liberty and Equality " had been current in the lodges of the Grand Orient — a formula that sounds wholly pacific, yet which holds within it a whole world of discord. For observe the contradiction: it is impossible to have complete liberty and equality, the two are mutually exclusive. It is possible to have a system of complete liberty in which every man is free to behave as he pleases, to do what he will with his own, to rob or to murder, to live, that is to say, under the law of the jungle, rule by the strongest, but there is no equality there. Or one may have a system of absolute equality, of cutting every one down to the same dead level, of crushing all incentive in man to rise above his fellows, but there is no liberty there. So Grand Orient Freemasonry, by coupling together two words for ever incompatible, threw into the arena an apple of discord over which the world has never ceased to quarrel from that day to this, and which has throughout divided the revolutionary forces into two opposing camps.

As to the word Fraternity, which completes the masonic formula, we find that this was added by a further Secret Society, the Martinistes, founded in 1754 by a Portuguese Jew, Martinez Paschalis (or Pasqually), who had evolved a system out of gnosticism, Judaized Christianity, and the philosophies of Greece and of the East.

This Order split up into two branches, one continued by Saint-Martin, a disciple of Martinez Paschalis, but also of Jacob Boehme, and a fervent Christian, and the other a more or less revolutionary body by which the lodge of the

[1] *La Comtesse de Rudolstadt*, ii. 219.

Philalèthes was founded in Paris. In the book of Saint-Martin, *Des erreurs et de la vérité*, published in 1775, the formula " Liberty, Equality, and Fraternity " is referred to as " le ternaire sacré."

The Martinistes, frequently referred to in French contemporary records as the Illuminés, were in reality dreamers and fanatics,[1] and must not be confounded with the Order of the Illuminati of Bavaria that came into existence twenty-two years later. It is by this " terrible and formidable sect " that the gigantic plan of World Revolution was worked out under the leadership of the man whom Louis Blanc has truly described as " the profoundest conspirator that has ever existed."

Adam Weishaupt, the founder of the Illuminati, was born on the 6th of February, 1748. His early training by the Jesuits had inspired him with a violent dislike for their Order, and he turned with eagerness to the subversive teaching of the French philosophers and the anti-Christian doctrines of the Manicheans. It is said that he was also indoctrinated into Egyptian occultism by a certain merchant of unknown origin from Jutland, named Kölmer, who was travelling about Europe during the year 1771 in search of adepts.[2] Weishaupt, who combined the practical German brain with the cunning of Machiavelli, spent no less than five years thinking out a plan by which all these ideas should be reduced to a system, and at the end of this period he had evolved the following theory:

Civilization, Weishaupt held with Rousseau, was a mistake: it had developed along the wrong lines, and to this cause all the inequalities of human life were due. " Man," he declared, " is fallen from the condition of Liberty and Equality, the State of Pure Nature. He is under subordination and civil bondage arising from the vices of Man. This is the Fall and Original Sin." The first step towards regaining the state of primitive liberty consisted in learning to do without things. Man must divest himself of all the trappings laid on him by civilization and return to nomadic

[1] "The Martinistes, whose tendencies were purely scientific, passed frequently for madmen and despised politics" (Papus, *op. cit.* p. 55).
[2] *Les Sectes et sociétés secrètes*, by the Comte Le Couteulx de Canteleu (1863), p. 152.

conditions — even clothing, food, and fixed abodes should be abandoned. Necessarily, therefore, all arts and sciences must be abolished. " Do the common sciences afford real enlightenment, real human happiness? or are they not rather children of necessity, the complicated needs of a state contrary to Nature, the inventions of vain and empty brains? " Moreover, " are not many of the complicated needs of civilization the means of retaining in power the mercantile class (Kaufmannschaft), which if allowed any authority in the government would inevitably end by exercising the most formidable and despotic power? You will see it dictating the law to the universe, and from it will perhaps ensue the independence of one part of the world, the slavery of the other. For he is a master who can arouse and foresee, stifle, satisfy, or lessen needs. And who can do that better than tradesmen? "

Once released from the bondage civilization imposes, Man must then be self-governing. " Why," asked Weishaupt, " should it be impossible to the human race to attain its highest perfection, the capacity for governing itself? " For this reason not only should kings and nobles be abolished, but even a Republic should not be tolerated, and the people should be taught to do without any controlling authority, any law, or any civil code. In order to make this system a success it would be necessary only to inculcate in Man " a just and steady morality," and since Weishaupt professed to share Rousseau's belief in the inherent goodness of human nature this would not be difficult, and society might then " go on peaceably in a state of perfect Liberty and Equality." For since the only real obstacle to human perfection lay in the restraints imposed on Man by artificial conditions of life, the removal of these must inevitably restore him to his primitive virtue. " Man is not bad except as he is made so by arbitrary morality. He is bad because Religion, the State, and bad examples pervert him." It was necessary, therefore, to root out from his mind all ideas of a Hereafter, all fear of retribution for evil deeds, and to substitute for these superstitions the religion of Reason. " When at least Reason becomes the religion of men, then will the problem be solved."

After deliverance from the bondage of religion, the loosening of all social ties must follow. Both family and national life must cease to exist so as to "make of the human race one good and happy family." The origins of patriotism and the love of kindred are thus described by Weishaupt in the directions given to his Hierophants for the instruction of initiates:

At the moment when men united themselves into nations they ceased to recognise themselves under a common name. Nationalism or National Love took the place of universal love. With the division of the globe and its countries benevolence restricted itself behind boundaries that it was never again to transgress. Then it became a virtue to spread out at the expense of those who did not happen to be under our dominion. Then in order to attain this goal, it became permissible to despise foreigners, and to deceive and to offend them. This virtue was called Patriotism. That man was called a Patriot, who, whilst just towards his own people, was unjust to others, who blinded himself to the merits of foreigners and took for perfections the vices of his own country. So one sees that Patriotism gave birth to Localism, to the family spirit, and finally to Egoism. Thus the origin of states or governments of civil society was the seed of discord and Patriotism found its punishment in itself. . . . Diminish, do away with this love of country, and men will once more learn to know and love each other as men; there will be no more partiality, the ties between hearts will unroll and extend.[1]

In these words, the purest expression of Internationalism as it is expounded today, Weishaupt displayed an ignorance of primeval conditions of life as profound as that of Rousseau. The idea of palaeolithic man, whose skeleton is usually exhumed with a flint instrument or other weapon of warfare grasped in its hand, passing his existence in a state of "universal love," is simply ludicrous. It was not, however, in his diatribes against civilization that Weishaupt surpassed Rousseau, but in the plan he devised for overthrowing it. Rousseau had merely paved the way for revolution; Weishaupt constructed the actual machinery of revolution itself.

It was on the 1st of May 1776 that Weishaupt's five

[1] *Nachtrag . . . Originalschriften (des Illuminaten Ordens), Zweite* Abtheilung, p. 65.

years of meditation resulted in his founding the secret
society that he named, after bygone philosophical systems,
the Illuminati.[1] All the members were required to adopt
classical names: thus Weishaupt took that of Spartacus,
the leader of an insurrection of slaves in ancient Rome;
his principal ally, Herr von Zwack, privy councillor to the
Prince von Salm, became Cato; the Marquis di Constanza,
Diomedes; Massenhausen, Ajax; Hertel, Marius; the
Baron von Schroeckenstein, Mahomed; the Baron Mengen-
hofen, Sylla, etc. In the same way the names of places
were changed to those celebrated in antiquity; Munich, the
headquarters of the system, was to be known as Athens;
Ingoldstadt, the birthplace of Illuminism, as Ephesus, or
to the adepts initiated into the inner mysteries of the
Order, as Eleusis; Heidelberg as Utica, Bavaria as Achaia,
Suabia as Pannonia, etc. For greater secrecy in correspondence the word Illuminism was to be replaced by the
cypher ⊙, and the word lodge by ☐. The calendar also
was to be reconstructed and the months known by names
suggestive of Hebrew origin — January as Dimeh, February as Benmeh, etc. For the letters of the alphabet a complete code of figures was constructed, beginning with *m* as
number 1, and working back to *a* and on to *z*.

The grades of the Order were a combination of the
grades of Freemasonry and the degrees belonging to the
Jesuits. Weishaupt, as has already been said, detested the
Jesuits, but recognizing the efficiency of their methods in
acquiring influence over the minds of their disciples, he
conceived the idea of adopting their system to his own purpose. " He admired," says the Abbé Barruel, " the institutions of the founders of this Order, he admired above all
those laws, that régime of the Jesuits, which under one
head made so many men dispersed all over the universe
tend towards the same object; he felt that one might
imitate their methods whilst proposing to himself views
diametrically opposed. He said to himself: ' What all these
men have done for altars and empires, why should I not
do against altars and empires? By the attraction of

[1] A German sect of this name professing Satanism, with which Weishaupt's Order may have been connected, existed in the fifteenth century.

mysteries, of legends, of adepts, why should not I destroy in the dark what they erect in the light of day?' "

Weishaupt at first entertained hopes of persuading other ex-Jesuits to join the society, but having succeeded in enlisting only two he became more than ever the enemy of their Order, and injunctions were given to his adepts to admit no Jews or Jesuits to the sect of the Illuminati unless by special permission. "Ex-Jesuits," he wrote emphatically, "must be avoided as the plague."

It was in the training of adepts that Weishaupt showed his profound subtlety. Proselytes were not to be admitted at once to the secret aims of Illuminism, but initiated step by step into the higher mysteries — and the greatest caution was to be exercised not to reveal to the novice doctrines that might be likely to revolt him. For this purpose the initiators must acquire the habit of "talking backwards and forwards" so as not to commit themselves. "One must speak," Weishaupt explained to the Superiors of the Order, "sometimes in one way, sometimes in another, so that our real purpose should remain impenetrable to our inferiors."

Thus to certain novices (the *novices écossais*) the Illuminati must profess to disapprove of revolutions, and demonstrate the advantages of proceeding by peaceful methods towards the attainment of *world domination*. But to the Minerval the plan of world power must not be revealed; on the contrary, one of the opening sentences in the initiation for this grade runs as follows: "After two years' reflection, experience, intercourse, reading of the graduated writings and information, you will necessarily have formed the impression that the final aim of our society is nothing less than to win power and riches, to undermine secular or religious government and to obtain the mastery of the world." *Qui s'excuse s'accuse* indeed! The passage then goes on to say vaguely that this is not the case and that the Order only demands of the initiate the fulfilment of his obligations. Nor must antagonism to religion be admitted; on the contrary, Christ was to be represented as the first author of Illuminism, whose secret mission was to restore to men the original liberty and equality they had lost in the Fall. "No one," the novice should be told, "paved so sure a way for liberty as our Grand Master Jesus of Nazareth, and if Christ exhorted his disciples to despise riches it was in order to prepare the world for that community of goods that should do away with property."

This device proved particularly successful not only with young novices, but with men of all ranks and ages. "The most admirable thing of all," wrote Spartacus triumphantly to Cato, "is that great Protestant and reformed theologians (Lutherans and Calvinists) who belong to our Order really believe they see in it the true and genuine mind of the Christian religion. Oh! man, what cannot you be brought to believe!" By this means, as Philo (the Baron von Knigge) later on pointed out, the Order was able " to tickle those who have a hankering for religion."

It was not, then, until his admission to the higher grades that the adept was initiated into the real intentions of Illuminism with regard to religion. When he reached the grade of Illuminated Major or Minor, of Scotch Knight, Epopte, or Priest he was told the whole secret of the Order in a discourse by the Initiator:

Remember that from the first invitations which we have given you in order to attract you to us, we commenced by telling you that in the projects of our Order there did not enter any designs against religion. You remember that such an assurance was given you when you were admitted into the ranks of our novices, and that it was repeated when you entered into our Minerval Academy. . . . You remember with what art, with what simulated respect we have spoken to you of Christ and of his gospel; but in the grades of greater Illuminism, of Scotch Knight, and of Epopte or Priest, how we have to know to form from Christ's gospel that of our reason, and from its religion that of nature, and from religion, reason, morality and Nature, to make the religion and morality of the rights of man, of equality and of liberty. . . . We have had many prejudices to overcome in you before being able to persuade you that the pretended religion of Christ was nothing else than the work of priests, of imposture and of tyranny. If it be so with that religion so much proclaimed and admired, what are we to think of other religions? Understand then that they have all the same fictions for their origin, that they are all equally founded on lying, error, chimera and imposture. Behold our secret. . . . If in order to destroy all Christianity, all religion, we have pretended to have the sole true religion, remember that the end justifies the means, and that the wise ought to take all the means to do good which the wicked take to do evil. Those which we have taken to deliver you, those which we have taken to deliver one day the human race from all religion, are nothing else than a pious fraud which we reserve to unveil one day in the grade of Magus or Philosopher Illuminated.

But all this was unknown to the novice, whose confidence being won by the simulation of religion was enjoined to strict obedience. Amongst the questions put to him were the following:

If you came to discover anything wrong or unjust to be done under the Order what line would you take?

Will you and can you regard the good of the Order as your own good?

Will you give to our Society the right of life and death?

Do you bind yourself to absolute and unreserved obedience? And do you know the force of this undertaking?

By way of warning as to the consequences of betraying the Order a forcible illustration was included in the ceremony of initiation. Taking a naked sword from the table, the Initiator held the point against the heart of the novice with these words:

If you are only a traitor and perjurer learn that all our brothers are called upon to arm themselves against you. Do not hope to escape or to find a place of safety. Wherever you are, shame, remorse, and the rage of our brothers will pursue you and torment you to the innermost recesses of your entrails.

It will thus be seen that the Liberty vaunted by the leaders of the Illuminati had no existence, and that iron discipline was in reality the watchword of the Order.

A great point impressed upon the adepts — of which we shall see the importance later — was that they should not be known as Illuminati; this rule was particularly enforced in the case of those described as " enrollers," and by way of attracting proselytes they were further admonished to be irreproachable. " The Superiors of the Order are to be regarded as the most perfect and enlightened of men; they must not even permit any doubts on their infallibility." Therefore to the enrollers it was said: " Apply yourselves to inward and outward perfection," but also

" Apply yourselves to the art of counterfeit, of hiding and masking yourselves when observing others, so as to penetrate into their minds (Die Kunst zu erlernen, andere zu beobachten und auszuforschen)." These precepts were summed up in the one phrase: " Keep silence, be perfect, mask yourselves." How far the founder of the Order had himself attained perfection was subsequently revealed by the discovery of his papers, amongst which was found a letter from Weishaupt to Hertel in 1783, confessing that he had seduced his sister-in-law, and adding: " I am therefore in danger of losing my honour and that reputation which gave me so much authority over our world."

For a time this reputation for perfectibility was successfully maintained for the benefit of the members, who would have been revolted by a breach of morality, and only those likely to be attracted by it were to be allowed to know of the laxity permitted by the Order.

Women were also to be enlisted as Illuminati by being given " hints of emancipation."[1] " Through women," wrote Weishaupt, " one may often work the best in the world; to insinuate ourselves with these and to win them over should be one of our cleverest studies. More or less they can all be led towards change by vanity, curiosity, sensuality, and inclination. From this can one draw much profit for the good cause. This sex has a large part of the world in its hands."[2] The female adepts were then to be divided into two classes, each with its own secret, the first to consist of virtuous women who would give an air of respectability to the Order, the second of " light women," " who would help to satisfy those brothers who have a penchant for pleasure." But the present utility of both classes would consist in providing funds for the society. Fools with money, whether men or women, were to be particularly welcomed. " These good people," wrote Spartacus to Ajax and Cato, " swell our numbers and fill our money-box; set yourselves to work; these gentlemen must be made to nibble at the bait. . . . But let us beware of telling them our secrets, this sort of people *must always*

---

[1] Heckethorn's *Secret Societies*, ii. 34.
[2] *Neuesten Arbeiten des Spartacus und Philo*, vi. 139.

be made to believe that the grade they have reached is the last." [1]

The sect was thus to consist of Weishaupt and the adepts who had been initiated into the inner mysteries, and, besides these, of a large following of simple and credulous people who could be kept in ignorance of the real goal towards which they were being driven. Weishaupt's method for obtaining proselytes is thus shown by a diagram in the code of the Illuminati:

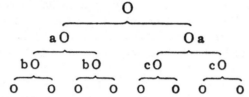

(Reproduced from *Originalschriften des Illuminaten Ordens,* Zweite Abtheilung, p. 60.)

Naturally the least educated classes offered a wide field for Weishaupt's activities. " It is also necessary," runs the code of the Illuminati, " to gain the common people (das gemeine Volk) to our Order. The great means to that end is influence in the schools. One can also succeed, now by liberty, now by striking an effect, and at other times by humiliating oneself, by making oneself popular, or enduring with an air of patience prejudices that one can gradually root out later." [2]

Espionage formed a large part of Weishaupt's programme. The adepts known as the " Insinuating Brothers " were enjoined to assume the rôle of " observers " and " reporters "; " every person shall be made a spy on another and on all around him "; " friends, relations, enemies, those who are indifferent — all without exception shall be the object of his inquiries; he shall attempt to discover their strong side and their weak, their passions, their prejudices, their connections, above all, their actions — in a word, the most detailed information about them." All this is to be entered on tablets that the Insinuant carries with him, and from which he shall draw up reports to be sent in twice a month to his Superiors, so that the Order

---

[1] Barruel, *Mémoires sur le Jacobinisme,* iii. 28, quoting *Originalschriften.*
[2] *Neuesten Arbeiten des Spartacus und Philo,* vii.

may know which are the people in each town and village
to whom it can look for support.

It is impossible not to admire the ingenuity of the system by which each section of the community was to be
made to believe that it would reap untold benefits from
Illuminism — princes whose kingdoms were to be reft
from them, priests and ministers whose religion was to be
destroyed, merchants whose commerce was to be ruined.
women who were to be reduced to the rank of squaws,
peasants who were to be made to return to a state of
savagery, were all, by means of dividing up the secrets of
the Order into watertight compartments, to be persuaded
that in Illuminism alone lay their prosperity or salvation,

Secrecy being thus the great principle of his system.
Weishaupt had not been slow to perceive the advantages
offered by an alliance with Freemasonry. During the
period when he was thinking out his plan the real aims of
masonry were unknown to him. " He only knew," says
the Abbé Barruel, " that the Freemasons held secret meetings, he saw them united by a mysterious link and recognizing each other as brothers by certain signs and certain
words, to whatever nation or religion they belonged; he
therefore conceived a new combination of which the result
was to be a society adopting for its methods — as far as it
suited him — the régime of the Jesuits and the mysterious
silence, the obscure existence of the Masons. . . ."

It was in 1777, nearly two years after he had founded
the Order of the Illuminati, that Weishaupt became a
Freemason, and towards the end of 1778 the idea was first
launched of amalgamating the two societies. Cato, that is
to say Herr von Zwack, who became a mason on November
27, 1778, talked the matter over with a brother mason, the
Abbé Marotti, to whom he confided the whole secret of
Illuminism; and two years later a further understanding
between Illuminism and Freemasonry was brought about
by a certain Freemason, Freiherr von Knigge, who in
July 1780 arrived at Frankfurt, where he met the Illuminatus Diomedes — the Marquis di Constanza — sent by the
Bavarian Illuminati to establish colonies in Protestant
countries. The two men compared notes on the aims of

their respective societies, and Knigge then expressed the wish to be received into the Order of the Illuminati. This met with the approval of Weishaupt, and Knigge, adopting the name of Philo, was thereupon initiated into the secrets of the first class of Illuminism — the Minervals. The zeal he displayed in obtaining proselytes delighted Spartacus. " Philo," he wrote, " is the master from whom to take lessons; give me six men of his stamp and with them I will change the face of the Universe."

As a result of the negotiations between Weishaupt and Knigge a kind of union was arranged between the two societies, and Spartacus agreed to Illuminism receiving the first three degrees of masonry. On the 20th of December 1781 it was finally decided that the combined Order should be composed of three classes: (*a*) the Minervals, (*b*) the Freemasons, and (*c*) the Mystery Class, which, as the highest of all, was divided into the lesser and greater mysteries, the former including the grades of " Priests " and " Regents," the latter the " Mages " and the " Men-Kings."

But it was not until the Congrès de Wilhelmsbad that the alliance between Illuminism and Freemasonry was finally sealed. This assembly, of which the importance to the subsequent history of the world has never been appreciated by historians, met for the first time on the 16th of July 1782, and included representatives of all the Secret Societies — Martinistes as well as Freemasons and Illuminati — which now numbered no less than three million members all over the world. Amongst these different orders the Illuminati of Bavaria alone had formulated a definite plan of campaign, and it was they who henceforward took the lead. What passed at this terrible Congress will never be known to the outside world, for even those men who had been drawn unwittingly into the movement, and now heard for the first time the real designs of the leaders, were under oath to reveal nothing. One such honest Freemason, the Comte de Virieu, a member of a Martiniste lodge at Lyons, returning from the Congrès de Wilhelmsbad could not conceal his alarm, and when questioned on the " tragic secrets " he had brought back with

him, replied: " I will not confide them to you. I can only
tell you that all this is very much more serious than you
think. The conspiracy which is being woven is so well
thought out that it will be, so to speak, impossible for the
Monarchy and the Church to escape from it." From this
time onwards, says his biographer, M. Costa de Beaure-
gard, " the Comte de Virieu could only speak of Freemasonry with horror."

The years of 1781 and 1782 were remarkable for the
growth of another movement which found expression at
the Congrès de Wilhelmsbad, namely, the emancipation of
the Jews. During these years a wave of pro-Semitism was
produced throughout Europe by Dohm's great book *Upon
the Civil Amelioration of the Condition of the Jews*, written
under the influence of Moses Mendelssohn and finished in
August 1781.[1] " It was thus," wrote the Abbé Lemann,
" that eight years before the Revolution the programme in
favour of Judaism was sent out by Prussia. . . . This
book had a considerable influence on the revolutionary
movement; it is the trumpet call of the Jewish cause, the
signal for the step forward." [2]

Graetz, the Jewish historian, himself recognizes the
immense importance of Dohm's work, " painting the
Christians as cruel barbarians and the Jews as illustrious
martyrs." [3] " All thinking people," he adds, " now began
to interest themselves in the Jewish question." Mirabeau,
a few years later on a mission to Berlin, formed a friendship
with Dohm and became an habitué of the salon of a young
and beautiful Jewess, Henriette de Lemos, wife of Dr.
Herz, and it was there that the disciples of Mendelssohn,
who had just died, pressed him to raise his voice in favour
of the oppressed Jews, with the result that Mirabeau published a book in London on the same lines as Dohm's.[4]

Meanwhile, in 1781, Anacharsis Clootz, the future

[1] Graetz, *History of the Jews*, v. 438; A. de la Rive, *Le Juif dans la
franc-maçonnerie*, pp. 40-43.

[2] Abbé Lemann, *L'Entrée des Israélites dans la société française*, Paris,
1886.

[3] Graetz, v. 373.

[4] *Sur Moses Mendelssohn, sur la réforme politique des Juifs; et en
particulier sur la révolution tentée en leur faveur en 1753 dans la Grande-
Bretagne*. À Londres, 1787.

author of *La République Universelle*, wrote his pro-Semitic pamphlet called " Lettre sur les Juifs."

The result of this agitation was seen later in the edicts passed through the influence of Mirabeau and the Abbé Grégoire by the National Assembly in 1791 decreeing the emancipation of the Jews. A more immediate effect, however, was the resolution taken at the masonic congress of Wilhelmsbad — which was attended by Lessing and a company of Jews [1] — that henceforth Jews should no longer be excluded from the lodges.[2] At the same time it was decided to remove the headquarters of illuminized Freemasonry to Frankfurt, which incidentally was the stronghold of Jewish finance, controlled at this date by such leading members of the race as Rothschild, Mayer Amschel — later to become Rothschild also — Oppenheimer, Wertheimer, Schuster, Speyer, Stern, and others.[3] At this head lodge of Frankfurt the gigantic plan of world revolution was carried forward, and it was there that at a large masonic congress in 1786 two French Freemasons afterwards declared the deaths of Louis XVI. and Gustavus III. of Sweden were definitely decreed.[4]

From the moment of the great coalition effected at Wilhelmsbad, Illuminism, aided largely by the activities of Knigge, was able to extend its ramifications all over Germany; the lodge of Eichstadt under Mahomed (the Baron Schroeckenstein) illuminated Baireuth and other Imperial towns; Berlin under Nicolai and Leuchtsenring illuminated the provinces of Brandenburg and Pomerania; Frankfurt illuminated Hanover, and so on. All these

---

[1] A. Cowan, *The X-Rays in Freemasonry*, p. 122; *Archives israélites* (1867), p. 466.

[2] A. de la Rive, *Le Juif dans la franc-maçonnerie*, p. 36. Hitherto Jews had only been admitted into the lodges of the Order of Melchisedeck, of which the three principal grades are given by the Marquis de Luchet as (1) The *Frères Initiés d'Asie;* (2) The *Maîtres des Sages;* (3) The *Prêtres Royaux* or *Véritables Frères Rose-croix*, or the grade of Melchisedeck.

The *Frères Initiés d'Asie* were an order of which the hieroglyphics were taken from Hebrew, the supreme direction was called " The small and constant Sanhedrim of Europe" (*Essai sur la secte des Illuminés* (1789), p. 212). Lombard de Langres says this secret society became affiliated to Illuminism, that its centre was at Hamburg, and that only the Grand Master knew the whole secret (*Des sociétés secrètes en Allemagne*, pp. 81, 82).

[3] Werner Sombart, *The Jews and Modern Capitalism*, p. 187.

[4] Charles d'Héricault, *La Révolution*, p. 104.

branches were controlled by the twelve leading adepts headed by Weishaupt, who at the lodge in Munich held in his hands the threads of the whole conspiracy.

But dissensions had now begun amongst the two principal leaders — Weishaupt and Knigge. Both were indeed born intriguers, but whilst Weishaupt preferred to work in the dark and wrap himself in mystery, Knigge loved to make a noise in the world and to meddle with everything. It was inevitable that two such men could not continue to work together harmoniously, and before long Knigge's persistent attempts to pry into Weishaupt's secrets and to usurp a share of his glory roused the animosity of his chief, who ended by depriving Knigge of his post as director of the provinces and placing him in a subordinate position. Whereat " Philo," on the 20th of January 1783, wrote indignantly to " Cato ": " It is the Jesuitry of Weishaupt that causes all our divisions, it is the despotism that he exercises over men perhaps less rich than himself in imagination, in ruses, in cunning. . . . I declare that nothing can put me on the same footing with Spartacus as that on which I was at first." As a matter of fact Knigge was in no way behind Weishaupt in what he described as " Jesuitry," but revolted by the tyranny of his leader he finally left the Illuminati in anger and disgust. " I abhor treachery and profligacy," he wrote again to Cato, " and I leave him to blow himself and his Order into the air."

Public opinion had now, however, become thoroughly roused on the subject of the society, and the Elector of Bavaria, informed of the danger to the State constituted by its adepts, who were said to have declared that " the Illuminati must in time rule the world," published an edict forbidding all secret societies. In April of the following year, 1785, four other Illuminati, who like Knigge had left the society, disgusted by the tyranny of Weishaupt, were summoned before a Court of Inquiry to give an account of the doctrines and methods of the sect. The evidence of these men — Utschneider, Cossandey, Grünberger, and Renner, all professors of the Marianen Academy — left no further room for doubt as to the diabolical nature of Illuminism. " All religion," they declared, " all love of country and loyalty to sovereigns, were to be annihilated, a favourite maxim of the Order being:

> Tous les rois et tous les prêtres
> Sont des fripons et des traîtres.

Moreover, every effort was to be made to create discord not only between princes and their subjects but between ministers and their secretaries, and even between parents and children, whilst suicide was to be encouraged by inculcating in men's minds the idea that the act of killing oneself afforded a certain voluptuous pleasure. Espionage was to be extended even to the post by placing adepts in the post offices who possessed the art of opening letters and closing them again without fear of detection." Robison, who studied all the evidence of the four professors, thus sums up the plan of Weishaupt as revealed by them:

The Order of the Illuminati adjured Christianity and advocated sensual pleasures. " In the lodges death was declared an eternal sleep; patriotism and loyalty were called narrow-minded prejudices and incompatible with universal benevolence ";[1] further, " they accounted all princes usurpers and tyrants, and all privileged orders as their abettors . . . they meant to abolish the laws which protected property accumulated by long-continued and successful industry; and to prevent for the future any such accumulation. They intended to establish universal liberty and equality, the imprescriptible rights of man . . . and as necessary preparations for all this they intended to root out all religion and ordinary morality, and even to break the bonds of domestic life, by destroying the veneration for marriage vows, and by taking the education of children out of the hands of the parents."[2]

Reduced to a simple formula the aims of the Illuminati may be summarized in the following six points:

1. Abolition of Monarchy and all ordered Government.
2. Abolition of private property.
3. Abolition of inheritance.
4. Abolition of patriotism.

[1] Robison's *Proofs of a Conspiracy*, pp. 106, 107.
[2] *Ibid.* p. 375.

5. Abolition of the family (*i.e.* of marriage and all morality, and the institution of the communal education of children).

6. Abolition of all religion.

Now it will surely be admitted that the above forms a programme hitherto unprecedented in the history of civilization. Communistic theories had been held by isolated thinkers or groups of thinkers since the days of Plato, but no one, as far as we know, had ever yet seriously proposed to destroy everything for which civilization stands. Moreover, when, as we shall see, the plan of Illuminism as codified by the above six points has continued up to the present day to form the exact programme of the World Revolution, how can we doubt that the whole movement originated with the Illuminati or with secret influences at work behind them?

Here a curious point arises. Was Weishaupt the inventor of his system? We know that he was indoctrinated in occultism by Kölmer, but beyond this we can discover nothing. If indeed Weishaupt himself thought out his whole plan of world revolution — that " gigantic conception " as it is described by Louis Blanc — how is it that so vast a genius should have remained absolutely unknown to posterity? How is it that succeeding groups of world revolutionaries whilst all following in his footsteps, even those who we know positively to have belonged to his Order, never once have referred to the source of their inspiration? Is not the answer to the latter question that throughout the movement the adepts of the Order have always adhered to the stringent rule laid down by Weishaupt that they should never allow themselves to be known as Illuminati? The persistent efforts to conceal the very existence of the Order, or, if this proves impossible, to represent it as an unimportant philanthropic movement, has continued up to the very year in which I write.

With regard to the philanthropic nature of Illuminism it is only necessary to consult the original writings of Weishaupt to realize the hollowness of this assurance. Amongst the whole correspondence which passed between Weishaupt and his adepts laid bare by the Government of

Bavaria, we find no word of sympathy with the poor or suffering, no hint of social reform, nothing but the desire either for domination, for *world power*, or sheer love of destruction, and throughout all the insatiable spirit of intrigue. For this purpose every method was held to be justifiable, since the fundamental doctrine of the sect was that " the end sanctifies the means (*der Zweck heiligt die Mittel*)," which Weishaupt referred to in his code, declaring it to be a part of the Jesuit system — an imputation which the Abbé Barruel indignantly denies — and which inevitably led, as Robison points out, to the conclusion that " nothing would be scrupled at, if it could be made appear that the Order would derive advantage from it, because the great object of the Order was held as superior to every consideration."

As might be expected, Weishaupt loudly protested against the account of his society given by the four professors, declaring that they had not been initiated into its inner mysteries, but the discovery a little later of his correspondence with Zwack — from which quotations have already been given earlier in this chapter — threw a still more sinister light on the real aims of the Order. It was on the 11th of October 1786 that the Bavarian authorities descended upon the house of Zwack and seized the documents which laid bare the methods of the conspirators. Here were found descriptions of a strong box for safeguarding papers which if forced open should blow up by means of an infernal machine; of a composition which should blind or kill if squirted in the face; of a method for counterfeiting seals; recipes for a particularly deadly kind of "aqua toffana," for poisonous perfumes that would fill a bedroom with pestilential vapours, and for a tea to procure abortion. A eulogy of atheism entitled *Better than Horus* was also discovered, and a paper in the handwriting of Zwack describing the plan for enlisting women in the two classes mentioned above:

It will be of great service and procure much information and money, and will suit charmingly the taste of many of our truest members who are lovers of the sex. It should consist of two classes, the virtuous and the freer-hearted. . . . They must not know of each other, and must be under the direction of men, but without knowing it . . . through good books, and the latter (class) through the indulging of their passions in concealment.[1]

The Illuminati of course still proclaimed their innocence, and though not attempting to deny the authenticity of these documents, declared that they had been misinterpreted, and that the real purpose of the Order was to make of the human race " one good and happy family." But the damning evidence their papers contained made the plan of the Illuminati only too clear, which was no other than to bring about " the universal revolution that should deal the death-blow to society." " Princes and nations," Weishaupt had written, " shall disappear off the face of the earth; yes, the time will come when men will have no other laws than the book of nature; this revolution will be the work of the secret societies, and that is one of our great mysteries."

The fearful danger presented by the Illuminati now became apparent, and the Government of Bavaria, judging that the best manner of conveying a warning to the civilized world would be to allow the papers to speak for themselves, ordered them to be printed forthwith and circulated as widely as possible. A copy of this publication, entitled *Original Writings of the Order of the Illuminati*, was then forwarded to every Government of Europe, but, strange to say, attracted little attention, the truth being doubtless, as the Abbé Barruel points out, that the extravagance of the scheme therein propounded rendered it unbelievable, and the rulers of Europe, refusing to take Illuminism seriously, put it aside as a chimera.

The Government of Bavaria, however, continued its proceedings against the sect; several of its members were arrested; Zwack left the country on a mission to England; Weishaupt, with a price set on his head, took refuge with one of his royal adepts, the Duke of Saxe-Gotha. This apparent break-up of the society admirably served the purpose of the conspirators, who now diligently circulated the news that Illuminism had ceased to exist — a deception carried on ever since by interested historians anxious

[1] *Nachtrag . . . Originalschriften.* i. C.

to suppress the truth about its subsequent activities. The truth is that not until Illuminism had been apparently extinguished in Bavaria was it able to make its formidable influence felt abroad, and public anxiety being allayed it could secretly extend its organization over the whole civilized world.

CHAPTER II

THE FIRST FRENCH REVOLUTION

Illuminism in France — Cagliostro — Mirabeau — Intrigues of Prussia — The Orléanistes — The Reign of Terror — Clootz and Internationalism — Robespierre and Socialism — The plan of depopulation — After-effects of revolution.

Two years before the suppression of Illuminism in Bavaria its adepts had begun their work in France. The " magician " Cagliostro, generally reputed to be a Jew[1] from Sicily, had been enrolled as an Illuminatus in Germany. According to his own account given in the course of his interrogatory before the Holy See in Rome in 1790, " his initiation took place at a little distance from Frankfort in an underground room. An iron box filled with papers was opened. The introducers took from it a manuscript book on the first page of which one read: ' We, Grand Masters of the Templars —' Then followed a form of oath, traced in

[1] It has been denied that Cagliostro was a Jew, but no definite proof to the contrary has been produced. M. Louis Dasté in his book *Marie-Antoinette et le complot maçonnique*, p. 70, gives passages from various contemporaries affirming his Jewish origin. Friedrich Bülau (*Geheime Geschichten und Räthselhafte Menschen* (1850), vol. i. p. 311) says that his father was Peter Balsamo, the son of a bookseller in Palermo — Antonio Balsamo — who appears to have been of the Jewish race, but Joseph (*i. e.* Cagliostro) was brought up in a seminary as a Christian. Bülau adds that it was Cagliostro who brought about the admission of Jews to the masonic lodges. Cagliostro himself pretended to know nothing of his origin, declaring that he was brought up in Arabia, in the palace of the Muphti at Medina. Replying to Mme. de la Motte's assertion that he was a Jew, he stated: " I was brought up as the son of Christian parents — I have never been a Jew or a Mohammedan," but he did not say that he was not of Jewish race. Bulau further relates that Cagliostro on a visit to England formed a friendship with Lord George Gordon, who in the following year made a plan to burn down London and incidentally became a Jew. (See *Chambers's Biographical Dictionary*, article on Lord George Gordon; *Mémoire pour le Comte de Cagliostro*, p. 83 (1786 edition.)

blood. The book stated that Illuminism was a conspiracy directed against thrones and altars, and that the first blows were to attain France, that after the fall of the French Monarchy, Rome must be attacked. Cagliostro learnt from the mouths of the Initiators that the secret society of which henceforth he formed a part possessed a mass of money dispersed in the banks of Amsterdam, Rotterdam, London, Genoa, and Venice. He himself drew a substantial sum destined for the expenses of propaganda, received the instructions of the Sect and went to Strasbourg." [1] It was in Strasbourg that Cagliostro then made the acquaintance of the Cardinal de Rohan,[2] who quickly fell under the spell of the hypnotic power which formed Cagliostro's stock-in-trade and is still practised by propagandists of Illuminism. Soon after this the Cardinal introduced the magician to Mme. de la Motte,[3] and the " Affair of the Necklace " was the result. It was thus that the first blow at the French Monarchy was planned in the councils of the German Illuminati.

Two years later a further success was achieved for Illuminism by the acquisition of Mirabeau. That great adventurer had been sent by the French Government on a mission to Berlin, and whilst in Germany became acquainted with some of the Illuminati, amongst others Nicolai and Leuchtsenring. Finally at Brunswick he formed a friendship with Mauvillon, who initiated him into the highest mysteries of the Order.[4] With superb effrontery Mirabeau then published a pamphlet entitled *Essai sur la secte des Illuminés*, purporting to expose the follies of Illuminism but in reality describing the sect of the Martinistes, so as to throw a veil over the manœuvres of the real Illuminati of Bavaria.[5] On his return to France, Mirabeau (who had assumed the illuminated name " Leonidas "), in co-operation with Talleyrand, introduced Illuminism into his lodge, which he had called the " Philalèthes,"[6] again throwing dust in the eyes of the

[1] Louis Blanc, *Histoire de la Révolution Française,* ii. 81.
[2] *Mémoire pour le Comte de Cagliostro,* p. 34.
[3] *Ibid.* p. 44.
[4] Barruel, *Mémoires sur le Jacobinisme,* iv. 258; Robison, *op. cit.* 276.
[5] Clifford, *Application of Barruel's Memoirs of Jacobinism,* p. xvii.
[6] Barruel, *op. cit.* iv. 258, 373.

public, for, as we have seen, the " Philalèthes " was a lodge of the Martinistes — and it was then decided that all the masonic lodges of France should be illuminized. Finding this task, however, beyond his powers, Mirabeau sent to Germany for two more adepts — Bode, known as Amelius, and the Baron de Busche, known as Bayard. At the lodge of the " Amis Réunis," where the members of the masonic lodges from all over France congregated, the mysteries of Illuminism were unveiled by the two German emissaries and the code of Weishaupt was formally placed on the table.[1] The result of this was that by March 1789 the 266 lodges controlled by the Grand Orient were all " illumin- ized " without knowing it, for the Freemasons in general were not told the name of the sect that brought them these mysteries, and only a very small number were really initiated into the secret.[2]

In the following month the Revolution broke out.

No one will deny that France at this period was ripe for drastic reforms. It is true that Babeuf, the Socialist, afterwards declared that the people of France were no worse off than the people of other countries,[3] and that Arthur Young, whose earlier views on the Revolution, written under Orléaniste influence, are always quoted as the strongest indictment of the Old Régime, was later on led by fuller knowledge to assert that " the old government of France, with all its faults, was certainly the best enjoyed by any considerable country in Europe, England alone excepted."[4] Still an examination of facts shows that there was very real cause for discontent, more on the part of the peasants than of the industrial workers. The Game Laws, or *capitaineries* — by which the crops of the peasants could be trampled down by the hunt or destroyed by the game — the salt tax or *gabelle*, the enforced labour known as the *corvée*, the dues paid to the landlords, and a host of other agricultural grievances, but above all, the iniquitous inequality of taxation, were burdens that the people very naturally resented. But it must not be forgotten that the

---

[1] Barruel, *op. cit.* iv. 280.
[2] *Ibid.* iv. 281.
[3] *Pièces saisies chez Babeuf*, 142.
[4] Arthur Young, *The Example of France, a Warning to Britain*, p. 36.

King himself had continued to urge the abolition of these injustices, and that the attitude of the aristocracy as a whole was at this moment far from intractable. The philosophy of Rousseau had opened the eyes of many of the nobles to the need for reforms, and there was probably never a moment in the history of the world when a great regeneration might have been carried out with less violence.

The work of the revolutionaries was not, however, to accelerate reforms, but to arrest them in order to increase popular discontent and bring themselves into power. The manner in which they accomplished their designs has been described in detail in my study of the French Revolution, and for the purpose of the present work the history of this period must be condensed as far as possible so as to indicate only the course of the social revolution.

For, during the first three years of the great upheaval, the plan of Illuminism was obscured by the intrigues of political factions — the conspiracy of the Orléanistes to change the dynasty, and later the struggle of the Girondins to achieve political power. Meanwhile Prussia was playing an insidious part in the troubles of France.

For many years before the Revolution the cherished scheme of Frederick the Great had been to break the Franco-Austrian alliance of 1756, which barred his way to power, and to establish a unified Germany under Prussian domination. In 1778 the Empress Maria Theresa in a letter to her daughter Marie Antoinette wrote these prophetic words:

Every one in Europe knows to what point one can count on the King of Prussia and how far one can depend on his word. France has been able to perceive this under diverse circumstances. And yet that is the sovereign who aspires to erect himself as protector and dictator of Germany. What is still more extraordinary, the Powers do not think of uniting to prevent such a misfortune, from which, sooner or later, all will have to endure the disastrous consequences. What I put forward concerns all the Powers of Europe; the future does not appear to me under a smiling aspect. Yet to-day we endure the influence of *that military and despotic monarchy which recognizes no principle*, but which, in all that it does and all that it undertakes, always pursues the same goal, its own interest and its exclusive advantage. If this Prussian principle is allowed to continue to gain ground, what hope is there for those who will succeed us one day? [1]

As a result of warnings such as these Marie Antoinette adopted that anti-Prussian attitude for which she paid so dearly, and Frederick, centring all his hatred of Austria on the luckless Dauphine of France, circulated libels against her through his agent von der Goltz, who combined the rôle of ambassador and spy at the Court of Versailles. Such indeed was the thoroughness of Hohenzollern methods that he had even taken the trouble to enter into relations with an obscure thief in France named Carra, afterwards to become a leading revolutionary, who apparently proved so efficient that Frederick saw fit to reward him with a gold snuff-box in recognition of his services. The policy of Frederick the Great was faithfully carried out by his successor, Frederick William II., and Prussian agents, chief amongst them a Jew named Ephraim, were sent over to Paris to mingle with the revolutionary mobs and inflame their passions.

The intrigue that directed the opening stages of the Revolution was, however, the Orléaniste conspiracy, and it was by this faction that the artificial scarcity of grain was created during the spring and summer of 1789, and that the siege of the Bastille on July 14 and the march on Versailles on October 5 were organized. Now it has been objected by several critics that in my descriptions of these days I overrated the importance of the Orléaniste conspiracy, and that the feeble character of the Duc d'Orléans makes it impossible to see in him a determined conspirator. The latter fact is true, but it will be noticed that I did not attribute to the Duke himself the organization of the conspiracy, but to his supporters, notably Choderlos de Laclos. Since, however, in research of this kind no progress can be made unless one is willing to reconstruct one's view in the light of further knowledge, I frankly admit that in my *French Revolution* I underrated the importance of Illuminism, and it is therefore quite possible that part of the organization I attributed to the genius of Choderlos de Laclos was in reality the work of illuminized Freemasonry. This would

[1] Deschamps, *op. cit.* pp. 22-28, quoting from the German press.

in no way affect the descriptions of the mechanism by which the so-called popular risings were brought about, but would supply a further explanation of its efficiency.

But since the Duc d'Orléans, whilst lending himself to the plan of usurping the throne of France, was at the same time Grand Master of the Grand Orient, and all the revolutionary leaders, Orléaniste or otherwise, were members of the lodges, it is obviously impossible to disentangle the threads of the two intrigues. How can we know which of the Duke's supporters were genuinely working for a change of dynasty and which for the overthrow of monarchy and all ordered government? The plan of Weishaupt was always to make use of princes to further their own ends, and it would be interesting to discover whether the loans raised by the Duc d'Orléans in Amsterdam and England, wherewith, as the Revolution proceeded he replenished his coffers, came from the funds of the Illuminati in those places.

To whatever agency we attribute it, however, the mechanism of the French Revolution distinguishes it from all previous revolutions. Hitherto the isolated revolutions that had taken place throughout the history of the world can be clearly recognized as spontaneous movements brought about by oppression or by a political faction enjoying some measure of popular support, and therefore endeavouring to satisfy the demands of the people. But in the French Revolution we see for the first time that plan in operation which has been carried on right up to the present moment — *the systematic attempt to create grievances in order to exploit them.*

The most remarkable instance of engineered agitation during the early stages of the Revolution was the extraordinary incident known to history as " The Great Fear," when on the same day, July 22, 1789, and almost at the same hour, in towns and villages all over France, a panic was created by the announcement that brigands were approaching and therefore that all good citizens must take up arms. The messengers who brought the news post-haste on horseback in many cases exhibited placards headed " Edict of the King," bearing the words "The King orders all châteaux to be burnt down; he only wishes to keep his own!" And the people, obedient to these commands, seized upon every weapon they could find and set themselves to the task of destruction. The object of the conspirators was thus achieved — the arming of the populace against law and order, a device which ever since 1789 has always formed the first item in the programme of the social revolution.

It is said that the idea originated with Adrien Dupont and has therefore been attributed to the Orléaniste conspiracy, but Dupont was not only an *intime* of the Duc d'Orléans, but an adept of illuminized Freemasonry, and the organization of the " Great Fear " may well have been masonic. This explanation seems the more probable when we remember that the plan of the lodges even before they became illuminized had been " to make a revolution for the benefit of the *bourgeoisie* with the people as instruments." With this end in view the conspirators held up the food supplies, blocked all reforms in the National Assembly, and organized demonstrations directly opposed to the interests of the people. From the attack on the factory of Reveillon in April 1789 to the murder of the baker François in October, nearly every outrage was directed against men who had fed and befriended the poor.

Under the domination of the Tiers État — almost entirely composed of *bourgeoisie* far more occupied with their own grievances against the nobles than with the sufferings of the people — the legislation carried out by the National Assembly cannot be described by so mild a word as " reactionary "; it was frankly and ruthlessly repressive of all Socialistic or even democratic ideas. Not only was property safeguarded by new laws, but suffrage was extended only to citizens possessing certain incomes, whilst the trade unions that had existed peacefully under the name of " working-men's corporations " were rigorously suppressed by the famous " Loi Chapelier " on June 14, 1791.

By this glaringly anti-democratic act working-men were forbidden to " name presidents, keep registers, make resolutions, deliberate or draw up regulations on their pretended common interests," or to agree on any fixed scale of wages. The wording of the first Article runs as follows:

The annihilation of all kinds of corporations of citizens belonging to the same state or profession being one of the fundamental bases of the French Constitution, it is forbidden to reestablish them on any pretext or under any form whatsoever.

This law was passed without a word of protest from Robespierre or any of the so-called democrats of the Assembly.[1]

As to the " Constitution " held up before the eyes of the people as the supreme benefit the Revolution was to confer on them, it will be noticed that every step on the road to its final promulgation was marked by a fresh outbreak of revolutionary agitation. No sooner had its first principles been placed before the Assembly by Mounier, Clermont Tonnerre, and other honest democrats than a price was placed on the heads of these men by the revolutionaries of the Palais Royal, and an attempt was made to march on Versailles. When two years later the King finally accepted the Constitution, this immense concession to the demands of the people, which if the Revolution had been made by the people would undoubtedly have ended it, became the signal for a fresh outbreak of revolutionary fury, expressed by the hideous massacre known as the " Glacière d'Avignon." Can we not believe then that there may be some truth in the Père Deschamps' statement that " the cry of ' Constitution ' has been in all countries the word of command of the Secret Societies," that is to say, the rallying cry of revolution?[2] We shall find further confirmation of this theory later in the history of the revolutionary movement in Russia.

Thus during the first two years of the Revolution Illuminism concealed itself under the guise of popular tumults, but with the formation of the Jacobin Clubs all over France its scheme of domination becomes more apparent.

These societies, Robison in his *Proofs of a Conspiracy* declares, were organized by the revolutionary committees

[1] Buchez et Roux, *Histoire parlementaire*, x. 196.
[2] *Les Sociétés secrètes et la société*, by P. Deschamps and Claudio Jannet. p. 242.

under the direct inspiration of the Bavarian Illuminati, who taught them their "method of doing business, of managing their correspondence, and of procuring and training pupils." It was thus that at a given signal insurrections could be engineered simultaneously in all parts of the country or that the Faubourgs could be summoned forth at the word of command.

The plan of Weishaupt for enlisting women in the movement had been adopted from the beginning by the revolutionaries, and we see in the declamations of Théroigne de Méricourt,[1] and of the militant suffragette Olympe de Gouges, how cleverly the idea of "giving them hints of emancipation" was carried out. Madame Roland, likewise glorying in the political power the Revolution had brought her, little dreamt whither the movement was tending — to the disappearance from the stage of all women except the furies of the guillotine. Olympe and Madame Roland paid for their illusions with their heads; Théroigne, publicly flogged in the Tuileries gardens by the *tricoteuses* of Robespierre, lost her reason and died raving mad in the Salpêtrière some years later. For in times of revolution it is not the women of brains and energy who can ever take a leading part, but only those whose disordered imaginations and perverted passions inspire them with a ferocity more horrible than that of man.

The Jacobins, in playing on these passions amongst the women who assembled at the meetings held three times weekly at their "Sociétés Fraternelles," fanned their fury into flame and prepared those terrible bands of harpies who committed the atrocities of August 10th.

So complete had the organization of the Jacobin Clubs now become that during 1791 and 1792 all the masonic lodges of France were closed down and Philippe Egalité sent in his resignation as Grand Master. This was held advisable for several reasons: the Jacobins, once the masters of France, could not with safety tolerate the existence

---

[1] Théroigne thus expressed her views on the Revolution to an English contemporary: "Society is undergoing a change, a grand reorganization, and women are about to resume their rights. We shall no more be flattered in order to be enslaved; these arms have dethroned the tyrant and conquered freedom " (*France in* 1802, Letters of Redhead Yorke, p. 62).

of any secret association that might be used as a cover for counter-revolutionary schemes; moreover, as the great plan of Illuminism was by this time in process of fulfilment, what further need was there for secrecy? Projects formerly discussed with bated breath in the lodges could now be openly avowed in the tribune of the Jacobin Clubs, and nothing remained but to put them into execution.

It was not, however, until after the overthrow of the monarchy on the 10th of August that the work of demolition began on the vast scale planned by Weishaupt. From this moment the rôle of Illuminism can be clearly traced through the succeeding phases of the Revolution. Thus it is from the 10th of August onwards that we find the tricolour, banner of the usurper, replaced by the red flag of the social revolution, whilst the cry of " Vive notre roi d'Orléans! " gives way to the masonic watchword "Liberty Equality, Fraternity!" During the massacres in the prisons that followed in September the assassins were observed to make masonic signs to the victims and to spare those who knew how to reply. Amongst those not spared was the Abbé Lefranc, who had published a pamphlet unveiling the designs of Freemasonry at the beginning of the Revolution.

The proclamation issued by the Convention in December summoning the proletariats of Europe to rise in revolt against all ordered government was the first trumpet-call to World Revolution, and it was the failure to respond to this appeal that forced the Jacobins into a " national " attitude they had never intended to assume.

In November 1793 the campaign against religion, inaugurated by the massacre of the priests in September 1792 was carried out all over France. In the cemeteries the cherished motto of the Illuminati, " Death is an eternal sleep," was posted up by order of the Illuminatus " Anaxagoras " Chaumette. The Feasts of Reason celebrated in the churches of Paris were the mere corollary to Weishaupt's teaching that " Reason should be the only code of Man "; and Robison states that the actual ceremonies which took place, when women of easy morals were enthroned as goddesses, were modelled on Weishaupt's plan of an " Eroterion " or festival in honour of the god of Love.[1]

It was likewise to Weishaupt's declamations against " the mercantile tribe " that the devastation of the manufacturing towns of France and the ruin of her merchants can be traced, whilst the campaign against education formed a further part of the scheme for destroying civilization. The Terrorists in burning down the libraries and guillotining Lavoisier, on the plea that " the Republic has no need of chemists," were simply putting into practice Weishaupt's theory that the sciences were " children of necessity, the complicated needs of a state contrary to Nature, the inventions of vain and empty brains." " The system of persecution against men of talents was organized," a contemporary declared — organized, as was the whole system of the Terror, by the Illuminati and carried out by men who had accepted the guiding principle of the sect. For it was Weishaupt's favourite maxim, " The end justifies the means," that we find again in the mouths of the Jacobins under the form of " Tout est permis à quiconque agit dans le sens de la Révolution." The Reign of Terror was the logical outcome of this premise.

But this does not imply that all the Terrorists were Illuminati, that is to say, conscious adepts of Weishaupt. It is true that, as we have seen, all were Freemasons at the beginning of the Revolution, but it is probable that few were initiated into the inner mysteries of the Order. The art of Illuminism lay in enlisting dupes as well as adepts, and by encouraging the dreams of honest visionaries or the schemes of fanatics, by flattering the vanity of ambitious egoists, by working on unbalanced brains, or by playing on such passions as greed of gold or power, to make men of totally divergent aims serve the secret purpose of the sect. Indeed, amongst all the revolutionary leaders one man alone stands out as a pure Illuminatus — the Prussian Baron, Anacharsis Clootz.

[1] The idea seems to have been long current in Germany. " In 1751 an impious work, dedicated to Frederick II. (the Great), published as a frontispiece the scene of the adoration of a prostitute which was destined to be realised on the 20th of Brumaire 1793 on the altar of Notre Dame of Paris " (Deschamps, *Les Sociétés secrètes*, ii. 98, quoting *Der Goetze der Humanität oder das Positive der Freimaurerei*, Freiburg Herder, 1875, pp. 75-80).

In the utterances of Clootz we find the doctrines of Weishaupt expressed with absolute fidelity. Thus in his *République Universelle* the scheme of Weishaupt for welding the whole human race into " one good and happy family " is set forth at length: " One common interest! one mind! one Nation! " cries Anacharsis. " Do you wish," he asks again, " to exterminate all tyrants at a blow? Declare then authentically that sovereignty consists in the common patriotism and solidarity of the totality of men, of the one and only nation. . . . The Universe will form one State, the State of united individuals, the immutable empire of the great *Germany* — the Universal Republic." Or again: " When the Tower of London falls like the tower of Paris it will be all over with tyrants. All the people forming only one nation, all the trades forming only one trade, all interests forming only one interest," etc. It was Clootz, moreover, who played the most active part in the campaign against religion. Was it not he who had invented the word to " septemberize," regretting that they had not " septemberized " more priests in the prisons, and who openly declared himself " the personal enemy of Jesus Christ " ? The fact that he never revealed himself to be an Illuminatus and never referred to Weishaupt was in strict accordance with the rule of the Order, which we shall find adhered to by every adept in turn. " The Illuminati," Professor Renner had declared before the Bavarian Court of Inquiry, " fear nothing so much as being recognized under this name," and frightful punishment was attached to the betrayal of the secret. It is thus that historians, unaware of the sources whence Clootz drew his theories, or anxious to conceal the rôle of Illuminism in the revolutionary movement, describe him as an amiable eccentric of no importance. In reality Clootz was one of the most important figures of the whole Revolution if viewed from the modern standpoint, for it was he alone of all his day who embodied the spirit of anti-patriotism and Internationalism which, defeated in France of 1793, finally secured its triumph on the ruins of the Russian Empire of 1917.

It was Clootz's Internationalism that ended by antagonizing Robespierre. When at the Jacobin Club the

Prussian Baron declared that " his heart was French and *sans-culotte*," but at the same time proposed that as soon as "the French army came in sight of the Austrian and Prussian soldiers they should, instead of attacking the enemy, throw down their own arms and advance towards them dancing in a friendly manner," [1] Robespierre, " who was not without a certain penetration in his hatreds . . . acidly apostrophized him, saying that he distrusted all these foreigners who pretended to be more patriotic than the French themselves, that he suspected the good faith of a so-called *sans-culotte* who had an income of 100,000 livres," [2] and he ended by sending Clootz and his fellow-atheists Hébert, Chaumette, Ronsin, and Vincent to the scaffold.

Was Robespierre then not an Illuminatus? He was certainly a Freemason, and Prince Kropotkine definitely states that he belonged to one of the lodges of the Illuminati founded by Weishaupt. But contemporaries declare that he had not been fully initiated and acted as the tool rather than as the agent of the conspiracy. Moreover, Robespierre was the disciple not only of Weishaupt but of Rousseau, and under the inspiration of the *Contrat Social* had elaborated a scheme of his own which held none of the aimless destructiveness of the Illuminati. Thus Robespierre clearly recognized the necessity for the vast social revolution indicated by Weishaupt; but whilst Weishaupt fixed his eyes on the explosion and " smiled at the thought of universal conflagration," Robespierre regarded anarchy simply as a means to an end — the reconstruction of society according to the plan he had evolved with the co-operation of Saint-Just, which was simply an embryonic form of the system known later as *State Socialism*.

This statement will of course be challenged by Socialists, who have always — for reasons I shall show later — denied the Robespierrean origin of their doctrines. It is true of course that the word Socialism was not invented until some forty years later, but it would be absurd by means of such a quibble to disassociate Socialism from its

[1] *France in* 1802, Letters of Henry Redhead Yorke, p. 72.
[2] *Biographie Michaud*, article " Clootz."

earliest exponents. M. Aulard is no doubt perfectly right
in saying that Robespierre's Declaration of the Rights of
Man contains " all the essentials of French Socialism
founded on the principles of 1789 and such as Louis Blanc
popularized in 1848. It is for having proposed these
Socialistic articles, it is for having proposed this charter
for Socialism, and not for having vaguely declaimed
against the rich and sounded the praises of mediocrity,
that Robespierre after his death, as much in our own
century as in the time of Babeuf, became the prophet of
many of those amongst us who dreamt of a social renova-
tion, and he remained so until the period when German
influence made French Socialists temporarily forget the
French origins of their doctrines." [1] Robespierre may
indeed, in the language of Socialism, be described as more
" advanced " than his French successors of the early nineteenth century, for he anticipated the Marxian theory of
the class war, which was not again to find acceptance in
France until adopted by the Guesdists and Syndicalists
at the very end of the century. Robespierre's cherished
maxim, " The rich man is the enemy of the *sans-culotte*," [2]
contains the whole spirit of the class war. We have in fact
only to transpose the phrases current in 1793 into their
modern equivalents to recognize their identity with modern
Socialistic formulas. Thus the magic phrase " dictatorship of the proletariat " — of which it is doubtful whether
any one understands the precise meaning — was expressed
at that date by the words " Sovereignty of the People,"
and formed the text of Robespierre's gospel. " The
people," he wrote, " must be the object of all political
institutions." [3] All other classes of the community were
to be entirely unrepresented or, preferably, not to be
allowed to exist.

Even the theory of "wage slavery," later on proclaimed
by Marx, was already current during the Reign of Terror,
and on this point we have the evidence of a contemporary.

[1] Aulard, *Histoire politique de la Révolution Française*, iv. 47; see also
Aulard, *Etudes et leçons sur la Révolution Française*, ii. 51.
[2] *Papiers trouvés chez Robespierre*, i. 15.
[3] *Discours et rapports de Robespierre*, edited by Charles Vellay, p. 8;
see also p. 327.

" The plan of the Jacobins," wrote the democrat Fantin Désodoards, " was to stir up the rich against the poor and the poor against the rich. To the latter they said: ' You have made a few sacrifices in favour of the Revolution, but fear, not patriotism, was the motive.' To the former they said: ' The rich man has no bowels of compassion; under the pretext of feeding the poor by providing them with work he exercises over them a superiority contrary to the views of Nature and to Republican principles. Liberty will always be precarious *as long as one part of the nation lives on wages from the other*. In order to preserve its independence, it is necessary that every one should be rich or that every one should be poor.' " [1]

It will be seen then that the whole theory of the class war, and even the very phrases by which it was to be promoted, as also the necessity for abolishing the relationship of capital and labour, which is usually associated with Marx, were ideas that existed twenty-five years before his birth. We cannot doubt that it is to Robespierre and Saint-Just that they must be mainly attributed. Robespierre, as we know, definitely advocated the abolition of inheritance. " The property of a man," he said, " must return after his death to the public domain of society "; and although he was known to declare that " equality of wealth is a chimera," it was no doubt because he well knew that wealth can never be evenly distributed, and therefore that the only way to achieve equality is by the process known to-day as the nationalization of all wealth and property. " This," says the editor of his discourses, M. Charles Vellay, " is what the Revolution means to him — it is to lead to a sort of Communism, and it is here that he separates himself from his colleagues, that he isolates himself, and that resistance gathers around him." In 1840 the Socialist Cabet, who had received the Robespierriste tradition direct from the contemporary Buonarotti, expressed the same opinion:

All the proposals of the Comité de Salut Public during the last five months, the opinions of Bodson and of Buonarotti — both initiated into the profound views of Robespierre, both his admirers, and both Communists, — give us the conviction that Robespierre and Saint-Just only blamed the untimely invocation

[1] Fantin Désodoards, *Histoire philosophique de la Révolution Française,* iv. 344.

of Community by declared atheists (*i.e.* Clootz, Hébert, etc.), and that they themselves marched towards Communism by paths they judged more suited to success.[1]

Still more clinching evidence of Robespierre's real aim is, however, provided by the Communist Babeuf, who wrote these words in 1795:

He (Robespierre) thought that equality would only be a vain word as long as the owners of property were allowed to tyrannize over the great mass, and that in order to destroy their power and to take the mass of citizens out of their dependence *there was no way but to place all property in the hands of the government.*[2]

In the face of this statement how can any one deny that Robespierre was a State Socialist in precisely the sense in which we understand the term to-day? That the State was of course to be represented by Robespierre himself and his chosen associates it is needless to add, but what Communist or group of Communists have ever excluded the hypothesis of their own supremacy from their plan of a Socialist State? " L'Etat c'est nous " is the maxim of all such theorists.

On one point, however, Robespierre differed from most of the members of the same school of thought who came after him in that he showed himself a *consistent* Socialist, for he had the singleness of aim, aided by an entire want of moral scruples, to push his theories to their logical conclusion. A Labour extremist in this country recently described the modern Bolsheviks as " Socialists with the courage of their opinions," and the same description might be applied to Robespierre and Saint-Just. Thus Robespierre did not talk hypocritically of " peaceful revolution "; he knew that revolution is never peaceful, that in its very essence it implies onslaught met with resistance, a resistance that can only be overcome by an absolute disregard for human life. " I will walk willingly with my feet in blood and tears," said his coadjutor Saint-Just; and this, whether he admits it or not, must be the maxim of every revolutionary Socialist who believes that any methods are justifiable for the attainment of his end.

[1] *Histoire populaire de la Révolution Française*, by Cabet (1840).
[2] *Sur le système de la dépopulation*, p. 28.

The Reign of Terror was therefore not only the outcome of Illuminism but also the logical result of Socialistic doctrines. Thus, for example, the attacks on civilization carried out in the summer of 1793, the burning of the libraries and the destruction of treasures of art and literature, were all part of the scheme of Weishaupt, but they were also perfectly consistent with the Socialistic theory of the " sovereignty of the people." For if one considers that in the least educated portion of the community all wisdom and all virtue reside, the only logical thing to do is to burn the libraries and close down the schools. Of what avail is it to train the intellectual faculties of a child if manual labour alone is to be held honourable? Of what use to civilize him if in civilization is to be found the bane of mankind? It is idle in one breath to talk of the beauties of education and in the next to advocate the " dictatorship of the proletariat " and condemn all educated people as *bourgeois*.

Of this strange contradiction the Jacobins of France, like the Bolsheviks of Russia, at first were guilty. Magnificent schemes were propounded to the Convention for " écoles normales," " écoles centrales," etc.; regiments of professors were to be commandeered for the instruction of youth; but all these schemes came to nought, for by the end of 1794 public education was said to be non-existent,[1] owing obviously to the fact that meanwhile the emissaries of the Comité de Salut Public had busied themselves destroying books and pictures and persecuting all men of education.

This campaign against the *bourgeoisie* found its principal support in Robespierre. It was he who first sounded the call to arms which has since become the war-cry of the social revolution. " Internal dangers come from the *bourgeois;* in order to conquer the *bourgeois* we must rouse the people, we must procure arms for them and make them angry." [2] The natural consequence of this policy carried out against the mercantile *bourgeoisie* by the attacks on the manufacturing towns of France was of course to create

[1] Joseph de Maistre, *Mélanges inédits*. pp. 122, 124, 125, quoting contemporary documents.
[2] *Papiers trouvés chez Robespierre*. ii. 15.

vast unemployment. Already the destruction of the aristocracy had thrown numberless workers on the streets, so that by 1791 nearly all the hands that had ministered to the needs or caprices of the rich were idle, and thousands of hairdressers, gilders, bookbinders, tailors, embroiderers, and domestic servants wandered about Paris and collected in crowds " to debate on the misery of their situation."

The situation must always arise, if the leisured classes are suddenly destroyed either by killing them off or by a ruthless conscription of capital. Socialists are fond of describing luxury workers as parasites; obviously then if one destroys the animal on which the parasite lives one must destroy the parasite too. It is possible that by a very slow and gradual redistribution of wealth luxury workers might be more or less absorbed into the essential trades, but even this is very doubtful. At any rate the attempt to abolish the luxury trades at a blow must inevitably lead to unemployment on a vast scale, for not only will the luxury workers themselves be idle, but, since all classes are interdependent, many of the workers in the essential trades who depend on them for a livelihood will be idle likewise. Any sudden dislocation of the industrial system must therefore mean national bankruptcy.

This is precisely what happened in France — as even Socialist writers admit. Malon in his *Histoire du socialisme* illustrates, by a picture of a scene in a Paris street, the situation described by Michelet in the words:

The Revolution was to open a career to the peasant but closed it to the workman. The first pricked up his ear at the decrees which placed the goods of the clergy on sale; the second, silent and sombre, dismissed from his workshop, wandered about all day with folded arms.[1]

The condition of the industrial workers was still further aggravated by the legislation of the Terror. Not only was the Loi Chapelier against trade unions confirmed and severely enforced by the Comité de Salut Public under the domination of Robespierre, but the workers were obliged to toil very much harder than ever before. This point, systematically ignored by historians, constitutes one of the

[1] Malon, *Histoire du socialisme*, i. 267, 297.

chief ironies of the period and illustrates the ingenious method by which the so-called advocates of the People's Sovereignty contrived to dupe the People to their own undoing. Thus, under the pretext of abolishing the obsolete customs and superstitions of the Old Régime, the workers were deprived of all the holidays they had enjoyed in honour of the Saints or the festivals of the Church. Under the monarchy not only every one of these days but also the day following it had been a holiday, and neither on Sunday nor on Monday was any work done.

By substituting " decadi," that is to say one day in every ten, for Sunday and making it only a half-holiday, the new masters of France added three and one-half working days to every fortnight. The result per year is shown in an amusing article of the *Moniteur* for September 9, 1794, entitled " National Idleness," of which the following is an extract:

Easter, Christmas, All Saints, days of the Virgin, of Kings, Saint Martin, fifty thousand patrons of parishes and priories . . . all these fêtes and their morrows have been suppressed; by expelling the saints from their shrines and all the priests from their confessionals thirty-six half Sundays are left us (*i.e.* the thirty-six *decadis* which occurred in the course of the year, which were half-holidays). The Revolution has consecrated to work at least a hundred and twenty days which the Pope and his Elder Son (the title given to the King of France) left to idleness in France. This national idleness was a tax on misery, a tax that diminished the revenues of the State and increased expenses for alms, assistance, and hospitals. Permission to work is a charity which costs nothing to the public treasure and which will bring to it considerable funds. All is new in France — weather, mankind, the earth, and the sea. . . . *The Republican year gives to work four months more than the papal and monarchic year.*[1]

It is not necessary to be a believer in the principle of Ca' Canny as a remedy for unemployment to recognize that the result of this legislation was to reduce the number of hands required and leave the vast reserve of labour which enables the employer to make his own terms with the workers. It will be seen that this expedient which State Socialists are fond of denouncing as one of the evils of

[1] *Moniteur*, xxi. 699.

Capitalism was practised under the régime of that first experimenter in State Socialism — Maximilien Robespierre.

But towards the end of 1793 it became evident that there was no possibility of absorbing the residuum created, for the attacks on the manufacturing towns of France had dealt the final blow to trade and the Republic found itself faced by hundreds of thousands of working-men for whom it could not find employment. It was then that the Comité de Salut Public, anticipating the Malthusian theory, embarked on its fearful project — *the system of depopulation.*

That this plan really existed it is impossible to doubt in the face of overwhelming contemporary evidence. In *The French Revolution* I quoted in this connection the testimony of no less than twenty-two witnesses — all revolutionaries; [1] and since then I have found further corroboration of the fact in the letters of an Englishman, named Redhead Yorke, who travelled in France in 1802 and made particular inquiries on this question from the ally of Robespierre, the painter David:

I asked him whether it was true that a project had been in contemplation to reduce the population of France to one-third of its present number. He answered that it had been seriously discussed and that Dubois Crancé was the author.

In another passage Yorke states:

Monsieur de la Métherie assured me that during the time of the Revolutionary Tribunals, it was in serious contemplation to reduce the population of France to 14,000,000. Dubois Crancé was a very distinguished and enthusiastic partisan of this humane and philosophical policy.[2]

It will be noticed that there is here a discrepancy in the exact figures; the population of France at that period being twenty-five millions, the proposal to reduce it to one-third was to bring it down to approximately eight millions. The difference then lies between the projects of reducing it *by* one-third or *to* one-third — issues which Yorke evidently

[1] *The French Revolution*, pp. 426-428.
[2] *France in* 1802, Letters of Redhead Yorke, edited by J. A. C. Sykes (Heinemann), 1906, pp. 102, 127.

confused; but it was precisely on this point that the opinions of the Terrorists differed. Thus we are told that d'Antonelle of the Revolutionary Tribunal advocated the former and more moderate policy, but that a reduction to eight millions, that is to say to one-third, was the figure generally agreed on by the leaders.

The necessity for this lay not only in the fact that there was not even enough bread, money, or property to go round, but also, after the destruction of the aristocracy and *bourgeoisie*, not enough work.

" In the eyes of Maximilien Robespierre and his council," says Babeuf, " depopulation was indispensable because the calculation had been made that the French population was in excess of the resources of the soil and of the requirements of *useful industry*, that is to say, that with us men jostled each other too much for each to be able to live at ease; that hands were too numerous for the execution of all works of *essential utility* — and this is the horrible conclusion, that since the superabundant population could only amount to so much . . . a portion of *sans-culottes* must be sacrificed; that this rubbish could be cleared up to a certain quantity, and that means must be found for doing it."

The system of the Terror was thus the answer to the problem of unemployment — unemployment brought about on a vast scale by the destruction of the luxury trades.

If the hecatombs carried out all over France never reached the huge proportions planned by the leaders, it was not for want of what they described as " energy in the art of revolution." Night and day the members of the Comité de Salut Public sat round the green-covered table in the Tuileries with the map of France spread out before them, pointing out towns and villages and calculating how many heads they must have in each department. Night and day the Revolutionary Tribunal passed on, without judgment, its never-ending stream of victims, whilst near by the indefatigable Fouquier bent over his lists for the morrow, and in the provinces the proconsuls Carrier, Fréron, Collot d'Herbois, Lebon toiled unremittingly at the same Herculean task.

Compared to the results they had hoped to achieve the

mortality was insignificant; compared to the accounts given us by " the conspiracy of history " it was terrific. The popular conception of the Reign of Terror as a procession of powdered heads going to the guillotine seems strangely naïve when we read the actual records of the period. Thus during the great Terror in Paris about 2800 victims perished, and out of these approximately 500 were of the aristocracy, 1000 of the *bourgeoisie*, and 1000 working-class. These estimates are not a surmise, since they can be proved by the actual register of the Revolutionary Tribunal published both by Campardon and Wallon, also by the contemporary Prudhomme,[1] and they are accepted as accurate by the Robespierriste historian Louis Blanc.[2]

According to Prudhomme the total number of victims drowned, guillotined, or shot all over France amounted to 300,000 and of this number the nobles sacrificed were an almost negligible quantity, only about 3000 in all.[3]

At Nantes 500 children of the people were killed in one butchery, and according to an English contemporary 144 poor women who sewed shirts for the army were thrown into the river.[4]

Such was the period during which Carlyle dared to assure us that " The Twenty-Five Millions of France " had " never suffered less."

But this frightful mortality was not the only dreadful feature of the Terror — ruin, misery, starvation were the lot of all but the band of tyrants who had seized the reins of power, and this state of affairs continued long after the reign of Robespierre ended. The conception of France rising like a phoenix from that great welter of blood and horror is as mythical as the allegory from which it is taken and has existed only in the minds of posterity. Not a single contemporary who lived through the Revolution has ever pretended that it was anything but a ghastly failure. The conspiracy of history alone has created the myth.

Yet in France the truth is at last beginning to be

[1] Prudhomme, *Crimes de la Révolution*, vol. vi. Table VI.
[2] Louis Blanc, *Histoire de la Révolution*, xi. 155.
[3] Prudhomme, *Crimes de la Révolution*, vol. vi. Table VI.
[4] Playfair's *History of Jacobinism*, p. 789.

known. Thus M. Madelin, the most impartial and enlightened of modern historians, has described the condition of France at the end of the Terror in these forcible words:

France is demoralized. She is exhausted — this is the last trait of this country in ruins. There is no longer any public opinion, or rather this opinion is made up only of hatred. They hate the Directors (members of the Directory) and they hate the deputies; they hate the Terrorists and they hate the *chouans* (the Royalists of La Vendée); they hate the rich and they hate the anarchists; they hate the Revolution and the counter-revolution. . . . But where hatred reaches paroxysm is in the case of the newly rich. What is the good of having destroyed Kings, nobles, and aristocrats, since deputies, farmers, and tradesmen take their place? What cries of hatred! . . . Of all the ruins found and increased by the Directory — ruins of parties, ruins of power, ruins of national representation, ruins of churches, ruins of finances, ruins of homes, ruins of consciences, ruins of intellects — there is nothing more pitiable than this: *the ruin of the national character*.[1]

Eight years after the ending of the Terror, France had not yet recovered from its ravages. According to Redhead Yorke, even the usually accepted theory of agricultural prosperity is erroneous.

Nothing can exceed the wretchedness of the implements of husbandry employed but the wretched appearance of the persons using them. Women at the plough and young girls driving a team give but an indifferent idea of the progress of agriculture under the Republic. There are no farmhouses dispersed over the fields. The farmers reside together in remote villages, a circumstance calculated to retard the business of cultivation. The interiors of the houses are filthy, the farmyards in the utmost disorder, and the miserable condition of the cattle sufficiently bespeaks the poverty of their owner.[2]

Everywhere beggars assailed the traveller for alms; in spite of the reduced population unemployment was rife, education was at a standstill, and owing to the destruction of the old nobility and clergy, and the fact that the new rich who occupied their estates were absentee landlords, there was no system of organized charity. Yorke is finally driven to declare:

The Revolution, which was brought about ostensibly for the

[1] Madelin, *La Révolution*, pp. 443, 444.
[2] *France in* 1802, p. 28.

benefit of the lower classes of society, has sunk them to a degree of degradation and misfortune to which they never were reduced under the ancient monarchy. They have been disinherited, stripped, and deprived of every resource for existence, except defeats of arms and the fleeting spoil of vanquished nations.

In another passage Yorke asks the inevitable question that arises in the minds of all thinking contemporaries:

France still bleeds at every pore — she is a vast mourning family, clad in sackcloth. It is impossible at this time for a contemplative mind to be gay in France. At every footstep the merciless and sanguinary route of fanatical barbarians disgust the sight and sicken humanity — on all sides ruins obtrude themselves on the eye and compel the question, " For what and for whom are all this havoc and desolation? " [1]

It will of course be said that Redhead Yorke was a " reactionary." As a matter of fact he was a constitutional revolutionary and had served a term of imprisonment in Dorchester Castle from 1795 to 1799 for having declared himself to be " a man who had been concerned in three revolutions already, who essentially contributed to serve the Republic in America, who contributed to that of Holland, who materially assisted that of France, and who will continue to cause revolutions all over the world." His visit to France in 1802, however, dispelled his illusions, and he had the courage to admit his change of views. His letters were not published till after his death.

Advocates of social revolution, to whom the revelations on the real facts of the Terror which have recently been published are extremely disconcerting, have adopted the convenient line of describing the first French Revolution as a " *bourgeois* movement." It is true that it was made by *bourgeois*, and at the beginning also by aristocrats — and that the people throughout were the chief sufferers; but this has been the case in every outbreak of the World Revolution. All revolutionary leaders or writers have been *bourgeois*, from Weishaupt to Lenin. Marx was a *bourgeois*, Sorel was a *bourgeois* likewise. No man of the people has ever taken a prominent part in the movement. But in the French " Terror," as in Russia to-day, the *bourgeoisie* were also the victims.

[1] *France in* 1802, p. 33.

" In that sort of epilepsy into which France had fallen,"
wrote Prudhomme, " not only the revolutionary nobles set themselves by preference against nobles, priests against priests,
merchants against merchants, rich against rich, but even the
sans-culottes once they themselves became judges did not any
the more spare the *sans-culottes* who had remained amongst the
crowd of citizens. How could the people have suspected the
system of universal depopulation? Until then it had not been
heard of in history. This great doctrine, however, was not
chimerical, it existed, it was visible, the leaders of opinion only
wished to reign over deserts." [1]

What power can have inspired this fearful system?
The pages of accepted history provide no clue to the problem. Only by a recognition of the secret forces at work
beneath the surface is it possible to understand how the
French nation fell a victim to the hideous régime of the
Terror. In the opinion of numberless enlightened contemporaries Illuminism alone explains the mystery. As
early as 1793 the *Journal de Vienne* pointed out the true
source of inspiration beneath the system of the Jacobins:

It is not the French who conceived the great project of
changing the face of the world; this honour belongs to the
Germans. The French can claim the honour of having begun its
execution, and of having followed it out to its ultimate consequences, which, as history is there to prove, were in accordance
with the genius of this people — the guillotine, intrigue, assassination, incendiarism, and cannibalism. . . . Whence comes the
eternal Jacobin refrain of universal liberty and equality, of the
suppression of kings and princes who are merely tyrants, of
oppression by the clergy, of necessary measures for annihilating
the Christian religion and establishing a philosophic religion — a
refrain that reminds every one of the declarations of Mauvillon,
a notable Illuminatus, touching Christianity, of those of Knigge
and Campe touching State religion? Whence comes it that all
this harmonizes with the " Original Writings " of the Illuminati
if there is no alliance between the two sects? Whence comes it
that Jacobinism has partisans everywhere, even in the most
distant countries, and how can we explain that these, as far as
researches can extend, have been in touch with Illuminism?

Aloys Hoffman, editor of this Journal, wrote: " I shall
never cease to repeat that the Revolution has come from
masonry and that it was made by writers and the Illuminati."

[1] Prudhomme, *Crimes de la Révolution*, i. p. xxiii.

That the objects of the conspiracy were precisely the same as they are to-day is shown by this remarkable extract from a letter of Quintin Crawfurd to Lord Auckland on May 23, 1793:

The present crisis is certainly the most extraordinary in its nature, and may be the most important in its consequences of any that is to be found on the page of history. It may decide the fate of the Religion and Government of most of the nations of Europe, or rather it may decide whether religion and government are to exist, or Europe be plunged again into a state of barbarism. Hitherto the basis of human polity was religion, the Supreme Being was everywhere adored, and the great maxims of morality respected; but when the order of civil society had attained a degree of perfection unknown in former ages, we see endeavours almost everywhere put in practice to destroy it, Atheism rising against Religion, Anarchy against government, vagabonds against the industrious, men who have nothing to lose against those who enjoy what they received from their ancestors or acquired by their labour, and this conflict brought at last into the field to be decided by the sword. On one hand we see the chief powers of Europe taking arms in defence of Religion and lawful authority, and on the other a multitude of disorganized barbarians endeavouring to undo them. Such, my Lord, with some political shades that might be added is a pretty faithful picture of what the French Revolution has produced hitherto.

.   .   .   .   .   .

What words could better describe the situation of Europe in this year of 1921?

But in spite of the vast demolition effected by the Terror, neither the disciples of Weishaupt nor their tools the revolutionary Socialists had achieved their purpose. One more effort must be made to bring about the " Universal revolution that should deal the deathblow to society." This attempt was made two years after the Terror ended by the Communist, Gracchus Babeuf.

CHAPTER III

THE CONSPIRACY OF BABEUF

Gracchus Babeuf — The Panthéonistes — Manifesto of the Equals — System of Babeuf — Plan of the Conspirators — The Great Day of the People — Discovery of the Plot — Execution of Babouvistes — Illuminism in England — Ireland — The United Irishmen — Bantry Bay — Illuminism in America.

FRANÇOIS NOËL BABEUF was born in 1762, and at the beginning of the Reign of Terror occupied the post of commissary in the Supply Department of the Commune, where he incurred the displeasure of the Comité de Salut Public by publishing a placard accusing the Committee of a plan to drive the people to revolt by means of a fictitious famine and so provide a pretext for killing them off.[1] For this offence Babeuf and his colleagues in the same department were thrown into prison at the Abbaye, but Babeuf, being apparently regarded as mentally irresponsible, was soon afterwards released, and once more proceeded to attack the party in power, which was no other than that of Robespierre, Couthon, and Saint-Just. This is the more remarkable since the political opinions of Babeuf were entirely in accord with those of the Triumvirate; for Robespierre's "Declaration of the Rights of Man" Babeuf entertained the warmest admiration. But where, at this point in his career, Babeuf joined issue with Robespierre was in the method by which this ideal system should be brought about; for the plan of reducing the population of France by some fifteen millions in order to be able to provide bread and work for the remainder, which Babeuf later described as "the immense secret" of the Terror, seemed to him too drastic, and in his pamphlet *Sur la dépopulation de la*

[1] *Babeuf et le socialisme en* 1796, by Edouard Fleury, p. 20.

53

France he denounced the *noyades, fusillades,* and *guillo-tinades* that had decimated the provinces — methods which he held should not have been adopted until pacific measures for winning the peasants over to Republicanism had at least been attempted.

But the régime that followed on the fall of Robespierre led Babeuf to readjust his views, for the Thermidoriens, with whom he had thrown in his lot, showed themselves to be Opportunists of the most flagrant description, and it was thus that after the Directory had been in power a few months Babeuf insulted Tallien and Fréron,[1] declared that the 9th of Thermidor had been an unmitigated disaster, and that the only hope for the people now lay in carrying out the unfinished plan of Robespierre for " the common happiness." Robespierre, he held, was the one " pure " revolutionary of his day;[2] all the rest — the Girondins, who had only wished to dethrone the King in order to usurp power and riches, the Orléanistes, led by Philippe Egalité and Danton, a faction " composed of men as monstrous as their chief . . . avid and prodigal of gold . . . auda-cious, liars, intriguers "[3] — had exploited the people for their own advantage; " Robespierre and his companions in martyrdom " alone had aspired to " the equal distribu-tion of work and pleasure "[4] which was the ideal of Babeuf. Accordingly, he now appealed to the people to rise against the Directory and maintain the Constitution of 1793 founded on Robespierre's " Declaration of the Rights of Man."

The publication of this call to insurrection led to the arrest of its author, and Babeuf was again thrown into prison, first at Plessis, then at Arras; but while in captivity he encountered a number of kindred spirits, with whose co-operation he was able to mature his plan for a further revolution — a social revolution for " the common happi-ness and true equality " (*le bonheur common et l'égalité réelle*).[5]

---

[1] Fleury, *op. cit.* p. 37.
[2] *Pièces saisies chez Babeuf,* i. 147.
[3] *Ibid.* i. 98, 106.
[4] *Conspiration pour l'égalité dite de Babeuf,* by Ph. Buonarotti, i. 88.
[5] Fleury, *op. cit.* p. 45.

M. Louis Blanc is no doubt right in pronouncing Babeuf to have been an Illuminatus, a disciple of Weishaupt, and it was thus in accordance with the custom of the sect that he had adopted a classical pseudonym, renouncing his Christian names of François Noël in favour of Gracchus,[1] just as Weishaupt had assumed the name of Spartacus, the Illuminatus Jean Baptiste Clootz had elected to be known as Anacharsis, and Pierre Gaspard Chaumette as Anaxagoras. The plan of campaign devised by Babeuf was therefore modelled directly on the system of Weishaupt, and on his release from prison — which was brought about by the amnesty of the " Treize Vendémiaire " — he gathered his fellow-conspirators around him and formed an association on masonic lines by which propaganda was to be carried on in public places, the confederates recognizing each other by secret signs and passwords.[2] At the first meeting of the Babouvistes — amongst whom were found Darthé, Germain, Bodson, and Buonarotti — all swore to " remain united and to make equality triumph," and the project was then discussed of establishing a large popular society for the inculcation of Babeuf's doctrines. In order to escape the vigilance of the police it was decided to assemble henceforth in a small room in the garden of the Abbaye de Sainte Geneviève lent by one of the members who had rented part of the building; later the society moved to the refectory of the Abbey, or, on nights when this hall was required for other purposes, meetings were held in the crypt, where, seated on the ground, by the light of torches, the conspirators discussed the great plan for overthrowing society. The proximity of this building to the Panthéon led to their being known under the name of the *Panthéonistes*.[3]

Unfortunately the confusion of mind prevailing amongst the advocates of " Equality " was so great that the meetings — which before long consisted of two thousand people — became " like a Tower of Babel." [4] No one knew precisely what he wanted and no decisions could be reached; it was therefore decided to supplement these huge

[1] Fleury, *op. cit.* p. 38.
[2] *Ibid.* pp. 69, 70.
[3] *Ibid.* p. 69.
[4] *Ibid.* p. 71.

assemblies by small secret committees, the first of which held its sittings at the house of Amar — one of the most ferocious members of the Comité de Sûreté Générale during the Terror — and here the scheme of social revolution was elaborated. Starting from the premise that all property is theft, it was decided that the process known in revolutionary language as " expropriation "[1] must take place; that is to say, all property must be wrested from its present owners by force — the force of an armed mob. But Babeuf, whilst advocating violence and tumult as the means to an end, in no way desired anarchy as a permanent condition; the State must be maintained, and not only maintained but made absolute, the sole dispenser of the necessities of life.[2] " In my system of Common Happiness," he wrote, " I desire that no individual property shall exist. The land is God's and its fruits belong to all men in general."[3] Another Babouviste, the Marquis d'Antonelle, formerly a member of the Revolutionary Tribunal, had expressed the matter in much the same words: " The State of Communism is the only just, the only good one; without this state of things no peaceful and really happy societies can exist."[4]

But Babeuf's activities had again aroused the attention of the Directory, and during the winter of 1795-6 the apostle of Equality was obliged to retire into hiding. Nevertheless from his retreat Babeuf still contrived, with the aid of his twelve-year-old son Émile, to edit his papers *Le Tribun du Peuple* and *Le Cri du Peuple*, and to direct the movement. At one of the meetings of the Panthéonistes, however, Darthé incautiously read the last number of *Le Tribun du Peuple* aloud, and this time no less a personage than General Bonaparte himself descended on the " den of brigands,"[5] as it was known to the police, and, after ordering it to be closed down before his eyes, went off with the key of the building in his pocket.

[1] This word was first coined by Thouret, a member of the National Assembly, in a debate on the goods of the clergy in 1790.
[2] Fleury, *op. cit.* p. 111.
[3] *Ibid.* p. 173.
[4] Antonelle in the *Orateur Plébeien*, No. 9. See *Pièces saisies chez Babeuf*, ii. 11.
[5] Buonarotti, *op. cit.* i. 107.

Babeuf then decided that a " Secret Directorate " must be formed,[1] of which the workings bear a curious resemblance to those of the Illuminati. Thus Weishaupt had employed twelve leading adepts to direct operations throughout Germany, and had strictly enjoined his followers not to be known even to each other as Illuminati; so Babeuf now instituted twelve principal agents to work the different districts of Paris, and these men were not even to know the names of those who formed the central committee of four, but only to communicate with them through intermediaries partially initiated into the secrets of the conspiracy. Like Weishaupt also Babeuf adopted a domineering and arrogant tone towards his subordinates, and any whom he suspected of treachery were threatened, after the manner of the secret societies, with the direst vengeance. " Woe to those of whom we have cause to complain! " he wrote to one whose zeal he had begun to doubt; " reflect that true conspirators can never relinquish those they have once decided to employ."[2]

By April 1796 the plan of insurrection was complete, and the famous *Manifesto of the Equals* drawn up ready for publication.

" PEOPLE OF FRANCE," this proclamation announced, " for fifteen centuries you have lived in slavery and consequently in unhappiness. For six years (*i.e.* during the course of the Revolution) you have hardly drawn breath, waiting for independence, for happiness, and equality. Equality! the first desire of Nature, the first need of Man and the principal bond of all legal association! . . .

" Well! We intend henceforth to live and die equal as we were born; we wish for real equality or death, that is what we must have. And we will have this real equality, no matter at what price. Woe to those who interpose themselves between it and us! . . .

" The French Revolution is only the forerunner of another revolution, very much greater, very much more solemn, which will be the last! . . . What must we have more than equality of rights? We must have not only that equality transcribed in the ' Declaration of the Rights of Man and of the Citizen,' we must have it in our midst, on the roofs of our houses. We will

[1] *Buonarotti* i. 114, 115.
[2] *Pièces saisies chez Babeuf*, ii. 163.

consent to anything for that, to make a clean sweep so as to hold to that only. Perish if necessary all the arts provided that real equality is left to us! . . .

" The agrarian law and the division of lands were the momentary wish of a few soldiers without principle moved by instinct rather than by reason. We tend to something more sublime and equitable, the *Common Happiness or the Community of Goods*. No more private property in land, the land belongs to no one. We claim, we wish for the communal enjoyment of the fruits of the earth: the fruits of the earth belong to every one.

" We declare that we can no longer endure that the great majority of men should work and sweat in the service and for the good pleasure of an extreme minority. Long enough and too long have less than a million individuals disposed of what belongs to more than twenty millions of their fellowmen, of their equals. Let it cease at last, this great scandal in which our nephews will not be able to believe. Vanish at last, revolting distinctions of rich and poor, of great and small, of masters and servants, of governors and governed. Let there be no other difference between men than that of age and sex. Since all have the same needs and the same faculties, let there be only one education, one kind of food. They content themselves with one sun and air for all; why should not the same portion and the same quality of food suffice for each of them? . . .

" PEOPLE OF FRANCE, we say to you: the holy enterprise that we are organizing has no other object but to put an end to civil dissensions and to public misery. Never has a more vast design been conceived and executed. From time to time a few men of genius, a few sages have spoken in a low and trembling voice. Not one of them has had the courage to tell the whole truth. The moment for great measures has arrived. The evil is at its height; it covers the face of the earth. Chaos under the name of politics has reigned for too many centuries. . . . The moment has come to found the Republic of the Equals, the great hostel open to all men. . . . Groaning families, come and seat yourselves at the common table set up by Nature for all her children. . . .

" PEOPLE OF FRANCE, Open your eyes and heart to the plenitude of happiness; recognize and proclaim with us the REPUBLIC OF THE EQUALS." [1]

This document was destined, however, not to be displayed to the eyes of the public, for the Secret Committee finally decided that it would be inexpedient to admit the people into the whole plan of the conspiracy; particularly

---

[1] Buonarotti, *op. cit.* ii. 130-134.

did they judge it inadvisable to publish the phrase which had been expressed in almost identical language by Weishaupt: " Perish all the arts, provided that real equality is left to us! " The people of France were not to know that a return to barbarism was contemplated. Accordingly a second proclamation was framed under the title of " ANALYSIS OF THE DOCTRINE OF BABEUF " — a far less inspiring appeal than the former Manifesto, and mainly unintelligible to the working-classes, yet, as M. Fleury remarks, " the veritable Bible or Koran of the despotic system known as Communism." [1] For herein lies the crux of the matter. No one reading these two documents of the Babouvistes can fail to recognize the truth of certain of their strictures on society — the glaring disparity between poverty and riches, the uneven distribution of work and pleasure, the injustice of an industrial system whereby, owing largely at this period to the suppression of trade unions by the revolutionary leaders, employers could live in luxury by sweated labour — but the point is: how did Babeuf propose to redress these evils? Briefly, then, his system, founded on the doctrine " Community of goods and of labour," [2] may be summarized as follows:

Every one must be forced to work so many hours a day in return for equal remuneration; the man who showed himself more skilful or industrious than his fellows would be recompensed merely by " public gratitude." [3] This compulsory labour was in fact not to be paid for in money but in kind, for, since the right to private property constituted the principal evil of existing society, the distinction of " mine " and " thine " must be abolished [4] and no one should be allowed to possess anything of his own. Payment could therefore only be made in the products of labour, which were all to be collected in huge communal stores and doled out in equal rations to the workers. [5] Inevitably commerce would be entirely done away with, and money was no longer to be coined or admitted to the

---

[1] *Babeuf et le socialisme en* 1796, by Edouard Fleury.
[2] Buonarotti, *op. cit.* i. 87.
[3] *Analyse de la doctrine de Babeuf*, Buonarotti, *op. cit.* ii. 146.
[4] *Ibid.* ii. 145.
[5] *Ibid.* i. 213.

country; foreign trade must therefore be carried on by coin now in circulation, and when that was exhausted, by a system of barter.[1]

Only work of essential utility was to be undertaken, and in order to ensure the requisite number of hands for each industry boys were no longer to be allowed to choose their professions but must be trained for whatever work was most urgently needed. The workers would then be drafted off in gangs to perform the labour assigned them " according to the needs of the nation and the supreme principle of equality."

Since in France agriculture was of the first importance, the greater number of inhabitants, both boys and girls, would be sent out to till the soil;[2] and it was hoped that by degrees Paris and all the large towns of France would disappear, for it was in towns that wage-slavery flourished and that " big capitalists " were able to surround themselves with luxury and display.[3] The hosts of parasites who had hitherto contributed to their enjoyment — shopkeepers, domestic servants, poets, painters, actors, dancers — would all now be obliged to seek a livelihood in the fields, and villages consisting of salubrious houses " remarkable for their elegant symmetry " would spring up all over France.[4]

The better to ensure a hardy race of toilers, children were to be given over to the State at birth and trained in institutions.

" In the social order conceived by the Committee," wrote Buonarotti, " the country seizes upon the individual at birth (*s'empare de l'individu naissant*) in order only to relinquish it at death. It watches over his first moments, assures him the milk and the care of her who gave him birth, keeps him from all that would injure his health or weaken his body, preserves him from false tenderness and conducts him by the hand of his mother to the national house where he will acquire virtue and the enlightenment necessary to a true citizen."[5]

[1] Buonarotti, *op. cit.* i. 238, 271, ii. 318.   [2] *Ibid.* i. 208-211.
[3] *Ibid.* i. 221. Note here the theory of " wage-slavery " again formulated: " From the perpetual exchange of services and salaries there arises on one side the habit of authority and of commanding, and on the other that of submission and servitude " (p. 222).
[4] Buonarotti, *op. cit.* i. 221-224.
[5] *Ibid.* i. 282. " Plus d'éducation domestique, plus de puissance paternelle " (*ibid.* i. 288).

In order to replace family affection by civic virtue in the mind of the child, it was further proposed to forbid him to bear the name of his father unless he were a man who had distinguished himself by great virtues.[1]

His education was to be of course only of the most primitive kind: reading, writing, enough arithmetic to enable him to work in a Government office if required; history — but only that relating to the evils ended by the Republic and the blessings of which it was a source — and such knowledge of law, geography, and natural history as would give him an idea of the wisdom of the institutions under which he lived. In order to embellish the fêtes arranged by the Government he should also be versed in music and dancing.[2]

Beyond this all avenues of knowledge were to be closed to him, for it was feared that " men might devote themselves to sciences," and thereby grow vain and averse from manual labour.[3] Had not Weishaupt declared the sciences to be " the complicated needs of a state contrary to Nature, the inventions of vain and empty brains "?

Such, then, was the scheme of Babeuf [4] for the liberation of the French people, and it is difficult to see wherein it differed from the serfdom under which their forefathers had groaned during the Middle Ages. There is in fact nothing to be said for Communism that does not equally apply to serfdom; in both the means of subsistence are assured, the spectre of unemployment is dispelled, in both the taskmaster may be kind or cruel, and in neither can the worker call his body or his soul his own. Was not then Babeuf's remedy worse than the disease? Were not even " the revolting distinctions of rich and poor " preferable to a dead level of slavery from which the one inspiring emotion of human life — hope — would be for ever removed?

It is at any rate impossible to imagine a system more distasteful to the French character than the labour colony thus devised by Babeuf. That the people of France, of all people the most acquisitive and the most retentive of their

---

[1] Buonarotti, *op. cit.* p. 219.　　　　[2] *Ibid.* i. 286-287.
[3] *Ibid.* i. 293.
[4] See summing up of system by Babeuf himself (*ibid.* ii. 220) in which he describes it as a " plan enchanteur."

possessions — the natural consequence of their inherent thrift and industry — should be willing to renounce the right to possess anything; that the pleasure-loving Parisians, to whom amidst all their privations the gay whirl of streets and *spectacles* was as the breath of life, should submit to be driven forth to seek a living on the desolate plains of the provinces, with no amusements to vary the monotony but the fêtes provided by the Republic — at which they were not to be allowed to wear festive attire, but to attend in their working clothes [1] for fear of violating the principle of absolute equality; that the nation distinguished for its poets and painters, its *savants* and *beaux-esprits*, should consent to become a race of unpaid manual labourers; above all, that a people who for six years had thrilled to the cry of " Liberty! " should now meekly place its neck under a yoke far more oppressive than that from which it had been relieved, would be grotesque if it were not so tragic.

But when one realises the misery of the people at this crisis and the countless disillusionments through which they had passed, one can feel nothing but burning indignation at the charlatans who thus set out to exploit their sufferings. For if these men had dealt honestly with the people, laying before them the real plan they had framed for their relief, the people would only have had themselves to blame if the conspirators had succeeded in carrying out their design.

But the people were not in the secret of the movement. Just as in the great outbreaks of the Revolution the mob of Paris had been driven blindly forward on false pretexts supplied by the agitators, so once again the people were to be made the instruments of their own ruin. The " Secret Committee of Direction " well knew that Communism was a system that would never appeal to the people; they were careful, therefore, not to admit their dupes among the working-classes into the whole of their programme, and believing that it was only by an appeal to self-interest and covetousness they could secure a following,[2]

[1] Buonarotti, *op. cit.* i. 225.
[2] *Ibid.* i. 97: " It was impossible to inspire the people with energy without talking to them of their interests and their rights."

they skillfuly played on the people's passions, promising them booty they had no intention of bestowing on them. Thus in the " Insurrectional Act " now drawn up by the Committee it was announced that " the goods of the *émigrés*, of the conspirators (*i.e.* the Royalists), and of the enemies of the people were to be distributed to the defenders of the country and the needy";[1] they did not tell them that in reality these things were to belong to no one, but to become the property of the State administered by themselves. Buonarotti in his naïve account of these manœuvres justifies the deception by observing that " the great point was to succeed," and so the Secret Directory judged it advisable to " fix the attention and sustain the hopes of the working-classes " by the promise to divide everything up amongst them.[2] The people then were not to be allowed to know the truth about the cause in which they were asked to shed their blood — and that they would be obliged to shed it in torrents no sane man could doubt.

It is here perhaps that Babeuf lays himself most open to the charge of mental irresponsibility. At one moment we find him declaring that the process can be carried out by perfectly pacific methods, at the next inciting the populace to violence of the most fearful kind. Thus when d'Antonelle suggested that, however urgent it might be to establish absolute equality, this ideal condition could only be brought about " by brigandage and the horrors of civil war, which would be a dreadful method," [3] Babeuf indignantly replied: " What do you mean by saying that one could only achieve real equality by brigandage? Is it really Antonelle who defines brigandage after the manner of the patriciate? Any movement, any proceeding that would bring about, if only partially, the disgorging of those who have too much for the profit of those who have not enough would not, it seems to me, be brigandage, it would be the beginning of a return to justice and real order." [4] As to d'Antonelle's further contention that in the confusion following on general pillage it would be impossible to carry

<hr />

[1] Buonarotti, *op. cit.* ii. 252.
[2] *Pièces saisies chez Babeuf*, ii. 16.
[3] *Ibid.* i. 155, 156.
[4] *Ibid.*

out any scheme of redistribution, Babeuf was equally incredulous. " What will they do after the upheaval, you will say; will they be capable of erecting the august temple of Equality? " Babeuf anticipated no difficulty here; they had only to read Diderot to discover how easy it would be to provide for the needs of a multitude of citizens; " all that is only a simple affair of numbering things and people, a simple operation of calculation and combinations and consequently susceptible of a very fine degree of order." [1]

But when it came to organizing the required insurrection Babeuf adopted a very different kind of language. In fact the former denouncer of Robespierre's " system of depopulation " now asserted that not only Robespierre's aims but his methods were to be commended.

> I confess to-day that I bear a grudge against myself for having formerly seen the revolutionary government and Robespierre and Saint-Just in such black colours. I think these men alone were worth all the revolutionaries put together, and that their dictatorial government was devilishly well thought out. . . . I do not at all agree . . . that they committed great crimes and made many Republicans perish. Not so many, I think. . . .[2] The salvation of twenty-five millions of men must not be weighed against consideration for a few equivocal individuals. A regenerator must take a wide outlook. He must mow down everything that thwarts him, everything that obstructs his passage, everything that can impede his prompt arrival at the goal on which he has determined. Rascals or imbeciles, or presumptuous people or those eager for glory, it is all the same, *tant pis pour eux* — what are they there for? Robespierre knew all that, and it is partly what makes me admire him.[3]

But where Babeuf showed himself the intellectual inferior of Robespierre was in the way he proposed to overcome resistance to his plan of a Socialist State. Robespierre, as he well knew, had spent fourteen months "mowing down those that obstructed his passage," had kept the guillotine unremittingly at work in Paris and the provinces, yet even then had not succeeded in silencing objectors. But Babeuf hoped to accomplish his purpose

---

[1] *Pièces saisies chez Babeuf*, ii. 23.

[2] It should be noted that in his pamphlet on *Le Système de la dépopulation* Babeuf had estimated the victims of the Terror at no less than a million.

[3] *Pièces saisies chez Babeuf*, ii. 52.

in one day — that *"great day of the people"* [1] wherein all opposition should be instantly suppressed, the whole existing social order annihilated, and the Republic of Equality erected on its ruins. If, however, the process were to be brief it must necessarily be all the more violent, and it was thus with none of the calm precision of Robespierre marking down heads for destruction that Babeuf set about his task. When writing out his plans of insurrection, his secretary Pillé afterwards related at his trial, Babeuf would rush up and down the room with flaming eyes, mouthing and grimacing, hitting himself against the furniture, knocking over the chairs whilst uttering hoarse cries of " To arms! to arms! The insurrection! the insurrection is beginning! " — it was an insurrection against the chairs, said Pillé drily. Then Babeuf would fling himself upon his pen, plunge it into the ink, and write with fearful rapidity, whilst his whole body trembled and the perspiration poured from his brow. " It was no longer madness," added Pillé, " it was frenzy! " [2] This frenzy, Babeuf explained, was necessary in order to work himself up to the required degree of eloquence, and in his appeals to insurrection it is difficult to see where his programme differed from the brigandage and violence he had deprecated in his reply to d'Antonelle.

" Why," he wrote in *Le Tribun du Peuple*, " does one speak of laws and property? Property is the share of usurpers and laws are the work of the strongest. The sun shines for every one, and the earth belongs to no one. Go then, my friends, and disturb, overthrow, and upset this society which does not suit you. Take everywhere all that you like. Superfluity belongs by right to him who has nothing. This is not all, friends and brothers. If constitutional barriers are opposed to your generous efforts, overthrow without scruple barriers and constitutions. Butcher without mercy tyrants, patricians, the Gilded Million, all those immoral beings who would oppose your common happiness. You are the People, the true People, the only People worthy to enjoy the good things of this world! The justice of the People is great and majestic as the People itself; all that it does is legitimate, all that it orders is sacred! " [3]

Inevitably Babeuf secured a certain following amongst the working-classes — the call to violence must ever find

[1] *Pièces saisies chez Babeuf*, ii. 21.
[2] Fleury, *op. cit.* p. 244.   [3] *Ibid.* p. 77.

an answering echo in the minds of the despairing, and the people of Paris at this crisis had good cause for despair. Food — owing to four years of war and seven of revolution — was at famine prices, the destruction of commerce carried on by the emissaries of the Comité de Salut Public in the manufacturing towns of France had raised all the commodities of life to the same prohibitive level and created vast unemployment; meanwhile the newly rich — the war profiteers, the army contractors, the adventurers who had made their fortunes out of the Revolution — revelled in luxury, their wives and mistresses swathed in pearls and diamonds, and little else besides, flaunted their charms and opulence before the hungry eyes of the poor. What wonder, then, that the soldiers cried out their " rulers were all rascals, all murderers of the people, that they were ready to exterminate them," or that the wretched inhabitants of the faubourgs declared all their ills " were to be attributed to the Revolution and that they were happier under the Old Régime "? [1]

To a people in such a mood as this it was easy to make the counsel of despair which consisted in smashing everything appear to be the simplest solution of all difficulties, and the agents of Babeuf, versed in all the methods of the Secret Societies for stirring up popular fury, succeeded in winning over a number of working-men to their views. One ingenious plan consisted in pasting up large incendiary placards around which accomplices known as *groupeurs* — or, as we might say, " crowd-collectors " — were employed to assemble as if by accident, and then to read the words aloud, pointing out the most important passages with their fingers.[2] The *Analyse de Babeuf* thus exposed met with much applause from the working-men, who could but dimly understand its real purport. At the same time inflammatory pamphlets dilating on the greed of the tradesmen and the infamies of the Government were circulated in the faubourgs, where the women of the people eagerly read them aloud to their men-folk whilst at work. So great was the enthusiasm thus created that the Babou-

[1] *Pièces saisies*, ii. 164.
[2] Fleury, *op. cit.* pp. 74, 131; *Pièces saisies*, ii. 106.

vistes entertained no doubt of being able to enlist the whole
proletariat in the movement, and by the beginning of May
it was estimated that an army of no less than 17,000 people
would assemble on the day of insurrection.[1] These forces
included 4500 soldiers and 6000 of the police, who by lavish
promises of booty had been won over to the conspiracy.

The following programme for the " Great Day " was
now drawn up by the Secret Directory: at a given moment
the revolutionary army was to march on the Legislative
Assembly, on the headquarters of the Army, and on the
houses of the Ministers. The best-trained troops were to
be sent to the arsenals and the munition factories, and also
to the camps of Vincennes and Grenelle in the hope that
the 8000 men encamped there would join in the movement.
Meanwhile orators were to hold forth to the soldiers, and
women were to present them with refreshment and civic
wreaths. In the event of their remaining proof against
these seductions the streets were to be barricaded, and
stones, bricks, boiling water, and vitriol thrown down on
the heads of the troops.[2] All supplies for the capital were
then to be seized and placed under the control of the
leaders; at the same time the wealthier classes were to be
driven from their houses, which were immediately to be
converted into lodgings for the poor.[3] The members of the
Directory were then to be butchered, likewise all citizens
who offered any resistance to the insurgents.[4] The insurrection thus " happily terminated," as Babeuf naïvely
expressed it,[5] the whole people were to be assembled in the
Place de la Révolution[6] and invited to co-operate in the
choice of their representatives. " The plan," writes
Buonarotti, " was to talk to the people without reserve and
without digressions, and to render the most impressive
homage to its sovereignty." [7] But lest the people per-
chance, blinded to its truest interests, might fail to recognize its saviours in the person of the conspirators, the
Babouvistes proposed to follow up their homage of the
people's sovereignty by demanding that " executive power
should be exclusively confided to themselves "; for, as

[1] Buonarotti, *op. cit.* i. 189.   [2] *Ibid.* i. 194.
[3] *Ibid.* i. 196.   [4] *Ibid.*
[5] *Ibid.* i. 197.   [6] *Ibid.* i. 156.   [7] *Ibid.* i. 200.

Buonarotti observed, " at the beginning of the revolution it is necessary, even out of respect for the real sovereignty of the people, to occupy oneself less with the wishes of the nation than to place supreme authority in strongly revolutionary hands." [1] Once in these hands it would of course remain there, and the Babouvistes with all the civil and military forces at their back would be able to impose their system of State serfdom on the submissive people.

It is fearful to imagine what blood might once again have reddened the streets of Paris if an unforeseen obstacle had not arisen in the path of the conspirators — namely, a traitor in the camp. This man, called Grisel, was a soldier in the 33rd Brigade who had been drawn against his will into the conspiracy. Strolling one April evening on the Quai des Tuileries, Grisel had encountered an old friend, a tailor named Mugnier, who was an enthusiastic Babouviste. Mugnier, convinced that he would find a sympathizer in Grisel, proceeded to pour forth complaints against the Government, and ended by introducing him to several of his fellow-conspirators. A few days later one of these men met Grisel in a café, and becoming loquacious under the influence of drink, confided to him part of the plan of the conspiracy. Grisel, fearing to make an enemy of so dangerous a man, dared not express his disapproval, and his new associates, encouraged by his apparent agreement with their views, invited him to one of their meetings at the café of the " Bains Chinois," whither they had removed after the closing down of the so-called " Panthéon." Here Grisel found himself in the thick of the conspiracy; violent speeches were made — both by men and women — revolutionary songs were sung, amongst others a dirge on the death of Robespierre. Meanwhile wine and cider flowed freely, and Grisel, invited to take part in the " orgy " as he afterwards described it, was hailed as an acquisition to the cause. One of the conspirators then handed him some of Babeuf's pamphlets for distribution amongst the soldiers and asked him to compose others for the same purpose. Grisel realized that it was too late to draw back, for the conspirators, having taken him into their confidence,

[1] Buonarotti, *op. cit.* i. 134.

would certainly dispose of him by a dagger-thrust if he now disassociated himself from their designs. Accordingly he set himself to the task assigned him, but not without first consulting his battalion-commander, who advised him to continue in his rôle of Babouviste. Grisel, warming to the work, thereupon composed a violent letter entitled *Franc-Libre à son ami La Terreur*, inciting the troops to rebellion, and in which he was careful to imitate the pompous and meaningless phraseology of the conspirators. This effusion met with the heartiest applause at the " Bains Chinois," and Grisel, who had hitherto been only partly initiated into the details of the insurrection, now found himself received into the inner councils of the leaders. At the first of these meetings, consisting only of five members — Babeuf, Germain, Buonarotti, Didier, and Darthé — Grisel saw the leader of the conspiracy for the first time, and looking at him with some curiosity noticed with surprise that Babeuf, of whose genius he had heard so much, presented an appearance of " extreme mediocrity," whilst his behaviour showed him to be more eccentric than original. In fact the whole band seemed to the newcomer a party of maniacs, and his first feeling was one of remorse at the idea of giving over the victims of mere mental disorder to justice. When, therefore, Babeuf unfolded his scheme of insurrection, entailing the wholesale massacre of the Government, the wealthy, and all existing authorities, Grisel, overcome with horror, ventured to expostulate, pointing out the terrible consequences of overthrowing the Government: " What will you put in its place? . . . Will there not be an interval between the fall of the Government . . . and that which you will put in its place? It will be complete anarchy; all the restraints of law will be broken. I pray you think it over. . . ." [1]

This moderation nearly proved fatal to Grisel, and seeing the threatening glances directed towards him, he hastily repaired his error by plunging into a violent harangue in which he proposed to burn down all the châteaux around Paris before falling on the members of the Directory. The suggestion did not, however, find favour

[1] Fleury, *op. cit.* pp. 175, 176.

with the conspirators, who saw in the destruction of the
châteaux an end to their hopes of booty; nevertheless
Grisel had now regained their good opinion and was
admitted to further meetings of the committee. At one of
these, Darthé read aloud the finished plan of insurrection,
to which further atrocious details had been added — every
one attempting to exercise any authority was instantly to
be put to death, the armourers were to be forced to give
up their arms, the bakers their supplies of bread, and those
who resisted hoisted to the nearest lantern; the same fate
was reserved for all wine and spirit merchants who might
refuse to provide the brandy needed to inflame the populace and drive them into violence.[1] " All reflection on the
part of the people must be avoided," ran the written directions to the leaders; " they must commit acts which will
prevent them from going back." [2]

Amongst the whole of this ferocious band, Rossignol,
the former general of the revolutionary armies in La
Vendée, showed himself the most bloodthirsty: " I will not
have anything to do with your insurrection," he cried,
" unless heads fall like hail . . . unless it inspires so great
a terror that it makes the whole universe shudder . . . "
— a discourse that met with unanimous applause.

The 11th of May had been fixed for the great day of
explosion, when not only Paris, but all the large cities of
France worked on by the agents of Babeuf were to rise
and overthrow the whole structure of civilization. But
Grisel had sought an interview with Carnot, and the Government, warned of the impending attack, was ready to
meet it. On the morning of the day appointed, a placard
was found posted up on all the walls of Paris bearing these
words:

THE EXECUTIVE DIRECTORY TO THE CITIZENS OF PARIS

Citizens, a frightful plot is to break out this night or
tomorrow at the dawn of day. A band of thieves and murderers
has formed the project of butchering the Legislative Assembly,
all the members of the Government, the staff of the Army, and
all constituted authorities in Paris. The Constitution of '93 is
to be proclaimed. This proclamation is to be the signal for a

---

[1] Fleury, *op. cit.* pp. 193-195. *Ibid.* p. 196.

general pillage of Paris, of houses as much as of stores and shops, and the massacre of a great number of citizens is to be carried out at the same time. But be reassured, good citizens; the Government is watching, it knows the leaders of the plot and their methods . . . ; be calm, therefore, and carry on your ordinary business; the Government has taken infallible measures for outwitting their schemes, and for giving them up with their partisans to the vengeance of the law.[1]

Then, without further warning, the police burst into the house where Babeuf and Buonarotti were drawing up a rival placard calling the people to revolt. In the midst of their task the arm of the law surprised and seized them, and on the following morning forty-five other leaders of the conspiracy were arrested likewise and thrown into the Abbaye. Alas for the support they had hoped for from the populace! The revolutionary army on which they had counted, impressed as the people always are by a display of authority, went over to the police in support of law and order. With the removal of the agitators the whole populace came to their senses and realized the full horror of the plot into which they had been inveigled.

" The working-man," a Government reporter writes, " no longer regards the conspiracy as a wild story, the pillage promised him makes him shrug his shoulders, and he feels that the brigands, hailing from no one knows where, would have pillaged the working-man himself. Their remark is, ' It would be better to stay as we are and to send all those rascals to the scaffold! ' When the project of the massacre is read and these words ' all reflection on the part of the people must be avoided; they must commit acts which will prevent them from going back,' the readers are overcome with anger. They see that the scoundrels wished to make them the victims. ' Let the Directory have them all hanged, and may Hell swallow them up! ' — that is their reflection. Some soldiers reading these dreadful documents say loudly: ' Soldiers of liberty will never have for friends thieves, brigands, and assassins! ' "[2]

The appeals of Babeuf's friends to the working-classes urging them to rescue the prisoners fell therefore on deaf ears. In vain hordes of viragos enlisted by the conspirators paraded the faubourgs, telling the working-men of Saint-Antoine that their comrades in Saint-Marceau were taking

[1] Fleury, *op. cit.* 216.   [2] Schmidt, *Tableaux de Paris,* iii. 197.

up arms, and proclaiming in Saint-Marceau that Saint-Antoine was rising; the working-men of both districts indignantly repulsed these furies, who admitted with tears they had been paid to stir up insurrection.

On the 27th of August 1796 all the leaders of the conspiracy to the number of forty-seven were removed to Vendôme to await their trial, which, however, did not begin until February 20 of the following year and lasted until the end of May. Babeuf's behaviour in court alternated between brazen defiance and pitiable weakness. Already at his cross-examination in Paris he had declared himself to be merely the agent of a conspiracy:

I attest they do me too much honour in decorating me with the title of head of this affair. I declare that I had only a secondary and limited part in it. . . . The heads and the leaders needed a director of public opinion, I was in the position to enlist this opinion. . . .[1]

Who were the mysterious chiefs referred to by Babeuf? The Illuminati? The Order, we know, was still active and co-operated with the society of the Philadelphes, which, according to Lombard de Langres, secretly directed the Babouviste conspiracy. Babeuf, whilst thus disclaiming responsibility, yet maintained his firm belief in Communism though admitting it to be an unattainable ideal. This final abandonment of his revolutionary programme, however, did not save him, and on the 27th of May 1797 sentence of death was passed on Babeuf and Darthé; seven of their fellow-conspirators were ordered to be deported, the rest acquitted. The two condemned men vainly attempted to stab themselves with stilettos they had concealed beneath their clothing, but were removed to their cells by the police, and on the 28th of May the " Chief of the Equals " and his companion perished on the scaffold.

So ended Babeuf, but not so Babouvisme. Buonarotti still survived to hand on the torch of conflagration to the revolutionary groups of the early nineteenth century.

To-day, however, owing to the pretensions of German Socialism, Babeuf, even in France, is almost forgotten or is remembered only as a madman. But why is Babeuf

[1] Fleury, *op. cit.* p. 230.

to be regarded as any madder than his more famous successors in the science of revolution? On the contrary, a close study of the Babouviste conspiracy reveals its author to have been far ahead of his times, a man who, if he had lived to-day, would undoubtedly be hailed as a herald of the dawn.

The fact is that, as students of the Russian Revolution will have observed, *Babouvisme and Bolshevism are identical;* between the two creeds there is no essential difference. The third Internationale of Moscow in its first Manifesto rightly traces its descent from Babeuf. We shall return to this point later in connection with the programme of the Bolsheviks.

It may be objected that the Babouviste rising was lacking in the International spirit of Bolshevism; it is true that Babeuf confined his energies to France in the matter of organizing the day of revolution, but that he dreamt of the movement subsequently developing on a far larger scale is evident from those momentous words of his Communist Manifesto: " The French Revolution is only the forerunner of another revolution, very much greater, very much more solemn, and which will be the last! "

.   .   .   .

The conspiracy of Babeuf was thus the expiring effort of the French Revolution to realize the great scheme of Weishaupt. The universal nature of that first upheaval has been too little realized by posterity. Everywhere Illuminism had found its adepts; in Holland, Belgium, Spain, Italy, Switzerland, Sweden, Russia, even as far as Africa, the disintegrating doctrines of Weishaupt had spread beneath the surface.[1] It was not merely the thrones of Europe that were shaken but civilization itself that trembled to its very foundations. England had entered largely into the projects of the conspirators; no less an adept than Cato-Zwack himself had, as we have seen, visited this country after his expulsion from Bavaria, and spent a year at Oxford University, which, less receptive to illuminated doctrines than it is to-day, accorded him scant appreciation.[2] But the efforts of his fellow-country-

[1] Barruel, *op. cit.* iv. 357-378.   [2] *Ibid. op. cit.* iv. p. 400.

men, Röntgen, Ibiken, and Regenhardt who followed,[1] met
with some degree of success, and Robison, himself a Freemason, admits with regret that a certain number of
British masons were won over by the German propagandists. Amongst these was the celebrated Thomas Paine,
who was later on to betray his connection with the Illuminati by his work, *The Age of Reason*, written in France
whilst the " Feasts of Reason " were taking place in the
churches of Paris. Largely, then, owing to the instrumentality of Paine several " illuminized " lodges were started
in England, which Robison, writing in 1797, declared to be
still in existence.[2] It is thus that we find noble lords at
their banquets drinking the health of the Sovereign People,
" whilst in their lairs other Brothers are meditating how
they shall set to work in order to put at the disposal of the
Sovereign People the possessions of their Brother Lords,
the treasures of the banks, and the shops of the rich merchants." [3] Barruel is no doubt right in describing these
upper class Subversives as the Brother Dupes (Frères-
Dupes) of the Order, it was not such men as Fox, Sheridan,
or even " the renegade Lord Stanhope " who desired to see
a levelling down of the wealth they themselves enjoyed;
but the plan of the Illuminati was always to use each section of the community for its own destruction. The real
aims of Illuminism were embodied not in the political
revolution devised by the Whigs to bring themselves into
power, but in the social revolution organized by the middle-
class malcontents, Paine, Price, and Priestly, and their
allies amongst the disgruntled manual workers. It was by
these men that, after the Revolution broke out in France,
revolutionary societies were started in England, the most
important being the London Corresponding Society,
founded in 1792 by a shoemaker named Hardy, with
branches all over the kingdom. Although conducting their
agitation under the pretext of reform, it is impossible to
see in this movement any connection with the working-
class grievances that underlay the Industrial Revolution

[1] *Application of Barruel's Memoirs of Jacobinism to the Secret Societies
of Ireland and Great Britain*, by the translator of that work (the Hon.
R. C. Clifford), London, 1798, p. xxii.
[2] Robison, *op. cit.* pp. 478, 479.　　　　[3] Barruel, *op. cit.* iv. 414.

some thirty years later; neither the doctrines nor the phraseology of these societies savour in any way of working-class mentality but are both obviously of foreign importation, whilst their plan of organization is simply that of the Illuminati. " These societies," writes a contemporary, " were formed on Weishaupt's corresponding scale," with a " Grand Council " to direct operations.[1] And we have only to read their correspondence to recognize the truth of the further assertion that " all their forms and even their modes of speech were servilely copied from the French "[2] — that is to say, from the French disciples of the Illuminati. It is certainly not British bootmakers or mechanics who devise such phrases as " Citizens of the World," the " Imprescriptible Rights of Man," or who would have bethought themselves of beginning a letter to the Convention of Paris with the words: " Illustrious senators, enlightened legislators, and dear friends! " The phraseology of Jacobinism is here clearly apparent. The " traitorous correspondence " that took place during the autumn of 1792, when immediately after the ghastly massacres of September the " English Jacobins " sent affectionate letters of good-will to their French brethren and even expressed the hope of setting up a National Convention in England, must not be traced to any native violence on the part of British working-men, but solely to the workings of Illuminism. Thus, owing to the international doctrines instilled in their minds by the adepts of Weishaupt, the English dupes who subscribed to these effusions little dreamt that the men to whom they addressed themselves were in reality their bitterest enemies.[3]

[1] Clifford, *Application of Barruel's Memoirs, etc.*, p. 33.
[2] Clifford, *op. cit.* p. 34.
[3] It should be remembered that at this date — September to December 1792 — the power of the Girondins, who had shown themselves friendly to England, was waning and Robespierre was gaining the ascendancy. And Robespierre's opinion of the English is thus concisely expressed in his speech to the Convention on January 30, 1794: " As a Frenchman and representative of the people I declare that I hate the English people — I declare that I shall increase as far as in me lies the hatred of my fellow-countrymen against them. What does it matter what they think of me? I only hope in our soldiers and in the profound hatred the French have for that people." Such were the " dear friends " at whose feet the English Jacobins saw fit to grovel.

Internationalism has always redounded to the discredit of England.

By way of further expressing their esteem for the Jacobins of France, the English revolutionary societies had collected large sums of money which they dispatched to Paris and also a quantity of arms made at Birmingham and Sheffield.[1] Fired by this example, the leading revolutionary society of Scotland, calling itself the " North Britons," two years later armed itself with pikes for the purpose of open insurrection. The plot, however, was discovered, and no less than 4000 pikes were found to have been ordered for Perth besides those wanted for Edinburgh.[2]

By this time, 1794, the victories of the Republican armies had rendered the French formidable allies, and, before long, plans for the invasion of Great Britain began to be discussed by the agents of the Illuminati. Then, as now, Ireland was recognized as the most vulnerable point of attack, and for three years an Irish Society had been at work in that country. This association, first known as the Irish Brotherhood, then as the " United Irishmen," was organized in June 1791 on the lines of the Illuminati. " The proposals for it," writes Clifford, " are couched in the style and exact terms of the Hierophants of Illuminism." They recommend the formation of an association, or, as it is styled, " a beneficent conspiracy " to serve the people; assuming " the secrecy and somewhat of the ceremonial attached to Freemasonry."[3] This was effected by means of a central society or lodge from which other lodges in the different towns radiated; chairmen or Masters presided over the lodges, and secretaries were appointed belonging only to the higher degrees. " The concatenation

---

[1] Oswald's speech to the Jacobins of September 30, 1792 (Aulard's *Séances des Jacobins,* iv. 346). It was Oswald, an English Jacobin, who seems to have suggested the idea of the terrible " Loi des Suspects " to the Convention and even advocated a more extreme measure still, namely to *put to death* every suspected man in France. This suggestion, emanating from a vegetarian (for Oswald had adopted the diet of the Brahmins after some years spent in India), drew from Thomas Paine the ironical remark, " Oswald, you have lived so long without tasting flesh that you have now a most voracious appetite for blood " (*Letters of Redhead Yorke,* 1906 edition, p. 71).

[2] Clifford, *op. cit.* p. 35.   [3] *Ibid.* pp. 1, 2.

of the degrees," Clifford goes on to observe, " perfectly coincides with Weishaupt's plan," and he illustrates the fact by a reproduction of the pyramidic scale of adepts, starting with the one controlling brain at the top and widening out into the lower ranks of the less initiated, resembling the one shown in the code of the Illuminati: [1]

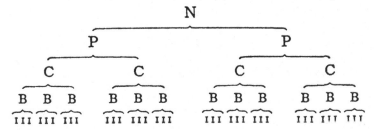

Committees were then formed all over Ireland, but " no person whatever could mention the names of the Committee-men: they were not even known to those who had elected them in the case of the National or Executive Committee. . . . Thus was the Society entirely governed by unknown Superiors." [2] The exact similarity between this system and the organization of the Babouviste conspiracy will be readily perceived. The official leader of the movement in Belfast was Wolfe Tone, in Dublin Napper Tandy, and, at first, Parliamentary Reform and Catholic Emancipation were held out as the only objects of the society, but in time plans of a more subversive nature were admitted. Thus, when military co-operation with the French was contemplated and it became necessary to win over the troops, the soldiers were adjured " to be true to the French Republic." " The better to propagate the system it was held out to the military that, when the French should come, the soldiers were to be such as them; that there were to be no rich but *All Equality*." [3] Accordingly the barracks were to be burnt down, the country set on fire from end to end, and all arms seized until the French should land. It should be noted that by this date, July 1797, even the appearance of liberty under the name

[1] Cf. diagram in *Nachtrag . . . Original Schriften*, p. 60.
[2] Clifford, *op. cit.* p. 6. [3] *Ibid.*

of Jacobinism had ceased to exist, and it was with the troops of the despotic Directory that the Irish soldiers were asked to coalesce.

In all this agitation the Irish peasants played no part at all; indeed, on the only occasion when the French effected a landing the people offered vigorous resistance. The contemporary account of the incident is so curious that it must be quoted verbatim:

" On the 24th of December (1796) the French really did make their appearance at Bantry; and, strange to say, they were not seconded in their attempts by the people; who universally rose in the south to oppose their invaders; but this is accounted for in a still more extraordinary manner. The Executive had received news that the French had deferred their expedition till spring; this circumstance threw them ' off their guard,' and in consequence of it no measures were taken to prepare the people for the reception of the French army. *The people were left to themselves.*" " I hope in God," adds Clifford, " that this avowal made by one of their intended Governors may prove a wholesome lesson to that same people, and encourage them to follow the loyal and genuine dictates of their hearts." [1]

Indeed so little were the Irish people initiated into the real aims of " the beneficent conspiracy " at work in their midst that even the County Committees were not in the secret as to the nature of the engagements entered into with the French.

What unhappy deluded people then were the lower associates who were informed of nothing, but were to be the mere agents of rebellion and murder, and were hurried on into this abyss of horror by a few political libertines who grasped at dominion, and wished to wade to the helm of the State through the blood of their countrymen! [2]

These words well describe the workings of the conspiracy which from 1791 onwards has never ceased to exploit the troubles of Ireland in order to bring about the destruction of England and of Christian civilization.

.   .   .   .

Whilst these events were taking place in Europe the

[1] Clifford, *op. cit.* 9, 10, quoting official report of the incident.
[2] *Ibid.* p. 12. This very curious pamphlet should be read by every one interested in the present state of affairs in Ireland, of which it offers an almost exact picture.

New World had been illuminized. As early as 1786 a lodge of the Order had been started in Virginia, and this was followed by fourteen others in different cities. But the horrors of the French Revolution, followed in 1797 by the books of Barruel and Robison, which supplied the key to events that had hitherto appeared inexplicable, opened the eyes of the American public to the truth of the conspiracy at work in its midst. The alarm that spread through the States was not, as it has been foolishly described, a case of " panic," but the recognition of a very real danger on which the clergy had the courage to warn their congregations from pulpits all over the country.

At Charlestown on May 9, 1798, the Rev. Jedediah Morse preached his famous sermon on Illuminism, taking for his text, " This is a day of trouble and of rebuke and blasphemy ":

Practically all of the civil and ecclesiastical establishments of Europe have already been shaken to their foundations by this terrible organization; the French Revolution itself is doubtless to be traced to its machinations; the successes of the French armies are to be explained on the same ground. The Jacobins are nothing more nor less than the open manifestation of the hidden system of the Illuminati. The Order has its branches established and its emissaries at work in America. The affiliated Jacobin Societies in America have doubtless had as the object of their establishment the propagation of the principles of the illuminated mother club in France.

In July of the same year Timothy Dwight, president of Yale, thus referred to the work of the French Revolution in his sermon to the people of New Haven:

No personal or national interest of man has been uninvaded; no impious sentiment of action against God has been spared; no malignant hostility against Christ and His religion has been unattempted. Justice, truth, kindness, piety, and moral obligation universally have been not merely trodden underfoot . . . but ridiculed, spurned, and insulted as the childish bugbears of drivelling idiocy. . . . For what end shall we be connected with men of whom this is the character and conduct? Is it that we may assume the same character and conduct? Is it that our churches may become temples of reason, our Sabbath a decade, and our psalms of praise Marseillaise hymns? . . . Is it that we may see the Bible cast into a bonfire, the vessels of the sacramental supper borne by an ass in public procession, and our children either wheedled or terrified, uniting in the mob, chanting mockeries against God, and hailing in the sounds of the " Ça ira " the ruin of their religion and the loss of their souls? . . . Shall our sons become the disciples of Voltaire and the dragoons of Marat, or our daughters the concubines of the Illuminati?

Dwight then refers to the misery wrought by the Republican troops in Belgium, Bolivia, Italy, and Switzerland — " the happiness of the last named, and its hopes cut off at a single stroke, happiness erected with the labour and the wisdom of three centuries. . . . What have they spread but crimes and miseries; where have they trodden but to waste, to pollute, and to destroy? "

Needless to say, these warnings were met with furious remonstrances from sympathizers with the principles of Illuminism. *The Independent Chronicle* spoke of " the incorrigible impertinence of the clergy in turning aside from their legitimate functions to spread alarm about Illuminism "; Jefferson — whom Morse declared to be himself an Illuminatus — strenuously denied all imputations against the Order, and described Weishaupt as " an enthusiastic philanthropist " and Barruel's revelations as " the ravings of a Bedlamite." The very violence of these disclaimers shows how truly the shafts had gone home. The line of defence adopted had been laid down some ten years earlier by Weishaupt. " The great care of the Illuminati after the publication of their secret writings," says Barruel, " was to persuade the whole of Germany that their Order no longer existed, that their adepts had all renounced not only their mysteries and conspiracies but all connection between themselves as members of a secret society." It is very curious to read these words written more than 120 years ago, for this is precisely the course that has been adopted throughout by the Illuminati. Still at the present day any reference to the rôle of Illuminism either in the French Revolution or after is immediately met with the assurance that the whole thing is a " mare's nest," and that in reality Illuminism was an unimportant and transitory movement, which finally ended with its suppression in Bavaria in 1786.

With regard to Barruel's and Robison's revelations, which we are asked to believe " fell flat " — but which in reality created so immense a sensation that the entire first edition of the translation of Barruel's Memoirs was sold out before the fourth volume reached the Press, whilst Robison's book went into at least four editions — every effort was made at the time of their appearance to counteract their effects and even to withdraw them from circulation. " The zealous brothers on the banks of the Thames asked for help from their German brothers " in order to destroy the copies of the obnoxious volumes.[1] Thereupon " Brother Boettiger " replied by an article in the *Monthly Magazine* for January 1798 in which he assured the British public that " every one concerned in unveiling Illuminism is now only pursuing a chimera on matters long since buried in profound oblivion, that since 1790 no one has paid the least attention to the Illuminati, that since that date there is no mention of them in the German lodges, and that, finally, proofs of this assertion are to be found in the papers of Bode, who had become the head of the Order." At least, as Barruel observes, Boettiger here admits " that the mysteries of Illuminism had become those of masonic lodges," and that the Order had not been annihilated in 1786 at the time of the discovery of its plots, as other writers of the sect had pretended, but that it had survived at any rate until 1790.

A further exoneration of the Illuminati which is frequently quoted to-day appeared some years later under the title of *De l'influence attribuée aux philosophes, aux Francs Maçons, et aux Illuminés sur la Révolution de France,* of which the author was no other than Jean Joseph Mounier, proposer of the Oath of the Tennis Court on June 20, 1789. According to this apparently reliable witness, neither Freemasonry nor Illuminism had the slightest influence on the Revolution, nor had philosophy either! Therefore, if we are to believe Mounier, the time-honoured opening to nearly every existing book on the French Revolution tracing its origins to the theories of Rousseau, Diderot, Voltaire, and so on, must be ruled out as fictions.

[1] Barruel, iv. 218.

When we come to examine Mounier's attitude more closely, however, certain considerations present themselves, too lengthy to enter into here, which detract somewhat from the value of his testimony. Of these the most important is the fact that Mounier wrote his book in Germany, where he was living under the protection of the Duke of Weimar, who had placed him at the head of a school in that city where Boettiger himself was director of the college,[1] and, according to the editor of Mounier's work, it was from Bode, who was also at Weimar and whom Boettiger declared to be the head of the Illuminati, that Mounier collected his information![2] And this is the sort of evidence seriously quoted against that of innumerable other contemporaries who testified to the influence of Illuminism on the French Revolution!

Space unfortunately forbids quotations from these authorities — Lombard de Langres, the Chevalier de Malet, Joseph de Maistre, the Comte de Vaudreuil, Zimmermann, Göchhausen, and many others — but an important point to notice is that they belonged to no one party, religion, school of thought, or nationality, but though widely differing in their political or religious point of view, agreed on this one question. Thus the argument frequently advanced that Barruel wrote simply in the interests of the Catholic Church is obviously absurd, since Robison, who was a Protestant, arrived independently at precisely the same conclusions, and the American ecclesiastics quoted above can certainly not be supposed to have spoken in obedience to the dictates of Rome.

It will still be objected that all these witnesses and those who came after them were " reactionaries " eager to discredit the Revolution by every possible means. Was Louis Blanc the Socialist a reactionary? And who has more clearly indicated the workings of the occult forces beneath the movement?[3] Was George Sand, revolutionary and Freemason, a " reactionary "? And it was George Sand who, in referring to " the European conspiracy of

[1] Mounier, *De l'influence attribuée, etc.*, p. lviii (1822 edition).
[2] *Ibid.* pp. 130, 212.
[3] See the whole chapter devoted to this question in the second volume of Louis Blanc's *Histoire de la Révolution Française.*

Illuminism " and "the gigantic conceptions of Weishaupt," declared that Illuminism, " drawing from the inventive genius of its leaders and from the traditions of the Secret Societies of mystic Germany, appalled the world by the most formidable and the most learned of political and religious conspiracies," which " shook all dynasties on their thrones." [1] And Madame Sand adds: " Had these societies more effect in France than in the heart of the Germany that had given them birth? *The French Revolution answers energetically with the affirmative.*" [2]

How, then, in the face of all this evidence — evidence which, as we shall see later, other Freemasons confirmed — is it possible to deny the influence of illuminized Freemasonry on the French Revolution? How can we doubt the truth of those terrible words of Barruel which the subsequent history of the world and, above all, its situation to-day has surely justified:

> You thought the Revolution ended in France, and the Revolution in France was only the first attempt of the Jacobins. In the desires of a terrible and formidable sect, you have only reached the first stage of the plans it has formed for that general Revolution which is to overthrow all thrones, all altars, annihilate all property, efface all law and end by dissolving all society.

Had not Weishaupt declared: " This revolution shall be the work of the Secret Societies, and that is one of our great mysteries " ?

But for a brief spell after the fall of Babeuf the work of the conspiracy was arrested. The XVIIIth of Brumaire dealt a crushing blow to Illuminism, and the same hand that had locked the door of the Panthéonistes' meeting-place closed down the Secret Societies. Thus the fifteen years during which Napoleon held the reins of power were the only period in the last 140 years during which Europe had peace from the devastating fire of Illuminism kindled by Weishaupt.

[1] *La Comtesse de Rudolstadt*, ii. 219.   [2] *Ibid.* p. 260.

CHAPTER IV

THE GROWTH OF SOCIALISM

Revival of Illuminism — The Tugendbund — The Alta Vendita — The Industrial Revolution — Rôle of the Jews — The Philosophers — Robert Owen — " New Harmony " — Saint-Simon — Pierre Leroux — Fourier — Buchez — Louis Blanc — Cabet — Vidal — Pecqueur — Proudhon — Trade-Union Terrorism.

AFTER the fall of Napoleon the smouldering flames of Illuminism broke out afresh all over Europe. The " German Union," inaugurated immediately on the suppression of the Illuminati in Bavaria, was in reality Weishaupt's Order reorganized under a different name, and in the early years of the following century other societies such as the Tugendbund and the Burschenshaft were started on much the same lines.[1] The Tugendbund, inaugurated in about 1812 and composed of all the most violent elements amongst the Illuminati, whose doctrines were those of Clootz and Marat, developed into a further Order known as the German Association and aiming at a United Germany.

It is here that for the first time we can clearly detect the connection between Prussianism and the secret forces of World Revolution, though, no doubt, it could be traced back to a much earlier date. As we have already seen, Frederick the Great, through his ambassador, von der

[1] Lombard de Langres, *Les Sociétés secrètes*, pp. 81, 102, 110-113. Metternich also regarded these German societies as the outcome of Illuminism. Writing in 1832 he says: "Germany has long suffered from the evil which to-day covers the whole of Europe. . . . The sect of Illuminés . . . has never been destroyed although the same (Bavarian) government has tried to suppress it and has been obliged to inveigh against it, and it has taken successively, according to circumstances and the needs of the times, the denominations of Tugendbund, of Burschenshaft, etc.," *Mémoires de Metternich*, v. 368.

Goltz, had worked indefatigably for the rupture of the Franco-Austrian alliance, but at the same time his intrigues were conducted through a more obscure channel, for Frederick was a Freemason, as also were his friends the philosophers of France, and it was thus largely through his influence that the disintegrating doctrines of Voltaire were propagated which paved the way for the anti-Christian campaign of Weishaupt. In 1807 Joseph de Maistre, who had the rare perspicacity to perceive the fearful danger of Frederick's policy to the peace and stability of Europe, wrote these remarkable words:

I have always had a particular aversion for Frederick II., whom a frenzied century hastened to proclaim a *great man*, but who was *au fond* only a *great Prussian*. History will note this prince as one of the greatest enemies of the human race who has ever existed.[1]

But de Maistre reckoned without that conspiracy of history which, controlled principally by German hands, was through the instrumentality of such agents as Carlyle, to maintain the prestige of Frederick in order to smooth the path for his successors.

After the death of Frederick the Great his policy was followed not only by his nephew Frederick William II., but by the disciples of Weishaupt. It was thus that the Illuminatus Diomedes (the Marquis de Constanza) wrote:

In Germany there must be only one or two princes at the most, and these princes must be illuminized and so led by our adepts and surrounded by them that no profane man may approach their persons.[2]

May not the Prussian Clootz's ambiguous reference to " the immutable Empire of the Great Germany — the Universal Republic "[3] be traced to the same source of inspiration? It is possible, indeed, that Clootz may have been not only the adept of Weishaupt, but, as both Robespierre and Brissot suspected, the agent of the King of Prussia. Certain contemporaries have in fact declared

---

[1] *Lettres inédites de Joseph de Maistre* (1851), p. 97.
[2] Deschamps, *op. cit.* ii. 397, quoting evidence given at the trial of the Illuminati.
[3] Clootz's speech to the Convention, September 9, 1792.

that Frederick William II. was actually an Illuminatus. Thus the Comte de Vaudreuil, writing to the Comte d'Artois from Venice in October 1790, remarked:

> What strikes me most is that the sect of the *Illuminés* is the cause and instigator of all our troubles; that one finds these sectaries everywhere, that even the King of Prussia is imbued with this pernicious system; that the man who possesses his chief confidence (Bischoffswerder) is one of its chief heads.[1]

And Robison states that his interest in the Illuminati was first aroused by an invitation to enter that Society from " a very honourable and worthy gentleman " who informed him " that the King of Prussia was the patron of the Order and that its object was most honourable and praiseworthy." Robison, however, declined the invitation because " there was something in the character and conduct of the King of Prussia which gave me a dislike to everything which he professed to patronize," and he was not surprised when later the same " honourable and worthy gentleman " confirmed his suspicions of the Order and said, " shaking his head very emphatically, ' Have nothing to do with it, we have been deceived, it is a dangerous thing.' "[2]

A connection between Prussianism and Illuminism can therefore be detected from the beginning but with the Tugendbund appears in the clear light of day. According to Eckert the ultimate ends of the two intrigues were not identical, but each used the other for its own plan of world power.

> This national sentiment latent in all (German) hearts, these efforts towards union of the different German States, masonry attempted to appropriate in order to direct them towards the overthrow of all thrones and of all nationalities. . . . The *Unity of Germany* became then the exclusive theme of the press; from the Tugendbund there issued, under high masonic direction, the German Association which absorbed it entirely.　. . . . . . .

> The object of this association (according to " the authentic Report of the Secret Associations of Germany " by Mannsdorf, one of the members of the upper lodges)

---

[1] *Correspondence du Comte de Vaudreuil et du Comte d'Artois*, i. 342.
[2] Robison, *Proofs of a Conspiracy*, p. 583.

was *to dethrone all the German princes with the exception of the King of Prussia*, to bestow on this last the Imperial Crown of Germany, and to give to the State a democratic constitution. The final goal of masonry was then to bring about " the real or Universal Republic and the destruction of all nationalities." [1]

It is easy to see that the Hohenzollerns might well make use of this intrigue in order to accomplish the first part of the programme — Prussian domination.

But Illuminism had not confined itself to Germany, and before the fall of Napoleon a further secret society was organized, under the name of the Carbonari, which soon fell under the control of the Illuminati. Though masonic in their origin, the Carbonari had not begun as a revolutionary body. Their founders were avowedly Royalists and Catholics who, possibly deluded as to the real aims of Illuminism, followed the precedent laid down by Weishaupt of taking Christ for their Grand Master. But before long the adepts of revolutionary masonry penetrated into their ranks and, taking the lead, acquired control over the whole association. " Italian genius," says Monsignor Dillon, " soon outstripped the Germans in astuteness, and as soon as, perhaps sooner than, Weishaupt had passed away, the supreme government of all the Secret Societies of the world was exercised by the Alta Vendita or highest lodge of the Italian Carbonari." [2] It was this formidable society, the " Haute Vente Romaine," which from 1814 to 1848 directed the activities of all the Secret Societies. Far more subtle, and therefore more formidable, than the Carbonari, the leaders of the Haute Vente conducted their campaign precisely on the lines of the Illuminati, of which they were indeed the direct continuation.[3] Thus, according to the custom of the earlier Order, followed by Anarcharsis Clootz and Gracchus Babeuf, the members of the Haute Vente all adopted classical pseudonyms, that of the leader, a corrupt Italian nobleman, being Nubius. This young man, rich, handsome, eloquent, and absolutely reckless,

[1] Deschamps, *op. cit.* ii. 227, 228.
[2] Monsignor George F. Dillon, *The War of Anti-Christ with the Church c·d Christian Civilization*, p. 63 (1884).
[3] *Ibid.* p. 63.

was " a visionary with an *idée fixe* of elevating a pedestal for his own vanity." [1] But it was not in the band of dissolute young Italians he gathered around him, but in his Jewish allies, that Nubius found his principal support. Throughout the early years of the nineteenth century Jews in increasing numbers had penetrated into the masonic lodges and also into certain Secret Societies. The Egyptian rite of Memphis had been founded before the French Revolution by the Jewish Illuminatus Cagliostro, and " in 1815 the Rite of Mizraim, consisting of ninety Jewish degrees, was established by the Jews in Paris. Ragon, the French Masonic authority, calls it Jewish masonry." [2]

Joseph de Maistre declared the Jews now to be playing an active part in Illuminism — a system which he had studied deeply and believed to be " the root of all the evil then afflicting Europe." [3] " There are certainly, according to all appearances," he wrote in 1816, " societies organized for the destruction of all the bodies of nobility, of all noble institutions, of all the thrones and of all the altars of Europe. The sect which makes use of everything seems at this moment to turn the Jews to great account and we must very much beware of them." [4] In the Haute Vente for the first time we find them taking the lead. Rich members of the Ashkenazim contributed to the funds of the society, lesser Jews acted as their cleverest agents.[5] Amongst the latter class, one who had assumed the pseudonym of Piccolo Tigre displayed the greatest energy. Masquerading as an itinerant jeweller and moneylender, Piccolo Tigre travelled about Europe carrying the instructions of the Haute Vente to the Carbonari and returning laden with gold for the money-boxes of Nubius. On these journeys Piccolo Tigre received the protection of the masonic lodges everywhere, although the greater number of the men who composed them were held by the Haute Vente in supreme contempt. " Beyond the Masons and unknown to them," writes Monsignor Dillon, " though

---

[1] J. Crétineau-Joly, *L'Eglise Romaine en face de la Révolution*, ii. 383.
[2] A. Cowan, *The X-rays in Freemasonry*, p. 160.
[3] *Lettres inédites de Joseph de Maistre*, p. 368.
[4] Joseph de Maistre, *Quatre chapitres inédits sur la Russie*, chap. iv.
[5] Monsignor Dillon, *op. cit.* p. 72. Crétineau-Joly, *op. cit.* ii. 131.

formed generally from them, lay the deadly secret conclave, which nevertheless used and directed them for the ruin of the world and of their own selves."

So important had the rôle of Piccolo Tigre become, that in 1822 we find him writing a letter of instruction to the Haute Vente Piedmontaise of which the following extract will serve to indicate the methods that he advocated and incidentally their similarity with those of the Illuminati:

In the impossibility in which our brothers and friends find themselves, to say, as yet their last word, it has been judged good and useful to propagate the light everywhere, and to set in motion all that which aspires to move. For this reason we do not cease to recommend you to affiliate persons of every class to every manner of association no matter of what kind, *only provided that mystery and secrecy shall be the dominant characteristics.* All Italy is covered with religious confraternities and with penitents of diverse colours. Do not fear to slip in some of your people into the very midst of these flocks, led, as they are, by a stupid devotion. Let our agents study with care the *personnel* of these confraternity men, and they will see that little by little they will not be wanting in a harvest. Under a pretext the most futile but never political or religious, create by yourselves, or better yet, cause to be created by others, associations having commerce, industry, music, the fine arts, etc., for objects. Reunite in one place or another — in the sacristies or chapels even — these tribes of yours as yet ignorant; put them under the pastoral staff of some virtuous priest, well known but credulous, and easy to be deceived. Then infiltrate the poison into those chosen hearts; infiltrate it in little doses and as if by chance. Afterwards, upon reflection, you will yourselves be astonished at your success.

The essential thing is to isolate a man from his family, to cause him to lose his morals. He is sufficiently disposed by the bent of his character to flee from household cares and to run after easy pleasures and forbidden joys. He loves the long conversations of the cafés, and the idleness of shows. Lead him along, sustain him, give him an importance of some kind, teach him discreetly to grow weary of his daily labours, and by this manœuvre, after having separated him from his wife and children and after having shown him how painful are all his duties, you will then excite in him the desire of another existence. Man is a born rebel. Stir up the desire of rebellion until it becomes a conflagration, but in such a manner that the conflagration does not break out. This is a preparation for the great work that you have to begin.

When you shall have insinuated into a few souls disgust for

family and for religion (the one nearly always follows in the wake of the other), let fall some words which will provoke the desire of being affiliated to the nearest lodge. This vanity of the citizen or of the *bourgeois* for being enrolled in Freemasonry is something so *banal* and so universal that I am always full of admiration for human stupidity. I am not surprised to see the whole world knocking at the door of all the Venerables and asking these gentlemen for the honour of being one of the workmen chosen for the reconstruction of the Temple of Solomon. To find oneself a member of a lodge, to feel oneself apart from one's wife and children, called upon to guard a secret which is never confided to one, is for certain natures a delight and an ambition.

The Alta Vendita desires that under one pretence or another, as many princes and wealthy persons as possible should be introduced into the Masonic Lodges. Princes of a sovereign house and those who have not the legitimate hope of being kings by the grace of God, all wish to be kings by the grace of a Revolution. The Duke of Orleans is a Freemason. . . . The prince who has not a kingdom to expect is a good fortune for us. There are many of them in that plight. Make Freemasons of them; these poor princes will serve our ends, while thinking to labour only for their own. They form a magnificent signboard.

It is upon the lodges that we count to double our ranks. They form, without knowing it, our preparatory novitiate. They discourse without end upon the dangers of fanaticism, upon the happiness of social equality and upon the grand principles of religious liberty. They launch amidst their feastings thundering anathemas against intolerance and persecution. This is positively more than we require to make adepts. A man imbued with these fine things is not very far from us. There is nothing more required than to enlist him.

It was thus by systematic demoralization that the leaders of the Haute Vente, like the Illuminati, hoped to establish their ascendancy over the " peoples " of Europe. But in order to understand the manner in which they set out to accomplish this purpose we must now examine the ground on which they had to work.

The Industrial Revolution

It is of the utmost importance to realize that the people at this period were suffering from very real grievances. These grievances weighed less, however, on the agricultural than on the industrial workers, whose conditions of life were often terrible. This fact no one has ever attempted to deny, and we need not have recourse to the writings of Socialists to gain an idea of the slavery endured by men, women, and children in the mines and factories of Europe during the years following on the Napoleonic wars, for we shall find the whole case stated with more accuracy and far greater eloquence in the letters of Lord Shaftesbury, whose whole life was devoted to the cause of the poor and oppressed.

What was the reason for this aggravation of the workers' lot? Partly the speeding up of industry brought about by the introduction of machinery; partly, in England, the rapidly increasing population, but in France to a large extent the situation must be directly attributed to the Revolution. We have already seen how the destruction of trade unions and increase in the days of labour by the abolition of national holidays had added to the workers' burden, but a further effect of the great upheaval had been the transference of power from the aristocracy to the *bourgeoisie* with disastrous consequences to the people. In a word the destruction of feudalism had inaugurated the reign of Commercialism. This is admitted by no less an authority than Marx himself.

The *bourgeoisie* has played in history a most revolutionary part. The *bourgeoisie*, whenever it has conquered power, has destroyed all feudal, patriarchal, and idyllic relations. It has pitilessly torn asunder all the many-coloured feudal bonds which united men to their "natural superiors," and has left no tie twixt man and man but naked self-interest and callous cash payment. It has drowned religious ecstasy, chivalrous enthusiasm, and middle-class sentimentality in the ice-cold water of egotistical calculation. It has transformed personal worth into mere exchange value, and substituted for countless dearly-bought chartered freedoms the one and only unconscionable freedom of Free Trade. It has, in one word, replaced an exploitation veiled by religious and political illusions by exploitation open, unashamed, direct, and brutal.[1]

Thus in the opinion of the leading prophet of modern Socialist thought, *it was the destruction of feudalism that led to the enslavement of the proletariat.* Exaggerated as this

[1] *Manifesto of the Communist Party*, by Karl Marx and Friedrich Engels, p. 9.

indictment of the *bourgeoisie* may be, there is a certain degree of truth in Marx's theory. The class that lives on inherited wealth is always the barrier to the exploitation of the workers. To the noble who paid 500 louis for his *carrosse*, or the duchess who never asked the price of her brocaded gown, where was the advantage of underpaying the workman or the dressmaker? " Sweating " results largely from the attempt to bring commodities within the reach of a class that cannot or will not pay a price allowing a fair rate of remuneration to the worker. After the revolution, when aristocracy with its careless expenditure and its traditional instincts of benevolence had taken refuge in garrets, these were the classes that supported industry, and it is thus against " the newly rich " that we find the bitterest complaints of the people directed.

At the same time, amongst the *bourgeoisie* had arisen a new influence that Marx is careful not to indicate, but about which the Socialist Malon is more explicit:

Feudalism signifies privilege granted in return for certain duties agreed upon; *judaized plutocracy* recognizes no duty, it has only one object, to appropriate the largest possible part of the work of others, and of the social accumulation in order to use and abuse it selfishly. That is its great moral indignity, and the signal for its approaching fall in the name of public welfare and of the interests of Humanity.

We shall find the same opinion expressed later by the Anarchist Bakunin.

The Jew was of course not alone in exploiting the workers; but the spirit of the Jew, permeating commerce in every country — in France, in Germany, above all in America — undoubtedly contributed to the industrial oppression against which Marx inveighs. Under the monarchy the Jews had been held in check by laws limiting their activities, but the edicts passed at the beginning of the Revolution, decreeing their complete emancipation, had removed all restraints to their rapacity.

By the Jewish race 1789 is therefore hailed as the year of deliverance. Without going so far as M. Drumont in saying that the Revolution delivered the people from the aristocrats in order to hand them over to the Jews, it cannot be denied that the power of the Jews over the people was immensely increased by the overthrow of the monarchy and aristocracy. Whether they deliberately contributed to this end it is impossible to say, but their influence was suspected by contemporaries, as may be seen by the following passage from Prudhomme, an ardent democrat and in no way to be accused of anti-Semitism:

The French Revolution did a great deal of good to the Jews; it entirely proscribed that antiquated prejudice which caused the remains of this ancient people to be regarded as a race of degraded men below all others. The Jews in France for a long while paid no longer at the barriers, as under the reign of Saint Louis, the same dues that were exacted from the cloven-footed. But every year each Jewish family was taxed 40 livres for the right of habitation, or protection and tolerance. This due was suppressed on the 20th of July, 1790. The Jews were, so to speak, naturalized French and took the rank of citizens. What did they do to show their gratitude? What they did before; they have not changed, they have not mended their ways, they contributed not a little to the fall of *assignats*. The disorder of our finances was a Peruvian mine for them; they have not abated their infamous traffic; on the contrary, civil liberty has only availed them to extend their stock-jobbing speculations. Public misery became a rich patrimony to them. . . . The Jews took impetus. The Government had need of them, and God knows how dearly they have made the Republic pay the resources that it demanded of them. What mysteries of iniquity would be revealed if the Jews, like the mole, did not make a point of working in the dark! In a word and to say all, the Jews have never been more Jews than since we tried to make of them men and citizens.[1]

But it was the peasants who became the chief sufferers from the domination of the Jews. Under the Old Régime, the feudal dues had proved oppressive, but in many instances the seigneurs were the benefactors and protectors of their vassals. The Jewish usurers on whom the peasant proprietors now depended to carry on if crops failed or weather proved unpropitious, showed no indulgence.

" As soon as he " (the peasant), writes Daniel Stern, " has

---

[1] *Crimes de la Révolution*, iii. 44. Burke relates that the Jews made large profits out of the plunder of the Churches, and that he is told " the very sons of such Jew-jobbers have been made bishops, persons not to be suspected of any Christian superstition " (*Reflections on the French Revolution*, p. 254). This may explain the apostasy of certain prelates on the 8th of November, 1793.

entered into commercial relations with this *rusé* race, as soon as he has put his name at the foot of a paper which he has read and re-read without perceiving the hidden clause that does for him, the peasant, in spite of all his *finesse*, will never succeed in recovering his liberty. Henceforth his activity, his intelligence, the benefits of Providence who sends him rich harvests will profit him nothing, but only his new master. The exorbitant interest on a very small capital will absorb his time and his labours. Every day he will see the comfort of his family diminish and his difficulties increase. As the fatal day approaches when the debt falls due the sombre face of his creditor warns him that he can expect no respite. He must make up his mind, he must go further along the road of perdition, borrow again, always borrow until ruin has been brought about, and fields, meadows, and woods, house, flocks, and home all have passed from his industrious hands into the rapacious ones of the usurer." [1]

In a word, the peasant inherited from the aristocrat; he was disinherited by the usurer. Here is the true history of the disinherited, not in France alone, but in Russia,[2] in Austria, in Poland; everywhere that the worker lives by tilling his own soil the abolition of feudalism has led to the domination of the money-lender, and the money-lender is in most cases a Jew. If, exasperated by this tyranny, the peasants from time to time have given way to violence and turned on their oppressors, is it altogether surprising? When in the fourteenth century the peasants rose against the *noblesse*, the blame, we are told, must rest solely with the nobles. Yet why is peasant fury when it took the form of a " jacquerie " to be condoned, and when it takes the form of a " pogrom " to be remorselessly condemned? Surely in one case as much as the other the plea of uncontrollable exasperation may be with justice put forward.

The industrial worker as well as the peasant found the

[1] *La Révolution de 1848*, by Daniel Stern, ii. 89 (La Comtesse d'Agoult).

[2] See the account given on his journey through White Russia in 1816 by the Grand Duke Nicholas, who, whilst admitting the support given to the Imperial authority by the Jews, remarks: " The general ruination of the peasantry of these provinces is attributable to the Jews, who are second in import to the landowners only; by their industries they exploit to the utmost the unfortunate population. They are everything here — merchants, contractors, pothouse-keepers, millers, carriers, artisans, etc., and they are so clever in squeezing and cheating the common people that they advance money on the unsown bread and discount the harvest before the fields are sown. They are regular leeches who suck up everything and completely exhaust this province," (E. A. Brayley Hodgett's *The Court of Russia in the Nineteenth Century*, i. 161).

Jew an exacting taskmaster. It was not only the introduction of machinery that at the beginning of the nineteenth century brought about the speeding up of industry, but the spirit of the new commercialism, which succeeded to the leisurely methods of the Old Régime. As M. Drumont has expressed it, if the workers paused for breath the cry went up from the statisticians: " What are we coming to? England manufactured 375 million trouser buttons last year and we have only produced 374 millions! "

This driving force behind the worker, this spirit of cut-throat competition, was largely attributable to the Jew.

At any rate, whether we regard the " Capitalistic system " as an evil or not, we cannot deny that the Jews were mainly responsible for it.

In order to appreciate thoroughly the insincerity of Marx with regard to this question, it is only necessary to glance through his book *Das Capital* and then the work of Werner Sombart on *The Jews and Modern Capitalism*. " The Jew," as Sombart remarks, " embodied modern Capitalism," [1] and he goes on to describe, step by step, the building up by Jewish hands of the system which superseded the Old Régime of amicable trading and peaceful industry; he shows the Jew as the inventor of advertisement,[2] as the employer of cheap labour,[3] as the principal participant in the stock-jobbing or *agiotage* that prevailed at the end of the first French Revolution.[4] But it is above all as the usurer that the Jew achieved power. " Modern Capitalism," says Sombart, " is the child of money-lending," [5] and the Jew, as we have seen, is the money-lender *par excellence*. The great fortune of the Rothschilds was built up on this basis. The principal " loan-floaters " of the world,[6] they were later the first railway kings.[7] The period of 1820 onwards became, as Sombart calls it, " the age of the Rothschilds," so that by the middle of the century it was a common dictum, " There is only one power in Europe, and that is Rothschild." [8]

Now how is it conceivable that a man who set out

[1] Werner Sombart, *The Jews and Modern Capitalism*, p. 50.
[2] *Ibid*. p. 139.   [3] *Ibid*. p. 150.   [4] *Ibid*. p. 101.
[5] *Ibid*. p. 189.   [6] *Ibid*. pp. 101, 103. [7] *Ibid*. p. 105
[8] *Ibid. The Jews and Modern Capitalism*, p. 99.

honestly to denounce Capitalism should have avoided all reference to its principal authors? Yet even in the section of his book dealing with the origins of Industrial Capitalism, where Marx refers to the great financiers, the stock-jobbing and speculation in shares, and what he describes as " the modern sovereignty of finance," he never once indicates the Jews as the leading financiers, or the Rothschilds as the super-capitalists of the world. As well might one sit down to recount the history of wireless telegraphy without any reference to Signor Marconi! How are we to explain this astounding omission? Only by recognizing that Marx was not sincere in his denunciations of the Capitalistic system, and that he had other ends in view. I shall return to this point later in connection with the career of Marx.

Such, then, was the condition of things at the beginning of the period known as the industrial revolution. The grievances of the workers were very real; the need for social reconstruction urgent, the gulf between poverty and riches greater than ever before, and the Government of France had no schemes of reform to offer. If only a great man had then arisen to lead the people back into paths of sanity and progress, to show them in that fatal year of 1789 new-born democracy had taken the wrong turning and wandered into a pathless jungle whence it could only emerge by retracing its footsteps, and starting afresh led by the light of its own day, not by the will o' the wisp of illuminized freemasonry!

Unhappily at this new crisis in the history of the working classes there was no one to point the way, no one who had the insight and the courage to rise and declare: " The great experiment of 1789 to 1794 has proved a failure, the principles on which it was founded have been weighed in the balance and found wanting, the goals it set before us have turned out to be *mirages* towards which we have marched too long with bleeding feet, the methods it employed were atrocious and must never be repeated, the men who led it were the enemies of the people and such as they shall never deceive us again. There is no hope for suffering humanity but to repudiate the Revolution and all its works, and to strike out a fresh path with new hopes, new aims founded not on the dreams of visionaries or the schemes of demagogues but on the true desires of the people."

Instead of rallying the people by such a trumpet-call as this, the men who now arose had nothing better to offer than the worn-out creed of their revolutionary predecessors. The doctrines that had proved fallacious, the visions that had turned out to be delusions, the battle-cries that had led the people to disaster were all to be again revived with the same assurance as if in the past they had been attended with triumphant success.

The Philosophers

The earliest pioneer of the movement in England, later to be known as Socialism, was the English cotton mill-owner, Robert Owen. At the outset of his career it seemed that Owen might really prove to be the man the people needed, the enlightened reformer who, sweeping aside the fallacious theories of the French Revolution, was to establish the industrial system on new lines. The work of Owen at New Lanark was wholly admirable, the proper housing of the workers, the better education of the children, and indeed of the whole population by the inculcation of ideas of thrift, sobriety, and cleanliness, brought about a complete regeneration of the town and excited universal admiration. In all these schemes their author encountered no resistance. Socialists are fond of declaring that " the upper classes " are perfectly indifferent to the welfare of the workers, and that nothing but revolutionary agitation will rouse them. The history of Robert Owen provides a striking instance to the contrary, for it was amongst the so-called " upper classes," dukes, bishops, statesmen, even crowned heads — for the Czar Nicholas I. visited him in person — that he received his principal support. New Lanark speedily became a place of pilgrimage for every one interested in social reform, and Owen found himself in danger of having his head turned by the adulation of the great.

It must be understood, however, that Owen's experiment was not conducted on Socialistic principles. Living in the big house and driving about in his carriage "like a prince amongst his subjects,"[1] Owen played the part simply of a benevolent autocrat.[2] His employés existing on the wage system were obliged to work eight to ten hours a day,[3] and were decorated with humiliating badges if they proved idle or inefficient. The proceeds of industry were not distributed amongst the workers, but gathered in by Owen himself and spent as he saw fit. It is true that from the model shop he erected in the town he drew no profit, goods being dealt out to customers at cost price, but with a lordly income Owen could well afford to indulge in this charitable hobby. No less honour must be attributed to him on this account, but the fact remains that Owen's philanthropy at New Lanark was conducted on the system Socialists condemn as "capitalistic."

At any rate the experiment proved triumphantly successful, but unhappily Owen allowed himself to be led from the path of sane and practical reforms into a wilderness of philosophic speculation. How are we to explain this unfortunate aberration? Only by the fact that Owen had fallen under the influence of the occult forces at work on the Continent, for if we examine his writings in the light of the doctrines described in the first chapter of this book, we cannot fail to perceive that his mind was permeated with Illuminism. Thus the fundamental point of Owen's teaching consists in the assumption that Man is the creature of circumstances, and that character results solely from environment. Therefore by removing him from evil conditions Man will inevitably be "transformed into an intelligent, rational and good being."[4] Further, the evil conditions that at present exist are simply the result of civilization, which, like Weishaupt, Owen held to be the bane of humanity. "All the nations of the earth, with all the boast of each respecting their advance in *what they call*

---

[1] *Life of Robert Owen*, by Sargant, p. 30.
[2] Cf. Holyoake, *The Co-operative Movement*, p. 13. "Owen . . . was one of the small class of benevolent Tories who regard power as including an obligation to use it for the advantages of the people."
[3] Sargant, *op. cit.* 217.
[4] *Life of Robert Owen by himself*, p. 60.

civilization, are to-day governed by force, fraud, false-hood, and fear, emanating from ignorance in governors and governed." [1] Consequently Owen declared: " You must think of me as not belonging to the present system of society, but as one looking with the greatest delight at its entire annihilation, so that ultimately not one stone of it shall be left upon another." [2]

All this is only another way of expressing Weishaupt's theory that " Man is not bad except as he is made so by arbitrary morality. He is bad because Religion, the State, and bad examples pervert him," and therefore it is nec-essary to bring about " the total destruction of the existing civil system."

Indeed certain passages of Owen are almost word for word the same as those that occur in the code of Weishaupt. For example, in the latter it was stated that the aim of the Illuminati was " to make of the human race, without any distinction of nation, condition or profession, *one good and happy family*," and Owen announced " that new state of existence upon earth, which, when understood and applied rationally to practice, will cordially unite all as *one good and enlightened family*." [3]

It is idle to attribute these extraordinary resemblances — of which many more examples might be given — to mere coincidence, and to suppose that the Yorkshire cotton-mill owner evolved the same conclusions and even the same phraseology as the Bavarian professor out of his own inner consciousness. And indeed, as Owen's biog-rapher points out, he himself " dimly indicates the pos-session of a philosophy which would regenerate society if men's minds were prepared to receive it. With a Pytha-gorean reticence, he reserves to himself and his initiated an esoteric doctrine of which the world is unworthy." [4] What could this doctrine be but Illuminism, which Owen, obedient to the custom of the Order, is careful not to reveal?

But it is in the matter of religion that Owen most clearly betrays the source of his inspiration. By no other

[1] *Life of Robert Owen by himself*, p. 77.
[2] *Ibid.* p. xxii.
[3] *Ibid.* p. 154.
[4] Sargant, *op. cit.* p. 76.

means can his campaign of militant atheism be explained. In a man of Weishaupt's moral character hatred of Christianity is not surprising, but that Owen, filled with ardour for the good of humanity, a sincere and tireless philanthropist, should have paid no tribute to the great Teacher of love and compassion is so extraordinary as to be inexplicable by any facts hitherto set forth by his biographers. But when we examine his theories, it is easy to see whence he derived them, for what are his ideas of a " Rational Society " and his perpetual allusions to reason but the old doctrine of Weishaupt that " Reason should be the only code of Man? " — a doctrine which had already found expression in Paine's *Age of Reason* and in the " Feasts of Reason " celebrated in the churches of Paris? It was then under this malign influence that Owen gave vent to sentiments utterly foreign to his natural character, as, for example, his declaration that " the religions of the world are horrid monsters and real demons of humanity which swallow up all its *rationality* and happiness." [1] Are we not forcibly reminded by such utterances of the diatribes of the Illuminatus Clootz on " the nullity of all religions " ? At moments Owen even rivals Clootz in violence. " Religion," Clootz had written, " is a social disease which cannot be too quickly cured. A religious man is a depraved animal," [2] and Owen echoes the sentiment by saying that " the fundamental notions of every religion . . . have made man the most inconsistent and most miserable being in existence. By the errors of these systems he has been made a weak, imbecile animal," etc. [3]

The occasion on which these words were uttered by Owen was the great public meeting where he had determined " to denounce all the religions of the world." [4] This day he long afterwards declared to have been the most glorious of his life, but in reality it simply had the effect of alienating from him public sympathy and destroying all his power for good. Led still further along the path of Illuminism, and, according to his biographer, " inflamed with an extravagant desire for notoriety," Owen, seven

[1] *Life of Robert Owen by himself*, p. 207.
[2] *La République universelle*, p. 27.
[3] Sargent, *op. cit.* p. 129.   [4] *Life of Robert Owen by himself*, p. 161

years later, abandoned his flourishing experiment at New Lanark in order to found a colony on Communistic lines in America.

For some years he had cherished the plan to " cut the world up into villages of 300 to 2000 souls," in which " the dwellings for the 200 or 300 families should be placed together in the form of a parallelogram," where "individualism was to be disallowed," and " each was to work for the benefit of all." [1] Attempts to found a colony on these lines in Ireland proved abortive, and accordingly in 1824 Owen sailed to the New World, where he bought a large tract of land named " Harmony " from some German colonists, disciples of the pastor Rapp. Here in the following year he started his " New Harmony Community of Equality." The Communist system was finally inaugurated, and other settlements on the same lines were started both in America and Scotland.

But Owen had calculated without taking human nature into account; the difficulty of eradicating the sense of property amongst the colonists proved an insuperable difficulty, and the noble desire to work for the common good with no thought of personal profit failed signally as an incentive.[2] Human passions had a strange way of springing to the surface even in the minds of the enthusiastic Communists who composed Owen's following; thus the organ of the community, *The Co-operative Magazine*, relates that one fine evening a member in the full flow of a discourse to an open-air meeting, on the theory that all forms of punishment shall be replaced by kindness, happened to perceive in the distance a small boy helping himself to the plums in the speaker's orchard, and instantly abandoning oratory, hurried towards the offender and administered a sound thrashing.[3]

Various attempts were made to organize the community on different Socialistic principles. For a time the system known to-day as Guild Socialism was practised in the town of New Harmony, whilst Communism was banished to the country.[4] But in all these experiments

---

[1] Sargant, *op. cit.* p. 171.
[2] *Ibid.* p. 254.
[3] *Ibid.* p. 240.
[4] *Ibid. op. cit.* pp. 252, 253.

human nature still remained the insuperable obstacle, and in 1827 Owen in despair resigned the management. The cause of his failure was attributed by convinced Communists to his own management. By Owen it was attributed to the character of the people who made up the community. His experience, he acknowledged, " had shown one thing: the necessity of great caution in selecting members. No societies with common property and equality could prosper, if composed of persons unfit for their peculiar duties. In order to succeed it was needful to exclude the intemperate, the idle, the careless, the quarrelsome, the avaricious, the selfish. . . ." In other words, Communist settlements must be composed of only perfect human beings. But as Owen's biographer observes: "One wonders whether for a society so weeded, any peculiar organization would be necessary. It is just the selfish and the intemperate who constitute the difficulty of our present arrangements."[1]

The colony founded by Owen's disciple, Abram Combe, at Orbiston, near Glasgow, and other Communist settlements started at Ralahine in County Clare in 1831, at Tytherley in Hampshire in 1839, proved failures for the same reason,[2] and Owen himself was obliged to recognise his cherished scheme as impracticable. Indeed, when on his way back to England in 1827 he had occasion to visit some slave plantations in Jamaica, he came to the conclusion that slavery was after all not such a bad system. For does not slavery provide all the blessings promised by Communism — the certainty of food and lodging, and freedom from " corroding care and anxiety " at the complete sacrifice of all personal liberty — but with the additional advantage of being a workable system?[3]

So ended the experiment of the man whom Socialists proudly name " the father of British Socialism." Considering the extraordinary dearth of practical philanthropists or of tangible results to be found in the annals of Socialism, it is natural that its exponents should be eager

---

[1] Sargant, p. 256.
[2] Sargant, *op. cit.* pp. 278-289. Orbiston started with co-operation but went over to Communism, and thenceforth, Sargant observes, " the project was doomed."   [3] *Ibid. op. cit.* p. 266.

to claim the famous founder of New Lanark as one of their number. But in this, as in most of their pretensions. Socialists have shown themselves singularly dishonest, for it was when Owen abandoned Capitalism in favour of Socialism that he failed. It is therefore not the Owen of New Lanark but the Owen of New Harmony whom Socialists can justly claim as their own. Rather than admit this painful truth, Socialist writers in describing the career of Robert Owen usually content themselves with expatiating at length on the brilliant success of New Lanark and omit all reference to New Harmony. It is a curious fact that no Socialist has so far devoted a book to a truthful account of past Socialistic experiments; all such failures are passed over in complete silence, and the theories on which they were founded are vaunted as if no attempt had ever been made to put them into practice.

A further claim Socialists are fond of making for Robert Owen is that of having founded the co-operative system. This is again a perversion of the truth. Owen's model shop in New Lanark was, as we have seen, simply a benevolent hobby such as a rich man drawing his profits direct from the industry in which the workers were engaged, and paying them a low rate of wages, could well afford. Owen did not believe in the co-operative system which was inaugurated by the famous Rochdale Pioneers at their little co-operative store in Toad Street in 1844. This was really the beginning of a great movement, and was followed by the Co-operative Society of Oldham in 1850 and by the co-operative societies, numbering 340,930 members, which were flourishing in 1874.[1]

In all this, however, neither Robert Owen nor Socialism can claim a share. It is true that some of the founders of co-operation had been influenced by Owen's example at New Lanark, but they did not share his Communistic theories, and Owen therefore " looked coldly " on the co-operative stores started by his so-called disciples.[2]

[1] Article on "Communism," by Mrs. Fawcett, in the *Encyclopædia Britannica* for 1877.
[2] Beatrice Webb, *The Co-operative Movement*, pp. 47, 56. See also Holyoake, *The Co-operative Movement*, p. 18, and *Co-operation in Rochdale*, p. 19. " Co-operation," Holyoake observes, " is not to be identified with

Co-operation then, as Holyoake says, is simply profit sharing,[1] — the system with which Socialists will have nothing to do and indeed oppose with all their might, except when, like Marx, they perceive its utility as a stepping-stone to Communism.

The essential difference between Co-operation and Communism is the system of the right to private property. Under the former system each person concerned in the business has the right to claim for his own his share of the profits; under the latter all profits go to the community. The former has frequently led to triumphant success; the second has invariably ended in total failure. As Mrs. Fawcett in her admirable article on " Communism " explained, the successful co-operative societies of the last century were promoted by real social reformers " who had proved by many failures the futility of Communism as an engine of social regeneration," and she adds: " There is no movement more distinctly non-communistic than co-operation. It strengthens the principles of capital and private property by making every co-operator a Capitalist and thus personally interesting him in the maintenance of the present economic condition of society." [2]

In other words, whilst Communism aims at the concentration of Capital in the hands of the State or of communists, Co-operation aims at the extension of Capital by distributing it amongst a larger number of individuals. And all experience teaches us that through Co-operation, not through Communism, lies the path to industrial peace.

Whilst this really progressive movement had been developing in England a succession of French philosophers were devising further schemes for the reorganization of industry, later to be classified under the generic term of Socialism.

First on the list comes the Comte de Simon, grandson of the famous author of the *Mémoires* relating to the court of Louis XIV. Born in 1760 with an unbalanced brain

Owen," but since it was his shop at New Lanark that suggested the idea to the future co-operators Owen may be said to have " originated co-operation without intending it or believing in it."

[1] Holyoake, *The Co-operative Movement*, p. 24.
[2] *Encyclopædia Britannica* for 1877.

inherited from an insane mother, Saint-Simon had early thrown himself into the wildest excesses and led the life of " an adventurer in quest of gold and glory," [1] but after a while, weary of orgies, he had turned his attention to the regeneration of the world, in which he believed himself destined to play the leading part. Since this book is not intended to form a history of Socialism, but only to indicate the relation between Socialistic theories and the course of the World Revolution, it would be beside the point to describe in detail the philosophy of Saint-Simon. Suffice it then to state briefly that according to his theory of industrial reconstruction there was no way to prevent the exploitation of man by man but to place, not only all property, but all human beings under State control, thus arriving " not at absolute equality but at a hierarchy " in which " each would be classed according to his capacity and rewarded according to his work " — a formula which was only another rendering of the Babouviste maxim: " Every one according to his strength; to every one according to his needs." [2]

In a word, Saint-Simonisme was simply a variation of our old friend Babouvisme, of which the tradition had been carried on by Babeuf's colleague Buonarotti. Saint-Simon's inspiration must, however, be traced still further back than the Chief of Equals, namely to Weishaupt, whose doctrines survived not only amongst the Babouvistes but, as we have seen, in the Haute Vente Romaine.

Saint-Simon, who, we know, was connected with this formidable secret society, accordingly continued the great scheme of Weishaupt by proclaiming the abolition of property, of inheritance, the dissolution of the marriage tie, and the break-up of the family — in a word, the destruction of civilization. Like Robert Owen, Saint-Simon frankly declared that the existing social system was dead and must be completely done away with. The French Illuminatus, however, did not fall into the error of his English contemporary, of alienating public opinion by the repudiation of Christianity; on the contrary, faithful to

---

[1] Thureau-Dangin, *La Monarchie de Juillet*, i. 221.
[2] Thureau-Dangin, *op. cit.* vi. 82.

the directions of Weishaupt, Saint-Simon, in his dook *Le Nouveau Christianisme*, set out to prove that his system was simply the fulfilment of Christ's teaching on the brotherhood of man, which had become perverted by the belief in the necessity for subduing the flesh; " therefore in order to re-establish Christianity on its true basis it was necessary to restore its sensual side, the absence of which strikes its social action with sterility." [1] It is easy to see how such a theory fits in with the plan of the Haute Vente for general demoralization.

Of course, as Weishaupt had foreseen, the method of identifying Christianity with Socialism proved immensely effectual. The wild-eyed revolutionary waving a red flag will never gain so many converts as the mild philosopher who preaches peaceful revolution carried out on the principles of Christian love and brotherhood. It was this old deception of representing Christ as a Socialist which made the strength of Saint-Simonism, and that, practised later on by the so-called Christian Socialists of our own country, not only drew countless amiable visionaries into Socialism, but at the same time drove many virile minds from Christianity to seek relief in Nietzscheism.

In reality no two principles could be more opposed than that of Christ, who taught that " a man's life consisteth not in the abundance of the things that he possesseth," and that of the purely materialistic philosophy which urges mankind to strive for one thing only — present welfare, and to indulge the grossest sensual passions. As to the perfectibility of human nature and the consequent " solidarity " between the workers borrowed by Saint-Simon from Weishaupt and Clootz, no one had ever shown the fallacy of this delusion more forcibly than Christ in His parable of the servant, who, being absolved from his debt towards his master, took his fellow-servant by the throat, saying, " Pay me what thou owest! "

Saint-Simonism carried within it the germs of its own destruction. In 1823 its founder vainly attempted to blow out his brains, but only succeeded in destroying the sight of one eye, and lingered on for two years in semi-blindness

[1] Malon, *Histoire du socialisme*, ii. 15.

and misery. After his death the " Family," as his disciples were wont to call themselves, headed by the " Père Enfantin," split up into opposing factions. It then transpired that the strangest scenes took place amongst them — reminiscent of the Anabaptists — " ecstasies, deliriums, transports "; finally, pursued by the police, the Family broke up amidst the hoots of the crowd.[1]

One of the first members to separate from Enfantin had been Pierre Leroux, who continued, however, to carry on Saint-Simonism with various elaborations. Out of the masonic trilogy Leroux selected " Equality " as the supreme object of desire, and this was to be obtained by a system of triads combining the three human faculties — sensation, sentiment, and knowledge. These were to be represented in the industrial world by trios composed of a workman, an artist, and a savant working together, the whole forming a " triad "; a number of these triads would make up a workshop, a number of workshops a commune, and all the communes collectively were to form a State. But as the State was to be the sole owner of the means of existence, the sole director of work, the triad system of Leroux resolved itself finally into a mere variation on the Communistic State of Robespierre, Babeuf, and Saint-Simon.

Meanwhile Charles Fourier, born in 1772, had devised another plan for the reorganization of society. Though not a Saint-Simonien, Fourier held with Saint-Simon that " civilization had taken the wrong road " (*avait fait fausse route*)[2], and a return to Nature should be effected by giving a free rein to all passions. Starting from the premise that everything which is natural — that is to say, in accordance with the purely animal side of human nature — is right and beneficial, Fourier advocated promiscuous intercourse between the sexes; even the Parc aux Cerfs of Louis XV. had, he considered, been needlessly condemned.[3] Greed, too, was particularly to be encouraged as " the mother of all industries," because it induced man to cultivate the ground and prepare food for himself.[4]

---

[1] Daniel Stern, *La Révolution de 1848*, i. 36.
[2] Thureau-Dangin, *op. cit.* vi. 96. [3] *Ibid.* vi. 99 [4] *Ibid. op. cit.* vi. 98.

It would be outside the scope of this book to follow
Fourier into all his bewildering speculations on the future
of our planet — that one day the moon would die of putrid
fever, the sea, purged of brine, turn into " a pleasant drink
like lemonade," and men, endowed with seven feet each,
would live to the age of 144, of which 120 were to be spent
in the exercise of " free love." [1]

The point to be considered here is Fourier's scheme for
the reconstruction of society. On one point, then, he is to
be commended, namely, that he deprecated any repetition
of the first French Revolution; alone of all his kind, Fourier
proclaimed the great experiment to have proved disastrous,
and never wearied of fulminating against its crimes and
follies. But in this he showed less insight than logic, for
Fourier had been a victim of the Terror — the small
grocer's shop he had set up in 1793 at Lyon had been
pillaged by the troops of the Convention, and he himself
had narrowly escaped the guillotine.

It was therefore by peaceful methods that he proposed
to destroy the existing Capitalistic system, and to establish in its place " domestic associations " of workers which
he named *phalansteries*, each composed of 1800 people,
subdivided into " series," " phalanges," and " groups." [2]
Amongst these perfect equality was to reign, no one was to
give orders, no one to be obliged to work, for in a community where all were able to indulge their passions freely
there would be no temptation to idleness. Fourier even
succeeded in surmounting the great stumbling-block of all
Socialist systems, the question of who was to do " the
dirty work " — this could be quite easily settled by
encouraging the aversion to cleanliness he had observed in
children, so that no tasks however unpleasant would be
repugnant to them.

This ideal condition of things clearly mapped out,
Fourier only awaited the necessary funds to put it into
execution, and accordingly he announced that he would be

[1] Thureau-Dangin, pp. 100, 101.
[2] See the hideous picture of one of these phalansteries — much resembling Owen's " parallelograms " — in Malon's *Histoire du socialisme*, ii.
297. Fourier's idea of the " *état harmonien* " was evidently taken from
Owen's " New Harmony " settlement (Stern, i. 36).

at home every day at 12 o'clock to receive any wealthy man who would supply him with 100,000 francs for the purpose. For ten years at the appointed hour Fourier patiently sat at home waiting for his expected millionaire, but none presented himself, and it was not until 1832 that he finally succeeded in raising the required sum from a certain Baudet Dulaury, and in the same year the first phalanstery was started at Condé-sur-Vesgre, but after the brief life of a year ended in total failure and had to be abandoned.

A little later on a Saint-Simonien named Buchez, who in 1836 became one of the leaders of the sect, embarked on a campaign for combining Socialism not merely with the vague Christianity of Saint-Simon but with rigorous Catholicism. "Starting from Jesus Christ and ending with Robespierre," [1] Buchez collaborated with Roux Lavergne in the famous *Histoire Parlementaire*, in which he palliated the crimes of the Comité de Salut Public on the same moral grounds that in his *Traité complet de philosophie* he had justified the Inquisition and the Massacre of St. Bartholomew, namely, that "the social aim justifies everything" [2] — a maxim adapted from that of the Jacobins, "all is justified for the sake of the revolution," derived in its turn from the doctrine adopted by Weishaupt that "the end justifies the means." We shall find many such genealogies in the language of Socialism.

The first followers of Buchez consisted mainly of young *bourgeois* — artists, students, doctors — but by degrees a certain number of working-men, whom it was his principal aim to enlist in the movement, became interested, and Buchez was then able to put his theories into practice by starting the "*associations ouvrières*" which had long been his dream. These were not to be Communistic in the sense of being State-controlled, but to be conducted on a system much resembling that which is known to-day as Guild Socialism.

The guiding principles of these associations being "Equality" and "Fraternity" — for Buchez, like Leroux,

---

[1] Daniel Stern, *La Révolution de 1848*, i. 42.
[2] Thureau-Dangin, *op. cit.* vi. 88.

had logically eliminated " Liberty " from the masonic formula — the workmen who composed them were invited to pool their tools and money and share their profits equally, only putting aside the sixth part to provide capital for carrying on the industry. In conformity with Buchez's conception of the teachings of Christ, the foreman, elected by the workers themselves, was to be the servant, not the master of all, hence " no more misery, no more inequality, no more conflicts between labour and capital." [1]

At first all went well, and so great was the enthusiasm aroused amongst the members of these associations that they now embarked on a " labour paper " named *L'Atelier* (The Workshop), edited and written by the workers themselves — an experiment unique in the annals of Socialism, unrivalled at any rate in the Socialist movement of to-day; for by no stretch of the imagination could the so-called " Labour organs," or the Labour articles expressed in the purest journalese, that figure in the modern press be supposed to emanate from the pens of working-men. The episode of the *Atelier* is all the more a tribute to the principles of true democracy, in that the views it presented gave evidence of a far greater degree of sanity than those of middle-class exponents of Socialism; for the writers, whilst applauding the past Revolution they had been taught to regard as the source of all social regeneration, deprecated a repetition of violence, and warned the workers against any connection with the secret societies.

A significant result of this parting company between Socialism and Illuminism was shown in the abandonment of the campaign of militant atheism that had distinguished the earlier revolutionary movement, and the readers of the *Atelier* were enjoined to regard the clergy no longer as " suspects " but as possible allies. " The Revolution has only to proclaim itself Christian, to desire only what Christianity commands," and the clergy will be obliged to unite with it.

Unhappily, in spite of these lofty ideals and the undoubted sincerity of the men who professed them, the " workers' associations " were doomed to failure, for the

[1] Thureau-Dangin, *op. cit.* vi. 89.

simple reason that their founder had reckoned without the weaknesses of human nature. After the first *élan* had subsided, the foreman became weary of being the servant of all. The workers found no stimulus to effort in the system of equal payment, and all chafed at the necessity for putting by a sixth part of the profit.[1] Finally, the difficulty of combining Christianity and revolution proved insuperable, and the workers, obliged to choose between the two, split into opposing camps, thus putting an end to the associations.

Meanwhile, another enthusiastic Robespierriste, Louis Blanc, was developing his scheme of working-men's associations on much the same lines, but with the difference that they were to be under State control.[2] Also the idea of Christianity was eliminated, for Louis Blanc repudiated religion in any form and derided Buchez as a sentimentalist.

It is usual to attribute to Louis Blanc the doctrine of " the right to work " (*le droit au travail*) which figured so prominently in the Revolution of 1848. In reality the idea dated from Robespierre, and may be found clearly set forth in Article X. of his " Declaration of the Rights of Man," on which the Constitution of 1793 was founded. Yet if Robespierre must be regarded as the author of the actual formula of the right to work — that is to say, of the duty of the State to provide every man with work, or with the means of subsistence when out of employment — the principle had been recognized long before the Revolution. Had not the Government of Louis XVI. provided work, at great expense to the State, by starting brickyards, workshops, etc., for the unemployed of Paris? Indeed, as Karl Marx, who stigmatizes the doctrine of " the right to work " as a " confused formula," truly observes: " What modern State does not feed its poor in one form or another? "[3]

Louis Blanc, then, in his book *L'Organisation du travail* originated nothing; his doctrines were those of Rousseau, Robespierre, and Babeuf, supplemented by the theorizings

---

[1] Thureau-Dangin, *op. cit.* vi. 93.
[2] Malon, *Histoire socialiste*, ii. 267.
[3] Marx, *La Lutte des classes en France*, p. 57.

of Saint-Simon, Fourier, Cabet, and Buonarotti, and his system that which was to be later known as State Socialism. The State, he held, must regulate the conditions of labour with a firm hand. " We wish for a strong government, because in the régime of inequality in which we are still vegetating there are the weak who need a social force to protect them." But in time the State was to undergo the process described later on by Lenin as " withering away." " One day if the dearest wish of our heart is not disappointed, one day will come when there will be no further need of a strong and active government because there will be no longer an inferior and minor class of society. Until then the establishment of a tutelary authority is indispensable." [1]

All Louis Blanc's schemes were founded on such Utopian premises.

But if his hopes for the future were tinged with too roseate a hue, his outlook on the present was one of unrelieved gloom. This attitude was no doubt partly owing to personal grievances. Nature had been unkind to him, for she had clothed his ardent soul with so puny a body that at thirty he was mistaken for thirteen, and full-grown men, judging him from his undersized frame and high piping voice to be a schoolboy, would pat him kindly on the shoulder and address him as " my lad." [2] This kind of humiliation had inspired him with a grudge against society; at the same time it would be unjust not to give him credit for a genuine and disinterested sympathy with the cause of the workers. His *Organisation du travail* breathes throughout a spirit of sincerity which offers a striking contrast to the cynical utterances of most modern Socialist writers, whose indictments of working-class grievances, like the harrowing details of bodily ills retailed in advertisements of quack medicines, seem to be actuated solely by the determination to sell the advertiser's panacea. Louis Blanc, obsessed with the worker's lot, unhappily allowed himself to fall a victim to that agony of pity which verges on neurasthenia.

[1] Louis Blanc, *L'Organisation du travail*, p. 20.
[2] Thureau-Dangin, *op. cit.* vi. 116; Daniel Stern, *La Révolution de 1848*, ii. 43.

Many sensitive natures brought in contact with the miseries of life have suffered from this tendency. Lord Shaftesbury, overwhelmed at times with the hopelessness of his task, knew these black moments of despair, but battled with them as a weakness that must not be allowed to sap his energies. The error of Louis Blanc, as of the Russian fanatics who came after him, was to give unbridled rein to morbid imaginings. To his clouded vision a poor man is necessarily a miserable man, all the conditions of his life are unbearable; of contentment combined with frugality he has no conception — the mason whistling as he goes to work, the fisherman singing as he puts out to sea, the country labourer tossing his rosy baby in his cottage garden do not exist for him. As long as some one possesses more than he does, a man must necessarily be miserable. This distorted view of the ills of life, combined with an exaggerated conception of his power to cure them, was the cause of Louis Blanc's subsequent failure and bitter disillusionment.

Quite a different type of Socialist was the genial " Papa Cabet," — a " *faux bonhomme*," says Thureau-Dangin, for Cabet was a born autocrat. The son of a barrel-maker, Étienne Cabet first saw the light at Dijon in 1788, and in 1834 went to England, where he became a convert to the ideas of Robert Owen.

After his return to France in 1839 Cabet sketched out his plan of a Communist settlement, modelled on Sir Thomas More's *Utopia*, in his *Voyage en Icarie*, and in the same year, 1840, published his great work on the French Revolution, showing the course of Communistic theories throughout the movement.[1] These ideas, which Cabet traces from Plato, Protagoras, the Essenians of Judea, More, Campanella, Locke, to Montesquieu, Mably, Rousseau, and other philosophers of the eighteenth century, formed, as we have shown in an earlier quotation from Cabet's work, the policy of Robespierre and, in a lesser degree, of Condorcet, Clootz, Hébert, and Chaumette. But it is above all Babeuf whom Cabet rightly regards as the principal exponent of Communism, and in

[1] *Histoire populaire de la Révolution Française*, in four vols.

this connection he provides an interesting explanation of a subterfuge employed in nearly all histories of Socialism.

Now, as every one knows, the word Socialism had not come into use at the beginning of the nineteenth century, and its doctrines were classified under such generic headings as " Babouvisme," " Saint-Simonisme," " Fouriérisme," etc. It was not until about 1848 that " Socialism " began to be employed as a comprehensive term embracing all these variations on the same theme.[1] Nevertheless, it is customary to describe Socialism as originating with Robert Owen, Saint-Simon, and Fourier. Why? Since none of these men called themselves Socialists, and Saint-Simon died twenty years before the word was invented, there seems no more reason to include them under the term than their predecessors of the eighteenth century from whom they took their theories. To the attentive student of social history it seems obvious that histories of Socialism, after tracing its origins in antiquity and in the doctrines of the French philosophers, should begin their account of the movement with its earliest exponents in the French Revolution. Why so resolutely dissociate Socialism, or its equivalent Communism, from Robespierre and Babeuf? Cabet answers this pertinent inquiry with a question:

> Why, in order to represent a doctrine that one believes to be the most beautiful and the most perfect, choose a man (Babeuf) who was perhaps not quite perfect, and whose life, attacked by a party of the patriots (*i.e.* revolutionaries) themselves, may at least furnish pretexts for attacks from the adversaries of community? Why choose a proscribed name of which all the enemies of the people have made a bugbear? To transform Communism into Babouvisme is it not to fall into a trap and obligingly increase difficulties already so great? For the same reason . . . we have considered it a mistake to invoke the name of Robespierre just as Bodson blamed Babeuf for invoking the name of this martyr. . . .[2]

Yes, decidedly for the credit of Communism it is better to keep Robespierre and Babeuf dark and to date the

[1] Malon (*Histoire du socialisme*, i. 31) says the word was first used in this sense by Pierre Leroux in 1848 in contra-distinction to Individualism, but Daniel Stern, *La Révolution de 1848*, i. 33, says it was not current till after this date. The verb " to socialize " had, however, as we shall see a few pages further on, been coined twelve years earlier.

[2] Cabet, *Histoire populaire, etc.*, iv. 331.

origins of Socialism from the teachings of such amiable visionaries as Owen, Saint-Simon, and Fourier! The admission is certainly naïve!

Cabet himself was a theorist of the same pacific order, and, although expressing his firm belief in the practicability of Communism despite its repeated failures in the past, declared:

> But we are profoundly convinced at the same time that a minority cannot establish it by violence, that it can only be realized by the power of public opinion, and that far from hastening its realization violence can only retard it. We think that one should profit by the lessons of history, that as Babeuf and his companions foresaw — (did they foresee it?) — their conspiracy was the final blow to democracy. We find it dead under the Directory, under the Consulate, under the Empire, and under the Restoration.[1]

Would that our so-called " advanced thinkers " of to-day would recognize the wisdom of this reflection!

It was therefore in a perfectly pacific spirit that Cabet gathered around him a circle of enthusiasts calling themselves Icarians, all profoundly imbued with the Babouviste tradition and eager, under the guidance of its latest exponent, to put it into practice. Realizing that materialism was a doctrine that would never make a popular appeal, Cabet followed the precedent of Weishaupt by declaring: " The present Communists are the disciples, the imitators, the continuers of Jesus Christ. Therefore respect a doctrine preached by Jesus Christ. Examine it. Study it."[2]

The old maxim of the Babouvistes was again adopted by the community: " From every one according to his strength, to every one according to his needs " (De chacun selon ses forces, à chacun selon ses besoins).[3]

In 1847 Cabet judged that the moment had come to carry his great scheme into execution, and on February the 3rd of the following year a band of sixty-nine enthusiastic Icarians started forth for Texas, where they eagerly set to work at clearing the ground for a settlement. Unfortunately they had selected a malarial district, a great number of the colonists were struck down by fever, the only doctor

[1] Cabet, op. cit. i. 334.

[2] Malon, Histoire du socialisme, ii. 172.   [3] Ibid. ii. 165.

of the party went mad, and several of the sick died for want of medical aid.[1] Accordingly the community decided to abandon the few miserable huts they had succeeded in erecting and to migrate to another part of the country.

The procession, divided into three columns, set forth on a tragic retreat from Texas to New Orleans, where they were joined by Cabet himself and about 200 more Icarians, and under his leadership moved on to the old Mormon town of Nauvoo in Illinois, where they finally settled in March 1849. Soon after this Cabet was recalled to France in order to defend himself in a lawsuit brought against him by some of the Icarians he had left behind, who accused him of appropriating 200,000 francs of their funds.[2] The court ended by acquitting him, and Cabet was able to return to Nauvoo, which was now prospering, for this time the colonists, finding ready-made houses awaiting them, were able to embark at once on various communal enterprises. Farms and workshops sprang up, also a distillery, a theatre, a school for the children. For five years all went well and by 1855 the colonists had increased to over 500 people. Communism seemed solidly established at last. But once again the inevitable occurred, for the history of Communist settlements is painfully monotonous in its reiteration, and in Nauvoo, as earlier in New Harmony, later in New Australia, the autocratic spirit of the leader began to make itself felt. Cabet indeed had, as Malon the Socialist observes, " such a hatred for every instinct of liberty " that he forbade the workers to have tobacco or brandy or even to speak during working-hours.[3]

Nauvoo had in fact become an absolute monarchy, for no one but Cabet was allowed to have any voice in public affairs. Not unnaturally the community revolted, and in 1856 organized a ballot which deprived Cabet of his leadership by a majority of votes. The dethroned monarch left Nauvoo, followed by the faithful minority of 200, but died — according to Larousse — of grief,[4] the same year, at St. Louis. The remainder of the Icarians now migrated from Nauvoo to Iowa, and in spite of continued dissensions

[1] Malon, *Histoire du socialisme*, ii. 174-175.
[2] *La Grande Encyclopédie*, article on " Cabet." [3] Malon, ii. 176.
[4] *Dictionnaire Larousse*, article on " Cabet."

struggled on without a further break-up until 1879, when their number was reduced to fifty-two. By this time, however, the exalted ideals with which they had embarked on the enterprise were almost forgotten, only a few of the old men retained something of their earlier Communistic ardour, which enthusiastic visitors from time to time fanned again into flame; the young men meanwhile grew up impatient at the arrest of all progress, and ended by forming themselves into a hostile camp of Progressives in opposition to the " Non-Progressives," who clung to the old order.[1] This scission led up to a definite rupture in 1879, when twenty-eight members left the colony and the remaining twenty-four struggled on painfully until their final extinction in 1888.

So ended one more attempt to put Communism into practice. By the middle of the last century, indeed, every form of Socialism which we hear proclaimed to-day as the last word in modern thought had already been propounded if not put to the test.

Space forbids the enumeration of the countless theorists — Désamy, Raspail, Talandier, Auguste Comte, and many others — who filled those years with the noise of their declamations on the regeneration of society. Those who care to plunge into this sea of words — and words — and words — all more or less rearrangements of the same old formulas and phrases — can do so in the pages of Malon's vast *Histoire du socialisme*, where they will find every conceivable variation of the Socialist theme set forth with a bewildering wealth of detail. They will then find that the French Socialists of 1825 to 1848 had anticipated all the theories of modern Socialism, which are habitually attributed to the Social Democrats of Germany. Thus as early as 1836 an obscure writer named Pecqueur had already coined the word to " socialize," so dear to the heart of the modern Bolshevik, and in 1838 published a treatise named *Des intérêts du commerce, de l'industrie et de l'agriculture et de la civilisation en général*, etc., in which he proposed that all banks, mines, railways, and by degrees all great industries, should be socialized: " In social economy the true

[1] Malon, *op. cit.* pp. 179-182.

good will be the progressive socialization of the sources of all riches, of instruments of work, of the conditions of general welfare." [1]

Again: " Capital must end by being entirely social, and each person must always receive a part of the produce according to his time of work." [2]

A little later Vidal took up the same theme, specializing on the theory that Marx was later to make famous under the name of wage-slavery. In his book *Vivre en travaillant*, published in 1848, Vidal, following in the footsteps of Pecqueur, demanded the " socialization of the land " and the " socialization of capitals," which was to lead to " collective capital " [3] — in other words, Communism tricked out in fresh phrases.

How is it that, in spite of continued failures, the idea of Communism persisted all through this period? M. Thureau-Dangin no doubt rightly attributes it to the Babouviste tradition, which he shows to have continued right up to the end of the century, and indeed we may say to the present moment:

In studying Fouriérisme, Saint-Simonisme, and the other schools deriving from them that called themselves pacific we have found one of the origins of revolutionary socialism. This origin is not the only one. There is another, which, whilst less apparent, can nevertheless be recognized, and for this we must go back to Gracchus Babeuf, who, under the Directory, loudly preached the abolition of property, and the dividing up of all lands and all riches. This affiliation has escaped the attention of most contemporaries, but to-day we have the proof that from the " Equals " of 1796 to the Socialists at the end of the Monarchy of July (*i.e.* the monarchy of Louis Philippe) the tradition was continued without interruption. One man was found in fact to receive it from the hands of Babeuf, to preserve it with a sort of savage piety and transmit it to new generations: this was Buonarotti [4]

It was Buonarotti who in 1828 published the *History of the Conspiracy of the Equals* (quoted in the last chapter of this book,) which was for ten years " the gospel of the French proletariat " studied in all the workshops, so that

---

[1] Malon, *Histoire du socialisme*, ii. 205.   [2] *Ibid.* p. 206.
[3] *Ibid.* ii. p. 197.   [4] Thureau-Dangin, *op. cit.* vi. 106-108.

the working-men became infected with Babouvisme. [1]

But in tracing this propaganda to Buonarotti's Babouvistic fervour M. Thureau-Dangin stops short of the truth and it is Malon who supplies the real explanation to the persistence of Communist tradition. Babeuf, it will be remembered, was an Illuminatus acting, according to his own confession, under orders from invisible chiefs, and it was by these same agencies that the work he had begun was carried on. " The idea of community (*i.e.* Communism)," says Malon, " *had been transmitted in the dark through the secret societies*," [2] and elsewhere he adds that Buonarotti had " inspired nearly all the secret societies during the first thirty-five years of the century." [3]

It is therefore not only as the coadjutor of Babeuf, but as the adept of Illuminism, that Buonarotti must be regarded.

But whilst Communism under the various forms described above continued its course through the succeeding groups of revolutionary Socialists, Illuminism had developed along another line more in conformity with its original purpose, namely, *Anarchy*. Of this creed Proudhon had become the chief exponent. Hitherto, although anarchic doctrines had been freely preached by Marat, Clootz, and Hébert, the appellation of " Anarchist " had been claimed by no one, but remained a term of opprobrium which even an *enragé* of 1793 would have indignantly resented. It was left to Proudhon to adopt the name of Anarchy (*i.e.* without government) as the profession of a political faith in contradistinction to Communism. [4]

The difference between the two systems must be clearly understood if we are to follow the conflicts that marked the course of the revolutionary movement from this moment onwards.

Briefly then, whilst Communism declares that all land, wealth, and property must be taken out of private hands and placed under the control of the State, Anarchy advocates precisely the opposite principle, the complete abolition of the State and the seizure of wealth by the

---

[1] Malon *op. cit.* ii. 147.   [2] *Ibid.* p. 163.   [3] *Ibid.* p. 147.
[4] Thureau-Dangin, *op. cit* vi. 132.

people. Once again we come back to the old masonic formula — Liberty and Equality. Communism, which is the application of the principle of absolute Equality, regards humanity only in the mass, and would cut all men down to one dead level; Anarchy, which proclaims complete Liberty, would leave every man free to live as he pleases, to do as he will with his own, to rob or to murder. The former is rigid bureaucracy; the latter, Individualism run mad.

Now it is obvious that between the two creeds there can be no understanding, that indeed they are more opposed to each other than either is opposed to the existing social system. For under the constitutional governments enjoyed by all civilized countries to-day a certain degree of both Liberty and Equality prevails, and so, in England at any rate, our form of government may be said to represent the happy mean between two principles which, if pushed to extremes, must remain for ever irreconcilable.

It was thus that the masonic formula, after leading mankind into the morass of revolution, from the middle of the nineteenth century onwards divided the revolutionary forces into the two hostile camps indicated in the chart accompanying this book under the parallel columns of Socialism and Anarchy. This rift, which had first made itself felt in 1794 when Robespierre turned on the Anarchists who had paved his way to power, now with the advent of Proudhon opened out never to close again. The rest of the history of world revolution up to the present day largely consists in the war between the State Socialists and Anarchists, whose bitter hatred of each other exceeds even the hatred of either for the " Capitalist system " both are eager to destroy.

By Proudhon, surnamed by Kropotkine " the Father of Anarchy," [1] this hatred was, above all, logically directed against Robespierre, the Father of State Socialism, and expressed in no mild terms:

[1] " They have reproached me with being the Father of Anarchy. They wish to do me too much honour. The Father of Anarchy is the immortal Proudhon, who propounded it for the first time in 1848." — Kropotkine before the Cour d'Appel of Lyon, *Procès des anarchistes* (1883), p. 100.

All the runners after popularity, mountebanks of the revolu-tion, have taken for their oracle Robespierre, the eternal denun-ciator, with the empty brain, the serpent's tooth. . . . Ah! I know him too well, this reptile, I have felt too well the wriggling of his tail, to spare in him the secret vice of democrats, the cor-rupting ferment of every Republic — *Envy*.[1]

For the nineteenth-century devotees of Robespierre, Proudhon had nothing but loathing and contempt, and therefore during the years preceding the 1848 revolution occupied an almost isolated position. " I am neither a Saint-Simonien, nor a Fouriériste, nor a Babouviste," he wrote in 1840; and again: " I have no desire to increase the number of these madmen." The system of Fourier he described as the " last dream of debauchery in delirium "; Louis Blanc was " the most ignorant, the vainest, the emptiest, the most impudent and nauseous of declaimers." " Far from me then, Communists! " he cries, " your pres-ence stinks in my nostrils, the sight of you disgusts me." [2]

The only point in which Proudhon found himself in accord with the Socialists was in his declamations against property, and in this be believed himself to be entirely original. " Property," he declared, " is theft! It is not once in a thousand years that such a saying is made. I have no other treasure on earth except this definition of property, but I hold it more precious than the millions of Rothschild! "

Unhappily Proudhon's treasure was not his own, for he had borrowed it almost verbatim from Brissot, who in 1780 had written: " Exclusive property is a theft in Nature. The thief, in the natural state, is the rich man." [3] Moreover Brissot himself had not originated the idea, which may be found in the writings of both Weishaupt and Rousseau. So much for Proudhon's one cherished possession.

In his blasphemies likewise Proudhon had not even the merit of originality, for we seem to hear " the personal enemy of Jesus Christ," Anacharsis Clootz, in such phrases

[1] P. J. Proudhon, *Idée générale de la révolution au XIXième siècle* (1851), pp. 188, 189.
[2] Thureau-Dangin, *La Monarchie de Juillet*, vi. 128.
[3] *Recherches philosophiques sur le droit de propriété et le vol.*

as these: "God — that is folly and cowardice; God is tyranny and misery; God is Evil." [1] And going one step further he cries: " To me then Lucifer, Satan! whoever you may be, the demon that the faith of my fathers opposed to God and the Church." [2]

It is Proudhon, racked with a demon of hatred, bitterness, and revenge, in whom the devastating fire of world revolution is incarnated, a devil that drives him from the company of his fellow-men to dwell like the Gadarene demoniac in the wilderness.

One man there was who sought out Proudhon in his savage isolation, Michel Bakunin, — the first of that band of Russians later to be known by the name adopted by Proudhon, that of " Anarchist " — and often before the outbreak of 1848 these two would sit far into the night discussing the world revolution that was to overthrow the existing order. Proudhon's resolution: " I shall arm myself to the teeth against civilization; I shall begin a war that will end only with my life! " [3] may be regarded as the battle-cry of the party led later on by Bakunin surnamed " the genius of destruction."

But neither Anarchists nor Socialists could alone have availed to bring about the revolutionary outbreaks that marked the first half of the nineteenth century; theory, however violent, must ever prove powerless to put in motion the concrete machinery needed for the subversion of law and order, and as in the first French Revolution it was the Secret Societies that provided the real driving force behind the movement.

It is possible that some of the leaders of thought during that period, known as " the dawn of Socialism," remained unconscious of the secret influence behind them; others, however wittingly, co-operated with them. Buonarotti, as we have seen, was one of the principal leaders of the Secret Societies; Saint-Simon and Bazard " consulted Nubius as a Delphic oracle." Mazzini, professing Christian and patriot though he was, had joined the ranks of the Car-

[1] Thureau-Dangin, *op. cit.* vi. 139.
[2] Proudhon, *La Révolution au XIXième siècle*, p. 290.
[3] Thureau-Dangin, *op. cit.* vi. 127.

bonari, where his activities merely excited the derision of the Haute Vente. For the methods of the Carbonari were not those of the Haute Vente, which held that the mind rather than the body should be the point of attack.

" The murders of which our people render themselves guilty in France, Switzerland, and also in Italy," writes Vindex to Nubius, " are for us a shame and a remorse . . . we are too advanced to content ourselves with such means. . . . Our predecessors in Carbonarism did not understand their power. It is not in the blood of an isolated man or even of a traitor that it must be exercised; it is on the masses. . . . Let us . . . never cease to corrupt. Tertullian was right in saying that the blood of martyrs was the seed of Christians . . . do not let us make martyrs, but let us popularise vice amongst the multitudes. Let them breathe it in by their five senses, let them drink it, let them be saturated in it. . . . Make vicious hearts and you will have no more Catholics. Keep the priest away from labour, from the altar, from virtue. . . . Make him lazy, and *gourmand*. . . . You will thus have a thousand times better accomplished your task than if you had blunted the point of your stiletto upon the bones of some poor wretches. . . .

" It is corruption *en masse* that we have undertaken; the corruption of the people by the clergy and the corruption of the clergy by ourselves, the corruption that ought one day to put the Church in her tomb. The best dagger with which to strike the Church is corruption. To the work, then, even to the very end." [1]

It was thus that Mazzini excited the derision of the Haute Vente, for, as Nubius writing to " Beppo " on April 7, 1836, observed:

You know that Mazzini has judged himself worthy to co-operate with us as in the grandest work of our day. The Vente Suprême has not decided thus. Mazzini behaves too much like a conspirator of melodrama to suit the obscure rôle we resign ourselves to play until our triumph. Mazzini likes to talk about a great many things, about himself above all. He never ceases writing that he is overthrowing thrones and altars, that he fertilizes the peoples, that he is the prophet of humanitarianism, etc., etc., and all that reduces itself to a few miserable defeats or to assassinations so vulgar that I should send away one of my lacqueys if he permitted himself to get rid of one of my enemies by such shameful means. Mazzini is a demigod to fools before whom he tries to get himself proclaimed the pontiff of fraternity of which he will be the Italian god. . . . In the

[1] Crétineau-Joly, ii. 147.

sphere where he acts this poor Joseph is only ridiculous; in order to be a complete wild beast, he will always want for claws. He is the *bourgeois gentilhomme* of the Secret Societies. . . .[1]

Mazzini on his part suspected that secrets were being kept from him by the chiefs of the Haute Vente, and Malegari, assailed by the same fears, wrote from London in 1835 to Dr. Breidenstein these significant words:

We form an association of brothers in all points of the globe, we have desires and interests in common, we aim at the emancipation of humanity, we wish to break every kind of yoke, yet there is one that is unseen, that can hardly be felt, yet that weighs on us. Whence comes it? Where is it? No one knows, or at least no one tells. The association is secret, even for us, the veterans of secret societies.

Not only amongst the revolutionary leaders but in the industrial centres a new and mysterious power was making itself felt — the tyranny of Trade Unionism. Strikes not to be explained by the existing industrial grievances broke out continually in Scotland and the manufacturing towns in the North of England during those years of 1834 to 1860 and were conducted with a ferocity hitherto unknown in the history of the working-classes; men who would not co-operate were not merely boycotted but murdered, their houses burnt down and their wives and children driven half-clad into the streets at midnight.[2] These outrages reached their height in 1859 and at Sheffield continued for fifteen years. In Manchester the brickmakers' hands were pierced and maimed by needles mixed in the clay they handled.[3]

It would be absurd to attribute such methods to honest Trade Union leaders animated solely by an ardent or even a fanatical desire to improve the workers' lot. A number of these men indeed came forward to deny complicity and in some cases offered a reward for the detection of the criminals.[4]

---

[1] Crétineau-Joly, *op. cit.* ii. 145.
[2] Heckethorn's *Secret Societies*, ii. 224.
[3] Justin M'Carthy, *A History of Our Own Times*, iv. 152.
[4] *Ibid.* See the trial of the leaders by the Commission that sat in Sheffield in June 1867, reported in the *Annual Register* for that year. Note the references to " the mandates of the secret tribunals " and the descriptions of the terror displayed by the witnesses when questioned on this point.

The truth is clear that Illuminism, following its usual course of insinuating itself into every organization framed for the benefit of humanity, and turning it to an exactly opposite purpose, was using Trade Unionism, which had been designed to liberate the workers, for their complete enslavement.

In the minds of contemporaries no doubt exists that a hidden and malevolent agency was at work. Alison, writing in 1847 of the despotism exercised by the " ruthless trade unions " in condemning thousands of people " to compulsory idleness and real destitution," adds:

Nearly the whole of the loss arising from these strikes fell on the innocent and industrious labourers, willing and anxious to work, but deterred from doing so by the threats of the unions, and *the dark menaces of an unknown committee*. The mode in which these committees acquire such despotic authority is precisely the same as that which made the Committee of Public Safety despotic. Terror — terror — terror ——" [1]

Justin M'Carthy in his history of the same period confirms this assertion:

It began to be common talk that among the trades associations there was systematic terrorizing of the worst kind, and that *a Vehmgericht more secret and more grim than any known to the middle ages* was issuing its sentences in many of our great industrial communities.[2]

So Socialist leaders and working-men alike played the part of helpless puppets pulled by wires from behind, held in the hands of their sinister directors.

We shall now see how the course of world revolution coincided with the activities of these same secret agencies.

[1] Alison's *History of Europe*, i. 255.
[2] Justin M'Carthy, *A History of Our Own Times*, iv. 152.

CHAPTER V

THE REVOLUTION OF 1848

Russian Secret Societies — The Dekabrist rising — The French Revolution of 1830 — The *bourgeoisie* before 1848 — The Secret Societies — Apathy of the Government — The outbreak of February — Fall of the Monarchy — The Social Democratic Republic — National workshops — Associations of working-men — The 17th of March — The 16th of April — The 15th of May — The days of June — Reaction — The European conflagration.

THE first visible result of the work of the Secret Societies in the nineteenth century occurred in Russia, whither the doctrines of illuminized freemasonry had been carried by Napoleon's armies and by Russian officers who had travelled in Germany.[1] It was owing to the intrigues of these societies that the band of true reformers calling themselves " The Association of Welfare " was dissolved and two new parties were formed, the first known as the Northern Association demanding constitutional monarchy, the second called the Southern Association under Colonel Pestel, who was in direct communication with Nubius — which aimed not only at a Republic but at the extermination of the whole royal family.[2] Many attempts indeed were made on the life of Alexander I. through the agency of the Secret Societies,[3] and after his death in 1825 an insurrection broke out, led by the " United Slavs " who were connected with the Southern Association and the Polish Secret Societies at Warsaw.[4] The pretext for this outbreak, known as " The

---

[1] *La Russie en 1839*, by Astolphe de Custine, ii. 42; *The Court of Russia in the Nineteenth Century*, by E. A. Brayley Hodgetts, i. 116.
[2] *The Revolutionary Movement in Russia*, by Konni Zilliacus, p. 8; Brayley Hodgetts, *op. cit.* i. 122.
[3] Deschamps, *op. cit.* ii. 242; Frost's *Secret Societies*, ii. 213.
[4] Zilliacus, *op. cit.*; Brayley Hodgetts, *op. cit.* i. 123.

Dekabrist rising " because it occurred in December, was the accession to the throne of Nicholas I. at the request of his elder brother Constantine, and a crowd of mutinying soldiers were persuaded to march on the Winter Palace and protest against the acceptance of the crown by Nicholas, represented to them by the agitators as an act of usurpation. The manner in which the movement was engineered has been described by the Marquis de Custine, who travelled in Russia a few years later:

> Well-informed people have attributed this riot to the influence of the Secret Societies by which Russia is worked. . . . The method that the conspirators had employed to rouse the army was a ridiculous lie: the rumour had been spread that Nicholas was usurping the throne from his brother Constantine, who, they said, was advancing on Petersburg to defend his rights by armed force. This is the means they took in order to decide the revolutionaries to cry under the windows of the Palace: " Long live the Constitution!" The leaders had persuaded them that this word Constitution was the name of the wife of Constantine, their supposed Empress. You see that an idea of duty was at the bottom of the soldiers' hearts, since they could only be led into rebellion by a trick.[1]

This strange incident tends to confirm the assertion of Père Deschamps that the word " Constitution " was the signal agreed on by the Secret Societies for an outbreak of revolution. It had been employed in the same manner in France in 1791, and, as we shall see, it was employed again in Russia at intervals throughout the revolutionary movement.

The Dekabrist rising was ended by three rounds of grape-shot, and five of the ringleaders were hanged. In no sense was it a popular insurrection, in fact the people regarded it with strong disapproval as an act of sacrilege, and so little did it aid the cause of liberty that General Levashoff declared to Prince Troubetzkoy " it had thrown back Russia fifty years." [2]

Further evidence of the connection between the French Revolution and the engineering of revolution in Russia is supplied by de Custine on his travels in the latter country

---

[1] De Custine, *op. cit.* ii. 42; Brayley Hodgetts, *op. cit.* i. 192.
[2] Brayley Hodgetts, *op. cit.* i. 201, 205.

fourteen years later. Now in those days before the abolition of serfdom, the peasants on an estate were bought and
sold with the land, and since the Emperor's serfs were the
best treated in the whole country the inhabitants of estates
newly acquired by the Crown became the objects of envy
to their fellow-serfs. In this year of 1839 the peasants,
hearing that the Emperor had just bought some more land,
sent a deputation to Petersburg, consisting of representatives from all parts of Russia, to petition that the districts
from which they came should also be added to the royal
domains.

Nicholas I. received them kindly, for whilst adopting
repressive measures towards insurrection his sympathies
were with the people. We must not forget that it was he
who visited Robert Owen at New Lanark to study his
schemes of social reform. When, therefore, the peasants
petitioned him to buy them he answered with great gentle-
ness that he regretted he could not buy up all Russia, but
he added: " I hope that the time will come when every
peasant of this Empire will be free; if it only depended on
me Russians would enjoy from to-day the independence
that I wish for them and that I am working with all my
might to procure for them in the future."

These words, interpreted to the serfs by " savage and
envious men," led to the most terrible outbreak of violence
all along the Volga. " The Father wishes for our deliverance," cried the deluded deputies on their return to their
homes, " he only wishes for our happiness, he told us so
himself; it is therefore the seigneurs and their overseers
who are our enemies and oppose the good designs of the
Father! Let us avenge ourselves! Let us avenge the
Emperor."

And forthwith the peasants, imagining they were
carrying out the Emperor's intention, threw themselves
upon the seigneurs and their overseers, roasted them alive,
boiled others in coppers, disembowelled the delegates, put
everything to fire and sword and devastated the whole
province.[1]

Now when we compare this incident with the " Great

[1] *La Russie en 1839*, ii. 219-220.

Fear " that took place in France precisely fifty years earlier (*i.e.* in July 1789) how can we doubt the connection between the two? In both the pretext and the organization are identical. The benevolent intentions of Louis XVI., interpreted by the emissaries to the provinces in the words, " The King desires you to burn down the châteaux; he only wishes to keep his own "; the placards paraded through the towns, headed " Edict of the King," ordering the peasants to burn and destroy, and the massacres and burnings that followed — all this was exactly repeated in Russia fifty years later quite obviously by the same organization that had engineered the earlier outbreak. How otherwise are we to explain it?

Five years after the Russian explosion of 1825 the second French Revolution took place, which, however, hardly enters into the scope of this book. The revolution of 1830 was in the main not a social but a political revolution, a renewed attempt of the Orléaniste conspiracy to effect a change of dynasty and as such formed a mere corollary to the insurrections of July and October 1789. It is true that beneath the tumults of 1830, as beneath the Siege of the Bastille and the march on Versailles, the subversive force of Illuminism made itself felt, and that during " the glorious days of July " the hatred of Christianity expressed by the Terror broke out again in the sacking of the " Archevêché," in the pillage and desecration of the churches, and in the attacks on religion in the provinces. But the driving force behind the revolution that precipitated Charles X. from the throne was not Socialist but Orléaniste; it was a movement led by the tricouleur of July 13, 1789, not by the red flag of August 10, 1792, emblem of the social revolution; its strength lay not with the workmen but with the *bourgeoisie*, and it was the *bourgeoisie* who triumphed.

The régime that followed has well been named " the *bourgeois* monarchy." For Louis Philippe, once the ardent partisan of revolution, followed the usual programme of demagogy, and as soon as the reins of power were in his hands turned a deaf ear to the demands of the people. It was thus that in 1848, organized by the Secret Societies, directed by the Socialists, executed by the working-men and aggravated by the intractable attitude of the King and his ministers, the second great outbreak of World Revolution took place.

There was then, just as in the first French Revolution, real grievances that rankled in the minds of the people; electoral reform, the adjustment of wages and hours of labour, and particularly the burning question of unemployment, were all matters that demanded immediate attention. The people in 1848 even more than in 1789 had good cause for complaint.

But in justice to the *bourgeoisie* it must be recognized that they were in the main sympathetic to the cause of the workers. " Bourgeois opinion," even the Socialist Malon admits, " was . . . open to renovating conceptions. Before 1848 the French *bourgeoisie* had as yet no fear of social insurrections; they readily allowed themselves to indulge in innocent Socialist speculations. It was thus that Fouriérisme, for example, founded entirely on seeking the greatest sum of happiness possible, had numerous sympathizers in the provincial bourgeoisie." [1]

Like the aristocrats of 1788 who had voluntarily offered to surrender their pecuniary privileges, and on the famous 4th of August 1789 themselves dealt the death-blow to the feudal system by renouncing all other rights and privileges, so the *bourgeoisie* of 1848 showed their willingness to co-operate not merely with reforms but with the most drastic social changes directly opposed to their own interests.

" In the first weeks of 1848," Malon says again, " it was not only the proletarians who spoke of profound social reforms; the *bourgeoisie* that Fouriériste propaganda (but above all the novels of Eugène Sue and of George Sand) had almost reconciled with Socialism, thought themselves the hour had come, and all the candidates talked of ameliorating the lot of the people, of realizing social democracy, of abolishing misery. Great proprietors believed that the Provisional Government was composed of Communists, and one day twenty of them came to offer Garnier Pagès to give up their goods to the community." [2]

But the art of the revolutionaries has always been to check reforms by alienating the sympathies of the class in

---

[1] Malon, *Histoire du socialisme*, ii. 295.   [2] *Ibid.* ii. 520.

power, and they had no intention of allowing the people to be contented by pacific measures or to look to any one but themselves for salvation.

As on the eve of all great public commotions, a great masonic congress was held in 1847.[1] Amongst the French masons present were the men who played the leading parts in the subsequent revolution — Louis Blanc, Caussidière, Crémieux, Ledru Rollin, etc., and it was then decided to enlist the Swiss Cantons in the movement so that the centre of Europe should form no barrier against the tide.

It was by the Secret Societies that the plan of campaign was drawn up and the revolutionary machine set in motion. Caussidière, a prominent member of these associations, and at the same time Prefect of Police in Paris during the tumults of 1848, has himself provided us with the clearest evidence on this point.

"The Secret Societies," he writes, "had never ceased to exist even after the set-back of May 12, 1838. This freemasonry of devoted soldiers had been maintained without new affiliations until 1846. The orders of the day, printed in Brussels or sometimes in secret by compositors of Paris, had kept up its zeal. But the frequency of these proclamations, which fell sooner or later into the hands of the police, rendered the use of them very dangerous. Relations between the affiliated and the leaders had thus become rather restricted when, in 1846, the Secret Societies were reorganized and took up some initiative again. Paris was the centre around which radiated the different ramifications extending into the provincial towns. In Paris and in the provinces the same sentiment inspired all these militant phalanxes, more preoccupied by revolutionary action than by social theories. Guns were more talked of than Communism, and the only formula unanimously accepted was Robespierre's 'Declaration of the Rights of Man.' The Secret Societies found their real strength in the heart of the people of the working-classes, which thus had its vanguard, a certain disciplined force always ready to act, their co-operation was never wanting to any political emotion and they were found in the forefront of the barricades in February."[2]

But the working-classes were not admitted to the inner councils of the leaders; the place of the vanguard was on

[1] Deschamps, *op. cit.* ii. 281, quoting Gyr, *La Franc-Maçonnerie*, p. 368, and also Eckert.

[2] *Mémoires de Caussidière*, i. 38, 39.

the barricades when the shooting began, not in the meetings where the plan of campaign was drawn up.

Amongst these secret agencies the Haute Vente naturally played the leading part, and two years before the revolution broke out Piccolo Tigre was able to congratulate himself on the complete success of his efforts to bring about a vast upheaval.

On the 5th of January 1846 the energetic agent of Nubius writes in these hopeful terms to his chief:

The journey that I have just accomplished in Europe has been as fortunate and as productive as we had hoped. Henceforth nothing remains but to put our hand to the task in order to reach the *dénouement* of the comedy. . . . The harvest I have reaped has been abundant . . . and if I can believe the news communicated to me here (at Livorno) we are approaching the epoch we so much desire. The fall of thrones is no longer a matter of doubt to me now that I have just studied the work of our societies in France, in Switzerland, in Germany, and as far as Russia. The assault which in a few years and perhaps even in a few months from now will be made on the princes of the earth will bury them under the wreckage of their impotent armies and their decrepit thrones. Everywhere there is enthusiasm in our ranks and apathy or indifference amongst the enemies. This is a certain and infallible sign of success. . . . What have we asked in return for our labours and our sacrifices? It is not a revolution in one country or another. That can always be managed if one wishes it. In order to kill the old world surely, we have held that we must stifle the Catholic and Christian germ, and you, with the audacity of genius, have offered yourself with the sling of a new David to hit the pontifical Goliath on the head.[1]

Piccolo Tigre was perfectly right in his estimate of the " apathy and indifference " of the ruling classes, and in the success this attitude promised to the conspirators. No civilized modern government can be overthrown by violence if it realizes the danger that threatens it and firmly resolves to defend itself. It is not resistance but weakness that produces revolution, for weakness invites audacity and audacity is the essence of the revolutionary spirit. " Osez! " said St.-Just, " ce mot est toute la politique de la Révolution. " (" Dare! this word is the whole policy of

[1] Crétineau-Joly, *L'Eglise Romaine en face de la Révolution*, ii. 387.

revolution.") So whilst the revolutionary forces were mustering, the Government of France remained sublimely oblivious to the coming danger. On the surface few signs of popular effervescence were apparent. The incendiary doctrines of the agitators seemed to have made little headway amongst the great mass of the people. The peasants, indeed, with their passionate love of possession, saw little to attract them in the communal ownership of the land and continued to dig and plant with undiminished ardour. Only in the towns the fire of revolutionary Socialism was smouldering silently, unnoticed or ignored by those in power. The government, reassured by the loyal spirit of the army and deluded by the perfect calm that reigned in the streets, made no preparations for defence. The circulation of seditious papers was known to be small, the theories of Buchez and of Louis Blanc were believed to have taken no hold on the masses — one could afford to shrug one's shoulders at the number of their following. As to Proudhon the police had declared in 1846: " His doctrines are very dangerous, there are gun-shots at the end of them; fortunately they are not read." Perhaps the most unconcerned person was the King himself. " No human power," wrote M. Cuvillier Fleury, " could have made him read a page of M. Louis Blanc, of M. Pierre Leroux, of M. Buchez, or of M. Proudhon." [1]

So with sublime insouciance the " monarchy of July " awaited the explosion.

This is not the place to relate in detail the political events which led up to the four months revolution of 1848. Ministerial corruption — always the bane of France from the first revolution onwards — opposition to electoral reform, indifference to the interests of the people provided quite sufficient grounds for insurrection. In vain de Tocqueville warned the Chamber of Deputies whither this state of public affairs must lead them: " My profound conviction is that we are sleeping on a volcano." And after quoting various scandalous instances of corruption he went on to say:

[1] Imbert de Saint-Amand, *Marie Amélie et la société française en 1847*, pp. 102-110.

It is by such acts as these that great catastrophes are prepared. Let us seek in history the efficacious causes that have taken away power from the governing classes; they lost it when they became by their egoism unworthy to retain it. . . . The evils I point out will bring about the gravest revolutions; do you not feel by a sort of intuition that the soil of Europe trembles once more? Is there not a breath of revolution in the air? . . . Do you know what may happen in two years: in one year, perhaps to-morrow? . . . Keep your laws if you will, but for God's sake change the spirit of the Government. That spirit leads to the abyss.[1]

No truer words were ever spoken. Corrupt and selfish politicians will always be the most useful allies of Anarchists. We cannot doubt that Proudhon and Blanqui rejoiced over the callous attitude of the Government as heartily as de Tocqueville deplored it. The very real grounds for popular discontent would serve, as de Tocqueville clearly saw, to " magnify doctrines which tend to nothing less than the overthrow of all the foundations on which society rests."

The ministerial banquets planned by the heads of the masonic lodges [2] for the 22nd of February and forbidden by the government provided the pretext for insurrection. When in the morning of that day the obedient army of the proletariat assembled in answer to the summons of the revolutionary papers *Le National* and *La Réforme*, the cry of " A bas Guizot! " that rose from their ranks was less a protest against Guizot's policy than a call to revolution for revolution's sake. Deluded by the promises of the Utopian Socialists, inflamed by the teachings of the Anarchists, it was now no longer electoral reform nor even universal suffrage that could satisfy the people; it was not a mere Republic they demanded or a change of ministry, it was the complete overthrow of the existing system of government in favour of the social millennium promised them by the theorists, and which the agitators had urged them to establish by force of arms.

The dismissal of Guizot by the King on the 23rd of February did nothing, therefore, to allay popular agitation, and according to the usual revolutionary programme the

[1] Émile de Bonnechose, *Histoire de France*, ii. 647
[2] Deschamps, *op. cit.* ii. 282.

insurgents proceeded to barricade the streets and to pillage the gunsmiths' shops.

But even then it proved difficult to bring about a conflict, for the sympathies of the *bourgeoisie* were still with the people, and the National Guards, seeing in the working-men their brothers, showed reluctance to use force against them.[1] This feeling of *camaraderie*, contemptuously described by Marx as " charlatanry of general fraternity," [2] was dispelled by the menacing attitude the working-men were persuaded to assume, and inevitably the demonstrations that followed — the hoisting of the red flag, the marching of processions amongst which could be seen the glint of steel and brandishing of sabres — led to a collision with the troops. In the confusion a number of the insurgents fell victims to the fire of the irritated soldiery. This skirmish, described as " the massacre of the Boulevard des Capucines," gave the signal for revolution.

Throughout that night of February 23-24 the Secret Societies were at work issuing their orders; meanwhile Proudhon busied himself drawing up a plan of attack.[3] Dawn found the city in a state of chaos, the trees of the boulevards were broken to the ground, the paving-stones torn up, excited bands of insurgents — working-men of the faubourgs, students, schoolboys, deserters from the National Guard — collected round the Tuileries, shots were fired in at the windows of the young princes. This was the moment chosen by Louis Blanc and his friends to issue a protest against the employment of troops in civil commotions, which, handed from barricade to barricade, immensely enboldened the audacity of the revolutionaries, who now proceeded to seize munitions and attack the municipal Guard, killing a number of them. The hesitating policy of the government and the declarations of the agitators inevitably affected the morale of the troops, and by the middle of the morning they ceased to offer any further resistance and left the people in possession of the field. Already Proudhon and Flocon had posted up a placard demanding the deposition of the King, and amongst the

[1] *Cambridge Modern History*, vol. xi. 97.
[2] Marx, *La Lutte des classes en France*, p. 40.
[3] *Cambridge Modern History*, vol. xi. p. 99.

leaders — Caussidière, Arago, Sobrier, and others — the word "Republic" made itself heard. In vain Louis Philippe, profiting by the error committed by his predecessor Louis XVI. in precisely the same circumstances, mounted a gorgeously caparisoned horse in order to inspect the troops assembled in the Tuileries gardens and promised reforms to the excited populace; the hour of the Orléaniste dynasty had struck, and at one o'clock the royal family chose the prudent course of flight.

Thus in the space of a few hours the monarchy was swept away and the "Social Democratic Republic" was proclaimed.[1]

But now the men who had brought about the crisis were faced with the work of reconstruction — a very different matter. For it is one thing to sit at one's desk peaceably writing about the beauties of revolution, it is quite another to find oneself in the midst of a tumultuous city where all the springs of law and order have been broken; it is one thing to talk romantically about "the sovereignty of the people," it is less soothing to one's vanity to be confronted with working-men of real flesh and blood insolently demanding the fulfilment of the promises one has made them. This was the experience that fell to the lot of the men composing the Provisional Government the day after the King's abdication. All advocates of social revolution, they now for the first time saw revolution face to face—and liked it less well than on paper.

The hoisting of the red flag by the populace — described by Lamartine as "the symbol of threats and disorders" — had struck terror into the hearts of all except Louis Blanc, and it was not until Lamartine in an impassioned speech had besought the angry multitude to restore the *tricouleur* that the red flag was finally lowered and the deputies were able to retire to the Hôtel de Ville and discuss the new scheme of government.

In all the history of the "Labour Movement" no more dramatic scene has ever been enacted than that which now took place. Seated around the council table were the

---

[1] Louis Blanc, *La Révolution de 1848*, p. 23; *Mémoires de Caussidière*, p. 62.

men who for the last ten years had fired the people with
enthusiasm for the principles of the first Revolution —
Lamartine, panegyrist of the Gironde, Louis Blanc the
Robespierriste, Ledru Rollin, whose chief source of pride
was his supposed resemblance to Danton.

Suddenly the door of the council chamber burst open
and a working-man entered, gun in hand, his face con-
vulsed with rage, followed by several of his comrades.
Advancing towards the table where sat the trembling
demagogues, Marche, for this was the name of the leader
of the deputation, struck the floor with the butt end of his
gun and said loudly: " Citizens, it is twenty-four hours
since the revolution was made; the people await the results.
They send me to tell you that they will brook no more
delays. They wish for the right to work — the right to
work at once."

Twenty-four hours since the revolution had been made,
and the New Heavens and the New Earth had not yet been
created! The theorists had calculated without the immense
impatience of " the People," they had forgotten that to
simple practical minds to give is to give quickly and at
once; that the immense social changes represented by
Louis Blanc in his *Organisation du travail* as quite a simple
matter had been accepted by the workers in the same
unquestioning spirit; of the enormous difficulties incidental
to the readjustment of the conditions of the labour, of the
time it must take to reconstruct the whole social system,
Marche and his companions could have no conception.
They had been promised the " right to work," and the
gigantic organization that brief formula entailed was to be
accomplished in one day and instantly put into operation.

Louis Blanc admits that his first emotion on hearing
the tirade of Marche was that of anger;[1] it were better if
he had said of shame. It was he more than any other who
had shown the workers the land of promise, and now that it
had proved a mirage he, more than any other, was to
blame. Before promising one must know how to perform
—and to perform without delay.

It was apparently Lamartine whom the working-men

[1] Louis Blanc. *La Révolution de 1848*, p. 31.

regarded as the chief obstacle to their demand for " the right to work," for throughout his speech Marche had fixed his eyes, " blazing with audacity," on those of the poet of the Gironde. Lamartine, outraged by this attitude, thereupon replied in an imperious tone that were he threatened by a thousand deaths, were he led by Marche and his companions before the loaded cannons down beneath the windows, he would never sign a decree of which he did not understand the meaning. But finally conquering his irritation, he adopted a more conciliatory tone, and placing his hand on the arm of the angry workman he besought him to have patience, pointing out that legitimate as his demand might be, so great a measure as the organization of labour must take time to elaborate, that in the face of so many crying needs the government must be given time to formulate its schemes, that all competent men must be consulted. . . .

The eloquence of the poet triumphed, gradually Marche's indignation died down; the workmen, honest men touched by the evident sincerity of the speaker, looked into each other's eyes questioningly, with an expression of relenting, and Marche, interpreting their attitude, cried out, " Well, then, yes, we will wait. We will have confidence in our government. The people will wait; they place three months of misery at the service of the Republic! " [1]

Have more pathetic words ever been uttered in the whole history of social revolution? Like their forefathers of 1792 these men were ready to suffer, to sacrifice themselves for the new-formed Republic represented to them as the one hope of salvation for France, and animated by this noble enthusiasm they were willing to trust the political charlatans who had led them on with fair promises into abortive insurrection. Even whilst Lamartine was urging patience, Louis Blanc, still intent on his untried theories, had retired into the embrasure of a window, where, with Flocon and Ledru Rollin, he drew up the decree, founded on the 10th article of Robespierre's " Declaration of the Rights of Man," by which the Provisional Government

Daniel Stern, *op. cit.* i. 379.

undertook to " guarantee work to all citizens." Louis Blanc was probably the only man present who believed in the possibility of carrying out this promise, yet all ended by subscribing to it, and the same day the decree was publicly proclaimed throughout Paris.

Two days later the *National Workshops*, which were to provide the promised employment, were opened under the direction of Émile Thomas and of M. Marie. The result was inevitably disastrous, necessary work being insufficient, the workmen were sent hither and thither from one employer to another, useless jobs were devised that necessarily proved discouraging to the men engaged on them, whilst the workers in the skilled trades for whom no employment could be found had to be maintained on " an unemployment dole." This last measure, the most demoralizing of all, had the effect of attracting thousands of workers from all over the country, and even from abroad, into the capital.[1]

The organization of the National Workshops and their lamentable failure has frequently been ascribed by opponents of Socialism to Louis Blanc. This is inaccurate. The manner in which these workshops were conducted was not that advocated by Louis Blanc in his *Organisation du travail*, and must be ascribed solely to MM. Marie and Thomas. But the principle on which they were founded, namely the duty of the State to provide work or payment for every man, was nevertheless the one adopted by Louis Blanc from Robespierre. Once this premise is accepted many of the difficulties that contributed to the failure of the National Workshops are bound to follow. The mere fact that a man has no longer to depend on his own efforts to seek and find employment must inevitably lead to lack of enterprise and to idleness on the part of those who do not want to work; moreover, if payment is to be received whether a man is in or out of employment it will be obviously a matter of indifference to the slacker whether he keeps his job or loses it.

That in a civilized state no man should be allowed to

---

[1] Daniel Stern, *op. cit.* i. 484. See also report of May 29 given in *The Economist* for June 3, 1843 (vi. 617).

starve because he cannot find work is clearly evident, but that some degree of privation should attach to unemployment is absolutely necessary to the very existence of industry.

The truth is, as Mermeix points out, the Provisional Government of 1848 had promised the impossible because " a government cannot guarantee work since it does not depend on it to provide consumers." [1] Moreover, the funds with which it pays out unemployment doles can only be raised in the form of taxation which automatically reduces the spending power of the community, thus creating further unemployment.

Magnificent, then, as the recognition of " the right to work " may be in theory, no Government has so far been able to put it into practice without aggravating the evil it has set out to cure.

If, therefore, Louis Blanc cannot be held responsible for the methods of the National Workshops, it is impossible to deny that his precipitate action in formulating the proclamation of " the right to work " largely contributed to the chaos that followed. Moreover, we shall see that when at last he was able to put his own theories into practice the experiment proved not much more successful than that of MM. Thomas and Marie.

It was on the 10th of March that a committee began its sittings at the Luxembourg, presided over by Louis Blanc with the workman Albert as vice-president. Before this board employers and employed were summoned to attend and put forward their claims or grievances; builders and their workmen, master bakers and baker boys, omnibus owners and drivers, all arrived in crowds to discuss the questions of hours and payment. In general the employers showed themselves magnanimous and perfectly ready to co-operate in any reasonable reforms,[2] but this, as Mme. d'Agoult observes, could not satisfy the ambition of Louis Blanc, " which dreamt of changing the world." [3] A sane and practical man with the interests of the people really at heart, given his opportunity, might have laid forever the

[1] Mermeix (G. Terrail), *Le Syndicalisme contre le socialisme*, p. 51.
[2] " The employers gave evidence of the most conciliatory disposition " (Daniel Stern, *op. cit.* ii. 49).   [3] *Ibid.* p. 48.

foundations of an improved industrial system, but Louis Blanc seated in the historic armchair of the Chancelier Pasquier could only fall back, like his predecessors of 1789, on the fatal gift of eloquence, and at every moment " began again the epic recital of the Revolution and the tableau of the great things accomplished by the people." [1]

Strange this tendency of Socialism that imagines itself progressive to hark back eternally to the past!

The working-men on their part showed themselves in the main perfectly sane and reasonable, demanding protection from the exploitation of middle-men, and a reduction in the hours of labour to ten or eleven a day, giving for their reason a theory tenable perhaps at a period when working days consisted of fourteen or fifteen hours, but which to-day has been perverted into the disastrous system known as " Ca' Canny," namely that " the longer the day is the fewer workers are employed, and that the workers who are occupied absorb a salary which might be divided amongst a greater number of workers." They also " criticised excessive work as an obstacle to their education and the intellectual development of the people."

At any rate, whether sound or not in their political economy, the people of Paris at this crisis showed themselves in no way prone to violence; the people did not wish for bloodshed and for barricades, for burnings and destruction. Reduced to its simplest expression, they asked for two things only — bread and work: what juster demand could have been formulated? And they were ready, as Marche had said, to wait, to suffer, to sacrifice themselves not only for their own ultimate welfare but for the glory of France. Misled as they had been by visionaries, illusioned as they were on the benefits of the first French Revolution, they asked for no repetition of its horrors but only to be allowed to work in peace and fraternity.

" Citizens, . . ." wrote the cloth printers to the Provisional Government at the end of March 1848, " we, workers ourselves, printers on stuff, we offer you our feeble co-operation, we bring you 2000 francs to help towards the success of your noble creation. . . . Let them be reassured those who may believe in a

[1] Daniel Stern, *op. cit.* p. 41.
[2] *Mémoires de Caussidière*, i. 286.

return to the bloody scenes enacted in our history! Let them be reassured! Neither civil war, nor war abroad shall rend the entrails of our beautiful France! Let them be reassured on our National Assembly, for there will be neither Montagnards nor Girondins! Yes, let them be reassured and let them help to give to Europe a magic sight, let them show the universe that in France there has been no violence in the revolution, that there has only been a change of system, that honour has succeeded to corruption, the sovereignty of the people and of equity to odious despotism, force and order to weakness, union to castes, to tyranny this sublime device: ' Liberty, Equality, Fraternity, progress, civilization, happiness for all and all for happiness! ' " [1]

What might not have been done with a people such as this, so filled with gay enthusiasm, with noble patriotism, if only they had had leaders worthy of them? But on one side Louis Blanc, helpless and hesitating now that he was brought face to face with realities, pushing aside sane reforms in favour of unrealizable ideals, and on the other Blanqui, Proudhon, wild beasts crouching to spring, waiting to rend and destroy that very civilization for which the people were ready to sacrifice their all!

But Louis Blanc, obsessed with his idea of " working-men's associations," led the people from the path of true reform into the wilderness. The National Workshops, he afterwards declared, were a failure because they were not conducted on the Socialistic lines he advocated, and the Government refused to give him funds to put his own theories into practice. But, as Mme. d'Agoult explains, what the Government really refused to M. Blanc was " a budget and a ministry " which would have satisfied his ambitions. The Government *did* provide M. Blanc with funds to start " associations of working-men " on his own lines, and gave him a perfectly free hand in organizing them. The first of these experiments was made at the Hôtel de Clichy, which M. Blanc was allowed to transform from a debtors' prison into an enormous national tailors' shop; he was then given capital free of interest, " subsistence money " was advanced to the workers, and an order for 25,000 uniforms for the National Guards was placed by the Government. The usual contractor's price for these uniforms was eleven francs each, " a sum found sufficient

[1] Daniel Stern, *op. cit.* i. 514.

to provide the profit of the master tailor, remuneration for his workshop and tools, interest on his capital and wages for the workmen." [1] But now that the profits of the rapacious capitalist were to be eliminated it was expected that a handsome balance would remain over after the cost of materials had been defrayed, and this was to be divided equally amongst the workers. Unhappily when the first order was completed the cost proved to be far higher than under the old capitalistic system, and the uniforms worked out at 16 instead of 11 francs each. Moreover, though " the principle of glory, love, and fraternity was so strong that the tailors worked twelve and thirteen hours a day, and the same even on Sundays," the ragged new recruits to the army were kept waiting so long for their uniforms that, driven to exasperation, they went several times to Clichy and quarrelled violently with the tailors over the delay. " This," says Mme. d'Agoult, " was the origin of the scission between the ' people ' in blouses and the ' people ' in uniforms which led at last to a mortal combat." [2]

Louis Blanc's other experiments were attended with not much more success. His " association of arm-chair makers " dwindled in one year from 400 members to 20, and out of 180 associations in all only 10 survived until 1867. [3]

A further breach was brought about between the soldiers and the industrial workers by the attempt of the Government to establish " equality " in the army. On the 14th of March it had passed the decree ordering the smartest battalions of the National Guards to renounce their distinctive uniforms and likewise all insignia of superior rank. More preposterous still, the election of new officers was to be made henceforth by universal suffrage. [4]

The result was of course an explosion of indignation amongst the soldiers, and on the 16th of March a procession of 4000 to 5000 National Guards marched on the Hôtel de Ville to protest against the decree. Here they

[1] *Problems and Perils of Socialism*, by J. St. Loe Strachey, quoting contemporary account on this experiment in *The Economist* for May 20, 1848 (vol. vi. p. 562).
[2] Daniel Stern, *op. cit.* ii. 165.
[3] Heckethorn, *Secret Societies*, ii. 222, 223.
[4] Daniel Stern, *op. cit.* ii. 55; Caussidière, *op. cit.* i. 176.

encountered a crowd of workmen and young boys, with whom they came into collision; insults and blows were exchanged, and the breach between the *bourgeoisie* and the people was now definitely created.

This breach was necessary to the Socialist leaders if they were to retain their ascendancy, and the revolution was not to end in the peaceful amelioration of the workers' lot. Accordingly they seized the opportunity offered by popular excitement to organize a demonstration for the following day, and as in the first French Revolution the people were ordered out *en masse*. A huge crowd was to assemble in the Place de la Concorde and march to the Hôtel de Ville in order to congratulate the members of the Provisional Government and demand the postponement of the elections, which might possibly remove the Socialists from power. This programme, naïvely drawn up by the Socialists themselves — Louis Blanc, Caussidière, and Ledru Rollin — was issued to all the different districts of Paris on the evening of the 16th.

But already the organizers of the procession found themselves outdistanced by the clubs acting under the orders of the Secret Societies, and whilst the people were being invited by the members of the Provisional Government to come and demonstrate in favour of their remaining in office Blanqui was concerting another agitation for the purpose of ejecting them. It was thus that, when the immense procession arrived at the Hôtel de Ville on the 17th of March, Louis Blanc and his colleagues found themselves confronted not by congratulatory and admiring bands of workers but by a hostile army, at the head of which were found their enemies and rivals to power — Barbès, Blanqui, Cabet, Sobrier, and others — " whose expression," says Louis Blanc, " held something sinister."

In vain Louis Blanc took refuge in his habitual revolutionary eloquence, declaring that the only desire of the Provisional Government was "to march with the people, to live for them, if necessary to die for them"; the crowd, wearied of such protestations, gave way to prolonged murmurs. "The people," cried one of them, "expect more than *words*."[1]

[1] Caussidière, *op. cit.* i. 182.

But words in the end prevailed, and floods of oratory poured forth by Ledru Rollin and Lamartine finally had the effect of calming the agitation of the crowd, which towards five o'clock in the afternoon gradually melted away to the cries of "Vive Louis Blanc, Vive Ledru Rollin!"

Caussidière afterwards described this " day of March 17 " as the " pacific victory of the people by calm and reason "; in reality it was a victory for the Socialists of the Provisional Government. From the people's point of view the day had proved as abortive as most of the " great days " of the first revolution, in which they had acted simply as the tools of political adventurers. " The greater number of the workmen," says Mme. d'Agoult, " who had joined spontaneously in the manifestation in a sincere and naïve spirit of Republican fraternity, were persuaded that they had given the Government a mark of respect and had defended them against royalist plots." For themselves they had gained nothing but an increase of hostility on the part of the *bourgeoisie*, who had watched with growing anxiety the menacing aspect of the procession.

The result of " the day of March the 17th " was to throw back irretrievably the cause of the Paris workmen. So far they had gained certain points in their programme — the establishment of the " social and democratic Republic," the promise of universal suffrage at the coming elections, the recognition by the Provisional Government of " the right to work," and the application of this principle in the National Workshops, which, however unsatisfactory from the point of view of the State, had relieved unemployment. Had the revolution ceased early in March before the passing of the impolitic decree concerning the National Guards, it must have ended in a triumph for the workers. But the action of the Socialists in throwing this apple of discord between the people and the *bourgeoisie* turned the tide in favour of reaction. Not only in Paris but all over the country the display of force exhibited by the procession of March 17 created widespread alarm. The provinces had no intention of falling again, as in 1793, under the domination of the Paris populace, and a strong Conservative spirit was aroused that boded ill for the success of Socialist candidates at the elections. "From this moment," writes the Comtesse d'Agoult, "there begins for the proletariat a series of reverses in which it is to lose all the advantages it had won in a few hours, and of which it had made use generously, it is true, and with greatness, but without discernment or foresight." [1]

This was the whole cause of the working-men's failure in 1848. Instead of acting on their own initiative, instead of pressing the advantages they had really gained, they allowed themselves to be led into fruitless agitation by a band of political charlatans who were mainly occupied in quarrelling amongst themselves.

Thus whilst Louis Blanc continued to represent himself to the people with his usual eloquence as the sole representative of their cause, the partisans of Ledru Rollin (amongst them George Sand the novelist) intrigued to establish a revolutionary government under his dictatorship, and Blanqui stirred up the workmen to resist the convocation of the National Assembly. Meanwhile Lamartine, seeing his own power waning, endeavoured to frighten Ledru Rollin "with visions of Blanqui sharpening his dagger in the background," and at the same time continued to confer secretly with Blanqui in the hope of winning him over to his side. Amidst all this confusion of plans the people counted for nothing, but each faction hoped by a further " popular manifestation " to triumph finally over its rivals.

On the 16th of April the people of Paris were once more summoned forth on the pretext of electing fourteen officers for the staff of the army, according to the new decree of election by popular suffrage. At 10 o'clock in the morning a procession of 8000 working-men assembled in the Champ de Mars, holding aloft their banners with Socialist devices such as: " Abolition of the exploitation of man by man," " Equality," " Organization of work," etc. This army, which had started out quite peaceably, now stirred up by Blanqui, increased to 40,000 and then proceeded to march on the Hôtel de Ville, whereat a panic spread throughout the city. Scare news was passed from mouth to mouth:

[1] Daniel Stern, *op. cit.* ii. 154.

" The Faubourg St. Antoine has risen in revolt! The Communists have taken the Invalides, they are setting fire to it; 200,000 proletarians in arms are preparing to sack Paris! "

On arrival at the Place de Grève before the entrance to the Hôtel de Ville a number of troops, however, were drawn up, and now the scission that had been created between the soldiers and the working-men became again apparent. The inclination to fraternize with their comrades in blouses that earlier in the Revolution had marked the attitude of the troops had changed to active hostility, and from their ranks arose the cry: " Down with the Communists! Down with Blanqui! Down with Louis Blanc! "

The tide had turned irrevocably against the workers. As the dejected battalions of the industrial " proletariat " filed past the Hôtel de Ville through the serried ranks of the soldiery and finally dispersed, no doubt remained that the day had ended in defeat and it was to the Socialists the workers owed their humiliation. The working-men had not on their own initiative assumed the menacing attitude that alarmed the citizens of Paris; they had not devised the truculent mottoes inscribed upon their banners. It was Blanqui with his ferocious methods of agitation, it was Louis Blanc with his foolish theorizings, who had turned their just demands for social reform into war on the community and created the gulf that yawned between the workmen and the rest of Paris. Up to the outbreak of the 1848 revolution the *bourgeoisie*, as we have seen, had regarded the aspirations of the " people " with the greatest sympathy; the work of the Socialists was to destroy this understanding and to consolidate not only the *bourgeoisie* but the whole non-industrial population in a mass antagonistic to the workers. It is from this moment that we can date that narrowing down of the word " people " to signify only the " industrial proletariat,"[1] the sense in which it has been used throughout by Marxian Socialists, and that has contributed so largely to the divorce between Socialism and democracy.

The 16th of April was followed by a great wave of

[1] Daniel Stern, *op. cit.* ii. 15.

reaction in all quarters of the city. The authors of the manifestation became the objects of indignant denunciations; a furious crowd carried a coffin beneath the window of Cabet. "One half of Paris," wrote the Prefect of the Police, "wishes to imprison the other."[1] Even the allies of the Socialists were suddenly smitten with misgivings, and it was George Sand, the disciple of Babeuf and Pierre Leroux, who was believed to have written these words in the *Bulletins de la République* for the 20th of April:

> As to the Communists, against whom so many cries of reprobation and of anger have been heard, they were not worth the trouble of a demonstration. That a little number of sectarians should preach the chimerical establishment of the impossible equality of fortunes need not surprise or alarm one. At all periods misguided minds have pursued the realization of this dream without ever attaining it.[2]

The reaction was not confined to Paris alone. All over France the tide turned irrevocably against Socialism, and in the elections that followed the people showed themselves overwhelmingly in favour of the moderates. But the revolutionaries had gained one point, namely that they had put an end to what Marx described as "the charlatanry of universal fraternity," and the gulf between the industrial proletariat and the rest of the nation yawned more widely than ever.

When the new National Assembly met on the 4th of May the extremists Proudhon, Cabet, Louis Blanc, and Blanqui were all rejected by the electors, as also the "Labour" candidates in favour of Communism who had been put forward by the Committee of the Luxembourg: and it was Lamartine who now received the plaudits of the crowd. This was largely owing to the attitude of Louis Blanc, who had made it clear that he aimed at nothing less than "the absolute domination of the proletariat,"[3] a proposition that, placed before a spirited nation possessing an energetic and intelligent *bourgeoisie*, must necessarily encounter determined opposition.

Louis Blanc, moreover, possessed the irritating characteristic, common to many Socialists, of imagining that he

[1] Daniel Stern, *op. cit.* ii. 179-180.   [2] *Ibid.* p. 183.
[3] *Ibid., op. cit.* ii. 207.

alone was animated by sincere love for the people, and
his discourse to the Assembly on the 10th of May, again
demanding " a ministry of work and progress," was so
tinged with this peculiar form of egoism as to provoke cries
of protest. Finally the whole Assembly rose in a body,
whilst from all sides shouts went up: " You have not the
monopoly of love for the people! We are all here for the
social question, we have all come in the name of the people!
The whole Assembly is here to defend the rights of the
people! " [1]

The new assembly thus found itself crushed between
two forces — on one hand the *bourgeoisie* rendered intractable by the menace of Communism, on the other the revolutionaries who, now legally excluded from the government,
were obliged to cast about for a further pretext to stir up
the people. This was provided by a revolt in Poland which
the Prussian troops had ruthlessly suppressed on the 5th
of May, and the working-men of Paris were summoned to
assemble in their thousands as a protest against this display of arbitrary authority. Accordingly, on the 13th a
procession of 5000 to 6000 people, led by Sobrier and
Huber, a professional agitator of equivocal antecedents,
marched to the Place de la Concorde, shouting: " Vive la
Pologne! " The working-men in the crowd, who had
started out in all good faith to agitate, as they had been
told to do, in favour of oppressed Poland, were animated
by no revolutionary intentions and never dreamt of overthrowing the Assembly elected by universal suffrage. But,
as usual, agents of disorder had mingled in their ranks,
strangers of sinister appearance ready to side either with
police or mob in order to provoke a riot, well-dressed
women not of the people were observed inciting the crowd
to violence.[2]

At the bridge of the Concorde the procession seemed to
hesitate, but Blanqui, now placing himself at its head,
cried loudly, " Forward! " and the whole mass surged
towards the palace occupied by the Assembly. The small
number of National Guards assembled proved powerless
to stem the oncoming tide of 150.000 men and women,

[1] Daniel Stern, pp. 237-238.   [2] *Ibid. op. cit.* ii. 258.

which pressed onwards with such force that a number of
people were crushed to death at the entrance of the Palace.

It was then that Lamartine, braver than his predecessors the revolutionaries of 1792, came forward out of the
Assembly and faced the people.

" Citizen Lamartine," said one of the leaders, Laviron,
" we have come to read a petition to the Assembly in
favour of Poland. . . . "

" You shall not pass," Lamartine answered imperiously.

" By what right will you prevent us from passing?
We are the people. Too long have you made fine phrases;
the people want something besides phrases, they wish to
go themselves to the Assembly and signify their wishes."

How true was the word uttered by a voice in the crowd
at this juncture: " Unhappy ones, what are you doing?
You are throwing back the cause of liberty for more than
a century! "

In vain the men who had raised the storm now tried to
quell it. Whilst the crowd pressed onwards into the hall
of the Assembly, Thomas, Raspail, Barbès, Ledru Rollin,
Buchez, Louis Blanc struggled amidst the suffocating
heat of the May day and the odour of massed humanity to
make their voices heard. Louis Blanc at the table declared
that " the people by their cries had violated their own
sovereignty "; the crowd responded with shouts of:
" Vive la Pologne! Vive l'organisation du travail! "
Louis Blanc, attacked with the weapon he himself had
forged, was reduced to impotence; it was no longer the
theorist who had deluded them with words that the people
demanded, but Blanqui, the man of action, the instigator
of violence and fury. " Blanqui! Where is Blanqui? We
want Blanqui! " was the cry of the multitude. And
instantly, borne on the shoulders of the crowd, the strange
figure of the famous agitator appeared — a little man prematurely bent, with wild eyes darting flame from hollows
deep sunk in the sickly pallor of his face, with black hair
shaved close like a monk's, his black coat buttoned up to
meet his black tie, his hands encased in black gloves —
and at this sinister vision a silence fell upon the crowd.
Blanqui, suiting himself to the temper of his audience,

thereupon delivered a harangue demanding that France should immediately declare war on Europe for the deliverance of Poland — truly a strange measure for the relief of public misery in Paris! Meanwhile Louis Blanc, with a Polish flag thrust into his hands, was making a valiant effort to recover his popularity. An eloquent discourse on " the sovereignty of the people " had at last the desired effect, and amidst cries of " Long live Louis Blanc! Long live the social and democratic Republic! " he too was hoisted on to the shoulders of the people and carried in triumph. But the emotion of the moment proved too great for the frail body; Louis Blanc, his face streaming with perspiration, attempted in vain to address the crowd, but no sound came from his lips and, finally lowered to earth, he fell fainting on a seat.

The dementia of the crowd, urged on by the " Clubistes," now reached its height. Whilst Barbès vainly attempted to deliver a speech the tribune was assailed by a group of maniacs, who with clenched fists threatened each other and drowned his voice in tumultuous cries. To add to the confusion the galleries began to break down under the weight of the increasing crowd and a bursting water-tank flooded the corridor.

At this juncture Huber, who had likewise fallen into a long swoon, suddenly recovered consciousness, and, mounting the tribune, declared in a voice of thunder that the Assembly was dissolved in the name of the people.

At the same moment Buchez was flung out of his seat, Louis Blanc was driven by the crowd out on to the esplanade of the Invalides, Raspail fainted on the lawn, Sobrier was carried in triumph by the workmen, and Huber disappeared.

Then followed the inevitable reaction. The troops arrived on the scene and dispersed the crowd, Barbès was arrested. Louis Blanc, with tumbled hair and torn clothes, succeeded in escaping from the National Guards and took refuge in the Assembly, only to find himself assailed with cries of indignation.

" You always talk of yourself! You have no heart! "

Whilst these extraordinary scenes had been taking

place at the Assembly another crowd of 200 people had invaded the Prefecture of Police, where Caussidière, following the example of Pétion on the 10th of August, remained discreetly waiting to see which way the tide turned before deciding on the course he should take. Faced by an angry mob of insurgents the wretched Caussidière, hitherto in the vanguard of revolution, now began to talk of " constitutional authority " and threatened to run a rebel through the body with his sabre.[1]

With the aid of the Republican Guard the Prefecture of Police was finally evacuated, and throughout Paris the troops set about restoring order. " The repression," writes the Comtesse d'Agoult, " is without pity because the attack has been terrible " — words ever to be remembered by the makers of revolution. The fiercer the onslaught the fiercer must be the resistance, and anarchy can only end in despotism. Even the revolutionary leaders are obliged to admit the reactionary effects of May the 15th, and the people themselves, always impressed by a display of authority, sided with the victors. When on the 16th of May the arrested conspirators leave for Vincennes " they hear, on going through the Faubourg St. Antoine, the imprecations of the crowd of men, women, and children who, in spite of the extreme heat of the day, follow the carriages with insults in their mouths as far as the first houses of Vincennes."

But this revulsion of popular feeling was only momentary; before long the Socialists had re-established their ascendancy over the people. In the by-elections on June the 5th Pierre Leroux, Proudhon, and Caussidière were all successful, and the situation was further complicated by the election of Louis Napoléon Bonaparte.

It was now that the Imperialist schemes of the Bonapartistes first became apparent, and that the cry of " Vive l'Empereur! " was first heard. The leaders of this faction, no less than those of the Socialists, realized that the overthrow of the existing government must be brought about by a popular insurrection, and the usual weapon of class hatred was employed by both with equal unscrupulous-

---

[1] *Mémoires de Caussidière*, ii. 136.

ness. Side by side with the hawkers of such gutter-press journals as the *Robespierre*, the *Père Duchesne*, the *Carmagnole*, the *Journal de la Canaille*, the vendors of the *Napoléon Républicain* pressed their wares on the soldiers, warning them that " the bourgeois Terror " would represent them as the murderers of their brothers and invoking the red flag of social revolution.[1]

The government elected by the system of universal suffrage so long demanded thus found itself between two fires, and the whole revolutionary movement turned into a contest between the warring political parties.

The industrial situation had now become chaotic. Trade was paralysed by the feeling of general insecurity and by continual strikes of workmen, whilst the men employed in the National Workshops showed an increasing tendency to revolt. This method of absorbing unemployed labour had, as we have seen, from the beginning proved a failure; and at last, after a vain attempt to improve matters by dismissing the provincial workmen who had crowded into Paris, and by reintroducing the system of piece-work, the Government announced its intention of abolishing the National Workshops. A decree to this effect was passed on the 21st of June and inevitably brought about the final crisis. On the evening of the same day bands of workmen again assembled, and to the rival cries of " Vive Barbès! " and " Vive Napoléon! " planned a fresh demonstration.

Then followed the three fearful days of June the 22nd to the 25th. Barricades were once more erected in the streets, and war to the knife was declared on the Republic. As in every outbreak of the World Revolution, the insurgents were composed of warring elements, all resolved to destroy the existing order and all animated by opposing aims. Thus, according to the report of Panisse, the head of the division for general security, the crowds that took part in the insurrection included, besides the workmen driven by hunger and despair to revolt, a number of honest and credulous people duped by the agitators — " Communists, dreamers of a Utopia amongst which each has his system

[1] Daniel Stern, *op. cit.* ii. 341.

and disagreeing with each other; " Legitimists, demanding
the restoration of the Bourbon dynasty in the person of the
Duc de Chambord; Bonapartistes, partisans of a regency;
and, finally, " the scum of all parties, convicts and wastrels;
in a word, the enemies of all society, men vowed by
instinct to ideas of insurrection, theft, and pillage." [1]

Against this terrible army the troops, led by the Generals Cavaignac and Lamoricière, reinforced by National
Guards from all over France, displayed the greatest vigour,
and on the 26th of June, after terrible fighting which left
no less than 10,000 killed and wounded in the streets of
Paris, Cavaignac remained master of the situation and a
military dictatorship assumed control.

It is unnecessary to follow the French Revolution of
1848 through its final political stages — the election of
Prince Louis Napoléon to the Presidency of the Republic
in December of the same year, the *coup d' État* carried out
by him three years later (on December 2, 1851), by which
the Constitution of 1848 was overthrown, and, finally, the
proclamation of the Empire on December 10, 1852, with
the prince as Napoléon III. at its head. Throughout this
period the fire of social revolution could only smoulder
feebly, and with the accession of the Emperor was temporarily extinguished in France. The régime that followed,
like that which succeeded to the first French Revolution,
was one of absolute repression. The Socialist leaders were
arrested, no less than 25,000 prisoners were taken by the
Government and a great number deported without trial.
At the same time the Secret Societies were put down with
an iron hand, all the liberties guaranteed to the French
people, including the liberty of the press, were abolished
by the Constitution of 1852, and this despotism was
accepted by a majority of 7,000,000 to 600,000 votes. For
as in 1800 the nation, wearied of revolution, was ready to
throw itself at the feet of a strong man who would restore
order and give it peace once more.

The revolution of 1848 thus ended in the total defeat of
the workers, and for this it is impossible to deny that the
principal blame lay with the Socialist leaders — above all

[1] Daniel Stern, ii. 598.

with Louis Blanc. It is only just to recognize the excellent intentions of the man, who devoted all his energies to the reorganization of labour on an ideal system, yet it must surely be admitted that social experiments of this kind can only be judged by results. The scientist who fails in a laboratory experiment may be pardoned for failure, but in the case of men who juggle with human lives failure is crime. If a duke were to invent a novel system of drainage, and, without assuring himself of its efficacy, were to install it in all his tenants' cottages, thereby killing them off by diphtheria, he would not be regarded as a noble enthusiast whose only crime was excess of zeal, but as a criminal fool for whom no mercy should be demanded. Why then should reckless ventures, merely because they are conducted in the name of Socialism, ensure the immunity of their authors? Louis Blanc may well have been a sincere and well-meaning man, the fact remains that through his application of impracticable schemes and obstinate belief in his own infallibility he led the working-classes to disaster. No one has recognized this truth more clearly than the anarchist Proudhon, who in these words has apportioned to this dangerous dreamer the blame he so truly deserves:

A great responsibility will rest in history on Louis Blanc. It was he who at the Luxembourg with his riddle "Equality, Fraternity, Liberty," with his abracadabra "Every one according to his strength, to every one according to his needs!" — began that miserable opposition of ideologies to ideas, and who roused common sense against Socialism. He thought himself the bee of the revolution and he was only the grasshopper. May he at last, after having poisoned the working-men with his absurd formulas, bring to the cause of the proletariat, which on a day of error fell into his feeble hands, the obol of his abstention and his silence![1]

But a further reproach to be brought against Louis Blanc and his colleagues of 1848 is their habit of perpetually reverting to the past. "Let us respect the past," said Victor Hugo, " provided it is content to be dead; but if it wishes to be alive, we must attack it and try to kill it." Socialists who are quite willing to apply this maxim

[1] *La Révolution au XIXième siècle*, p. 108.

to the noblest traditions of the past reject it when it is a matter of reviving exploded subversive doctrines or methods. So the men of 1848, instead of considering the needs of the present hour, instead of pressing forward to more enlightened schemes of social reform, persisted in harking back eternally to the principles of the first French Revolution; soaked in the doctrines of their revolutionary predecessors all craved to emulate them, and thus the so-called popular demonstrations organized by them in Paris between February and June of 1848 were directly modelled on those of 1789 to 1792. On this point both Marx and Proudhon are in accord. "The Revolution of 1848," says Marx, "could do nothing better than parody first 1789 and then the revolutionary tradition of 1793-1795;"[1] and Proudhon covers with ridicule the manner in which the "souvenirs" of 1793 were constantly evoked by the leaders. It was "a universal mania," Mme. d'Agoult observes likewise, "from the 24th of February onwards to refer everything back to our first revolution." The failure of 1848 lay, therefore, not in over-zeal for progress, but in reactionariness, in blind attachment to past and dead traditions.

.   .   .   .

The outbreak of revolution in Paris had given the signal for the European conflagration. On the 1st of March insurrection began in Baden, on the 12th in Vienna, on the 13th riots took place in Berlin, on the 18th a rising in Milan, on the 20th in Parma, on the 22nd a Republic was declared in Venice, on the 10th of April a Chartist demonstration was organized in London, on the 7th of May troubles began in Spain, on the 15th in Naples, and during the course of the year no less than sixty-four outbreaks of serfs occurred in Russia.

Of course, in the pages of official history we shall find no explanation of this sudden recurrence of the revolutionary epidemic, which is once more conveniently ascribed to the time-honoured theory of contagious popular enthusiasm for liberty. Thus the *Cambridge Modern History*, describing the revolution in Germany,

[1] Marx, *La Lutte des classes*, p. 192.

observes: " The Grand Duchy of Baden was the natural starting-place for the revolutionary movement, which, once set on foot, seemed to progress almost automatically from State to State and town to town."

Precisely; but we are given no hint as to the mechanism which produced this automatic action all over Europe. The business of the official historian is not to inquire into causes but to present the sequence of events in a manner unintelligible to the philosopher but satisfying to the uninquiring mind of the general public.

That the European Revolution of 1848 was the result of masonic organization cannot, however, be doubted by any one who takes trouble to dig below the surface. We have already seen how Mazzini and the " Young Italy " movement had proved the blind instruments of the Haute Vente Romaine, and how the same society operating through the lodges had prepared the ground in every country. In France the part played by Freemasonry in the revolutionary movement was quite frankly recognized, and the Supreme Council of the Scottish rite presenting themselves before the members of the Provisional Government on the 10th of March received the congratulations of Lamartine in these words:

I am convinced that it is from the depths of your lodges that have emanated, first in the shade, then in the half-light, and finally in the full light of day, the sentiments which ended by producing the sublime explosion we witnessed in 1789, and of which the people of Paris have just given to the world the second and, I hope, the last representation.[1]

But, of course, the people were to be allowed to think they had acted on their own initiative. Thus the Jewish Freemason Crémieux, whom the Revolution had raised to a place in the Provisional Government, declared in a speech to the crowd that on the ruins of the shattered monarchy " the *people* took for the eternal symbol of revolution ' Liberty, Equality, Fraternity ' ";[2] it was only to the Freemasons themselves — this time a deputation of the Grand Orient, on the 24th of March — that he acknowledged the true origin of this device: " In all times

[1] Deschamps, *op. cit.* ii. 282.   [2] *Mémoires de Caussidière*, i. 131.

and under all circumstances . . . *Masonry* ceaselessly repeated these sublime words: 'Liberty Equality, Fraternity.' " [1]

In Germany as in France the principal leaders of the revolution — Hecker, Fickler, and Herwegh in Baden; Robert Blum in Saxony; Jacobi in Koenigsberg; von Gagern in Berlin — were all Freemasons who had been present at the aforesaid Masonic Congress in 1847.

The 1848 Revolution was thus the second great attempt of illuminized Freemasonry to bring about a world conflagration. But there was one country where the movement proved completely abortive; this was England. It is true that for many years the Chartist riots had created widespread anxiety, but the independent character of the English people had hitherto always prevented them from modelling their agitations on continental precedents; and " the People's Charter," aiming rather at political reform than at social disintegration, was essentially a national product. That agitators working for the overthrow of the existing social system had introduced themselves into the movement as earlier they had found their way into Trade Unionism cannot be doubted; it was this, however, that led to the final defeat of Chartism. When on the 13th of April 1848 a great demonstration was organized and a monster petition carried to Kennington Common, London prepared itself for self-defence and prudent tradesmen put up their shutters in expectation of riots, but the insignificant proportions of the assembled mob, and the discovery that a great number of the signatures appended to the petition were fraudulent, covered the whole affair with ridicule and the dreaded explosion ended in smoke. The truth is that in a country where reforms were in progress revolution could make little headway, and the passing of the Ten Hours Bill in 1847 had done much to quell agitation. Moreover, as we have already seen, the Co-operative movement had begun and was taking a strong hold on the imaginations of the British workers. It is not a little to the credit of our country that, whilst France continued to turn in a vicious circle of

[1] Deschamps, ii. 283.

abortive revolution, the English people, true to their traditions, had struck out a fresh path entirely on their own initiative, which but for Socialist opposition might have led — and may yet lead — to the regeneration of the industrial system.

Thus the situation stood at the end of 1848. Socialism in every conceivable form had been tried and found wanting. It had failed in the form of peaceful experiments under Robert Owen, St-Simon, Fourier, Pierre Leroux, and Cabet; it had failed still more signally when the attempt was made to establish it by revolutionary methods. So we find that at this crisis a change came over the revolutionary movement, and Socialism, a derelict concern, was taken over by a company. What that company was we shall see in the next chapter.

CHAPTER VI

THE INTERNATIONALE

Rôle of the Jews in Germany — German Social Democracy — Lassalle — Karl Marx — Engels — Russian Anarchy — Michel Bakunin — " The Working-men's Association " — Intrigues of Marx — The " Alliance of Social Democracy " — Bakunin and the " German Jew Company."

IN order to follow the new course on which the World Revolution now entered it is necessary to understand something of the events that had taken place in Germany during the memorable year of 1848.

We have already seen how the plan of a United Germany, with Prussia at its head, originating with Frederick the Great, had been carried on not only by his successor Frederick William II. but by the Illuminati, the Tugendbund, and the Masonic Lodges. Under Frederick William III., Master of the Grand Lodge of Prussia, a further pact was concluded between Prussia and Freemasonry.

The lodges judged that Prussia was of all the States of Europe the one most capable of carrying out their work, and they made it the pivot of their political action . . . the idea of a union under their domination never ceased to be the aim of all the lodges.[1]

But it seems that in Frederick William IV. they encountered a rebel. Without this hypothesis the agitation that took place in Berlin on the 18th of March 1848 is incomprehensible. Why should the King of Prussia have become the object of a hostile demonstration led to the cry of a " United Germany " in which Prussia was to be supreme? Why should he have rejected as " a crown of shame " (Schandkrone) the Imperial diadem subsequently

Deschamps, *op. cit.* ii. 400.

160

offered him by the National Assembly of Frankfurt and have pressed the claims of Austria to supremacy? May not the explanation be that Frederick William IV. had broken away from the traditions of the Hohenzollerns in refusing to ally himself with the subversive forces of which his predecessors had made such good use abroad, and that in preferring the claim of Austrian to Prussian supremacy his motive was reluctance to make himself the tool of the masons and to subscribe to their formula, as expressed by Mazzini: " Delenda est Austria " ? [1] The crown of shame which he declined to wear when offered to him by the Frankfurt Assembly under the President von Gagern, Freemason and Member of the Burschenschaft, was the Masonic crown worn by Frederick the Great and his two successors, offered by the Freemasons of France to the Duke of Brunswick and placed on the head of William I. in 1871.

But there was yet another consideration that may well have weighed with Frederick William IV. Freemasonry was not the only subversive force at work in Germany. Behind Freemasonry, behind even the secret societies that made of Freemasons their adepts, another power was making itself felt, a power that ever since the Congress of Wilhelmsbad in 1782 had been slowly gaining ground — the power of the *Jews*.

Until the middle of the nineteenth century the part played by the Jews in the revolutionary movement is more or less obscure. We have seen their mole-like working below ground during the first French Revolution, suspected by Prudhomme, we have seen them insinuating themselves into Masonic Lodges and secret societies, we have seen rich Jews financing the Haute Vente Romaine, and needy members of the tribe acting as agents of Nubius, but at the same time we have watched the building up of Capitalism by Jewish hands, and Jews in Russia supporting the authority of the Czar. How are we to explain this

---

[1] Deschamps et Claudio Jannet, *op. cit.* iii. 245, quoting instructions of Mazzini published in the *Journal des Débats* for May 16, 1851, where the following passage occurs: " *Delenda est Austria* is the first and last word for action against that empire. . . . We must get hold of Prussia by exciting her military pride and her irascibility."

double rôle of the Jews throughout the social revolution? The common theory that as victims of oppression they embraced with fervour the doctrine of " Liberty and Equality " formulated by the lodges is completely refuted by Disraeli in an illuminating passage:

" The Jews represent the Semitic principle; all that is spiritual in our nature. They are the trustees of tradition and the conservators of the religious element. They are a living and the most striking evidence of the falsity of that pernicious doctrine of modern times, the natural equality of man." " Cosmopolitan fraternity " — or, as we should say to-day, " International Socialism " — Disraeli goes on to observe, " is a principle which, were it possible to act on it, would deteriorate the great races and destroy all the genius of the world. . . . The native tendency of the Jewish race, who are justly proud of their blood, is against the doctrine of the equality of man. They have also another characteristic, the faculty of acquisition. Although the European laws have endeavoured to prevent their obtaining property, they have nevertheless become remarkable for their accumulated wealth. Thus it will be seen that all the tendencies of the Jewish race are conservative. Their bias is to religion, property, and natural aristocracy. . . ." [1]

In a word, then, the Jews are not genuine revolutionaries, but only throw themselves into revolutions for their own ends. Whilst professing to believe in Liberty and Equality they secretly deride such ideas, but make use of them to destroy existing governments in order to establish their own domination in religion, property, and power. Thus, according to Disraeli, it was they who played the principal part in preparing the 1848 conflagration:

The influence of the Jews may be traced in the last outbreak of the destructive principle in Europe. An insurrection takes place against tradition and aristocracy, against religion and property. Destruction of the Semitic principle, extirpation of the Jewish religion whether in the Mosaic or in the Christian form, the natural equality of men and the abrogation of property, are proclaimed by the secret societies who form provisional governments, and men of Jewish race are found at the head of every one of them. The people of God co-operate with atheists; the most skilful accumulators of property ally themselves with communists; the peculiar and chosen race touch the hand of all the scum and low castes of Europe! And all this because they wish to destroy that ungrateful Christendom

[1] *Life of Lord George Bentinck*, pp. 496, 497.

which owes to them even its name, and whose tyranny they can no longer endure.[1]

It is a favourite ruse of the Jews to represent the Christians as their only enemies; in reality the persecution of the Jews began long before the Christian era, nor has it since then been confined to countries where the Christian religion prevails.

If Christendom is to be accused of ingratitude for the privilege of harbouring numbers of the chosen people in her midst, the pagan world showed itself quite equally ungrateful. Egyptians, Persians, and Assyrians kept them in complete subjection; indeed, owing to their racial characteristics, it was found impossible even under the more liberal régime of Alexander the Great's successors to receive them into the community of nations.

" The sullen obstinacy with which they maintained their peculiar rites and unsocial manners," writes Gibbon, " seemed to mark them out a distinct species of men, who boldly professed, or who faintly disguised, their implacable hatred to the rest of human kind." [2]

Here, then, rather than in Christian intolerance, may be found at least a partial explanation of the persecution of the Jews. Nor was persecution confined to one side only in the war of Semite against Gentile, for, given the opportunity, the Jews showed themselves in no way behind other races in cruelty.

" From the reign of Nero to that of Antoninus Pius," Gibbon says again, " the Jews discovered a fierce impatience of the dominion of Rome which repeatedly broke out in the most furious massacres and insurrections. Humanity is shocked at the recital of the horrid cruelties which they committed in the cities of Egypt, of Cyprus, and of Cyrene, where they dwelt in treacherous friendship with the unsuspecting natives. . . . In Cyrene they massacred 220,000 Greeks; in Cyprus 240,000; in Egypt a very great multitude. Many of these unhappy victims were sawed asunder, according to a precedent to which David had given the sanction of his example."

Here follow details too horrible to transcribe.[3]

Under the humane rule of Antoninus Pius the Jews

[1] *Life of Lord George Bentinck*, pp. 497, 498, published in 1852.
[2] Gibbon's *Decline and Fall of the Roman Empire* (Oxford University Press edition), ii. 3. [3] *Ibid*. ii. 83.

" assumed the behaviour of peaceable and industrious subjects." But " their irreconcilable hatred of mankind, instead of flaming out in acts of blood and violence, evaporated in less dangerous gratifications. They embraced every opportunity of overreaching the idolaters in trade. . . ." [1]

Thus since the earliest times it is as the exploiter that the Jew has been known amongst his fellow-men of all races and creeds. Moreover, he has persistently shown himself ungrateful. As Gibbon again points out, in spite of the Jews' attachment to the Mosaic religion, their forefathers who first received the law given in thunder from Mount Sinai had " perpetually relapsed into rebellion against the visible majesty of their Divine King " — even though " the tides of the ocean and the course of the planets were suspended for the convenience of the Israelites," so that at last even the Almighty was led to declare : " How long will this people provoke me ? " [2]

The truth is, then, that the Jews have always formed a rebellious element in every State, and not more so in those where they were persecuted than in those where they were allowed to dwell at peace. In fact, a careful study of their character throughout history shows that the Jew is well able to endure persecution with serenity provided he is permitted to carry on his natural avocations without hindrance, whilst on the other hand he finds it impossible to exist under a benevolent régime that limits his activities. Thus in China, where the Jews were welcomed and allowed all the privileges of good citizens, the race found life unendurable because the Chinaman blandly declined to be exploited. The Jews therefore, finding it impossible to gain control of the principal wealth of the country, sought more congenial climes, and still to-day, outside the treaty ports, very few are to be found in China.

On the other hand, Germany has always been the favourite resort of the Jews. If they object to persecution, how can we explain this fact ? In no other country have they been so despised as in " the Fatherland," which does not recognize the Israelites amongst its progeny. We in

[1] *Gibbon's Decline and Fall of the Roman Empire,* ii. 85.   [2] *Ibid.* ii. 5.

England, living under a régime of tolerance and " live and let live " unparalleled in any other land, can hardly conceive the bitterness, or even the existence, of *Judenhetze*. " The social peril is the Jew," was a phrase currrent in Germany; " the Jew," said Treitschke, " is our misfortune." Yet in spite of these amenities the Jew has found in Germany more than in any other land his natural home.[1] The reason may perhaps be found in the foregoing explanation of the Jewish point of view given by Disraeli. If indeed the Jew is a natural aristocrat, a disbeliever in the doctrine of equality, and an admirer of forceful government, he finds in Prussian Imperialism a system which, though oppressive of his own liberties, wins, nevertheless, his confidence and his respect. Here in the land of the jackboot and the spur he encounters few of those enervating theories of humanitarianism, those disintegrating concessions to democracy which he regards as " deteriorating to the great races and the genius of the world." In a word, the Jew has always been inclined to regard Prussia as the best investment for his money. If only he could gain some measure of control over the great military machine his position in Europe was secure.

It is thus that, as M. Claudio Jannet observes, " the Jews had always shown themselves the most active in the work of the unification of Germany," and he quotes from an article " devoted to the exaltation of Israel," in the *Journal des Débats* for November 5, 1879, the following remarkable words:

In Germany from 1830 onwards the Jews play an important part: they are at the head of Young Germany. If German unity has been hastened by Prussian diplomacy and Prussian militarism, this work has been prepared, supported, and completed by them.[2]

Here, then, is the link between the apparently incompatible elements of Judaism and Imperial Germany. In spite

---

[1] Mr. Wickham Steed in *The Hapsburg Monarchy* (p. 172) relates that he once asked a learned Austrian Hebrew for an explanation of " the pro-German tendencies displayed by Ashkenazim Jews the world over. 'German,' said this pundit, ' is the basis of our jargon, and, next to Palestine, Germany is the country which we regard as our home. Hence our sentimental leaning towards Germany.' "

[2] Deschamps, *op. cit.* ii. 417.

of *Judenhetze* the Jews have always had a peculiar affinity with the Prussians, so that to-day, after the ending of the Great War, we find the *Deutsche Allgemeine Zeitung* confidently declaring that there is " no contradiction between the desiderata of the Jews and German interests." [1]

But before this alliance could be effected it was necessary for the Jews to establish their position in the State, and for this reason rather than from a spirit of revenge they threw themselves into the revolutionary movement. It was they who provided the driving force behind the masonic insurrection of 1848 in Germany, which started with the cry of Jewish emancipation and proclaimed as its ultimate purpose the supremacy of Prussia. This eventuality had been clearly foreseen by Disraeli, who in 1844 declared through the mouth of Sidonia, the Jewish hero of *Coningsby:*

That mighty revolution which is at this moment preparing in Germany and which will be in fact a greater and a second Reformation, and of which so little is as yet known in England, is entirely developing under the auspices of the Jews, who almost monopolize the professorial chairs of Germany.

The dialogue ends with the significant words:

So you see, my dear Coningsby, that the world is governed by very different personages from what is imagined by those who are not behind the scenes. [2]

Four years after these words were written the revolution broke out in Germany exactly as Disraeli had foretold, and if it did not assume the proportions he had anticipated, the year of 1848 inaugurated the emancipation of the Jews in Germany as surely as 1790 had inaugurated it in France.

The accession to the throne of William I., " the protector of masonry," and the ministry of Bismarck opened a fresh field to Jewish activities. For the new rulers of Prussia realized that the Jews could be very useful to their cause. Hohenzollern tradition had always recognized the utility of the despised race as agents. Frederick the Great had not disdained to employ a Jew named Ephraim for the purpose of coining false money [3] — probably the

[1] Date of January 30, 1919.
[2] *Coningsby* (Longman's edition), pp. 250-252.
[3] *The Despatches of Earl Gower*, edited by Oscar Browning (1885), p. 385.

same Ephraim whom his successor, Frederick William II., had sent as a paid agitator to finance the tumults of the French Revolution. According to a strongly pro-Semitic writer in the *Revue des Deux Mondes* for 1880, Bismarck had recourse to the Jews for replenishing his war-chests. " The Jews," the same writer goes on to observe, " were the only people who were able to use Bismarck so that all Liberal reforms in Germany from Sadowa onwards carried out with the acquiescence of Bismarck turned to the profit of the Jews." [1]

It was this date of 1866 which sealed the definite alliance between Prussianism and Jewry. Sadowa had proved the efficiency of the Prussian military machine, and henceforth persecutors and persecuted were to march hand in hand to the conquest of world power.

But already Bismarck had found a valuable ally in the person of the Jewish " Socialist " Lassalle.

Ferdinand Lassalle, the son of a rich Hebrew merchant, was born in 1825. Tormented from his youth by hatred of the Christian races, whose blood even as a schoolboy he hoped to shed, Lassalle early embarked on a revolutionary career. " Congenitally idle," dishonest, revengeful, an avowed atheist,[2] Lassalle declared himself a " revolutionary by principle " who " would not hesitate at a Reign of Terror as a means to secure his ends." [3]

After the German Revolution of 1848, in which he played a leading part, Lassalle settled in Berlin, where he lived in splendour, not caring to drink wine at less than twenty or thirty marks a bottle, and entertaining his friends at gorgeous banquets.[4]

The source of Lassalle's wealth was the Hatzfeldt property, on which he lived complacently; indeed he frankly declared that he would willingly have married any woman who could bring him two or three million thalers of revenue. Such was the man who posed as the champion of the working-classes.

But Bismarck had been quick to recognize the advan-

---

[1] " La Question des Juifs en Allemagne," by G. Valbert, in *Revue des Deux Mondes*, vol. xxxviii. p. 203.

[2] *Ferdinand Lassalle*, by George Brandes, pp. 10-12.

[3] *Ibid.* pp. 44, 46.   [4] *Ibid.* p. 88.

tage of harnessing the Jewish agitator to the Prussian
Imperial machine, and before long we find Lassalle sinking
his racial hatred against the Gentiles in favour of the worst
oppressors of his kind. By 1859 he had become an ardent
Prussian Jingoist, subscribing to the whole policy of Bismarck, aiming at the absolute annihilation of Austria,
" whose German provinces were to form an integral part
of the one and indivisible German Republic " — a phrase
strangely reminiscent of Anacharsis Clootz's vision of " the
great Germany, the Universal Republic " — yet at the
same time an enthusiastic propagandist for the Hohenzollerns.[1] Under these circumstances it is not surprising
that to the day of his death Bismarck always spoke of
Lassalle with gratitude and respect.

Even more valuable to the cause of German Imperialism was the founder of the creed now known as " Marxian
Socialism."

Karl Marx, the son of a Jewish lawyer whose real name
was Mordechai, was born at Trèves in 1818. In 1843 he
settled in Paris to study economics, but his revolutionary
activities led to his being expelled from France, and in 1845
he moved to Brussels, where, in collaboration with his
German friend Friedrich Engels, he reorganized the Communist League, and a few years later (in 1847) published
the now famous *Communist Manifesto*. Soon after this he
returned to Germany, where he took an active part in the
1848 Revolution, and in the same year we find him in
Berlin at the head of a secret Communist society wielding
the powers of life and death.[2] For this it is said that he was
condemned to death,[3] but succeeded in escaping to London, where he settled down for the rest of his life and
devoted himself to his great book *Das Kapital*. This pon-
derous work has been described as the " Bible of the working-classes." In reality the term, if employed at all, might
be more aptly applied to his earlier production, *The Communist Manifesto*. To the working-man *Das Kapital* must

[1] *Ferdinand Lassalle*, by Edouard Bernstein, pp. 47, 62.
[2] Edmond Laskine, *L'Internationale et le Pangermanisme* (quoting
Nettlau's *Bakunin*), p. 56.
[3] Louis Enault, *Paris brulé par la Commune*, p. 23; Beaumont Vassy,
La Commune de Paris, p. 9.

be completely unintelligible, for even Marxians of the educated class are totally divided as to its meaning. But to that small minority amongst the working-men that composes " the revolutionary proletariat " the meaning of *The Communist Manifesto*, described by Marxians as " the Charter of Freedom of the Workers of the World," is clear enough. Here are all the diatribes against the *bourgeoisie* and capitalists with which Marat, Hébert, and Babeuf had familiarized the people, and here in plain language are set forth the doctrines laid down in the code of Weishaupt — the abolition of inheritance, of marriage and the family, of patriotism, of all religion, the institution of the community of women, and the communal education of children by the State. This, divested of its trappings, is the real plan of Marxian Socialism, which, enveloped in the algebraical phraseology of *Das Kapital*, is less easy to discover.

In neither work had Marx originated anything. His theory of " wage-slavery " was, as we have seen, current during the first French Revolution, and had been continued by Vidal and Pecqueur, to whom the idea of the socialization of mines, railways, and transport was also due; his Communism was that of Babeuf, of Louis Blanc, and Cabet; his Internationalist schemes had been propounded by Weishaupt and Clootz, as also his attacks upon religion; his doctrine that " Labour is the source of all wealth " had been set forth by such early English writers as Locke, Petty, Adam Smith, and later by Robert Owen; [1] even his theory of surplus value was not his own but had been formulated with some vagueness by Owen, more definitely by the Chartists in their organ (*The Poor Man's Guardian*) in 1835, seven years before Marx began to write. [2] When we have traced these ideas to their original

[1] Sargant, *Life of Robert Owen*, pp. 170, 441-442. " The poor and working-classes," Owen wrote, " create all the wealth which the rich possess."

[2] Marx's plagiarisms are admitted even by his admirer the Syndicalist Sorel. " The new Marxian school," he writes, " perceived with a certain stupefaction that pretended inventions had been put down to the account of the master which originated with his predecessors or were even commonplaces at the time when *The Communist Manifesto* was drawn up. According to an author who ranks amongst well-informed people, ' . . . the accumulation (of capital in the hands of a few individuals) is one of the

sources, what then is left of Marx's system? Absolutely nothing but the form in which it was conveyed.

Werner Sombart has remarked on the peculiar aptitude of the Jewish race for making use of waste product. The Jews, it appears, are the *chiffoniers par excellence* of the world. This then was the particular art of Marx, who, as we know, collected all the materials for his book on Capital in the reading-room of the British Museum. It was there that he found his whole system ready to hand. Can we not see him, like some veteran Jewish rag-and-bone merchant, going over the accumulated débris of past social schemes, passing through his fingers the dry bones of dead philosophies, the shreds and tatters of worn-out doctrines, the dust and ashes of exploded theories, and with the practical cunning of the German and the Hebrew brain shrewdly recognizing the use that might be made of all this lumber by skilfully welding it into one subversive whole?

Marx then was an impostor from the beginning. Posing as the prophet of a new gospel, he was in reality nothing but a plagiarist, and a plagiarist without the common honesty to pay tribute to the sources whence he drew his material. For after pillaging freely from all the earlier Socialists Marx dismisses them with a sneer. For Owen, Fourier, and Cabet — the " Utopian Socialists " as he describes them — Marx has nothing but a light contempt, because they " consistently endeavour to suppress the class struggle and to reconcile antagonisms," [1] whilst amongst " the Republican asses of 1848 " [2] Louis Blanc is referred to as " a high priest of the Socialist synagogue." [3]

But it was for Proudhon that Marx reserved his bitter-

great discoveries of Marx, one of the finds of which he was the proudest.' (A. Métin, *Le Socialisme en Angleterre*, p. 191). With all due deference to this notable academician this thesis was known to the man in the street (*courait les rues*) before Marx had ever written anything, and had become a dogma in the Socialist world at the end of the reign of Louis Philippe. There are a quantity of Marxian theses of the same kind " (*Réflexions sur la violence*, pp. 173, 174).

[1] *Communist Manifesto* (edited in pamphlet form by Socialist Labour Party), p. 27.
[2] Letter from Marx to Engels, July 7, 1868, *Briefwechsel zwischen Friedrich Engels und Karl Marx* (published by Dietz of Stuttgart), iv. 65.
[3] Marx, *La Lutte des classes.*

est animosity, as Bakunin the Anarchist, whilst still under the spell of Marx, described in an illuminating passage:

His vanity . . . has no bounds, a veritable Jew's vanity. . . . This vanity, already very great, has been considerably increased by the adulation of his friends and disciples. Very personal, very jealous, very touchy, and very vindictive, like Jehovah the God of his people, Marx will not suffer that one should recognize any other God but himself; what do I say? that one should even render justice to another Socialist writer or worker in his presence. Proudhon, who has never been a God, but who was certainly a great revolutionary thinker, and who rendered immense services to the development of Socialist ideas, became for this reason the *bête noire* of Marx. To praise Proudhon in his presence was to cause him a mortal offence worthy of all the natural consequences of his enmity; and these consequences are at first hatred, then the foulest calumnies. Marx has never recoiled before falsehood, however odious, however perfidious it might be, when he thought he could make use of it without too great danger for himself against those who had the misfortune to incur his wrath.[1]

Such was the personal character of the man represented to us to-day as the saviour of the working-classes. How far was he consistent in his championship of the " proletariat " ? Here we come to the greatest irony of all in the career of Marx.

It has been seen that the principal theory proclaimed by Marx was the necessity for the overthrow of Capitalism, a system founded on the exploitation of the workers by whom all wealth is produced. Yet probably few of his followers have troubled to inquire whence Marx derived his own means of livelihood. We know that throughout his whole life he never did a stroke of manual labour — the only form of work that Marxians recognize as " productive " — and that his writings did not bring him in sufficient to maintain himself and his family in comfort. How then did Marx live? On the bounty of Friedrich Engels.

Engels has been described by the Socialist Guillaume, Secretary of the Internationale, as " a rich manufacturer accustomed to regard workmen as machine fodder and

---

[1] *Michael Bakunin, eine Biographie*, by Dr. Max Nettlau, i. 69, quoting letter from Bakunin in 1873 to the " Frères de l'Alliance en Espagne."

cannon fodder." [1] His large fortune had been made out of Lancashire cotton spinning, and it was he who supplemented the meagre earnings of his collaborator. [2] So we have the ludicrous situation of these two German opponents of Capitalism and industrial exploitation living complacently on capital accumulated from the exploitation of English workers! How in the face of this fact can any one retain a lingering belief in the genuineness of Marx's Socialism? Indeed the more we study Marx's writings — not those intended for publication, but the real expression of his opinions contained in his private correspondence — the more the conviction is borne in upon our minds that Marx never believed a word of the doctrines he professed, but that to him Socialism was merely a system to be made use of for his own ends.

It was thus that with the rise of German Social Democracy under the aegis of Lassalle, Marx, and Engels true Socialism — that is to say French Socialism — died, and its dry bones were taken over by the company which Bakunin described as " the German Jew Company," the " red bureaucracy." From this moment the vein of idealism that had run through the earlier stages of the revolutionary movement ceases entirely, and Socialism reduced from a Utopian dream to a cut-and-dried system, practical and unaspiring as the prospectus of a Germany company promoter, is seen in all its heartless materialism, its ruthless Prussianism, as it had first appeared in the code of Weishaupt.

. . . .

Meanwhile Illuminism had continued to develop along the line of Anarchy. No longer represented merely by the visionary Proudhon but by the fierce Slavonic force of Bakunin, Anarchy for the first time showed itself under its true colours. Hitherto even such anarchic writers as Marat and Hébert had professed to entertain some scheme of reconstruction. Proudhon had formulated an elementary theory of Syndicalism with which to replace the existing order; it was left to Bakunin to advocate the

[1] Guillaume, *Documents de l'Internationale*, iii. 153.
[2] *Reminiscences*, by H. M. Hyndman, pp. 278, 279.

system of Anarchy as a permanent institution, not as a transitory period necessary to traverse on the way to a regenerated social order.

Michael Bakunin (or Bakounine), born in 1814, belonged to the Russian nobility, and at the age of twenty entered the artillery school at St. Petersburg. He passed his examinations brilliantly, but, always an incorrigible idler, spent most of his time, when quartered in a provincial town, lying on his bed in his dressing-gown.[1] Before long he left the army, but took up no other profession, preferring to dabble in philosophy and to meddle in his friends' affairs, one of whom, Bielinski, driven to exasperation, wrote: "I should be capable of throwing him down and stamping on him with sabots."[2] Even his *intimes* and fellow-Anarchists Ogareff and Herzen had little good to say of him. "I infinitely regret having nourished this reptile . . ." wrote the former; "he is a man with whom it repels me to shake hands;" whilst Herzen described him briefly as a man "with talent but a detestable character and a *mauvais sujet*."[3] Incidentally Bakunin had applied the same description to Herzen.

Embroiled in all these private quarrels, too indolent to do any honest work, Bakunin ended by taking up the profession of a revolutionary — a career which, like many another of his kind, he found both easy and remunerative.

By dint of perpetually borrowing money from his friends, Bakunin was spared from exerting himself even in a literary way, and during the course of seven years, 1840–1847, his entire output of work consisted in six newspaper articles. Meanwhile his revolutionary energies found their vent in talk — endless, discursive talk — with his fellow-revolutionaries, lasting frequently all through the night, to the accompaniment of excellent Russian tea and sandwiches. It is thus that in 1847 we have already found him discussing with Proudhon and Sazanoff the prospect of "the universal revolution."

At this period Bakunin seems not to have formulated any definite revolutionary creed, and thus, although he

---

[1] *Correspondence de Michel Bakounine*, published by Michel Dragomanov (1896), p. 7.   [2] *Ibid.* p. 8.   [3] *Ibid.* p. 13.

vaguely regarded Communism as "logically impossible," he was quite content to throw in his lot with the Communists of Paris, amongst them his future antagonist Marx. Twenty-nine years later Bakunin described their first meeting in these words:

Marx and I are old acquaintances. I met him for the first time in Paris in 1844. . . . We were rather good friends. He was much more advanced than I was, as to-day he still is, not more advanced but incomparably more learned than I am. I knew nothing then of political economy, I had not yet got rid of metaphysical abstractions, and my Socialism was only that of instinct. He, though younger than I, was already an atheist, a learned materialist, and a thoughtful Socialist. It was precisely at this epoch that he elaborated the first foundations of his present system. We saw each other fairly often, for I respected him very much for his knowledge and for his devotion, passionate and serious though always mingled with personal vanity, to the cause of the proletariat, and I eagerly sought his conversation, which was always instructive and witty when it was not inspired by petty hatred, which, alas! occurred too frequently. There was never, however, any frank intimacy between us. Our temperaments did not permit of it. He called me a sentimental idealist, and he was right; I called him a vain man, perfidious and crafty, and I was right also.[1]

It is easy to read between the lines here, to see how from the beginning Bakunin was simply a tool in the hands of Marx. The shrewd German Jew clearly recognized the value of the Russian as a huge dynamic force to be made use of and then cast aside when it had served his purpose.

Before the Revolution of 1848, Bakunin, like Marx, was expelled from Paris, but after the explosion of February he contrived to return and join himself to the extreme party, with whom he passed his nights preaching revolution, equality of salaries, the levelling down of all classes in the name of Equality.

But Caussidière and Flocon, exasperated by his tirades, finally sent him off on a mission to the Slavs, in the hope of his breaking his neck. "What a man! What a man!" said Caussidière. "The first day of a revolution he is a treasure, the second he is only good to shoot."

[1] *Michael Bakunin, eine Biographie*, by Dr. Max Nettlau, i. 69. (This work is unpublished, and only 50 copies were reproduced in lithograph from manuscript. One of these is in the British Museum.)

Herzen, who records this expression of opinion, adds that Caussidière himself needed shooting the day before the revolution began.[1]

Bakunin's journey eastwards effectively rid France of his presence for many years; for after taking part in the revolutionary outbreaks in Russia, Prague, and finally in Dresden, he was arrested at Chemnitz and imprisoned first at Altenburg, then at Koenigstein, then taken in chains to Prague, transferred to Olmütz, where he remained chained to the wall for five months, and last of all given over to the Russian Government, by which he was imprisoned in the fortress of Peter and Paul in May 1851. Two months later Count Orloff came to visit him and urged him to write a confession of his misdeeds to the Emperor as to a father confessor. Bakunin complied, but Nicholas I. on reading the document observed briefly: " He is a brave boy with a lively wit, but he is a dangerous man and must be kept under lock and key." Accordingly Bakunin remained in prison, for a time in St. Peter and Paul, later at Schlüsselbourg, where he remained three years, during which time he contracted scurvy and all his teeth fell out.

On the accession of Alexander II. a fresh demand was made for a reprieve, but the new Emperor, on being shown Bakunin's " confession " to his predecessor, remarked, " I see not the least repentance in this letter," and sent him to Siberia.

Here Bakunin spent four quite pleasant years; free to move about, he actually, for the only time in his life, took up a little work, and finally married a Polish girl who " shared all his aspirations." " I am completely happy," he wrote in 1860. " Ah! how sweet it is to live for others, especially when it is for a charming woman."

But peace and quiet could not content the restless spirit of Bakunin for long. The revolutionary fever was on him and he craved to be back again at his old game of agitation. The emancipation of the serfs, which took place in the following year, stirred him but mildly; in this immense concession to the cause of liberty he saw only a means of shaking the Imperial authority, and at the end

[1] *Correspondance de Bakounine*, pp. 41, 42.

of this same year he succeeded in escaping from Siberia, whence he travelled across Japan and America to London. Here Bakunin, received with open arms by Ogareff and Herzen, found himself once more in a congenial atmosphere. Surrounded by conspirators of all nationalities he was able to get to work on fresh plots, on schemes for stirring up the Poles, and organizing revolutions everywhere. Herzen has thus described his activities at this crisis:

Bakunin renewed his youth; he was in his element. It is not only the rumbling of insurrection, the noise of the clubs, the tumult in the streets and public places, nor even the barricades that made up his happiness; he loved also the movement of the day before, the work of preparation, that life of agitation, yet at the same time rendered continuous by conferences — those sleepless nights, those parleyings and negotiations, rectifications, chemical ink, cyphers, and signs agreed upon beforehand.

And Herzen, who took revolution more seriously, adds that Bakunin " excited himself exactly as if it were a question of preparing a Christmas tree — that annoyed me." [1]

It is easy to understand that to a man of Bakunin's temperament an existence of this kind — maintained as ever by the charity of his friends — was infinitely preferable to a life of honest toil such as most human beings are condemned to lead. Indeed in the above description we find the key to many an agitator's career, and we cannot wonder that as long as revolution provides constitutional idlers with a lucrative and amusing profession the world should continue to toss on the waves of unrest.

I have dwelt at some length on the character and career of Bakunin because more than any one he seems to me to embody the spirit of Anarchy — a spirit widely different, indeed diametrically opposed to that of State Socialism. The Anarchist is undoubtedly a more amiable being than the State Socialist; instead of wishing to cut every one down to the same pattern, he desires, on the contrary, to give all men unbounded liberty to develop along whatever lines they please — the idler should be free to idle and live on other men's labour, the drunkard to drink himself into

[1] *Correspondance de Bakounine*, p. 67.

a condition of maudlin imbecility, the murderer to cut throats until he wearies of the pastime, the thief to continue helping himself to other people's goods until he has accumulated enough to satisfy him. Exaggerated Individualism is the keynote of his system: liberty, not equality, is his goal. His belief in the amiability of human nature endows him with a *bonhomie* not to be found amongst the Communists, who regard their fellow-men as creatures to be dragooned into obedience to the dictates of the State, by which of course they mean themselves. The difference between the two is that which exists between the amiable eccentric who, believing in the innate benevolence of the entire animal kingdom, wishes to open all the cages in a menagerie and leave the wild beasts free to roam about the world, and the lion-tamer who loves at the crack of his whip to see king of beasts and performing poodle alike meekly rotating on a merry-go-round.

It is easy, therefore, to understand that Anarchists, far more than their dour opponents the State Socialists, have succeeded in endearing themselves to the people with whom they came in contact. The vision of " the Russian giant " in his big hat was remembered affectionately long afterwards by the inhabitants of Lugano, where Bakunin spent some years, and later on his disciple Prince Kropotkine made himself beloved in London drawing-rooms.

The truth is that to the Western mind such beings are impossible of comprehension. Deceived by the outward urbanity of the Anarchists, it fails to realize that beneath the smiling surface there lurks a tiger ready to be aroused by the smell of blood; it cannot believe that people can really exist who love violence for its own sake, who crave to burn and murder and destroy.

But in Eastern Europe creatures of this kind have always existed, and we find the exact prototype of Bakunin in the Baron Ungern von Sternberg who had pursued a career of crime at the beginning of the century in his island of Dago. The favourite pastime of this robber baron, who had vowed hatred to the whole human race, the Emperor in particular, was to lure ships to their destruction by means of a lighthouse installed in the tower of his castle.

As soon as a vessel was on the point of wrecking, the baron descended to the beach, embarked secretly with several clever and determined men whom he kept to help him in his nocturnal expeditions; he received the foreign mariners, finished them off in the darkness instead of rescuing them, and after having strangled them he pillaged their ship; all this less by cupidity than by pure love of evil, by a disinterested zeal for destruction. Disbelieving in everything, and above all in justice, he regarded moral and social disorder as the closest analogy to the state of man here below and civil and political virtues as harmful chimeras, since they only oppose Nature without subduing it.[1]

This was precisely the creed of Bakunin, who, if he had lived a hundred years earlier, before brigandage had been sanctified by the revolutionary Socialists and Anarchists of France, would doubtless have found a vent for his energies on the same lines as the robber baron, instead of masquerading as a champion of the people.

Such a dynamic force as Bakunin provided could not fail to be of immense value to the revolutionary movement, and it was thus that, during his stay in London, Marx — who incidentally had taken the opportunity of Bakunin's incarceration at Koenigstein in 1850 to declare that he was an agent of the Russian Government — came round to his lodgings and assured him that he had not intended to calumniate him in the past.

The fact is that Marx was now very busy at the great scheme of his life and needed all the co-operation he could muster — this scheme was the organization of the famous " Internationale."

In order to understand the origin of this association it is necessary to go back two years, that is to say to 1862, the year of the Great Exhibition in the Cromwell Road.

Now whilst Anarchists and State Socialists were striving for the mastery over the revolutionary movement, the working-men of France had begun dimly to realize that if they hoped to improve their lot it was to themselves they must look for salvation and not to the theorists who had hitherto led them to disaster. Accordingly in 1862 a deputation of French working-men was sent to England on a visit to the Great Exhibition to study technical questions

[1] *La Russie en 1839*, by Astolphe de Custine, i. 175.

connected with labour, and during the course of their stay they had the opportunity to observe the utility of Trade Unions in protecting the interests of the workers. This system was denied to them, for the " coalitions of working-men " suppressed in the first French Revolution still remained under the ban, and the Frenchmen now resolved to form a new association on their own account. Although imbued with the " mutualist " theories of Proudhon their programme was in no way revolutionary, and they hoped by pacific means to bring about a reorganization of the industrial system. An interesting little book which has now become very rare, *The Secret History of the International*, published in 1872, had admirably described the attitude towards the social problem of two of these men, Tolain and Fribourg, bronze-workers of Paris who visited London in 1864.

> They talked of peace, of study, of arrangement, of association. . . . A better knowledge of each other, a more frequent interchange of thought, a clearer view of the great laws which govern rise and fall in wages, and a means of stretching friendly hands from town to town, from sea to sea in case of need — these are the ends we have in view, they urged, not secret plots and wine-shop agitations.[1]

The path of peaceful progress was paved the more smoothly by the action of Napoleon III., who in May of this same year repealed the laws against Trade Unions and replaced them by a fresh edict threatening with punishment any concerted attempt, either on the part of employers or employed, to paralyse industry by malicious strikes or lock-outs. This year of 1864, as Mermeix points out, was thus " a great date in the history of the workers in France," for the new law " at last establishes equality of rights between the masters and the working-men," and if firmly applied should have accustomed them to respect each other. " It would not have permitted the method of ' direct action,' which is nothing but a series of fraudulent manœuvres concerted and carried out." [2] There was, therefore, at this moment less reason than ever to have

[1] *The Secret History of the International*, by Onslow Yorke, *alias* Hepworth Dixon (1872).
[2] Mermeix (G. Terrail), *Le Syndicalisme contre le socialisme*, pp. 53-56.

recourse to violent methods for the redress of social evils. But the work of the World Revolutionists is always to strangle true reforms at their birth, and the new liberty accorded to the workers proved the signal for fresh agitation on their part. In the " Working-men's Association" they saw the very instrument they needed for carrying out their plans. Karl Marx was then in London and frequently to be found in the clubs and cafés where the working-men forgathered. " In evil hour," says the *Secret History*, " the Paris *bronziers* met this learned and unsmiling Jew." From that moment the cause of the workers was lost.

It was not that Marx immediately introduced himself into the movement. On the contrary, at the meeting in St. Martin's Hall on September 28, 1864, when the " Internationale " was definitely founded, Marx played no part at all. " I was present," he wrote to Engels, " only as a dumb personage on the platform." But he was named, nevertheless, a member of the sub-committee, the other members being Mazzini's secretary — a Polish Jew named Wolff — Le Lubez, a French Freemason, Cremer, the secretary of the English Masons' Union, and Weston, the Owenite. At the first meeting of this committee Wolff placed before it the statutes of Mazzini's working-men's associations, proposing them as the basis of the new association; Le Lubez suggested amendments described by Marx as " perfectly childish." " I was firmly resolved," he wrote, " not to leave a single line if possible of all their balderdash." In a few weeks he had succeeded in establishing his authority. " My propositions were all accepted by the commission; they only insisted on the introduction in the Preamble of the statutes, of two phrases on duties and rights, and on truth, morality, and justice; but I placed them in such a way that it can do no harm." [1] The " provisional statutes of the Internationale " thus amended by Marx were then sent from London to Paris in the following November and accepted by the members of the association.

In all these manœuvres Marx had again displayed his

James Guillaume, *Karl Marx, pan-Germaniste*, p. 9 (Librairie Armand Collin, 1915).

skill in making use of the ideas of others to serve his own purpose. Just as he had succeeded in appropriating the theories of earlier Socialists and passing them off as his own invention, so he now contrived to gain the reputation of having founded the Internationale, an achievement we shall find habitually attributed to him by Marxian writers. But on this point we have further the conclusive evidence of James Guillaume, a Swiss member of the association and its principal chronicler:

It is not true that the Internationale was the creation of Karl Marx. He remained completely outside the preparatory work that took place from 1862 to 1864. He joined the Internationale at the moment when the initiative of the English and French workmen had just created it. Like the cuckoo he came and laid his egg in a nest which was not his own. His plan from the first day was to make the great working-men's organization the instrument of his personal views.[1]

But Marx was not the only intriguer to introduce himself into the movement. Monsieur Drumont has admirably described the manner in which middle-class theorists, entirely unsympathetic to the workers, succeeded in capturing the association:

In its origin the French Internationale was far from being revolutionary, from seeking disturbances in the streets, from liking insurrection for insurrection's sake. The Emperor Napoleon III., the only sovereign since 1789 who had sincerely interested himself in the working-classes, who understood their sufferings and desired to improve their lot, had followed the progress of the new association with sympathy. . . . It was only after a time that *bourgeois* agitators could make the Internationale deviate from its goal. This fact is ceaselessly repeated in everything the proletarians attempt. The *bourgeois* Capitalist exploits them as workers; when they deliberate together in order to consider means for improving their lot, the *bourgeois* Revolutionary, that is to say the needy *bourgeois* who wants to become a Capitalist, always finds a way of introducing himself into these associations and of making them serve for the satisfaction of his ambitions.[2]

It was through the secret societies that these *bourgeois* elements found their way into the new association.

---

[1] James Guillaume, *Karl Marx, pan-Germaniste*, p. 11 (Librairie Armand Collin, 1915).

[2] Édouard Drumont, *La Fin d'un monde*, p. 127.

Fribourg himself has declared that " the Internationale everywhere found support in Freemasonry,"[1] that is to say, in the lodges of the Grand Orient, and M. Louis Énault records that " in March 1865 all the secret associations of Europe and North America were merged in the ' International Association of Working-men,' ' The Marianne,' the ' Frères de la République ' of Lyons and Marseilles, the Fenians of Ireland, the innumerable secret societies of Russia and Poland, the remains of the Carbonari, joined up with the new society. This fusion was made."[2]

The Internationale, though itself an open and avowed association, thus became through its absorption of these existing secret organizations a huge semi-secret society — that is to say, it formed the outer shell that covered a ramification of conspiracies alien to the ideas of its founders and of which the secrets were known only to its middle-class directors.[3]

The anti-religious policy adopted by the Internationale was the work of these secret influences. In this same year of 1865 a great students' Congress took place in Liége, at which Fontaine declared:

What we wish for, we revolutionaries and socialists, is physical, moral, and intellectual development of the human race. Note that I say physical first, intellectual afterwards. We wish, in the moral order, by the annihilation of all prejudices of religion and the Church, to arrive at the negation of God and at free examination.[4]

And Lafargue, after chanting the praises of " our grand master Proudhon " at a further sitting of the Congress held in Brussels, had ended with the cry: " War on God! Hatred towards God! That is progress! We must shatter Heaven like a vault of a paper!"[5]

A number of these men — proudly claimed by the Freemasons as members of their Order — crowded into

---

[1] *L'Association Internationale des Travailleurs*, by E. E. Fribourg (1871). p. 31.

[2] Louis Énault, *Paris brûlé par la Commune* (1871), p. 24.

[3] P. Deschamps on this account describes the Internationale as a secret society (*op. cit.* ii. 541), and Heckethorn includes it in his work on " Secret Societies."

[4] P. Deschamps, *op. cit.* ii. 527a.   [5] *Ibid.* p. 528b.

the Internationale, which thus became permeated with the spirit of Illuminism. At a meeting of the association Garibaldi, venturing to propose that " faith in God should be adopted by the Congress," met with a stony silence, and was obliged to qualify the suggestion with the explanation that by the religion of God he meant the religion of Reason — the worship of the goddess of Reason, he added later, such as was practised in the French Revolution.[1]

The working-men took no part in these blasphemies. When Jaclard declared that outside Atheism there was no hope for man — " To be religious is to be ridiculous " — Fribourg, the bronze-worker, Chaudey, and Lemonnier " combated these views in the name of liberal Paris and of liberal France." " For," as the author of the *Secret History* truly adds, " these are not so much the views of working-men as of professors and philosophers." Indeed the vine-growers of Neuchâtal so little understood the aims of the Internationale as to declare naïvely that the principal article of their branch of the association should be: "Every vine-dresser must have a Bible and not neglect divine service " — a suggestion received with derision by their middle-class directors.[2]

It is difficult to write of these things calmly. For to deceive the people, whose simple faith and lack of education prevent them seeing whither they are being led, is as cowardly as to guide a blind man into a ditch. Yet this is what the exploiters of the Internationale did for the working-men. The identity of these middle-class interlopers who assembled at the Second Congress of the association in Lausanne in 1867 has thus been given by the author of the *Secret History;*

One delegate from Belgium, six delegates from England, seventeen from France, six from Germany, two from Italy, and thirty-one from Switzerland, came together in a room of the Casino at Lausanne. Three only of the deputies from England were of English name. England was mainly represented by two German tailors and a French fiddle-maker. Germany was represented by two doctors, one professor, an hotel-keeper, a machinist, and a gentleman of no profession that he cared to

[1] *Documents et souvenirs de l'Internationale*, by James Guillaume, ii. 47-49.   [2] *Ibid*. i. 248.

name. Italy was represented by two doctors, Stamfa and Tomasi. Four professors, three journalists, and a commercial agent represented the toilers of Zürich and Geneva. Observe that here is not a gathering of the craftsmen, bent on study of the questions which affect them in their hours of work and in their rate of pay, but an assembly of middle-class dreamers and theorists.

The " English " deputies here referred to are further described by James Guillaume. The tailor Eccarius, friend and disciple of Marx, was " a long personage with an unkempt beard, hair falling carelessly over his eyes, always stuffing his nose with tobacco " ; the other German tailor, Lessner, was " the true type of bearded democrat with burning eyes " — " his rôle seemed to be to protest perpetually. During discussion Eccarius speaks slowly with an imperturbable phlegm; Lessner cannot contain himself and exhales his passionate soul in a torrent of violent and bitter words; before an unintelligent contradictor Eccarius shrugs his shoulders, Lessner bounds about and seems to wish to devour his adversary." Eugène Dupont, the Frenchman and future president of the Congress, belonged to quite a different type — " a young man of thirty resembling all young men with a moustache." " I remark in him," adds Guillaume, " nothing but an innocent fondness for punning." [1] Another London member, this time an Englishman, not present at this Congress, was an eccentric millionaire named Cowell Stepney, " deaf as a post," an enthusiastic Communist and member of the General Council.[2]

The International Association of Working-men had become a farce. In vain the real workmen from Paris had protested at the First Congress in Geneva against the invasion of their ranks by men who were not manual workers, declaring that if the workers' Congress " were to be composed in greater part by economists, journalists, lawyers, and employers, the thing would be ridiculous and would annihilate the Association." [3] Marx, who in his " Preamble of the Provisional Rules of the Internationale" had himself declared that " the emancipation of the work-

---

[1] Guillaume, *Documents*, etc., i. 30, 31.   [2] *Ibid.* i. 80, 139, note.
[3] *Ibid. Karl Marx, pan-Germaniste*, p. 24.

ing-classes must be brought about by the working-classes themselves," waxed indignant at what he described as " the manœuvre of Tolain and Fribourg " in " invoking the principle that only working-men can represent working-men," and the French workmen's motion was defeated by 25 votes to 20.[1]

Marx indeed did not conceal his contempt for the originators of the Internationale

" The working-men, particularly those from Paris," he wrote a month after the Congress to his young Jewish friend Dr. Kugelmann, " belong as luxury workers (*i.e.* engravers on bronze) no doubt strongly to the old filth (*dem alten Dreck angehören.*) Ignorant, vain, pretentious, garrulous, swollen with pomposity, they were on the point of spoiling everything, having rushed to the Congress in numbers which in no way corresponded to that of their adherents. In the report I shall clandestinely rap them over the knuckles." [2]

As M. Guillaume truly observes: " All Marx is already in this letter."

The English delegates fared no better at his hands, for in the following year we find him writing in this strain to Engels:

I shall go personally to the next Congress at Brussels so as to give the *coup de grâce* to those asses of Proudhoniens . . . in the official Report of the General Council — for in spite of their efforts the Parisian chatterboxes have not been able to prevent our re-election — I shall give them the stick. The swinehounds amongst the English trade unionists who thought we were going too far will not catch us up easily. . . . Things are advancing, and at the first revolution, which is perhaps nearer than it seems, we, that is to say, you and I, will have this powerful instrument in our hands. . . . We can really be well satisfied![3]

In the light of these passages it is amusing to find one of Marx's admirers explaining that " the essence of

[1] Guillaume, *Karl Marx, pan-Germaniste*, p. 25.
[2] Letter from Marx to Kugelmann on October 9, 1866, *l'Internationale et le Pan-Germanisme*, by Edmond Laskine (1916), p. 24, quoting *Mouvement Socialiste*, 1902, pp. 17-46. Also Adolphe Smith, *The Pan-German Internationale*, p. 5.
[3] Laskine, *op. cit.* pp. 26, 27, quoting *Der Briefwechsel zwischen Kar Marx und Friedrich Engels* (Dietz, Stuttgart), iii. 406.

Marxian Socialism is that the working-classes must themselves work out their own salvation." [1]

It was, moreover, not only the industrial "proletariat" of France that Marx despised, but also those dwellers in the country districts who remained contentedly at work on their own bit of land — an arrangement, of course, directly opposed to the principles of Communism.

"The Bonapartes," he had written contemptuously after 1852, " are the dynasty of the peasants, that is to say, of the mass of the French nation." This dynasty, he goes on to point out, is therefore represented not by the revolutionary peasant "who wishes to overthrow the old order," but by " the conservative peasant," who, "stupidly bound by the old order, wishes to see himself saved and protected with his portion of the soil under the shadow of the Empire." [2]

If then it was the prosperity of the French peasant that roused Marx's ire, we might at least expect him to extend some sympathy towards the poor and destitute amongst the working-classes. Not at all. This portion of the people is designated by him as the " Lumpenproletariat," that is to say, the " ragged proletariat," for which, as Bakunin pointed out with indignation, " Marx, Engels, and all the school of Social Democrats of Germany display a profound contempt." [3] What section of the " proletariat " then did Marx approve? Obviously the section that showed itself submissive to his dictates.

The respective attitudes of Marx and of Bakunin towards the people much resembled those of Robespierre and Marat, their predecessors in the rival schools of State Socialism and Anarchy. To Robespierre the people whose " sovereignty " he proclaimed consisted simply of his own following amongst the men, and more particularly the women, of the Paris Faubourgs; to Marx, the proletariat, whose dictatorship he advocated, was represented by the small number of working-men who showed themselves willing to play into the hands of their German and Jewish

---

[1] *Violence and the Labour Movement*, by Robert Hunter, p. 148.
[2] Marx, *La Lutte des classes*, p. 345.
[3] Bakunin, *L'Etat et l'anarchie*, i. 8.

exploiters. But both to Marat and to Bakunin the people meant merely the turbulent elements amongst the populace — wastrels, criminals, drunkards, thieves, and vagabonds. Bakunin proposing his favourite toast, " To the destruction of all law and order and the unchaining of evil passions! " [1] might well have been the soul of the Spanish dwarf reincarnated in the body of the Russian giant. For criminals he expressed his predilection quite frankly:

" Only the proletariat in rags is inspired by the spirit and force of the coming social revolution, and in no way the *bourgeois* stratum of the working masses." His hopes even in the moujiks of Russia were disappointed, owing to the patriarchal conditions of their lives and their respect for the Emperor, so that it is to the brigands that he looks for salvation.

The only man who in the midst of the Russian people has the audacity to revolt against the Commune is the brigand. Thence brigandage constitutes an important phenomenon in the history of the Russian people — the first revolutionaries of Russia, Pougatcheff and Stenka Razine, were brigands.[2]

" Robbery," Bakunin writes again, " is one of the most honourable forms of Russian national life. The brigand is the hero, the defender, the popular avenger, the irreconcilable enemy of the State, and of all social and civil order established by the State. He is the wrestler in life and in death against all this civilization of officials, of nobles, of priests, and of the crown." [3]

In all this Bakunin showed himself a true and faithful follower of Weishaupt — was the robber baron of Dago perhaps an Illuminatus too? — and it is here that we find the explanation of his creed. Until the dawn of Illuminism crime and virtue, good and evil, held their opposing positions in the conceptions of the human mind. Even in pagan Greece Kerkuon and Procrustes found no apologists, but ranked simply as monsters of whom it was necessary to rid the world. It was left to Weishaupt to confuse the

---

[1] Guillaume, *Documents de l' Internationale*, i. 130.
[2] *Correspondance de Bakounine*, p. 38.
[3] *Words addressed to Students*, by Bakunin and Netchaïeff (1869).

issues, to glorify by the name of " useful larceny " [1] what had hitherto been described by the ugly name of theft, and to Brissot, the adept of illuminized Freemasonry, to declare theft to be a virtue. And it was Weishaupt who had first set out to destroy that religion and civilization which Bakunin and the Baron von Sternberg alike detested.

Bakunin then must not be regarded as a solitary demoniac, but as an exponent of those doctrines of Illuminism which found a fruitful soil in his wild Russian nature. On this point we have definite evidence, for the Socialist Malon, who was a member of the Internationale and personally acquainted with the Russian Anarchist, has explicitly stated that " *Bakunin was a disciple of Weishaupt.*" [2] It is only necessary to study the writings of Bakunin in order to recognize the truth of this statement.

Moreover, in the same year of 1864 that the Internationale was founded, Bakunin and his disciple Netchaïeff started a society on precisely the lines of the Illuminati. The plan of such conspirators has always been to envelop one secret society in another on the system of a nest of Chinese boxes, the outer one large and visible, the inner ones dwindling down to the tiny, almost invisible cell that contains the secret. This was the plan of Weishaupt, effected by his grades of adepts, initiated by successive stages into the greater and the lesser mysteries; and this too was the plan of Bakunin and his confederate Netchaïeff. The society organized by them consisted of three orders: (1) the International Brothers, (2) the National Brothers, and (3) the International Alliance of Social Democracy, which in its turn covered the inner secret society called the " Fraternal Alliance," over which Bakunin exercised supreme control.

We have only to compare the programme of the International Social Democratic Alliance with the plan of Weishaupt to recognize the evident connection between the two. Placed in parallel columns the aims of both will be seen to be identical:

[1] Barruel, *Mémoires sur le Jacobinisme*, iv. 18.
[2] Article on the Internationale, by Malon, in the *Nouvelle Revue*, xxvi. 752.

WEISHAUPT	BAKUNIN
The order of the Illuminati abjured Christianity. . . . In the lodges death was declared an eternal sleep; patriotism and loyalty were called narrow-minded prejudices incompatible with universal benevolence; further, they accounted all princes usurpers and tyrants, and all privileged orders as their abettors. They meant to abolish the laws which protected property accumulated by long-continued and successful industry; and to prevent for the future any such accumulation. They intended to establish universal liberty and equality, the imprescriptible rights of man, and as preparation for all this they intended to root out all religion and ordinary morality, and even to break the bonds of domestic life by destroying the veneration for marriage vows, and by taking the education of children out of the hands of the parents.	The Alliance professes Atheism. It aims at the abolition of religious services, the replacement of belief by knowledge and divine by human justice, the abolition of marriage as a political, religious, and civic arrangement. Before all, it aims at the definite and complete abolition of all classes and the political, economic, and social equality of the individual of either sex. The abolition of inheritance. All children to be brought up on a uniform system, so that artificial inequalities may disappear. . . . It aims directly at the triumph of the cause of labour over capital. It repudiates so-called patriotism and the rivalry of nations and desires the universal association of all local associations by means of freedom. The final aim of this society was " to accelerate the universal revolution."

Now how is it possible to suppose that the extraordinary similarity between these two programmes can be due to mere coincidence? In the Alliance of Bakunin, as in the *Communist Manifesto* of Marx, we find again all the points of Weishaupt — abolition of property, inheritance, marriage, and all morality, of patriotism and all religion. Is it not obvious that the plan had been handed down to the succeeding groups of Socialists and Anarchists by the secret societies which had carried on the traditions of the Illuminati, and that Bakunin, and still more his coadjutor Netchaïeff, was simply an Illuminatus?

Netchaïeff, moreover, is a type of no small importance to the history of social revolution. Uninspired by such anarchic philosophy as that proclaimed by Weishaupt and Bakunin, Netchaïeff showed himself a pure destructionist whose ferocity was untempered by the genial moods of Bakunin. "He was a liar, a thief, and a murderer — the incarnation of Hatred, Malice, and Revenge, who stopped at no crime against friend or foe that promised to advance what he was pleased to call the Revolution."[1] In the *Revolutionary Catechism* he composed in conjunction with Bakunin the following passages occur:

The revolutionary must let nothing stand between him and the work of destruction. . . . For him exists only one single pleasure, one single consolation, one reward, one satisfaction — the success of the revolution. Night and day he must have but one thought, but one aim — implacable destruction. . . . If he continues to live in this world it is only in order to annihilate it all the more surely.

For this reason no reforms were to be advocated; on the contrary, " every effort is to be made to heighten and increase the evil and sorrows which will at length wear out the patience of the people and encourage an insurrection *en masse*."[2] The second category of the association was therefore to be composed of " people to whom we concede life provisionally in order that by a series of monstrous acts they may drive the people into inevitable revolt."[3] In other words, oppressors of the people were to be encouraged.

To the sane mind it is almost impossible to believe that any man could put forward such theories, but this is precisely the advantage obtained by the advocates of World Revolution — their doctrines are so monstrous that they appear unbelievable to the world in general. Yet here is no possibility of misrepresentation, for the *Revolutionary Catechism* may be seen in print by any one who cares to look at it.

But like many another conspirator, from Weishaupt onwards, Bakunin found himself outwitted by his coadjutor. Perfectly unscrupulous as to the means he employed he had at first welcomed Netchaïeff as " a force," but by degrees he came to realize the danger he himself incurred

---

[1] Hunter, *Violence and the Labour Movement*, p. 16.
[2] *Alliance de la Démocratie Socialiste, etc., publiée par ordre du Congrès International de la Haye* (1873), p. 90.　　　　　　[3] *Ibid*.

by allying himself with a man who failed to recognize even the principle of " honour among thieves." Towards 1870 Bakunin discovered that Netchaïeff, whilst pretending to be his most devoted disciple, had all the while been a member of another society still more secret than the Alliance Sociale Démocratique, and of which he had never divulged the inner mysteries to his master.

" Netchaïeff," Bakunin wrote to Talandier, "is a devoted fanatic, but at the same time a very dangerous fanatic, and one with whom an alliance could only be disastrous to every one. This is why: He was first a member of an occult committee which really had existed in Russia. This committee no longer exists; all its members have been arrested. Netchaïeff alone remains, and alone he constitutes what he calls the committee. The Russian organization having been destroyed, he is trying to create a new one abroad. All this would be perfectly natural, legitimate, and very useful, but the way he goes to work is detestable. Keenly impressed by the catastrophe which has just destroyed the secret organization in Russia, he has gradually arrived at the conclusion that in order to found a serious and indestructible society one must take for a basis the policy of Machiavelli, and adopt in full the system of the Jesuits — bodily violence and a lying soul.

" Truth, mutual confidence, serious and severe solidarity exist only between about ten individuals who form the *sanctum sanctorum* of the society. All the rest must serve as a blind instrument and as matter to be exploited by the hands of these ten men really solidarized. It is permitted, and even ordered, that one should deceive them, compromise them, steal from them, and even if needs be ruin them — they are conspiracy-fodder (*chair à conspiration*). . . ."

Then Bakunin goes on to describe Netchaïeff's methods:

In the name of the cause he must get hold of your whole person without your knowing it. In order to do this he will spy on you and try to get hold of your secrets, and for that purpose, in your absence, left alone in your room he will open all your drawers, read all your correspondence, and when a letter seems interesting to him, that is to say, compromising from any point of view for you or for one of your friends, he will seal it and keep it carefully as a document against you or against your friend. . . . When convicted of this in a general assembly he dared to say to us: " Well, yes, it is our system. We consider as enemies, whom it is our duty to deceive and compromise, all those who are not completely with us. . . ." If you have introduced him to a friend, his first thought will be to raise discord, gossip and intrigue between you — in a word, to make you quarrel. Your friend has a wife, a daughter, he will try to seduce her, to give her a child, in order to drag her away from official morality and throw her into an attitude of forced revolutionary protest against society. All personal ties, all friendship are considered by them as an evil which it is their duty to destroy, because all this constitutes a force which, being outside the secret organization, diminishes the unique force of the latter. Do not cry out that I am exaggerating; all this has been amply developed and proved by me.[1]

It will be seen that all these were the exact principles and methods laid down by Weishaupt for the Illuminati.

Now it is curious to find the description of the inner ring of secret intrigue described by Bakunin in the above-quoted letter exactly corroborated by a very different authority, namely, the book of Gougenot des Mousseaux, entitled *Le Juif, le Judaïsme et la Judaïzation des peuples chrétiens*, published just a year earlier, in 1869.

It was in December 1865, that is to say, a year after Bakunin had formed his Alliance in conjunction with Netchaïeff, that Des Mousseaux received a letter from a Protestant statesman in the service of a great Germanic power, saying:

Since the revolutionary recrudescence of 1845, I have had relations with a Jew who, from vanity, betrayed the secret of the secret societies with which he had been associated, and who warned me eight or ten days beforehand of all the revolutions which were about to break out at any point of Europe. I owe to him the unshakable conviction that all these movements of " oppressed people," etc., etc., are devised by half-a-dozen individuals, who give their orders to the secret societies of all Europe. The ground is absolutely mined beneath our feet, and the Jews provide a large contingent of these miners. . . . The Jewish bankers will soon be, through their prodigious fortunes, our lords and masters. . . . All the great Radical news-papers of Germany are in the hands of Jews.[2]

It is impossible to suppose any collusion between men of opinions so divergent as the Royalist Catholic Des Mousseaux, his friend the Protestant statesman, and the Russian Anarchists Bakunin and Netchaïeff. We must, therefore, admit that each must have reached his conclu-

---

[1] *Correspondance de Bakounine*, published by Michel Dragomanov, pp. 325-327.　　[2] Gougenot des Mousseaux, *op. cit.* pp. 367, 368.

sions independently of the other, and the extraordinary similarity between their two accounts tends most certainly to confirm the assertion that this mysterious association really existed.[1] Of whom was it composed? According to Des Mousseaux it was largely controlled by Jews who had insinuated themselves into the Masonic Lodges and secret societies, and curiously enough it was in October of this same year, 1869, that Bakunin, who had been attacked by certain Jews in the Internationale, wrote his *Study on the German Jews*, where he repeats precisely the same story of Jewish intrigue. The passage in question runs as follows:

I begin by begging you to believe that I am in no way the enemy nor the detractor of the Jews. Although I may be considered a cannibal, I do not carry savagery to that point, and I assure you that in my eyes all nations have their worth. Each is, moreover, an ethnographically historic product, and is consequently responsible neither for its faults nor its merits. It is thus that we may observe in connection with the modern Jews that their nature lends itself little to frank Socialism. Their history, long before the Christian era, implanted in them an essentially mercantile and *bourgeois* tendency, with the result that, considered as a nation, they are *par excellence* the exploiters of other men's work, and they have a natural horror and fear of the popular masses, whom they despise, moreover, whether openly or in secret. The habit of exploitation, whilst developing the intelligence of the exploiters, gives it an exclusive and disastrous bent and quite contrary to the interests as well as to the instincts of the proletariat. I know that in expressing with this frankness my intimate opinion on the Jews I expose myself to enormous dangers. Many people share it, but very few dare publicly to express it, for the Jewish sect, very much more formidable than that of the Jesuits, Catholic or Protestant, constitutes today a veritable power in Europe. It reigns despotically in commerce, in the banks, and it has invaded three-quarters of German journalism and a very considerable portion of the journalism of other countries. Woe, then, to him who has the clumsiness to displease it![2]

But Bakunin had underestimated the control of the Jews over the press. The great anarchist might tilt with impunity against principalities and powers, might incite to murder, pillage, and rebellion, but the moment he

[1] See chart, society marked with note of interrogation.
[2] *Œuvres de Bakounine*, v. 241.

attempted to attack the Jews he was unable to obtain a hearing, and his *polémique* never saw the light until his works were published thirty or forty years later. The same failure had attended the efforts of the Hébertiste Tridon, who at about the same date wrote a denunciation of the Jews which could not be published during his lifetime.[1]

It will be seen that for all their destructive energy the French and Russian anarchists were no match for the German Jews of the Internationale into which Bakunin and his Alliance had been admitted in August 1869. Indeed Bakunin clearly stood in awe of Marx, for in the above-quoted letter he is careful to specify that he includes in his strictures only " the crowd of Jewish pygmies " who had penetrated into the Socialist movement, and exempts " the two Jewish giants Marx and Lassalle," and ten months earlier he had written to Marx himself in terms of the most servile flattery :

You ask whether I continue to be your friend. Yes, more than ever, dear Marx. . . . You see, dear friend, that I am your disciple, and I am proud of it.[2]

But in a letter to Herzen on October 28, 1869, Bakunin explains his attitude to Marx and his reason for conferring on him the title of giant.

Marx, who detests me and who, I imagine, loves no one but himself . . . is nevertheless a man very useful to the Internationale. . . . If at the present moment I had undertaken a war against Marx three quarters of the members of the Internationale would have turned against me, and I should have been at a disadvantage. . . .[3]

Although from the beginning Marx had hoped to make the Working-Men's Association " the instrument of his personal views," it was not until 1868 that he succeeded in definitely directing its policy along his line of State Socialism. At the first two congresses, of Geneva in 1866 and Lausanne in 1867, the theories of the French Proudhoniens still prevailed; the Congress at Brussels in 1868 showed, however, the parting of the ways by declaring that the

---

[1] Drumont, *La France juive*, p. 13.
[2] Guillaume, *Documents, etc.,* i. 103.
[3] *Correspondance de Bakounine*, p. 290.

machines and instruments of work should belong to the workers, but all public services — railways, mines, etc. — to the community. This programme was therefore a blend of the system later to be known as Syndicalism and of the Communism of Vidal and Pecqueur which had been adopted by Marx.

At the Fourth Congress in Basle in 1869 the policy of the Association veered still further towards Communism by the abolition of private property in land and of inheritance. The programme of Weishaupt had thus been accepted almost in its entirety by the Internationale.[1]

Fribourg, who with the other French workers of the association opposed the abolition of private property in land, points out that the history of the Internationale must be divided into two periods, the first up to the Congress of Lausanne " mutualist," that is to say, demanding free control of industry, the second period Russo-German, when the association " became Communist, that is to say authoritative." [2] From this policy, as also from the principle of class hatred upheld both by Marx and Bakunin, Fribourg disassociates himself and his comrades entirely. " I insist," he writes, " that it should be known that no upright mind could have conceived the idea of giving birth to a society of war and hatred." [3] And since this is what it had become, Fribourg declares that by 1869 " the Internationale of the French founders was dead, quite dead." [4] " The working-men's International," remarks Dühring, " was no longer working-class, in the sense that it manœuvred, used, and exploited the workers of different countries."[5]

Such then were the intrigues of the men who called themselves the champions of the " proletariat."

[1] M. Louis Énault (*Paris brûlé par la Commune*, p. 27) and the Vicomte de Beaumont Vassy (*La Commune de Paris*, p. 325) both reproduce the programme of the Internationale as published in 1867 in which the five points of Weishaupt, viz.: " The abolition of all religion, of property, of the family, of heredity, of the nation (*i. e.* of patriotism) " are exactly reproduced. The document which they quote is stated to have been signed by the secretary of the Internationale and to have been published in the form of a pamphlet entitled *Le Droit des travailleurs.* I have been unable to discover this pamphlet in the British Museum or elsewhere.

[2] Fribourg, *L'Association Internationale des Travailleurs*, p. 2.
[3] *Ibid.*   [4] *Ibid.* p. 140.
[5] Eügen Dühring, *Kritische Geschichte der Nationalökonomie*, p. 566.

All talk of conditions of labour, all discussion of the practical problems of industry had been abandoned and the Internationale became simply an engine of warfare against civilization. By its absorption of the secret societies and of the doctrines of Illuminism all the machinery of revolution passed into its keeping. Every move in the game devised by Weishaupt, every method for engineering disturbances and for spreading inflammatory propaganda, became part of its programme.

So just as the Jacobin Club had openly executed the hidden plan of the Illuminati, the Internationale, holding within it the same terrible secrets, carried on the work of World Revolution in the full light of day.

CHAPTER VII

THE REVOLUTION OF 1871

The Franco-Prussian War — Internationalism — Karl Marx, pan-Germanist — The Commune — Conflict between Marx and Bakunin — End of the Internationale.

WE have seen in the last chapter that as a means for the reorganization of industry the Internationale had failed signally of its purpose. What then of its Internationalism? How far was the brotherhood of man which had constituted one of its fundamental doctrines to avail as a barrier against militarism?

The conviction that war is a relic of barbarism and should be done away with, has been held by humanitarians at every stage in the history of civilization; the question is how so obviously desirable an end can be accomplished. In France, as we have seen, groups of enthusiasts as far back as the Confrères of the twelfth century had declared it possible, and the Constituent Assembly of the First Revolution had devoted their energies to the formation of a " League of Perpetual Peace." " Let all men be free as we are," a deputy had cried, " and we shall have no more wars! " Forthwith the decree was passed that the French nation should never again undertake any war of conquest.

Mirabeau alone had shown the futility of such resolutions in his immortal reply: " I ask myself," he said to the Assembly, lulled in its dreams of pacifism, " I ask myself whether because we suddenly change our political system we shall force other nations to change theirs. . . . Until then perpetual peace will remain a dream and a dangerous dream if it leads France to disarm before a Europe in arms."[1]

[1] Albert Sorel, *L'Europe et la Révolution Française*, ii. 87.

197

Mirabeau's prophetic instinct was justified when eighty years later the same dangerous dream led the French workers of the Internationale to weaken before a Prussia in arms.

The idea of " a strike of the peoples against war " was proposed as early as 1868 at the Congress of the Internationale in Brussels, and Dupont, the mouthpiece of Marx, closed his presidential address with the words:

The clerics say: "See this Congress, it declares that it wishes neither for government, armies, nor religion." They say the truth, we wish for no more governments because governments crush us with taxes; we wish for no more armies because armies massacre us; we wish for no more religion because religion stifles intelligence.[1]

When, therefore, two years later the first rumblings of the Franco-Prussian War were heard, the French workers fondly imagined that the Internationale would intervene and stop the conflict. Accordingly with touching *naïveté* they published in their paper *Le Reveil* on the 12th of July 1870 an address to the people of Germany begging them to desist from strife:

Brothers of Germany, in the name of peace do not listen to the subsidized or servile voices which seek to deceive you on the true spirit of France. Remain deaf to senseless provocations, for war between us would be a fratricidal war. Remain calm, as a great and courageous people can do without compromising its dignity. Our divisions would only bring about on both sides of the Rhine the complete triumph of despotism.[2]

When, however, a week later, on July 19, Napoleon III. was tricked by Bismarck into declaring war on Prussia, the German Social Democrats rallied in a body to the standard of Imperialism, and the so-called " Central Committee of the German International Sections " sitting at Brunswick issued a proclamation on the 24th of July referring to " the legitimate aspirations of the German people for national unity," and ending with the words: " Long live Germany! Long live the International struggle of the proletariat." [3]

Deluded by the last hypocritical protestation, *Solidarité*, the organ of the Internationale, still expressed its hopes for the future.

[1] Guillaume, *Karl Marx, pan-Germaniste*, p. 51.
[2] *Ibid.* p. 84. [3] Guillaume, *Documents*, ii. 70.

Two great military powers are about to devour each other. Since we have obtained this immense result, that the two peoples whom their masters have declared to be in a state of war, instead of hating each other, hold out the hand of friendship, we can await the *dénouement* with confidence.[1]

But it was not until the tide of war had turned definitely in favour of Prussia that the Committee of Brunswick saw fit to respond with a plea for peace. It is true that isolated working-men in Germany expressed their sympathy with the French people, and that the Socialists Bebel and Liebknecht were later on thrown into prison for protesting against the war after it had broken out, nevertheless Liebkneckt himself, before it was too late, had urged Prussia on to aggression. Thus in the *Volksstaat* for July 13, 1870, he " had reproached Bismarck and the King of Prussia for showing themselves too conciliatory towards France and of damaging the prestige of Germany by a too humble attitude." [2]

The fact then remains that as a preventive to war the Internationale proved completely futile for the very reason given by Mirabeau eighty years earlier. The French Internationalists had reckoned without the German national spirit, and Guillaume, writing in *Solidarité* on March 28, 1871, is obliged to confess:

What an infinitesimal minority is formed by these men with convictions (Bebel and Liebkneckt)! How many are there in Germany, alas! of whom we can call ourselves the brothers? The immense majority of the German working-men, are they not intoxicated like the *bourgeoisie* by Bismarck's victories? And are we not obliged today, whilst making an honourable exception of the friends we have just mentioned, to consider the German people in the mass as an obstacle to the Revolution? [3]

It was not till two years later that the Latin members of the Internationale discovered to their pained surprise that the " Central Committee of the German International Sections " was not, as they had imagined, the German branch of the Internationale but merely an unofficial group with no organization, for the German Government had taken the precaution to forbid the formation of an

[1] Guillaume, *Documents, etc.*, ii. 69.
[2] Laskine, *L'Internationale et le pan-Germanisme*, p. 202.
[3] Guillaume, *Documents, etc.*, ii. 137.

Internationale amongst its own people.[1] Thus, although Germans controlled the policy of the Internationale abroad, the Internationale was not allowed to exist in Germany! As Mr. Adolphe Smith has well expressed it in relation to the 1917 situation·

That Socialism, as " made in Germany," and destined mainly for foreign exportation, would facilitate the invasion not only of Russia, but also of France, Italy, and even England, was not very apparent at first. Yet this might have been suspected, for it was evident that the *Socialist Internationale, whenever it was controlled by Germans, became a pan-German association.*[2]

The real meaning of Internationalism became in time apparent to the French workers. The hand of Bismarck had been strongly suspected in the great strike at Creuzot.[3]

", Strikes, always strikes, and still more strikes," Fribourg wrote in 1871, " no more study nor anything that resembles it. . . . Foreign Internationals who hold the ground, support the movement, found violent newspapers, an epidemic of disturbances rages in France and paralyses production."[4]

What was the rôle of Marx in this question of Internationalism? In order to realize his full perfidy we must refer again to the Preamble to the Statutes of the Internationale drawn up by him. The first principle, that " the emancipation of the workers must be brought about by the workers themselves," he had violated, as we have seen, by insisting on the admission of non-workers to the Association; the further principle of " a fraternal union between the workers of different countries " was now at stake, and Marx repudiated this likewise.

The truth is that Marx had never believed in universal brotherhood any more than he had believed in the dictatorship of the proletariat — these were slogans to be made use of but not carried into practice. Thus just before Sadowa he had written to Engels:

The Proudhonien clique amongst the Paris students preaches peace, declares war an anachronism, nationalities vain words, attacks Bismarck. . . . As disciples of Proudhon — my good

[1] Guillaume, *Documents, etc.*, ii. 137.
[2] *The Pan-German Internationale*, p. 3.
[3] *La Commune de Paris*, by the Comte de Beaumont Vassy, p. 13.
[4] Fribourg, *L'Association Internationale des Travailleurs* (1871).

friends Lafargue and Longuet are amongst them — they wish to abolish misery and ignorance, ignorance with which they themselves are afflicted all the more that they make a parade of a so-called " social science," *they are quite simply grotesque*.[1]

The appeal of the French working-men to their brothers of Germany in 1870 was now declared by Marx to be " pure Jingoism."

" The French," he wrote to Engels on July 20, " need a' thrashing (die Französen brauchen Prügel).   If the Prussians are victorious, the centralization of the power of the State will be useful to the centralization of the German working-class. Besides, German preponderance will transport the centre of gravity of the working-class movement from France to Germany, and it is sufficient to compare the movement in the two countries from 1866 until the present moment in order to see that the German working-class is superior to the French as much from the point of view of theory as of organization.

The preponderance in the theatre of the world of the German proletariat over the French proletariat would be at the same time the preponderance of our theory over Proudhon's.[2]

Now it is curious to notice that Nietzsche, who as the prophet of autocracy, Imperialism, and warfare has usually been regarded as the opposite pole to Marx, had expressed himself at the above-quoted date, namely in 1866, at the time of Prussia's victory over Austria at Sadowa, in the following words:

We hold the cards; but as long as Paris remains the centre of Europe things will remain in the old condition. It is inevitable that we should make an effort to upset this equilibrium, or at least try to upset it. If we fail, then let us hope to fall, each of us, on a field of battle, struck by some French shell.[3]

How are we to explain the extraordinary resemblance between the point of view expressed in these two passages? Can we attribute it to mere coincidence, or shall we find a common inspiration at work behind both writers? It is impossible to study the lives and writings of Marx and Nietzsche without recognizing a certain resemblance between the two men; both were continually at war with the rest of the human race, both had been embittered by

---

[1] Laskine, *L'Internationale et le pan-Germanisme*, p. 23; letter of June 7, 1866.
[2] *Der Briefwechsel zwischen Marx und Engels*, iv. 296.
[3] *Life of Nietzsche*, by Daniel Halévy (Eng. trans.), p. 53.

early experiences, and both were animated by a fierce and undying hatred towards Christianity arising from the same cause, namely that both worshipped *force*. If Marx incarnated the destructive spirit we associate with Bolshevism, Nietzsche was in reality an inverted Bolshevik, a man who had narrowly escaped being a violent revolutionary Socialist. Whilst Nietzsche desired to maintain the uneducated classes in a state of slavery, Marx aimed at the enslavement of the *intelligentzia*; whilst Nietzsche advocated the autocracy of Superman, Marx professed to believe in the dictatorship of the proletariat; whilst Marx devoted his energies to stirring up class hatred from below, Nietzsche by his " class consciousness of a higher class " [1] strove to promote it from above. In a word, both were in revolt against the existing social order tempered by Christian forbearance and compassion, which they regarded as debilitating to man's highest faculties.

This meeting of extremes explains the fact that Nietzsche found an affinity in Mazzini whilst Marx entered wholeheartedly into the aims of Bismarck. It is impossible not to suspect a common inspiration behind them both, working for the advancement of pan-German interests.

At any rate in 1870 Marx faithfully served the cause of German Imperialism. Indeed the French branch of the Internationale in London actually denounced him as an agent of Bismarck, and Marx wrote to Engels on August 3, 1870, saying that he was not only accused of being a Prussian agent but of having received £10,000 from Bismarck. Fortunately, adds the author of *The Pan-German Internationale*, who quotes these admissions, " all this private correspondence has been recently printed by the Socialist publisher, Dietz of Stuttgart. We are thus able to obtain, not from what others have said but from what the principals themselves wrote, a clear indication of their motives and acts." [2]

In the light of these revelations it is difficult to see in

---

[1] *Friedrich Nietzsche*, by Georges Brandes (Eng. trans.), p. 30.

[2] Adolphe Smith, *The Pan-German Internationale*, p. 5; see also Laskine, *L'Internationale et le pan-Germanisme*, p. 83. Note that both these writers are themselves Socialists. Edmond Laskine is said to be a Russian Jew; he was educated in France.

Marx's revolutionary violence the Jewish spirit of revenge for the persecution of his race to which it has frequently been attributed. If Marx resented persecution, why did he throw in his lot with the country in which *Judenhetze* was most rampant? It is possible that Bismarck knew how to exploit his racial hatred against Christian civilization, but the fact remains that, as two modern writers have expressed it, Marx was, or at any rate became, " a German of the Germans, and Marx has done more for the Fatherland " — which incidentally had exiled him! — " than all the hordes of German agents that have filtered across the world." [1]

In this attitude he was naturally supported by Engels — " Marx's evil genius," as Mrs. Marx was wont to describe him — a constitutional militarist. Thus when the Internationale of Paris again protested to the German people against the invasion of French territory, and this time the German Social Democrats at Brunswick responded with the proposal of " an honourable peace with the French Republic," Engels wrote indignantly to Marx:

It is just the old infatuation, the superiority of France, the inviolability of the soil sanctified by 1793, and from which all the French swinishnesses (les cochonneries françaises) committed since then have not been able to take away the character, the sanctity of the word Republic. . . . I hope that these people will return to good sense once their first intoxication has passed, otherwise it will become devilishly difficult to continue international relations with them. [2]

By Marx and Engels the French working-men were therefore abjured to dissociate themselves from the war and to forget the memories of 1792. Meanwhile the German workers must be kept quiet.

" Longuet (the French Socialist)," Engels wrote again, " is very amusing! Because William I. has granted them a Republic now they want to make a revolution in Germany! . . . If we have any influence in Paris we must prevent the working-men from moving until peace is made. . . ." [3]

[1] *Bolshevik Russia*, by G. E. Raine and E. Luboff, p. 17.
[2] Guillaume, *Karl Marx, pan-Germaniste*, p. 95.   [3] *Ibid.* p. 99.

And next day he adds:

The war by being prolonged is taking a disagreeable turn. The French have not yet been thrashed enough, and yet on the other hand the Germans have already triumphed a good deal.

It is true that, in the end, Marx in a letter to the *Daily News* on January 16, 1871, professed some sympathy with the martyred nation, and even expressed the opinion that the complete supremacy of Prussia not only over the people of France but of the rest of Germany would be fatal to the cause of liberty, but as by this time the triumph of Prussia was a *fait accompli* — for two days later the King of Prussia was crowned Emperor of Germany at Versailles — such protestations could be made with impunity. The fact remains that, as M. Guillaume expresses it:

In 1870 Marx and Engels, German patriots before everything applauded the victories of the German armies. . . . And they took advantage of their position to try, in the name of the General Council of the Internationale, to dissuade the French proletariat from fighting against the invaders. . . . Their attitude at this moment was a real treachery towards the Internationale for the profit of pan-German interests. These are things that it is necessary to make known to all Republicans, Socialists or otherwise, in France and elsewhere.[1]

It will be seen, then, that Internationalism as devised by Weishaupt, interpreted by Clootz, and carried out by Marx and Engels, and in our own day by the agent of Germany, Nicholas Lenin, has served two causes only — German Imperialism and Jewish intrigue.

.   .   .   .

After the defeat of the French armies at Sedan on September 1, 1870, the Empire was swept away and social revolution dealt the final blows to crushed and suffering France.

The first outbreak of revolution occurred in the provinces, and at Lyons was carried out by the Bakunists. Like the war-horse smelling the battle afar, Bakunin himself at Locarno heard the revolutionary Socialists of Lyons calling, and borrowing some money, according to his usual custom, hastened to the scene of action. Here he found himself once more in his element. The city was in a state

[1] Guillaume, *Karl Marx, pan-Germaniste*, p. iv.

of chaos; " none of the leaders of the Internationale had any clear idea what they intended to do; " public meetings of extraordinary violence were taking place, at which " the most sanguinary motions were put forward and received with enthusiasm; " [1] in a word, it was a state of affairs after Bakunin's own heart.

But once again the *bourgeoisie* rose in defence of law and order; and the *Comité de Salut Public*, that had occupied the Town Hall, was obliged to evacuate. The rôle of Bakunin himself was thus derisively described by Marx:

> On the 28th of September, the day of his arrival, the people had seized the Hôtel de Ville. Bakunin installed himself there; then the critical moment arrived, the moment awaited for so many years, when Bakunin was able to accomplish the most revolutionary act the world has ever seen. He decreed the *abolition of the State*. But the State, in the shape and kind of two companies of *bourgeois* National Guards, entered by a door that it had been forgotten to guard, cleared the hall, and made Bakunin hastily take the road for Geneva.[2]

Bakunin, therefore, bruised and battered — for he had been severely handled in the fray — returned to Italy a chastened man. Yet wild as appears his scheme of saving France from Prussia by " the complete destruction of the whole administrative and governmental machine," [3] we must admit that he displayed a certain perspicacity with regard to the future of French Socialism:

> " I begin to think now," he wrote to Palix, " that it is all up with France. . . . She will become a viceroyalty of Germany. In the place of her real and living Socialism we shall have the *doctrinaire* Socialism of the Germans, who will say no more than the Prussian bayonets permit them to say." [4]

But the final triumph of German Social Democracy was reserved for three years later.

Whilst these events were taking place in Lyons, the Third Republic had been proclaimed after the abdication of Napoleon III. On the 17th of September the Siege of

[1] Guillaume, *Documents, etc.*, ii. 92.

[2] *Alliance de la Démocratie Socialiste, etc., publiée par ordre du Congrès Internationale de la Haye* (1873), p. 21.

[3] Guillaume, *Documents, etc.*, ii. 98.   [4] *Ibid.*

Paris began. Six weeks later, on the 31st of October, great popular indignation was created by the belief that the Government had attempted to conceal the news of the surrender of Bazaine and the capitulation of Metz. At the same time it was announced that the recent victory outside Paris had been turned into a defeat and Le Bouget recaptured by the Germans; further, that M. Thiers was coming to Paris, under a flag of truce, to negotiate an armistice. Then the people who had endured so much throughout the siege, feeling that all their sacrifices had been in vain, rose against the Government, and the anarchic elements, exploiting the outraged patriotism of the Parisians, threw the city into confusion. National unity was thus destroyed, and the Prussians, emboldened by these dissensions, immediately increased the severity of their terms, demanding the ceding of Alsace and Lorraine and a heavy war indemnity.[1] Meanwhile their troops were carrying terror and desolation throughout the provinces of France — burning, pillaging, destroying, and killing without mercy those who offered the least resistance.

According to the terms of the armistice declared after the coronation of the Emperor William I., the garrison of Paris, with the exception of 12,000 men, was ordered to be disbanded, but the National Guards, known to be infected with revolutionary doctrines, were to be retained. It was thus that some of the French soldiers refused to march against the Prussians, declaring that they preferred to reserve themselves for fighting Frenchmen; that civil war was to be preferred to war against a foreign enemy.[2] But it was observed that these doctrines, the outcome of German Social Democracy, exercised no influence over the German mind, for whilst the French disciples of Internationalism fell back in battle not one Prussian faltered.[3]

The triumphal entry of the Prussians into Paris on March 1 was the signal for the revolution to break out; and on the 18th of March the National Guards, acting on this occasion in a spirit of outraged patriotism at the incompetence of the Government in the matter of national

[1] Bonnechose, p. 707.   [2] Louis Énault, *Paris brulé*, p. 16.
[3] Heckethorn's *Secret Societies*, ii. 250.

defence, took possession of the guns ranged in the Place des Vosges lest they should fall into the hands of the Prussians, and carried them up to the heights of Montmartre.

At the same time a central committee of National Guards, formed on the plan of the Committee of Insurrection that had organized the plan of attack on August 10, 1792, seized the reins of power. In vain the Government ordered fresh troops to recapture the guns. The soldiers went over to the side of revolution, and barbarously murdered their generals Lecomte and Thomas. Once more the *tricouleur*, defeated, gave way to the red flag of the social revolution.

Four days later the affray known as the " Massacre of the Place Vendôme " took place, when a procession of " the Friends of Order " — an immense demonstration composed of unarmed National Guards, civilians, women, and children, bearing the *tricouleur* as a rallying sign against disorder — were fired on by the insurgents and — according to certain contemporaries — thirty of their number killed.[1]

From this moment the revolutionaries were masters of Paris. The Hôtel de Ville was seized, the Government driven out of Versailles and the Commune established in its place.

It is impossible to follow the events of 1871 with the same precision as those of 1848 owing to the chaotic nature of the movement. Whilst 1848, in spite of the diversity of views that prevailed amongst the leaders, remained essentially a Socialist revolution, 1871 developed more along the lines of Anarchy. It is true that at the outset some attempt was made by Marx and Engels to control the movement.

" When the Commune insurrection began in Paris," writes Prince Kropotkine, " the General Council insisted upon directing the insurrection from London. It required daily reports about the events, gave orders, favoured this and hampered that, and thus put in evidence the disadvantage of having a governing body, even within the association." [2]

[1] Bonnechose, *Histoire de France*, ii. 722; Louis Énault, *Paris brûlé par la Commune*, p. 33; John Leighton, *Paris under the Commune*, p. 54.
[2] *Memoirs of a Revolutionary*, ii. 66.

But these orders of Marx seem to have been disregarded, and it was German Illuminism rather than German Social Democracy that gained the ascendancy. When on the 26th of April a deputation of Freemasons arrived to congratulate the Commune, the old war-cry of Illuminism, " The Universal Republic," inaugurated by Anarcharsis Clootz, greeted their appearance.[1]

Brother Thirifocque, the orator of the procession, declared that " the Commune was the greatest revolution it had been given to the world to contemplate; that it was the new Temple of Solomon which Freemasons were bound in duty to defend." To which Lefrançais, member of the Commune, replied that he himself had been received into the *Loge Ecossaise*, and had long been convinced that the aim of the association was the same as that of the Commune — social regeneration.[2]

In accordance with the principles of "universal masonry" national interests were soon lost to sight and French patriotism became dominated by the spirit of the World Revolution. Here again 1871 differed essentially from 1848, for whilst that earlier movement, led entirely by Frenchmen, retained its national character throughout, the Commune quickly became an assemblage of cosmopolitan elements entirely unrepresentative of the spirit of France.

Amongst the foreigners in the service of the Commune there were 19 Poles, 10 Italians, 7 Germans, 2 Americans, 2 Russians, 2 Wallachians, 2 Portuguese, 1 Egyptian, 1 Belgian, 1 Hungarian, 1 Spaniard, and 1 Dutchman.[3] Generically its elements were divided into Internationals, Jacobins, and professional agitators. Amongst this heterogeneous crowd — " the *déclassés* of the whole world," writes a contemporary [4] — there could be no unity of action or of purpose.

Nevertheless the French Communards numbered sev-

---

[1] Leighton, *Paris under the Commune*, p. 221: " An enthusiastic cry of *Vive la Franc-Maçonnerie! Vive la République Universelle!* is re-echoed from mouth to mouth."

[2] Deschamps, ii. 421, 422.

[3] Leighton, *op. cit.* (quoting the *Figaro*) p. 75; Énault, *Paris brûlé*, p. 315.

[4] *Paris brûlé*, p. 42.

eral sincere patriots. It is impossible indeed to conceive of any movement taking place in Paris without the romantic and passionately patriotic spirit of the French making itself felt, and the incompetence of the Government had driven many enthusiasts over to the side of the revolution. Unhappily this enthusiasm had led to fanaticism. Thus Flourens, killed by a mounted patrol whilst leading a troop of insurgents to Versailles, has been described by an English contemporary as " an enthusiast in search of a social Eldorado, who would put himself at the service of the most forlorn cause." " In the bitter cold winters he fed and clothed the poor of Belleville, going from attic to attic with money and consolation." But the turbulence of his nature had thrown him into agitation. " He was a man of barricades. He did not seem to think that paving-stones were made to walk on; he only cared to see them heaped up across the street for the protection of armed patriots. . . . Wherever there was a chance of being killed he was sure to be. . . . He was a madman, but he was a hero." [1]

In justice to the men of 1871 we must admit their bravery. These French Communards did not, like their predecessors who composed the Commune of 1792, sit safely behind thick walls or take refuge in cellars whilst the crowd they had set in motion bore the brunt of the battle on the great days of tumult; the men of 1871 went boldly out into the streets to face the fire of the soldiery, and many died fighting, fired with enthusiasm to the last.

But alas! to what purpose? If the Government had proved incompetent the Commune proved more incompetent still. And as in all anarchic movements it was inevitably the most violent — more than this, the most criminal — elements that obtained control, M. Énault declares that no less than 52,000 foreigners and 17,000 released convicts took part in the scenes that followed.[2]

Under these influences the war on civilization planned by Weishaupt and inaugurated by the Terror of 1793 broke out afresh. As in 1848, all the memories of that earlier period — fatal precedent from which the French seemed

---

[1] Leighton, *op. cit.* 115, 116.   [2] *Paris brûlé*, p. 28.

destined never to depart — were once again evoked. A
" Comité de Salut Public " was formed, the calendar of
1793 revived, and with a pitiable poverty of imagination
even the names of the newspapers were copied from those
of the first Revolution — the *Cri du Peuple* of Babeuf, the
Père Duchesne of Hébert, in which the gutter verbiage of
the famous " stove merchant " was faithfully reproduced
by his imitator Vermesch.

Naturally the de-Christianization of Paris inaugurated
in 1793 entered again largely into the programme. The
same desecration of the churches took place; the images
of the saints were broken or tricked out in ignoble disguises,
the pictures torn, plate and ornaments pillaged; parties
played at cards on the high altar, orators mounted the
pulpit to blaspheme God. In the church of Saint Eustache,
where the font had been filled with tobacco and the statue
of the Holy Virgin dressed up as a " *vivandière*,"a crowd
of " female patriots," of the same class as those who had
seduced the soldiery in 1789, declaimed the doctrines of the
social revolution: " Marriage, citizenesses, is the greatest
error of ancient humanity. To be married is to be a slave.
. . ." A tall gaunt woman, with a nose like the beak of
a hawk and a jaundice-coloured complexion, demanded
amidst thunders of applause that the Commune should no
longer recognize marriage by according pensions to the
legitimate as well as the illegitimate wives of the National
Guards: " The matrimonial state is a perpetual crime
against morality. . . . We, the illegitimate companions,
will no longer suffer the legitimate wives to usurp rights
they no longer possess and which they ought never to have
had at all. Let the decree be modified. All for the free
women, none for the slaves! " [1]

The honest women of the people took no part in these
revolting scenes; indeed the " Ladies of the Market "
showed themselves some of the most determined opponents of disorder.[2] In the poor streets of Paris respect for
religion still held sway, and women wept to see their
children's coffins lowered into the grave without a prayer.
There are mothers, writes our English contemporary,

[1] Leighton, *op. cit.* p. 282.   [2] *Paris brûlé*, p. 208.

" quite unworthy of course to bear the children of patriots, who do not want their dear ones to be buried like dogs; who cannot understand that to pray is a crime, and to kneel down before God an offence to humanity, and who are still weak enough to wish to see a cross planted on the tombs of those they have loved and lost! Not the cross of the nineteenth century — a red flag! " [1]

This attitude on the part of the people of Paris naturally proved exasperating to the makers of World Revolution. Bakunin, like his prototype Marat, despaired of them altogether.

" The cause is lost," he wrote from Locarno, on the 9th of April; " it seems that the French, the working-class itself, are not much moved by this state of things. Yet how terrible the lesson is! But it is not enough. They must have greater calamities, ruder shocks. Everything makes one foresee that neither one nor the other will be wanting. And then perhaps the demon will awake. But as long as it slumbers we can do nothing. It would really be a pity to have to pay for the broken glasses, it would in fact be quite useless. Our task is to do the preparatory work, to organize and spread out so as to hold ourselves in readiness when the demon shall have awoken." [2]

But as far as the true people of Paris were concerned the demon never did awake, and it was a gang of foreign adventurers, " the most horrible horde that ever invaded civilization," [3] which carried out the pillage and burnings, the outrages and murders that followed on each other throughout those dreadful three days of May

Bakunin's claim to responsibility in these happenings finds confirmation in the words of Fribourg, one of the original founders of the Internationale: " Personally we firmly believe that the decrees of spoliation, the arbitrary arrests, the shooting of the hostages, and the systematic incendiarism of the capital are the work of the Russo-German party." [4] In other words, they were the work of German Illuminism and of its development in the Alliance Sociale Démocratique.

[1] Leighton, p. 117. Note adds: " Early in April the Commune forbade divine service in the Panthéon. They cut off the arms of the cross, and replaced it by the red flag during a salute of artillery."

[2] *Correspondance de Bakounine*, p. 350.   [3] *Paris brûlé*, p. 28.

[4] Fribourg, *L'Association Internationale des Travailleurs*, p. 143.

The prelude to this final stage of the revolution was the entry of the Versailles troops into Paris, five days after the destruction of the Colonne Vendôme. On the 16th of May the famous monument, erected in honour of French victories and now declared to be an insult to the principle of Internationalism, had been overthrown by order of the Commune — influenced, it was said, by Prussian gold [1] — whilst German officers looked on, rejoicing.[2] This outrage to the national traditions of France infuriated the army of Versailles, which had been recently reinforced by returned prisoners from Germany, and on the 21st of May an entry was made to the capital through the Porte de Saint-Cloud. The " bloody week " of street fighting followed. By the third day the Versailles troops had reached the approaches to the Tuileries, and it was then that the generals of the Commune, Brunel and Bergeret, set fire to the palace and the Rue Royale.

Once again the idea of war on cities, that had originated with Weishaupt, that had been carried out by the Terrorists of 1793 and revived by the Nihilists who had advocated the burning of towns, was put into practice with terrible effect. Amongst the dregs of the populace, wretched, drink-sodden old women, degenerate boys, armed with paraffin, set out to burn down Paris.[3] The plan had evidently long been premeditated in Germany; eight months before that terrible night of May 23, a cartoon had appeared in the shop windows of German towns depicting Paris in flames, with Germania above triumphant, and, beneath, the words: " Gefallen, gefallen ist Babylon die Stolze " (Babylon the mighty is fallen, is fallen!)[4]

Nearly a hundred years earlier, Weishaupt, the archenemy of civilization, had declared, " The day of conflagration will come!" Now it had come, and Paris, once the centre of the world's civilization, was to be burnt to the ground.

It cannot be doubted that the total destruction of the

[1] Heckethorn's *Secret Societies*, ii. 253.
[2] Bonnechose, *Histoire de France*, ii. 729.
[3] Heckethorn's *Secret Societies*, ii. 258, 262; Leighton, *op. cit.* p. 339.
[4] This cartoon is reproduced in *Le Fond de la société sous la Commune*, by C. A. Dauban.

city was desired by the enemies of France, and if this plan was not realized the havoc worked was terrible enough. The Palace of the Tuileries reduced to ashes, the Ministry of Finances, the Palace of the Legion of Honour, the Palais de Justice, the Hôtel de Ville with its treasures of art and priceless national archives—in a word the glory of old France lost to the world for ever — numerous houses in the Rue de Bac, the Rue de Lille, the Rue Royale, turned into rows of blackened ruins; and so little did the incendiaries concern themselves with the cause of the people that the Bureau de l'Assistance Publique, that existed solely to relieve distress, besides several houses belonging to it, of which the revenues belonged to the poor, were consumed by the flames. The granaries containing corn, wine, oil, and other provisions destined to relieve the sufferings of Paris famished by the siege shared a like fate.[1]

On the evening of the following day the horrible massacring of hostages was carried out. Six victims, including the Archbishop of Paris and four other priests who had been imprisoned seven weeks earlier, were shot down [2] in cold blood at the prison of La Roquette; in vain the poor women of the district with tears and cries besought for the life of their pastor the aged Abbé Deguerry, curé of La Madeleine; the massacrers, faithful to the traditions of September 1792, dragged him to his death amidst the curses and invectives of his parishioners.[3] All died with the courage of their eighteenth century predecessors in martyrdom. At the last moment the Archbishop, hearing the word liberty uttered by one of his murderers, said with dignity, " Do not pronounce that word of liberty; it belongs only to us who die for liberty and faith."[4]

As in September 1792, men of the people were not spared, and on the 27th of May a general massacre of the prisoners, including 66 gendarmes, took place. Amongst these was an unfortunate man, the father of eight children, accused of having stolen the blouse and blue trousers he wore, who met with a fearful death at the hands of a mob led by a revolutionary Amazon armed with a *chassepot*.[5]

---

[1] *Paris brûlé*, p. 203.   [2] Bonnechose, *op. cit.* ii. 733.
[3] Beaumont Vassy, *La Commune de Paris*, p. 118.
[4] Bonnechose, ii. 733.   [5] Leighton, *op. cit.* p. 327.

But the plan of the Illuminati for the destruction of civilization was once more frustrated. Civilization had risen in self-defence as civilization will always rise, and the fiercer the onslaught the more furious will be the reaction. When the struggle between the revolutionary army of the Commune and the forces of law and order had ended in a victory for the latter, thousands of victims strewed the streets of Paris; according to Prince Kropotkine, no less than 30,000 men, women, and children perished in the fray. But what were these to the Anarchists who, according to Marx, regarded the people as " cannon fodder " (*chair à canon*) on the day of revolution? [1]

So ended the third experiment in revolutionary government carried out on unhappy France. Even Mr. Adolphe Smith, who had hoped great things of the Commune admits its incompetence. Sanguine revolutionists after 1871, he writes, " began to realize the innate weakness of mere theories divorced from administrative capacity."

They saw that even when in possession of one of the fairest cities of Europe — with the bank of France in their hands, an enthusiastic army at their command, weapons and munitions of war innumerable — while the country was disorganized, the regular army flying in terror before the insurrection for it could not rely upon its own soldiers — still the Commune, though so strong and successful, was unable to accomplish anything. The leaders frittered away the precious moments for action in futile discussions and squabbles, till the reaction, gathering strength, organized its scattered forces and crushed them. The similitude of this with the position of Petrograd before and after the Bolsheviks seized the reins of government will not fail to be noticed by every observer. [2]

Yet in spite of its ghastly fiasco the régime of the Commune met with unanimous applause from the Internationale; at Zürich, Geneva, Brussels, Leipzig, members vied with each other in extolling the bloody deeds committed during those terrible months of March to May. An English Internationalist declared that "' the good time was really coming," and that " soon we shall be able to dethrone the Queen of England, turn Buckingham Palace

[1] *L'Alliance Sociale Démocratique*, p. 15.
[2] Unpublished work by Mr. Adolphe Smith entitled *The Betrayal of the International*.

into a workshop and pull down the York Column as the noble French people had pulled down the Vendôme column." [1]

Bakunin, who now apparently considered that the demon had awoken, admiringly described the French proletariat as " the modern Satan, the author of the sublime insurrection of the Commune." [2]

Marx, not to be left out of the movement, which in reality had, in its negation of the State, been conducted on principles opposed to his avowed opinions, now published a panegyric of the Commune entitled *The Civil War in France*, in which he referred to the State as " that parasite which exploits and hinders the free movements of society." How are we to reconcile this with Marx's advocacy of State Socialism? [3]

Guillaume, commenting on Marx's sudden *volte-face*, asks whether he had really become converted to the principles of federalism, and quotes Bakunin as declaring that the power of the Commune had proved so formidable that even the Marxians had been obliged to take off their hats to it. But the measure of Marx's sincerity in writing his panegyric of the Commune was revealed later when his correspondence with his friend Sorge was published in 1906. It seems that at the end of 1871 several refugees of the Commune who had fled to London and Geneva refused to obey his commands. Thereupon Marx wrote to Sorge:

And that is my reward for having wasted nearly five months working for the refugees, and for *having saved their honour* by the publication of the Address on the Civil War. [4]

Thus Marx, with his superb talent for using everything that could serve his purpose, turned the anarchic régime of the Commune to account. But now the moment had come to suppress that dynamic force which threatened his supremacy and to concentrate his attention on the Anarchists of the Internationale.

[1] Heckethorn's *Secret Societies*, ii. 252.
[2] Guillaume, *Documents*, ii. 253.
[3] First formulated in his *Communist Manifesto:* " to centralize all instruments of production in the hands of the State."
[4] Guillaume, *Documents*, ii. 192.

ANARCHY v. SOCIALISM

The years that followed on the revolution of 1871 were mainly occupied by the struggle between the two groups represented by Marx and Bakunin.

Until this date the words " Anarchy " and " Anarchist," though claimed by Proudhon and Bakunin, were seldom used, and the word " Socialist " was employed to cover both the warring factions. But from 1871 onwards we find the rival camps ranging themselves definitely beneath their opposing standards, and Socialism more and more becoming the label of the Marxists. The difference between the aims of the two creeds has thus been clearly defined by Malon: [1]

The State Socialism of Marx was comprised in the conquest of political power, that is to say of the State, by the working-class which has for its historic mission to put an end to the class war by the abolition of classes, and to the present economic miseries and contradictions by " the nationalization of production and distribution of wealth."

Bakunin, on his part, summed up his programme in these words:

Abolition of the State in all its religious, juristic, political, and social realizations; reorganization by the free initiative of free individuals in free groups. It was this formula that became later that of Anarchy.

And we might add, still later, that of Syndicalism. So the old antagonism between Liberty and Equality flamed out afresh in the great struggle between Marx and Bakunin which was to rend the Internationale in twain. Thus Bakunin, referring to the State Socialism of the Marxists, vehemently declared it to be " the vilest and the most formidable lie which our century has engendered — the official democratism and the *red bureaucracy*." [2] " I abominate Communism," he had declared to the Peace Congress at Berne in 1869, " because it is a denial of freedom and I cannot understand anything human without freedom." [3] On the other hand, Maurice Hess, the Marxian, had pointed out that between the Collectivists

[1] Article on the Internationale in *La Nouvelle Revue*, xxvi. 753.
[2] *Correspondance de Bakounine*, p. 219.
[3] E. V. Zenker, *Anarchism* (Eng. trans., 1898), p. 148.

and the Anarchists of the Internationale " there was all the difference which exists between civilization and barbarism, between liberty and despotism, between citizens condemning every form of violence and slaves addicted to the use of brutal force." [1]

It was not, however, only the bureaucracy of the Marxians that roused the wrath of Bakunin, but their pan-Germanism, which since 1870 had become more and more apparent. " The dream of the Socialists who swear by the head of Marx," he wrote to *La Liberté* of Brussels in 1872, " is the German hegemony, is German omnipotence (*la toute puissance germanique*), at first intellectual and moral, and later on material." [2]

But it was the Marxians who began the attack.

Already in the spring of 1871 Marx, Outine, Hess, Licbknecht, Bebel, in a word all the Germans and German-Jews of the Internationale,[3] displayed less concern over the régime of the Commune than over their own war on the Alliance Sociale Démocratique. To turn Bakunin and his followers out of the Internationale and remain himself in possession of the field now became the great aim of the man whom his Jewish disciples were fond of referring to as " the modern Moses." [4]

Fortunately for Marx a pretext was provided by the discovery that Netchaïeff, Bakunin's former ally, had been guilty of fraud, and at the Congress of the Internationale in London in 1871 the General Council, led by Marx took the resolution to make an inquiry into the participation of Bakunin and the Alliance Sociale Démocratique in the Affaire Netchaïeff. The Jew Nicholas Outine was ordered to draw up the report. Outine, who throughout acted consistently as the " acolyte of Marx," had already made an attempt to eject the Alliance from the Internationale

---

[1] *Oeuvres de Bakounine*, v. 223.   [2] iv. *Ibid*. 341.

[3] Guillaume, referring to the Jews in the Internationale, enumerates as the most important Marx, Outine, Maurice Hess, Borkheim, the editor of the *Zukunft*, a Socialist paper entirely controlled by Jews, Hepner, editor of the *Volksstaat*, and Frankel, member of the Paris Commune. Guillaume adds: " Calumniated and vilified by a pack of intriguers, we have been obliged to state that some of the most violent (*les plus acharnés contre nous*) were German and Russian Jews who seemed to hold together by a sort of *esprit de corps* " (*Documents de l'Internationale*, ii. 157 note).

[4] Guillaume, *Documents*, ii. 297.

by a ruse. At a meeting of the Geneva sections of the association that same spring, he and his allies had declared that the Alliance had never been received into the Internationale at all, and when in reply to this statement the secretary of the Alliance produced the original letters signed by Eccarius and Jung in the name of the Internationale announcing that the General Council had admitted the Alliance on the 25th of August 1869, Outine calmly replied that the letters were forgeries and brought forward a Russian Jewess, Mme. Dmitrieff, who had just arrived from London, in support of this assertion.[1]

A conference was finally arranged between the two factions on the 25th of July, 1871, at which Jung himself presided and Marx and Engels were present. The documents were again produced, and this time Jung was obliged to confess that he had signed the second, whilst Engels, after a quarter of an hour of prevarications, mumbled that it was impossible to deny either of the letters. As to Marx, Guillaume observes: " The great man, usually so sure of himself in the midst of his courtiers, was dumbfounded. He was caught in the *flagrant délit* of a lie and his act was authentically proved." [2]

Marx afterwards retaliated by accusing Bakunin of duplicity, declaring that in 1869 he had believed the Alliance to have been dissolved whilst in reality it continued to work in secret, and that " by means of this freemasonry its existence was not even suspected by the great mass of the Internationals." [3]

It is impossible to disentangle the truth from all this web of lying and intrigue; both sides had, as we know, accepted the doctrine that the end justifies the means, and both lied freely to obtain the mastery. Suffice it then to say that finally, at the Hague Congress of the Internationale held in 1872, the London General Council— " by a fictitious majority," says Prince Kropotkine — excluded the Bakuninists and the Jura Federation they had formed from the Internationale. The latter now moved its headquarters to New York and four years later

---

[1] Guillaume *Documents*, ii. 157.   [2] *Ibid*. ii. 176, 177.
[3] *L'Alliance Sociale Démocratique.*

quietly expired at Philadelphia. So ended the great association which for twelve years had spread terror throughout Europe. Long before its death the working-men had lost all faith in it, and the engineers of Brussels, led by it into an abortive strike, had denounced it as " the leprosy of Europe " and " the Company of Millionaires on paper."[1]

As a means for ameliorating the conditions of Labour it had proved from 1864 a fraud, as a barrier against international conflicts it had proved its futility in 1870, throughout its whole career it had existed merely as a hotbed of intrigue — mainly pan-German — and all its protestations of fraternity had led only to the old conflict between the rival forces of revolution. The inner history of the Internationale, like the history of all revolutionary organizations from the Terror onwards, is simply a series of petty rivalries and of miserable quarrels between the leaders, conducted without the faintest regard for the interests of the people whom such demagogues profess to represent. Readers have merely to glance through the voluminous *Documents de l'Internationale* by James Guillaume (4 vols. 1907), the best official record of the proceedings of the society, to convince themselves of the truth of this assertion. Further light has been thrown on the Marxian intrigues by Guillaume's recent brochure *Karl Marx, pan-Germaniste* (Armand Colin, 1915), and by Edmond Laskine's admirable work, *L'Internationale et le pan-Germanisme* (Floury, 1916). In France, therefore, the Marxian legend has been completely shattered, and it is doubtless owing to the fact that none of these books have been translated into English that a belief in Marx still survives in this country. Mr. Adolphe Smith's very valuable pamphlet is the only English work of this kind known to the present writer, and it should be scattered broadcast through the land.[2]

On the other hand, the Marxians' accusations against

[1] Heckethorn's *Secret Societies*, ii. 235.

[2] *The Pan-German Internationale*, articles by Adolphe Smith, Official Anglo-French Interpreter from 1882 at the Congresses of the Internationale. Reprinted from the *Times*, price 3d. Copies may be obtained from Adolphe Smith, 17 Scarsdale Terrace, Kensington, W.8. It is regrettable that Mr. Smith's larger work, *The Betrayal of the Internationale*, of which he has kindly allowed me to make use, has not yet been published.

the Anarchists may be read in the pamphlet *L'Alliance Sociale Démocratique*, published by order of the Congress of La Haye in 1873; the first part written by Engels and Lafargue, the conclusion by Marx and Engels with " the object of killing Bakunin dead (*le tuer raide mort*)." [1]

After perusing the case for both sides in this final dispute it is impossible to retain any illusions on the character of either Marx or his opponent; we need not, therefore, have recourse to anti-Socialist literature in order to realize to the full the perfidy and hypocrisy of that bogus company that called itself " The International Association of Working Men."

[1] Guillaume, *Documents*, iii. 148.

CHAPTER VIII

THE COURSE OF ANARCHY

Nihilism in Russia — Murder of Alexander II. — The revived Illuminati — Johann Most — Revolutionary Congress in London — Anarchist outrages in Western Europe — Fenianism — British Socialism.

ALTHOUGH Anarchy had been vanquished in the Internationale, it was Anarchy not State Socialism that after the revolution of 1871 obtained control of the revolutionary movement. Revolts against the Marxian autocracy of the Internationale— " the Marxist synagogue "[1] as Bakunin described it — broke out in Italy, Spain, Belgium, and in the Jura Federation that had been organized by the expelled Anarchists.[2]

But it was in Russia that Anarchy found its natural home, where the ground had been prepared by the propaganda of the Nihilists carried on indefatigably since the early 'sixties. Romantic Russian writers are anxious to make us believe that *Nihilism* — of which the name first appears in Turghenieff's novel, *Fathers and Sons*, in 1861 — was some kind of mystic creed indigenous to Russia, but to the readers of this book the tenets of the Nihilists will seem strangely familiar. Thus, for example, Bazaroff, the hero of Turghenieff's romance, explains that " it is necessary above all to clear the ground. Later, when all institutions have been destroyed, when a *tabula rasa* is complete, then existing forces, then humanity will crystallize again in new institutions which will no doubt be appropriate to surrounding conditions." The words have a reminiscent echo of Rabaud de St. Etienne's: " Every-

---

[1] Ettore Zoccoli, *L'Anarchia*, p. 116.
[2] Kropotkine, *Modern Science and Anarchism*, pp. 43, 62.

221

thing, yes, everything must be destroyed, since everything must be remade."

The Nihilist, Prince Kropotkine informs us, " declared war upon what may be described as ' the conventional lies of civilized mankind ' . . . he refused to bow before any authority except that of reason. . . ." Accordingly he " broke, of course, with the superstitions of his fathers " with regard to religion, whilst in the matter of social relations " he assumed a certain external roughness " — as a protest against conventional politeness. " Art was involved in the same sweeping negation," the Nihilist's attitude being expressed in the words: " A pair of boots is more important than all your Madonnas and all your refined talk about Shakespeare." [1]

The " equality of the sexes " was a fundamental doctrine of Nihilism which, as the Père Deschamps points out, is only another expression for the destruction of family life.[2] " According to the Nihilists, men and women live together in little groups where all is in common. In order to be wholly independent the woman must herself provide her livelihood." Maternity being an inequality of nature, " the Nihilist woman therefore willingly abandons " her offspring.[3]

Above all, of course, religion must be destroyed, and Stepniak admiringly describes the campaign carried on by the band of enthusiastic propagandists who preached materialism throughout Russia both in speech and print. "Atheism excited people like a new religion. The zealous went about, like veritable missionaries, in search of living souls, in order to cleanse them from the abomination of Christianity." [4]

Had not Anacharsis Clootz done likewise up to the very foot of the scaffold? What indeed is there in all this but the resuscitated plan of Illuminism? Père Deschamps' suggestion that Nihilism was simply the Eastern branch of Bakunin's Alliance Sociale Démocratique modelled on Weishaupt's Order, goes less to the root of the matter

[1] Kropotkine, *Memoirs of a Revolutionary*, ii. 86, 88.
[2] Deschamps, ii. 574.
[3] Fribourg, *L'Association Internationale des Travailleurs*, p. 184.
[4] Stepniak, *Underground Russia*, p. 5.

than his further explanation that the youthful philosophers of Russia had gone to the fountain-head by studying at German universities. Turghenieff himself had spent three years in Berlin reading Hegelian philosophy. It was therefore directly from Germany that Illuminism under its new name of Nihilism travelled to Russia. The very name itself had been foretold by Joseph de Maistre in the first years of the century when he declared that the doctrines of Illuminism would lead men to become "rienistes." [1]

Yet if the seed was not indigenous to Russia the soil was peculiarly adapted to its growth. The theory that "civilization is all wrong," however preposterous when applied to Western Europe, had something to commend it in the case of Russia. There civilization, consisting in a foreign veneer hastily applied to a rude natural surface, might appear even to non-anarchic minds "all wrong" — a process that needed redoing from the outset.

Civilization to be of any value must be necessarily of slow growth, must moreover begin at the bottom — in the hearts not in the manners of the people. England had her Alfred the Great, her Richard Cœur de Lion; France her Saint Louis and her Henry IV. These and other great founders of their civilizations had implanted deep down in the life of each nation those principles of humanity and compassion, of honour and of justice which in the latter country even the Revolution could not entirely eradicate.

Russia had never known these early influences; founded on Tartar instead of Roman ideas, she had remained sunk in barbarism until Peter the Great began his veneering process which, applied to the rude surface of Russian life, resulted in a form of culture both premature and unnatural. To change the simile, such civilization as Russia had attained in the nineteenth century was not the natural growth of the soil; it was a German civilization wholly foreign to the "genius" of her people. There was much that was good and wholesome in the life of the Russian peasants. De Custine declared that it was worth coming to Russia if only to see "the pure image of patriarchal

[1] Deschamps, ii. 586.

society " and the " celestial faces " of the old peasants
seated with dignity at the end of the day before the
threshold of their cottages.[1] " One must go into the inte-
rior of Russia to know what primitive man was worth and
all that the refinements of society have made him lose.
I have said and I repeat it . . . in this patriarchal
country, it is civilization that spoils man." [2]

It is easy then to understand how the " illuminated "
doctrine of a return to Nature might find an echo in the
least anarchic minds when applied to Russia, and if it had
been only this foreign and artificial civilization the Nihilists had set out to destroy, who could have blamed them?
If, further, they had had anything better to offer in its
place, who could have failed to applaud them? But the
tragedy of Russia is never to have been allowed to
develop along her own national lines; she had been made
by the Romanovs to imitate Western civilization, now she
was to be taught by the revolutionaries to imitate Western
methods of overthrowing it. Bakunin had raged against
German Petersbourgeois Imperialism (cet impérialisme
pétersbourgeois allemand), and it was German Illuminism
his followers brought to Russia in its stead. The tendency
to anarchy latent in the Russian nature, as exemplified in
the Baron Ungern von Sternberg, was to be exploited in
the interests of World Revolution. For, in spite of the
serenity described by de Custine as characteristic of the
Russian peasant in his normal moments, he responds only
too readily to suggestions of violence. And when we
consider this peculiarity, when we remember the tendency
to drunkenness and to brutality that underlies his surface
impassiveness we realize the fearful danger of taking
from him the only restraints he knew — respect for God
and the Czar.

Was the Imperial Government, then, to tolerate the
campaign of insubordination and of militant atheism conducted by the Nihilists from 1866 onwards?

Can it be seriously maintained that any government
would have been doing its duty if it had not protected
the simple peasantry from these disintegrating doctrines?

[1] La Russie en 1839, iv. 9, 10.   [2] Ibid. iv. 97.

What could it do but arrest, imprison, exile, and suppress by all means in its power the germ-carriers who would have infected the whole life of the people? If the methods adopted resembled those of Eastern potentates rather than those of our own enlightened legislators, it must be remembered that the rulers of Russia can no more than their subjects be judged by Western standards. Moreover, without condoning the brutality of the repression exercised, it must be recognized that a *revers du médaillon* exists.

Let us put ourselves in the place of Nicholas I., who has been persistently represented as an intractible autocrat. Ascending the throne with the warning of the French Revolution ringing in his ears, he found himself immediately confronted by the Dekabrist outbreak, obviously engineered by secret forces — an experience that left a deep impression on his mind. Yet, in spite of this, have we not seen him visiting Robert Owen at New Lanark, and in 1839 receiving deputations of serfs begging to be transferred to the royal domains, assuring them, moreover, of his desire for their emancipation — alas, with what fatal results! No wonder, then, that we find him declaring: " Despotism exists in Russia since it is the essence of my government, but it is in accord with the genius of the nation." [1] Three hundred years earlier the Austrian ambassador to Moscow had asked whether it was the character of the Russian nation that had made autocrats, or autocrats that had made the character of the Russian nation,[2] and de Custine, echoing the question in 1839, gives as his opinion: " If the iron rod that directs this still brutalized people were to cease for an instant to weigh on it, the whole of society would be overthrown." [3]

We have only to study the history of Russia throughout the nineteenth century to realize that every step towards reform became the signal for a fresh outbreak of revolutionary agitation. The Nihilist movement followed directly on the era of reform inaugurated by Alexander II. The emancipation of the serfs in 1861 did nothing to allay agitation, and if, as we are assured, the measure failed to

---

[1] de Custine, *La Russie en* 1839, ii. 46.
[2] *Ibid.* i. 241.　　　　　　　　　　　[3] *Ibid.* ii. 217.

satisfy the peasants we must at least recognize the sincerity of the Emperor's intentions. To turn against him at this juncture was naturally to drive him into reaction and to arrest the whole movement of reform.

It cannot be too often repeated — violence begets violence; and if we are to see in Nihilism the outcome of repression, as truly must we recognize in so-called " Czarism " the result of agitation. The revolutionaries plotted secretly against the State, and the State defended itself by the secret methods of " the Third Section " ; the authorities forbade the circulation of seditious pamphlets, and the traffickers in forbidden literature redoubled their efforts to smuggle it into the country; each side pitted its wits against the other, and thus the vicious circle once created could not be arrested.

It was not, however, until after 1871 that the Russian revolutionary movement entered on its violent phases. The example of the Paris Commune then spread eastwards, and the revolutionaries, no longer known as Nihilists but as " Revolutionary Socialists," embarked on the series of outrages which marked the years 1873–1881.

Much has been written about the heroism, the self-sacrifice, the burning enthusiasm of the " Tchaikovsky Circle " that was inaugurated toward the end of 1872 at St. Petersburg with ramifications at Moscow and other large towns of Russia. This little band of propagandists that consisted solely of upper-and middle-class intellectuals certainly showed themselves capable of great courage and endurance when the movement passed from words to deeds, but at the outset it is evident, from the accounts given by the members themselves, that they derived no small amount of enjoyment from the novelty and excitement the new life provided.

One must know something of the Russian character from personal experience to understand this; to the Russian, intrigue, particularly of the political variety, is as the breath of life, and we have already seen how to Bakunin the preparing of revolution — the secret signs and codes, chemical inks, all-night discussions over tea and cigarettes — afforded a joy incomprehensible to the

Western mind. More especially was this passion to be found in the young women of the country who hitherto had exercised in the service of the Czars their talent for secret political intrigue; Catherine the Great had made great use of these " Northern Aspasias " acting as her unofficial ambassadors and spies, and under Nicholas I. the same " organized feminine diplomacy " was continued by " political Amazons " whose passion for meddling in affairs of State absorbed them to the exclusion of all other matters — even love.

It is easy to understand that to women of this type the revolutionary movement should have offered a career even more enticing; to the delights of intrigue were added the charm of novelty and the excitement provided by an element of danger. The young Russian girls with cropped hair, dressed in boyish garments, who crowded to Zürich as students —medical or otherwise— could enjoy all the sensation of an adventure, and on their return to Russia thousands of men and women students went to live in towns and villages to carry on Socialistic propaganda amongst the workers. To the young, the strong, and the adventurous this kind of life may well have proved congenial; indeed in Prince Kropotkine's own account of his adventures as a member of the Tchaikovsky Circle we cannot fail to detect an afterglow of exhilaration. Throwing a peasant's shirt and coat over his silk undergarments this aristocratic anarchist would slip out of the Winter Palace at night and betake himself to the slums of St. Petersburg where meetings of the workers were held.

To play at being peasants has frequently proved a pastime to jaded aristocracy, and Kropotkine, masquerading as " Borodin " in a sheepskin, consulted as an oracle by the other sheepskins, evidently found these evenings more entertaining than the dreary formalities of St. Petersburg society.

Peter Kropotkine, who may be regarded as the milder type of visionary anarchist, was born in 1842 at Moscow. Although a follower and an ardent admirer of Bakunin, Kropotkine in his private life showed himself greatly superior to his master. Unlike Bakunin he was a worker, though not in the sense he implied in his writings. To identify himself with the " proletariat " in such phrases as " *we* shall succeed in getting *our* rights respected " is of course the purest affectation. Kropotkine, who had never worked with his hands but only with his brain, was essentially an aristocrat of the same variety as the aristocrats of France who before 1789 loved to dilate on the necessity of destroying the existing order. The keynote of all Kropotkine's writings is unreality, never does he at any point come to grips with life, and it is here he differs from Bakunin. The " Russian giant "was a realist, and in advocating revolution he knew perfectly well what revolution meant— violence, bloodshed, confusion, chaos — all things in which his soul delighted. On human nature, as we have seen, he entertained no illusions, and it was for criminals that he expressed his warmest sympathy. Kropotkine, less practical, or perhaps less honest, expressed a boundless belief in human nature; a disciple of Rousseau as well as of Weishaupt, he held that " the inequality of fortunes and conditions, the exploitation of man by man, the domination of the masses by a few, had in the course of ages undermined and destroyed the precious products of the primitive life of society " [1] — a passage that might well seem to be taken verbatim from the famous essay on " l'Inégalité des Conditions."

With the same wild disregard for truth Kropotkine echoes Rousseau's panegyrics on the happiness and benevolence of savages,[2] " the fraternity and solidarity " that distinguishes tribal life, " the hospitality of primitive peoples, their respect for human life, compassion for the weak," and personal self-sacrifice. Arriving inevitably at the same conclusions as Weishaupt, Kropotkine argues that human nature being so inherently benign, all restraint should be removed, all law and government abolished, even murderers should go unpunished and criminals should " be soothed with fraternal care." [3] So identical are many of these theories with those of Weishaupt that it is impossible not to believe that, like Bakunin, he had fallen under

[1] Kropotkine, *Paroles d'un révolté*, p. 19.
[2] *Les Temps nouveaux*, p. 21.
[3] *Paroles d'un révolté*, pp. 223, 242, 244.

the spell of Illuminism and was consciously working for the sect that had as its object the " universal revolution which should deal the death-blow to society."

The connection between all the succeeding disciples of Weishaupt can only be established by comparing their writings, when it will become evident that passages so closely resembling each other cannot be attributed to mere coincidence, and the main ideas of World Revolution will be seen to descend in unbroken sequence from one revolutionary group to another. Indeed Kropotkine himself informs us that between the " Alliance Sociale Démocratique " of Bakunin and the secret societies of 1795 there was " a direct affiliation." [1] If, then, Nihilism was working in conjunction with Bakunin's association — and we cannot doubt it — it is easy to see how the theories of the Philadelphes percolated to the Tchaikovsky Circle.

It is thus that in Kropotkine's *Paroles d'un révolté*, where more than in any other of his writings his programme of revolution is set forth, we seem to hear again the voice of that earlier Illuminatus Gracchus Babeuf, member of the Philadelphes and continuer of the plan of Weishaupt. Although not a Communist like Babeuf, Kropotkine advocates, for example, the same system of trade by barter. " Do you wish tools and machinery?" he asks the peasants; " you will come to an understanding with the workers of the towns, who will send them to you in exchange for your products " [2] and we are seriously asked to imagine life conducted by means of this continual weighing up of values — the peasant requiring a scythe despatching to the town a sitting of turkeys' eggs, and the worth being deemed insufficient, receiving in exchange a chisel — which he does not happen to want!

Not merely in puerilities such as these does Kropotkine continue the tradition of Babeuf, but also in the organization of the coming revolution. Babeuf, it will be remembered, was the first to preach the " great day of the people " — the day whereon the maddened multitude should fling itself upon all wealth and property as the

[1] Kropotkine, *The Great French Revolution*, p. 580.
[2] *Paroles d'un révolté*, p. 166.

preliminary to Communism. This simple and expeditious method, long since abandoned by the Communists in favour of the gradual acquisition of political power, was now revived by the Anarchists with the object of inaugurating their rival system, and thus in his chapter on " Expropriation " we find Kropotkine reproducing almost verbatim the old programme of Babeuf.

" General expropriation alone," writes Kropotkine, " can satisfy the multitude of sufferers and oppressed. From the domain of theory they must be made to enter that of practice. But in order that expropriation should answer to its principle, which is to suppress all private property and to give back all to all, it must be accomplished on a vast scale. On a small scale we should see nothing but vulgar pillage; on a large one it is the beginning of social reorganization." [1]

But although Bakunin had declared that " robbery was one of the most honourable forms of Russian national life," and that " he who does not understand robbery can understand nothing in the history of the Russian masses," [2] it appears that the plan of laying violent hands on all property was one to which the people could not be expected yet to rise: " It would be a fatal error," Kropotkine observes regretfully, " to believe that the idea of expropriation has yet penetrated into the minds of all the workers and become one of those convictions for which an upright man is ready to sacrifice his life. Far from it !" [3] And he goes on to explain the necessity of educating the people up to this sublime ideal.

In order to persuade the Russian peasants to emulate those of France in the preceding century by seizing social riches, " we " — Revolutionary Socialists — he writes, " must work incessantly from this moment to disseminate the idea of expropriation by all our words and all our acts. . . . Let the word ' expropriation ' penetrate into every *commune* of the country, let it be discussed in every village, and become, for every workman and every peasant, an integral part of the word Anarchy, and then, only then,

---

[1] *Paroles d'un révolté*, p. 337.
[2] *Words addressed to Students*, by Bakunin and Netchaieff (1869).
[3] *Paroles d'un révolté*, p. 320.'

we shall be sure that on the day of the Revolution it will be on all lips, that it will rise formidable, backed by the whole people, and that the blood of the people will not have flowed in vain." [1]

Kropotkine's idol Marat himself could not have written a more direct incentive to violence, and when we consider that he was one of the leading members of the Tchaikovsky Circle, and that this was the kind of propaganda the band of heroic " missionaries " was engaged in carrying out amongst the people from 1872 onwards, we cannot wonder that the Government again saw fit to intervene.

Thirty-seven provinces, a Government circular declared, had been " infected "by the Socialist contagion,[2] and in 1878 wholesale arrests were ordered. Then the vicious circle began again: a propagandist, Boguljuboff, was knouted by the police, and a woman revolutionary Vera Sassulitch, retaliated by attempting to shoot Trepoff, the Prefect of Police in St. Petersburg; Sassulitch was acquitted, but Kowalsky, the leader of a band of revolutionaries in Odessa, was shot, and in revenge Mesentseff, head of the Third Section, was murdered by Kravchinsky (alias Stepniak) on the Nevsky Prospect.

Then followed a series of attempts on the life of Alexander II.: in September 1879 the conspirators, led by Sophie Perovskaia and Leo Hartmann, formed a plan to blow up the Imperial train just outside Moscow, but only succeeded in destroying a train which did not contain the Emperor; in the following year two other Terrorists, Halturin and Scheliaboff, succeeded in exploding a charge of dynamite beneath the dining-room of the Winter Palace, but again the Emperor escaped without injury.

Meanwhile Alexander II., with a newly appointed minister, Count Loris Melikoff, continued to work out plans for reform. Melikoff, whatever his shortcomings might be,was a man of far more liberal tendencies than his predecessors, and indeed we find a Finnish writer declaring that " some of the measures adopted by him should have shown to every thoughtful person that he was planning

---

[1] *Paroles d'un révolté*, p. 322.
[2] Stepniak, *Underground Russia*, p. 28.

the introduction of far-reaching reforms which might perhaps have led to the regeneration of Russia." [1] Whether this is so or not it is certain that Loris Melikoff was largely instrumental in deciding the Emperor to convoke an advisory assembly on the question of reforms, and, more important, it was Melikoff who finally on the 2nd of March 1881 laid before him the plan of a constitution.

Are we to believe that, as has been already suggested, the word " Constitution " was the rallying cry of the secret societies? We have seen that in the French Revolution both the framing of the Constitution in 1789 and its acceptance by the king in 1791 became the signals for fresh outbreaks of revolutionary fury; we have seen the Dekabrist outbreak of 1825 in Russia led by the same war-cry, and now again in Russia of 1881 the same strange phenomenon occurs.

No sooner had Melikoff embarked on his career of reforms than an attempt had been made to murder him, and on the very day that Alexander II. signed the Constitution he was cut down by the hand of an assassin.

Even Prince Kropotkine is obliged to recognize the Emperor's courage and noble self-sacrifice at that supreme moment when, at a signal from Sophie Petrovskaia, a bomb was thrown at the Imperial carriage as it passed along the road by the Catherine Canal; only the mounted Cossacks surrounding it received any injuries, and the coachman urged the Tsar to allow him to drive on out of danger. But Alexander refused to leave his followers to their fate and deliberately went forth to meet his death. As he walked towards the wounded and dying Cossacks lying in the snow beside his carriage a second assassin with inconceivable cowardice threw another bomb, and this time Alexander fell mortally wounded.

The same night the draft of the Constitution bearing the Emperor's signature was torn into a hundred fragments by one of his son's advisers.

So ended for the moment all hope of reform in Russia. Inevitable reaction followed on this dastardly crime. The conspirators — Scheliaboff, Ryssakoff, Sophie Petrov-

[1] *The Revolutionary Movement in Russia*, by Konni Zilliacus, p. 101.

skaia, and two others — were put to death, it is said with fearful cruelty.

But though we must execrate these barbarous methods of retaliation, we must surely admit that brutality was to be found on both sides. If we pity the so-called " martyrs" of Imperial despotism may we not also ask: What pity had these men and woman felt for *their* victims — not only for the " agents of despotism " they set out to destroy, but for the innocent men of the people sacrificed with them? What regard had they shown for human life in their attempts to wreck the Imperial train? What of the engine-driver and other employés involved in the disaster? What of the many people actually killed and wounded in this attempt that miscarried? What of the thirty soldiers on duty who perished in the explosion at the Winter Palace?

Let us pity, then, the "martyrs" whose tortures no circumstances can justify, but let us reserve some pity for those humble and forgotten victims whom no revolutionary writer seems to consider of the slightest consequence.

ANARCHY IN WESTERN EUROPE

In 1878 Western Europe experienced a repercussion of the Russian Terror, and the four leading Anarchists, Kropotkine, Cafiero, Malatesta, and Brousse, organized a worldwide scheme of violence described by them as the " Propaganda of the Deed," which found its first expression in an attempt on the life of King Humbert of Italy. This outrage was followed by two attempts of the same kind directed against the Emperor William I. of Germany. If we are to believe Socialist writers, neither Hödel nor Dr. Karl Nöbiling, who within a month fired at the Emperor in Berlin, had any connection with the Socialist or Anarchist movement, but served simply as a pretext for the anti-Socialist law which Bismarck passed triumphantly at the end of the year. This would be quite in keeping with German Imperial policy, which had always consisted in crushing at home the subversive forces it used so freely abroad, and it is quite possible that a half-witted youth such as Hödel — with photographs of the leading Socialists,

Liebkneckt and Bebel, placed in his pockets by the Berlin police — may have been hired for the deed, — *agents provocateurs* are, of course, a favourite resource of autocratic governments.

Bismarck was thus able to nip in the bud not only Socialism but Anarchy, which in the person of Johann Most threatened to become a danger.

Germany itself, as Zenker observes, " may be termed the most free from Anarchists of any country in Europe." [1] The " genius " of the German people is naturally disinclined to Individualism, and whether in the form of Prussian militarism or of State Socialism always favours mass formation. It was thus by the Social Democrats themselves that Most was finally expelled. It will be noticed that whenever agitators threaten seriously to disturb the peace in Germany they are either summarily suppressed or used for export — preferably to England. Whether in accordance with this plan or on his own initiative Most came to London in 1879, where he organized a society called the " United Socialists," on the principles of Marx's *Communist Manifesto*, and having for its motto the Marxian battle-cry, " Workers of all countries, unite ! " At the same time he founded a secret association under the name of the " Propagandist Club " with a view to preparing " the general revolution." [2]

Yet in London he found an even less fruitful field for his labours than in Berlin. " England, the ancient refuge of political offenders," wrote Zenker in 1895, " although it has sheltered Bakunin, Kropotkine, Reclus, Most, Penkert, Louise Michel, Cafiero, Malatesta, and other Anarchist leaders, and still shelters some of them; although London is rich in Anarchist clubs and newspapers, meetings, and congresses; yet possesses no Anarchism ' native to the soil,' and has formed at all times merely a kind of exchange or market-place for Anarchist ideas, motive forces, and the literature of agitation. London is especially the headquarters of German Anarchism; the English working-classes have, however, always regarded their ideas very

---

[1] E. V. Zenker, *Anarchism* (Eng. trans.), p. 238.
[2] Dr. Zacher, *Die Rothe Internationale*'(1884).

coldly, while the Government have always regarded the eccentric proceedings of the Anarchists, as long as they confined themselves merely to talking or writing, in the most logical spirit of the doctrine of *laisser-faire*." [1] Indeed, so sturdy was the resistance offered by British Labour to Most's doctrines that when he endeavoured to publish his paper *Freedom* no printer could be found to set up the type. Alas! with the spread " of education " (?) such obstacles have long since been removed!

In 1881 Prince Kropotkine visited London and found his reception equally discouraging. At his meetings he was obliged to talk to almost empty benches. Only in the towns of the North were anarchic doctrines met with some degree of enthusiasm. " The year I passed in London," he wrote despondently, " was a year of real exile. For one who held advanced Socialist opinions there was no atmosphere to breathe in. There was no sign of that animated Socialist movement which I found so largely developed on my return in 1886." [2]

What was it that provided the fresh impetus to the plan of World Revolution during those five years? In the past, as we have seen, the secret societies had provided the medium through which it was able to work, and after their absorption by the Internationale the so-called " Working Men's Association " had become the great cover for its activities. But now that the Internationale was dead it became necessary for the secret societies to reorganize, and it is at this crisis that we find that " formidable sect " springing to life again — *the original Illuminati of Weishaupt.*

The facts about this resuscitated order are very difficult to ascertain, for naturally they have been carefully kept from the public, and as in the case of the earlier

[1] *Anarchism*, p. 242. Zenker here displays remarkable discernment with regard to the attitude of the British Government, which is usually incomprehensible to foreigners, the prevalent idea on the Continent (especially in France) being that the tolerance displayed in this country towards alien agitators springs from a profound Machiavellian policy of encouraging subversive ideas for the weakening of rival powers. To the French mind our national naiveté is inconceivable; it cannot believe that we really regard these people as harmless eccentrics whom it would be tyrannical to suppress.

[2] *Memoirs of a Revolutionary*, ii. 251.

Illuminati of 1776 every effort has been made by interested writers to conceal the existence of the society, or, if it must be admitted, to represent it as a perfectly innocuous and unimportant association.

What we do know definitely is that the society was refounded in Dresden in 1880 [1] — not in 1896 as it has been asserted — but it seems that its existence was not discovered until 1899. That it was consciously modelled on its eighteenth-century predecessor is clear from the fact that its chief, one Leopold Engel, was the author of a lengthy panegyric on Weishaupt and his Order, entitled *Geschichte des Illuminaten Ordens* (published in 1906), and in 1903 the original lodge at Ingoldstadt was restored. The official organ of the association from 1893 onwards was *Das Wort*. The society is still in existence and is believed to number adherents not only on the Continent but in our own country.

Of course we shall be assured that this association had no connection with the course of the World Revolution; yet the fact remains that the year of 1880, in which it was refounded, inaugurated a recrudescence of the revolutionary movement both in Europe and America.

On the 20th of August of this same year a secret revolutionary congress was held at Wyden in Switzerland, which brought about a definite rupture between the two German groups — the Social Democrats, led by Liebknecht and Bebel, formally expelling the Anarchists, led by Johann Most and Hasselmann. The theory of the latter as summarized by Zacher will be seen to be identical with the plan of the first Illuminati: " They held the existing order of things to be so corrupt that they were ready to compass its overthrow by any means, however violent, without concerning themselves as to what should take the place of that which they destroyed. *Their ideal was universal chaos, which must have as its necessary consequence the war of all against all and the break-up of all civilization.*" [2]

The connection between these plotters and the Nihilists of Russia is also clearly apparent. Two days after the

[1] " Die Religion in Geschichte und Gegenwart," *Encyclopedia*, edited by Friedrich Schiele and Leopold Zscharnack (Tübingen, 1912); article on " Illuminaten."   [2] Zacher, *Die Rothe Internationale.*

assassination of Alexander II. Hasselmann had addressed a meeting in New York, from which a message of sympathy was sent to the Russian Nihilists containing this phrase: " Brothers, we thoroughly approve your procedure. Kill, destroy, make of everything a *tabula rasa* till your enemies and ours have been annihilated." [1] The exact formula of Nihilism will be here recognized.

The Social Democrats differed only from the Anarchists in believing that this consummation should be effected by a more gradual process; and herein, as Zacher points out, lies their sole claim to " moderation " — if the Socialist party " attempts before the outer world to play the rôle of a peaceable party of reform, this is nothing more than a strategical manœuvre in order to maintain a show of legality in the face of public opinion and not to frighten waverers away. . . . However divergent, therefore, may be the views of the two factions of German Socialists, *i.e.* the Social Democrats and Anarchists, with regard to the policy to be pursued and the final goal to be attained, yet they both rest upon the same foundation, that is, the conviction that the present system cannot continue and must therefore be overthrown, which can only take place by forcible means."

Moreover, by the respective organs of the two parties, the *Sozialdemokrat* of the so-called moderates and the *Freiheit* of the Anarchists, we find the original ideas of Weishaupt, Clootz, and Bakunin clearly expressed. Thus, for example, in the matter of religion the *Sozialdemokrat* for the 25th of May 1880 declares that " it must be candidly avowed Christianity is the bitterest enemy of Social Democracy. . . . When God is driven out of the brains of men, the whole system of privilege by the grace of God comes to the ground, and when Heaven hereafter is recognized as a big lie, men will attempt to establish Heaven here. Therefore whoever assails Christianity assails, at the same time, monarchy and capitalism." [2]

In the same manner the *Freiheit* for February 5, 1881, characterized Christianity as " a swindle invented by jugglers," and went on to observe: " Do but read the

[1] Zacher, *Die Rothe Internationale*, p. 28.   [2] *Ibid.* p. 25.

Bible through, supposing you can overcome the disgust that must seize you when you open the pages of the most infamous of all shameful books (" das infamste aller Schandbücher "), and you may soon observe that the God whom this twaddle inculcates is a million-headed, fire-spitting, vengeance-breathing, ferocious dragon." [1]

The war on the *bourgeoisie* waged by Marat, Robespierre, Clootz, and Hébert under the influence of the Illuminati is again declared by *Freiheit* for December 18, 1880: " It is no longer aristocracy and royalty that the people can intend to destroy. Here perhaps but a *coup de grace* or two are yet needed. No, but in the coming onslaught the object is to smite the entire middle-class with annihilation." Or again: " Extirpate all the contemptible brood! Such is the refrain of a revolutionary song. . . . Science now puts means into our hands which make it possible to arrange for the wholesale destruction of the brutes in a perfectly quiet and business-like fashion,"etc.[2]

In July 1881 the Anarchists assembled a small International Revolutionary Congress in London under the aegis of Johann Most and the German-Jewish Nihilist, Hartmann — author of the plot for blowing up the Czar's trains two years earlier — at which Prince Kropotkine was present as delegate from the Anarchists of Lyons. Amongst the resolutions passed were the following:

The revolutionaries of all countries are uniting into an " International Social Revolutionary Working Men's Association " for the purpose of a social revolution. The headquarters of the Association is at London, and sub-committees are formed in Paris, Geneva, and New York. . . . The committees of each country keep up regular correspondence amongst themselves and with the chief committee by means of intermediate addresses for the sake of giving continuous information; and it is their duty to collect money for the purchase of poison and arms, as well as to discover places suitable for the construction of mines, etc. To attain the proposed end, the annihilation of all rulers, ministers of State, nobility, the clergy, the most prominent capitalists, and other exploiters, any means are permissible, and therefore great attention should be given specially to the study of chemistry and the preparation of explosives, as being the most important weapons, etc.[3]

[1] Zacher, *Die Rothe Internationale*, p. 27. [2] *Ibid.* p. 26.
[3] Zenker, *Anarchism*, p. 231; Zacher, *Die Rothe Internationale*.

This was a little too much even for the confiding British Government, and Most was at last condemned to eighteen months' imprisonment. Disgusted at this treatment, and still more at his difficulties with the printing of his *Freheit*, " Most, grumbling, left thankless old England and went to the New World, where however he was, if possible, taken even less seriously." [1]

Prince Kropotkine also shook the dust of Britain off his feet. " My wife and I," he writes, " felt so lonely in London, and our efforts to awaken a Socialist movement in England seemed so hopeless, that in the autumn of 1882 we decided to remove again to France. We were sure that in France I should soon be arrested; but we often said to each other, " Better a French prison than this grave." [2]

People who see in the Russian revolutionary movement only the natural result of repression will do well to note this passage. The amazing degree of liberty accorded by the British Government to the foreign agitator elicits from him no word of gratitude or appreciation, nor does it seem to occur to him that the fact of England being a free country might have something to do with the difficulty of rousing in it a spirit of rebellion. To Kropotkine this land of liberty, even more than Czarist Russia, was " a grave."

It will be seen that the recrudescence of the revolutionary movement cannot then be attributed to any subversive tendencies on the part of the people, but coincides exactly with the reorganization of the Illuminati. Even the most incredulous must surely admit it to be a curious coincidence that the society was reconstructed in 1880 and that on January 1, 1881 — that is to say, the very year when Prince Kropotkine was lamenting the lack of Socialist enthusiasm amongst the British working-classes — Mr. Hyndman in the *Nineteenth Century* announced " The Dawn of a Revolutionary Epoch." It is evident that once again the people were not in the secret of the movement and that preparations were going forward without their knowledge in co-operation with foreign revolutionaries.

[1] Zenker, p. 243.

[2] *Memoirs of a Revolutionist*, ii. 254. In the light of this sentence it was amusing to find the British press referring to Prince Kropotkine in his obituary notices as " a sincere lover of England! "

The connection between the secret organizations of this date with German Illuminism is, moreover, clearly evident. Thus in London a lodge called by the same name as that to which the Illuminatus Gracchus Babeuf had belonged — the *Philadelphes* — carried on the rite of Memphis — founded, it is said, by Cagliostro on Egyptian occultism — and initiated adepts into the higher grades of illuminized Freemasonry.[1] It was here that Johann Most and Hartmann conducted their intrigues and that, in spite of the recalcitrance of the printers, they succeeded for a time in publishing their journal *Freheit*, and it was by associations of the same kind in New York, Chicago, and Philadelphia that both Most and Hartmann were received on their arrival in America. That these American associations were continuously in touch with the Anarchist movement in England is clear from the fact that delegates had been sent by them to attend the aforesaid International Congress in London in July 1881 " with the object of studying chemical methods which might be useful to the work of revolution." [2]

In all these plottings England seems to have been the chief objective, as the following extraordinary passage that appeared in the *New York World* a year or two later testifies:

" ÇA IRA! ÉCRASEZ LES INFAMES! "

The storm of revolution is looming and lowering over Europe which will crush out and obliterate for ever the hydra-headed monarchies and nobilities of the Old World. In Russia the Nihilist is astir. In France the Communist is the coming man. In Germany the Social Democrat will soon rise again in his millions as in the days of Ferdinand Lassalle. In Italy the Internationalist is frequently heard from. In Spain the marks of the Black Hand have been visible on many an occasion. In Ireland the Fenian and Avenger terrorise, and in England the Land League is growing. All cry aloud for the blue blood of the monarch and the aristocrat. They wish to see it pouring again on the scaffold. Will it be by the guillotine that cut off the head of Louis XVI.? Or by the headsman's axe that decapitated Charles I.? Or by the dynamite that searched out the vitals of Alexander the Second? Or will it be by the hangman's noose around the neck of the next British monarch?

[1] Deschamps, iii. 628.   [2] *Ibid*. iii. 629.

No one can tell but that the coming English *sans culottes*, the descendants of Wamba the Fool and Gurth the Swineherd, will discover the necessary method and relentlessly employ it. They will make the nobles — who fatten and luxuriate in the castles and abbeys, and on the lands stolen from the Saxon, sacrilegiously robbed from the Catholic Church and kept from the peasantry of the villages and the labourer of the towns — wish they had never been born. They will be the executioners of the fate so justly merited by the aristocratic criminals of the past and the present. The cry that theirs is blue blood and that they are the privileged caste will not avail the men and women of rank when the English Republic is born. They will have to expiate their tyrannies, their murders, their lusts, and their crimes in accordance with the law given on Sinai amid the thunders of heaven: " The sins of the fathers shall be visited upon the children even unto the third and fourth generations." [1]

Sir Lepel Griffin, who quotes " these ravings," adds the significant words: " It is necessary to note that the *New York World* is edited by a German."

If we do not believe in a connection between occult forces and world revolution how are we to explain these periodic outbursts of revolutionary fury proceeding not from the people but from the enemies of the country against which they are directed? According to Mr. Hyndman, in the aforesaid article, the movement was largely developing under the auspices of the Jews, and it is interesting to compare this prophecy with that of Disraeli that had immediately preceded the 1848 explosion, for the point of view in both will be seen to be identical:

The influence of the Jews at the present time is more noticeable than ever. . . . They are at the head of European capitalists. . . . In politics many Jews are in the front rank. The press in more than one European capital is almost wholly in their hands. The Rothschilds are but the leading name among a whole series of capitalists, etc. . . . But whilst on the one hand the Jews are thus beyond dispute the leaders of the plutocracy of Europe . . . another section of the same race form the leaders of that revolutionary propaganda which is making way against that very capitalist class represented by their own fellow-Jews. Jews — more than any other men — have held forth against those who make their living not by producing value, but by trading on the differences of value; they at this moment are acting as the leaders in the revolutionary move-

[1] *The Great Republic*, by Sir Lepel Henry Griffin (1884), pp. 3-4.

ment which I have endeavoured to trace. Surely we have here a very strange phenomenon. . . . Those, therefore, who are accustomed to look upon all Jews as essentially practical and conservative, as certain, too, to enlist on the side of the prevailing social system, will be obliged to reconsider their conclusions. But the whole subject of the bad and good effects of Jewish influence on European social conditions is worthy of a more thorough investigation than can be undertaken here. Enough, that in the period we are approaching not the slightest influence on the side of revolution will be that of the Jew.

That Jews belonging to both the revolutionary camps of Anarchy and of State Socialism were now co-operating in their efforts to overthrow the existing social system is seen from another passage in Mr. Hyndman's works, in which he describes a visit he paid to Karl Marx when the anarchist Hartmann was present.[1] That these two Jews both desired the downfall of the country which so foolishly offered them hospitality is further evident.

Already twelve years earlier Marx had formed his plan of attack on Great Britain. In the Instructions issued by the General Council of the Internationale signed by Dupont, the acolyte of Marx, and despatched from London to Geneva in 1870, this axiom had been laid down: " Although revolutionary initiative must come from France, England alone can serve as a lever for a serious economic revolution."

But this revolution was not to be brought about by the English workers, for the instructions go on to say:

The General Council being placed in the happy position of having its hand on the great lever of the proletarian revolution, what folly to let it fall into purely English hands![2]

This policy is then summed up in the following message by Marx:

1.   England is the only country in which a real Socialist revolution can be made.
2.   The English people cannot make this revolution.
3.   Foreigners must make it for them.
4.   The foreign members, therefore, must retain their seats at the London board.

---

[1] Hyndman's *Reminiscences*, p. 280.
[2] Deschamps, ii. 569.

5. The point to strike at first is Ireland, and in Ireland they are ready to begin their work.[1]

" These English," Dupont added, " have all the materials needed for a Socialistic revolution; what they lack are the generalizing spirit and the revolutionary fire."

The author of the *Secret History*, whence we glean this gem, observes:

What then? Karl Marx, Eugène Dupont, and George Eccarius, must clutch their power and keep their seats. They say so boldly. . . . These gentlemen were aware that a revolutionary march is not an easy thing in London, where the people are so individual in their tastes and tempers, and so stupidly attached to independent judgment, private property, and personal rights. But they were not without some hope. In turning to the West they saw a star descending to the Irish Sea. That star they followed with beseeching eyes: it trembled over Cork. " The only point where we can strike the great blow against official England is on Irish soil. In Ireland the movement is made a hundred times more easy for us by the two prime facts that the social question is that of rent, and that the people are more revolutionary and exasperated than in England. . . ."

A final phrase completed M. Dupont's account:

The position of the Internationale in face of the Irish question is very clear. Our first care is to push the revolution in England. To this end we must strike the first blow in Ireland.[2]

Through what agency was this blow to be struck? What was the organization on which the World Revolutionists depended for the execution of their plan? Again a secret society. From the French Revolution onwards it was always by secret societies that Continental agitators had carried on their work in Ireland. The Society of United Irishmen founded in 1791 was, as we have already seen, directly modelled on the method of Weishaupt, the Secret Societies under Fenton Lalor in 1848 had followed the same tradition, and now the Fenians, who had come into being between 1858 and 1870, were organizing themselves on the same model. This was the society on which Marx and his council depended for support. The statement will of course be indignantly denied by the conspiracy of history which seeks to prove Fenianism, like Nihilism,

[1] *The Secret History of the International*, by Onslow Yorke, p. 156.
[2] *Ibid*. p. 159.

to be indigenous to the soil in which it flourished, a movement wholly unconnected with the central organization of World Revolution.   But as it happens, the connection between Marx and the revolutionaries of Ireland is not a matter of surmise but of fact, for it rests not only on the above-quoted message dated January 1, 1870, but receives further confirmation from an entry in the records of the Internationale containing a message of sympathy addressed to the Fenians in December 1869 by the General Council of the Internationale in London.[1]   It was evidently, therefore, on the strength of the manner in which this overture was received that Marx a few weeks later despatched his confident declaration to Geneva.

But the Internationale had failed to bring about the desired revolution in Ireland, and it was not until the date we have now reached, 1882 — after Illuminism had been reconstructed — that Fenianism, which in about 1872 had become a secret society, known as the " Irish Republican Brotherhood," embarked on its course of dynamite outrages in Great Britain and America.   The patriotic Catholic prelate, Monsignor Dillon, in a course of lectures held in Dublin, thus eloquently warned Ireland of the danger to itself and to all Christian countries from the conspiracy that was seeking to destroy every national and religious ideal:

It is not an expression of Irish discontent finding a vent in dynamite which England has most to fear from anarchy. . . . The dark directory of Socialism is powerful, wise, and determined.   It laughs at Ireland and her wrongs.   It hates and ever will hate the Irish people for their fidelity to the Catholic faith.   But it seizes upon those subjects which Irish discontent in America affords to make them teach the millions everywhere the power of dynamite, and the knife, and the revolver, against the comparatively few who hold property.   This is the real secret of dynamite outrages in England, in Russia, and all the world over; and I fear we are but upon the threshold of a social convulsion which will try every nation where the wiles of the secret societies have obtained, through the hate of senseless Christian sectaries, the power for Atheism to dominate over the rising generation and deprive it of Christian faith, and the fear and the love of God.

[1] Guillaume, *Documents de l'Internationale*, i. 251.

Monsignor Dillon goes on to describe the manner in which the occult powers enlist their dupes, and shows the terrible fate of

the Irishman who first begins to listen to the seducer of the secret society, and afterwards becomes himself a seducer, a leader, perhaps a traitor, in the deadly conspiracy to ruin religion, to destroy God. His career is often this: At first a hopeful, young, ambitious student of his country's history, he begins to feel indignation at her wrongs, and wishes to right them. In a fatal hour he meets the tempter. He is sworn into the terrible sect. He gets a command, an importance in the organization. He is youthful, but the season of life wherein to make an honest livelihood passes rapidly in intrigue. He knows the course into which he has fallen is bad, is injurious to religion, but he hopes to repent. . . . But having lived his best days to conspire, he now must conspire to live, and inured to bad habits, he is at last ready for anything. . . .

By degrees he herds with the worst class of Atheistic and Socialist plotters.

And this is strange, for while the Irish conspirator may be as able to plot mischief as the worst of the miscreants with whom he associates in France, he differs from them in this, that in the secret of his soul he never loses his faith. They know this well, and they watch him, use him, but never fully trust him. Many a broken Irish heart the children of the Revolution in Paris have made already. Many a one of those Irish victims wishes again for the days of his boyish innocence and blessed faith. . . . God grant that . . . the race of wretched men who have so often in the past ensnared generous-hearted Catholic Irishmen in Ireland, in Great Britain, in America, and elsewhere, may end for ever. From such false agents, and from the machinations of all enemies to Irish Faith, we may well pray, GOD SAVE IRELAND.

· The New World, like the Old, was soon to experience the effects of the great conspiracy. In 1886 the Anarchists of America, led by Johann Most, gave evidence of their presence by a dynamite explosion in the Haymarket of Chicago. But it was not until 1891 that the series of Anarchic outrages described as the *période tragique* began in earnest. Was it again a mere coincidence that in July 1889 an International Socialist Congress in Paris decided that May 1, which was *the day on which Weishaupt founded the Illuminati*, should be chosen for an annual International Labour demonstration, and that it was with a demonstration organized by the Anarchists on May 1, 1891, that the *période tragique* began?

For three years a gang led by Ravachol continued to terrorize the population of Paris with bombs and dynamite outrages, a series of crimes that ended with the stabbing of President Carnot at Lyons on June 25, 1894.

Later on followed the attacks on crowned heads — the murder of the Émpress of Austria in 1898, of King Humbert of Italy in 1900, of King Carlos and the Crown Prince of Portugal in 1908, of the King of Greece in 1914.

Professor Hunter, who in his book *Violence and the Labour Movement* deals in an interesting manner with the psychology of the men who perpetrated these deeds, asks our sympathy with them on the score of their devotion to a cause. Quoting Emma Goldman's explanation that they were impelled " not by the teachings of anarchism but by the tremendous pressure of conditions making life unbearable to their sensitive natures," Professor Hunter goes on to ask how it is possible for society to take the lives of these " tormented souls," driven to desperation by the sorrow and suffering of the world.

Now to begin with, a great number of the perpetrators of Anarchist outrages cannot be placed in the category of tormented souls, but belong simply to the class of common criminals who, if they had lived a couple of centuries earlier, would have found a congenial career as footpads, cut-throats, or banditti. One group of German Anarchists in New York who lived by arson — that is to say by insuring their premises for amounts far in excess of their real value and then burning them down with kerosene — ended by murdering and robbing an old woman in Jersey City; Ravachol, the leader of the Paris Terrorist gang, was finally convicted and executed for strangling a mendicant hermit; whilst the motor bandits of 1912 led by Bonnot, whom we are also asked to regard as rebels against " society," seem to the lay mind indistinguishable from the highwaymen of romance.

But in the case of those " tormented souls " which it would perhaps be nearer the truth to describe as " unbalanced brains " who appear to be victims of an idea rather

than of mere criminal instincts, the point overlooked—
and we cannot help thinking wilfully overlooked—by
Professor Hunter is that they were not solitary fanatics
acting on irresistible individual impulse but the agents of a
conspiracy. The art of the secret societies has always been
to seek out physical and mental degenerates and work upon
their minds until they have roused them to the requisite
degree of revolutionary fervour. Bound at the same time
by terrible oaths, the wretched tools selected for each
crime set forth on their tasks knowing full well there could
be no turning back for fear of the vengeance of their
instigators. Even as recently as the attack on M. Clemenceau the weak-minded youth Cottin admitted that he was
a member of a secret society and his connection with the
Anarchist movement was clearly established by the papers
found at his lodgings.

It is not then these poor creatures who should be led to
the scaffold or caged in prison cells until they lapse into
imbecility; the lunatic asylum should be reserved for such
as these, the scaffold for the superiors of the secret societies
who direct their strokes. But hardly less guilty are the
sane and responsible Socialists like Professor Hunter who,
by their glorification of crime, impel other weak minds to
follow the same course.

.   .   .   .

Whilst Anarchy was thus making itself felt throughout
Europe, Socialism pursued a more leisurely course. As in
all revolutionary movements violence had won the day,
and the decline in popular favour that had begun with the
anti-Marxian demonstrations of 1872 continued to the end
of Marx's life. Although by 1881 he had spent thirty-two
years in London, he was " practically unknown to the
British public " [1] and counted no following amongst
British workmen. Moreover, at this date he contrived to
fall foul of one of his staunchest supporters amongst the
intelligentzia, Mr. Hyndman, whom he accused of pilfering
his works without acknowledgment. " His attacks,"
writes Mr. Hyndman, " of the most vindictive character,

[1] Hyndman's *Reminiscences*, p. 272.

were " " followed up by Engels with even more of vitriolic fervour for years." [1]

Of the various British Socialist organizations inaugurated during this period I do not propose to treat in detail. Neither the Social Democratic Federation, founded in 1883 by Mr. Hyndman, nor " The Fabian Society," formed by Mr. Sidney Webb in the same year, nor the " Christian Socialists " under the Rev. Stuart Headlam, originated any new doctrines, but merely elaborated the ideas of their Continental inspirers. Many members of these societies were probably not Socialists at all but merely honest social reformers, whilst the less sincere — " drawing-room Socialists " living in luxury and tilting against the social system to which they owed their mode of existence — took up Socialism as a novel form of excitement and carried little weight, for their inflammatory speeches met with scant appreciation even in the poorest quarters of London. That they succeeded in obtaining a certain following amongst malcontents — mainly of their own class — is undeniable, but it was not they who supplied the driving force behind the great revolutionary machine which thirty-four years later was to deliver the supreme attack dreamt of by Weishaupt for the destruction of civilization.

[1] Hyndman's *Reminiscences*, p. 283.

CHAPTER IX

SYNDICALISM

Quarrels amongst Socialists — The old Guilds — Revolutionary Syndicalism — Outcome of Anarchy —The General Strike — Georges Sorel — Syndicalism *versus* Socialism — Guild Socialism — " New Australia."

WHILST Socialism in England was thus pursuing a laborious course and still remained almost exclusively confined to drawing-rooms, the same doctrines met with continued and active hostility from the French peasants.

Mr. Hyndman in his *Reminiscences* describes M. Clemenceau as expressing his opinion that Socialism could never make way in France in his day.

Looking only at the towns you may think otherwise, though even there I consider the progress of Socialism is overrated. But the towns do not govern France. The overwhelming majority of French voters are country voters. France means rural France, and the peasantry of France will never be Socialists. . . . Always property, ownership, possession, work, thrift, acquisition, individual gain. Socialism can never take root in such a soil as this. North or South it is just the same. Preach nationalization of the land in a French village, and you would barely escape with your life, if the peasants understood what you meant.[1]

It is strange how frankly Socialists at times admit that, for all their talk of democracy, their plans for the people's welfare are diametrically opposed to those of the people themselves. Mr. Hyndman goes on to relate that M. Paul Brousse, when consulted on Clemenceau's " pessimist opinion " of the French peasants, agreed that " to preach nationalization in the villages would be suicidal,"

[1] *Reminiscences*, p. 321.

249

but seemed to think the peasants might be tricked into Socialism all the same.

The word Socialism need never be used at all; but the ideas of natural and communal organization and administration would soon find their road into his mind. In this way the peasant's conception of the sanctity of private and the curse of public ownership would gradually be shaken, and he would be on the path to practical Socialism before he knew what he was going on.[1]

Mr. Hyndman remarks that he thought this idea quite admirable.

But while the Socialists were making plans for " educating the people up " to their own lofty ideals the Socialist camp in France was itself divided into at least three warring factions — the Guesdists, the Broussistes (or Possibilistes), and the Blanquistes — which continued " to excommunicate each other." [2] In fact, as Mr. Hyndman goes on to inform us, the conflict became at times so bitter that the Guesdists and the Broussistes " could not meet in one hall without the certainty of bloodshed, or at any rate of severe contusions, following. A spirit of fraternity so marked by brotherly hatred had about it something of the ludicrous."

When therefore an International Socialist Congress took place " to bring about the unity of the workers of the world " it was found necessary to assemble in " two separate halls purposely chosen at some distance from one another to avoid the possible consequences of fraternal greetings." [3]

The two points on which these opposing factions differed the most violently were the necessity for the class war and the domination of German Social Democracy. On the first question the Broussistes held more moderate views, believing in the possibility of immediate reforms whilst preparing the way for Socialism by evolutionary methods; the Guesdists, however, as consistent Marxists, adopted for their fundamental principle "the doctrine of the class struggle, a doctrine," says Laskine, " imported from

[1] *Reminiscences*, p. 326.
[2] Mermeix, *Le Syndicalisme contre le Socialisme*, p. 90.
[3] *Reminiscences*, p. 441.

Germany and profoundly foreign to the spirit of French Socialists." [1]

In ranging himself under the banner of Marx, Jules Guesde had executed a complete *volte-face*; at the time of the Socialist revolt against the domination of Marx after the Commune, Guesde in a letter to the *Bulletin de la Fédération jurassienne*, published on April 15, 1873, had denounced " the Marxist proconsuls " and " the infamous rôle of the founding of power by Marx and the General Council " (of the Internationale),[2] but after a five years' sojourn in Switzerland — whither he had fled to escape imprisonment — Guesde returned to France an enthusiastic Marxist.

The methods by which Guesde and other French Socialists were won over by the subtler German Jews to the Marxian camp is thus referred to in a significant sentence by Marx himself:

" I need not tell you," Marx wrote to Sorge on November 5, 1880, " that the *secret strings* by which the leaders from Guesde and Malon to Clemenceau have been set in motion must remain between ourselves. We must not speak about them." [3]

According to Laskine it was Hirsch — a German Jew — who had brought about the conversion of Guesde; at any rate from 1876 onwards the Guesdists became simply the French branch of German Social Democracy.

This policy naturally estranged them from the French workers to whom the principles of bureaucratic Communism had always been repellent. Still, as in 1862, it was to Proudhon rather than to Marx that the more revolutionary elements inclined, whilst the great mass of French workmen saw in peaceful corporative association the true path of progress. It was the junction of these various currents that towards 1895 brought about a further development in the revolutionary movement — Syndicalism.

" Syndicalism," Mr. Ramsay Macdonald observes, " is largely a revolt against Socialism." [4] That such a revolt

---

[1] Laskine, *L'Internationale et le pan-Germanisme*, p. 218.
[2] *Ibid.* p. 122.
[3] *Ibid.* p. 167, quoting *Briefe an Sorge*, p. 170 Laskine points out that Marx was mistaken in thinking that Clemenceau had gone over to the Marxist camp.
[4] Ramsay Macdonald, *Syndicalism* (1910), p. 6.

should have taken place is hardly surprising. For over a hundred years the working-men of Europe had seen the middle and upper class men who constituted themselves their champions living in luxury — sleeping in the gilded beds of the Tuileries in 1794, housed in safety and comfort whilst the people perished on the barricades of 1848, enjoying pleasant trips to Switzerland as delegates of the Internationale, drawing continual subscriptions from the pockets of the workers in support of " congresses " or " leagues" or associations devised to benefit Labour — and now the time had come to ask: " What have we gained from all our sacrifices? What have these men done in return for the confidence we placed in them? "

Not unnaturally, therefore, the theory of Syndicalism, consisting in the immediate control of industry by the workers themselves, seemed greatly preferable to the tedious and doubtful method of electing Socialist deputies to represent them in Parliament. Moreover, in the Syndicalist ideas entertained by many of the French workmen there was nothing essentially revolutionary; their conception of reorganized industry approached more to the old idea of " guilds " and " corporations " than to the aggressive combines advocated by revolutionary Syndicalists. They thought regretfully of the days of the Old Régime before the introduction of cut-throat competition when men worked peacefully at their trades, bound together by ties of comradeship under *patrons* who showed some concern for their welfare. Wherever he belonged " the *compagnon* was almost certain, by virtue of his corporative privilege, to find employment. The regulations provided that he should not find competitors amongst his comrades. The knowledge of his trade, recognized after the tests through which he had passed, constituted a capital for him of which the revenues were almost certain. And if this *compagnon* wanted to make a tour of France he found help and relief. Provided that he justified his claim as member of a corporation, he was welcomed and a place found for him. Defective and imperfect like all human things, the economic organization of the Old Régime was nevertheless beneficent, and how much preferable to the want of organization into which the régime of liberty had brusquely precipitated the working-men after the Revolution." [1]

The suppression of the " corporations " by the law of 1791 — confirmed by further laws under the Terror, and in the Code of Napoleon I. — had dealt the death-blow to the guild system, and when at last Napoleon III. in 1864 removed the ban on trade unions, and the workers once more saw their chance of coalescing in defence of their common interests, the German Social Democrats of the first Internationale had turned the whole movement to the advantage of Communism — a system inherently repugnant to the French workers. As far as they were concerned the Syndicalist movement was thus in its origins an attempt to get back to the freer ideas of friendly corporations, just as in England the co-operative system inaugurated by the Rochdale Pioneers took an ever firmer hold on the minds of working-men.

It was in order to meet these demands that, after the death of the Internationale, a general Union des Chambres Syndicales was formed under the leadership of Barbaret in 1873, a wholly pacific organization which aimed at industrial harmony, and in 1876 a general congress of French workmen met in Paris, at which seventy unions and twenty-eight workmen's clubs from thirty-nine towns, with a membership stated to number a million workers, were represented by more than 800 delegates. " At the opening of the Congress it was expressly insisted on that not principles of social politics but the purely economical and practical interests of the working-men would engage the meetings," [2] and real improvements in the industrial system formed the subject of discussion.

But as in the case of the Internationale the World Revolutionists succeeded in obtaining control over the movement; Broussistes, Guesdists, but above all Anarchists ended by invading its ranks and blocking the path of peaceful progress.

It is no figure of speech to say that Syndicalism is

[1] Mermeix (G. Terrail), *Le Syndicalisme contre le Socialisme*, pp. 62, 63.
[2] Zacher, *Die Rothe Internationale.*

simply a further development of the creed of Anarchy, for it rests on the same basis — negation of the State. Its earliest exponents were avowedly Anarchists; in America the terms were in fact synonymous. Moreover, it was Proudhon, the " Father of Anarchy," who had first formulated the whole theory of Syndicalism: " According to my idea, railways, a mine, a manufactory, a ship, etc., are to the workers whom they occupy what the hive is to the bees, that is at the same time their instrument and their dwelling, their country, their territory, their property." For this reason Proudhon opposed " the exploitation of the railways whether by companies of Capitalists or by the State." [1]

Syndicalism is, therefore, government by trade unions, and must inevitably lead to anarchy. For not only are the workers to run industries but the whole country "On their own," and with no State to act as umpire it is obvious that chaos must result. The miners might raise the price of coal, the bakers the price of bread, and the rest of the community would have no means of redress, for in the conflict that would ensue between the different groups of workers the key industries alone could exercise any real authority. For the power of each industry would be in exact ratio to its ability to hold up the country, and since society cannot get on for a day without bread, coal, or transport, the miners, the railway-men, and the food purveyors would have an immense advantage over the workers engaged in such trades as boot-making, tailoring, or upholstery, who might strike in vain against extortion. Women-workers would of course have no voice at all.

It is not, however, the system of Syndicalism but the method by which it is to be brought about that constitutes its principal claim to be ranged in the category of anarchy. This method is the *General Strike*.

Now, as Mermeix has pointed out, there are three kinds of General Strike: (1) the Corporative General Strike of the workers, (2) the Parliamentary General Strike of the Socialists, and (3) the Revolutionary General Strike of the Syndicalist leaders. Let us deal with these one by one.

[1] Proudhon, *La Révolution au XVIIIe siècle*, p. 249.

(1) The Corporative General Strike as conceived by the workers was not originally a measure of violence. Strikes throughout the early history of the Labour Movement had been the workers' only method of obtaining redress from exploitation, and no one but a Robespierre or a Lenin would deny the worker's right to lay down his tools if the conditions of his labour appear to him unjust.

The Corporative General Strike was simply a development of this time-honoured method of expressing discontent which, carried out on a larger scale, would enable wokers in all industries to bring an effective support to the demands of their oppressed comrades. As Mermeix points out, the working-men's conception of the way in which the plan would work was very naïve:

Some day one would stay at home; one would not go to the workshop. The *bourgeois* who fattens on the sweat of the people would waste away because the people would cease to sweat, it would be " a strike of folded arms " ; one would not go down into the street in tumultuous crowds, one would not expose oneself to the brutalities of the police and the guns of the soldiery. One would walk out in a family party, to lunch on the fortification, in the woods of Vincennes, in the Bois de Boulogne or even further in the smiling suburbs where the exploiters have their country houses. Would not this method be much better than that of the Socialist politicians who first of all advised one to vote for them, their electoral success being the first stage on the way to final victory, and who, once elected, would think only of their re-election? The general strike would be the revolution carried out as a huge joke. One would divert oneself with the expressions of the employers growing day by day more disconsolate. One would watch them grow pale, yellow, distorted, and their rage would be powerless against the brave proletarians who would simply make use of their right to idleness — the right of Man, a natural and sacred right which the *bourgeois* has so long selfishly enjoyed alone. When it had had enough of it the class of leeches would ask to capitulate. The proletariat would dictate its conditions: " Give me back what you have stolen from me, that is to say, give me back everything and we will become good friends again. I will go back into your workshop to work not as one exploited for your profit, but to work as a free social producer." And the *bourgeoisie* could not do otherwise than subscribe to this treaty.[1]

That in reality the worker would grow pale, yellow

[1] Mermeix, *Le Socialisme contre le Syndicalisme*, pp. 135, 136.

would in fact be dead before the employer reached the ends of his resources, did not enter into the reckonings of the " brave proletarians," nor does it still today when the plan of the general strike is placed before them.

(2) The Parliamentary General Strike, as approved by certain Socialists, aims at quite a different *dénoument;* it is not to end in improved relations between the workers and employers or in an *entente* between the workers and the Government, but in the overthrow of the political party which holds the reins of power in favour of the Socialists themselves. A general strike conducted on these lines would not " dispossess the Socialist party of the command which it has arrogated to itself over the working-classes"; on the contrary it would confirm this command, and leave to it the rôle it has chosen of " business man to the proletariat." [1]

Even Mr. Ramsay Macdonald, arch-opponent of the revolutionary general strike, admits the expediency of the political variety. " The general strike," he observes, " can be declared for two purposes. It can be used to secure some specific demand — say an extension of the franchise, the resignation of the Government, or the defeat of a war party. . . . As a last resort, as a *coup de grâce*, it may be justifiable, and need not be unsuccessful." [2]

In order, therefore, to place Mr. Ramsay Macdonald and his friends at the helm of the State, to overthrow a Government that retains an insular prejudice against foreign invasion, and to paralyse national defence, it may be necessary to bring upon the country the immense suffering caused by a general strike, which, when carried out by Syndicalists, as Mr. Macdonald himself remarks, " hits the poor people heaviest, the middle-classes next, and the rich least of all." [3]

For revolutionary Socialists today, as in 1793, " tours les moyens sont bons."

(3) But the Revolutionary General Strike, the form of general strike advocated by the Syndicalists and that now forms the programme of extremist trade union leaders,

[1] Mermeix, *Le Socialisme contre le Syndicalisme,* p. 142.
[2] J. Ramsay Macdonald, *Syndicalism*, p. 61. [3] *Ibid.* p. 62.

aims neither at a reorganization of industry nor at a change
of government in the political sense, but at the complete
destruction of constitutional government by violence of the
most frightful kind. It is here that we come back to the
connection between Anarchy and Syndicalism; not only
is the Syndicalist system a development of the creed of
Anarchy, but its method for inaugurating it comprises the
exact programme of the earlier Anarchists.

Now it will be remembered that the idea of " useful
larceny " had first been suggested by Weishaupt, a principle applauded by Brissot and put into practice by Marat
when he urged the populace to pillage the shops. Babeuf,
though a Communist, had carried on the same tradition in
his plan of the " Great Day of the People," when the
people were to rise as one man and lay violent hands upon
property. From Babeuf onwards the scheme had been
logically abandoned by Communists — since Communism
aims not at mob rule but at bureaucracy — but continued
along the line of Anarchy. Proudhon in his revival of
Brissot's axiom " Property is theft," Bakunin in his glorification of robbery, and finally Kropotkine in his theory of
" The Great Expropriation," all followed out the same
idea, namely, that of a " Great Day " of revolution when
the maddened multitude, driven by want and desperation,
should rise against all wealth and property in one overpowering onslaught. Had not Bakunin and Netchaïeff
indicated this design in an illuminating sentence: " We
must increase and heighten the evils and sorrows so as
to wear out the patience of the people and drive them
to insurrection *en masse*." By this means only, the
social revolution could be accomplished and civilization,
obnoxious civilization, wiped out at one stroke.

But how were the people to be driven to this pitch of
exasperation? Obviously by hunger. The want of bread
alone, as the Orléanistes of 1789 had clearly perceived, can
be depended on to produce popular insurrection, and in the
eighteenth century famine had been easy enough to engi-
neer by buying up supplies, waylaying waggons of corn, or
throwing sacks of flour into the river. But a hundred years
later improved means of transport and the complicated

modern system of food distribution had made such primitive methods impracticable. How, then, were want and hunger to be brought about? Only by some gigantic *coup* that would paralyze the whole country and lead to the Great Expropriation dreamt of by the Anarchists. Syndicalism now provided the weapon by which this was to be accomplished — the *General Strike*.

Let us examine the programme of the revolutionary General Strike as resumed by Mermeix from the declarations of its advocates, and we shall see how exactly the " Grand Soir " of the Syndicalists corresponds with the Anarchists' idea of the Great Day of Revolution.

First of all, a series of isolated strikes is to take place in various industries by way of partially paralysing Capital and of unsettling Labour.

Then at a given signal the workers, roused to violence by want and idleness, are to invade the workshops, mines, factories, etc., and take possession of them. At this stage, of course, the Government will be obliged to call in the aid of the police and soldiery, and the fight will begin. The revolutionaries will cut the telegraph and telephone wires; railway lines will be torn up to prevent the transport of troops or provisions; at the same time it is hoped that a number of the soldiers will go over to the side of the revolution. By this means the capital will be starved out, the markets will be empty, and the inhabitants rendered savage by hunger may be expected to turn on the Government — and also on the *bourgeoisie*.

Of course there is always the possibility that the population, instead of turning on the Government, will turn upon the revolutionaries, but " this last prospect does not disconcert the partisans of revolution by the General Strike. The Parisians will fight amongst themselves; well, then, things will go all the better. *Everything that will make confusion worse would be an advantage*." And in the end, if the revolutionaries fail to overthrow the Government, the havoc they will work will be irretrievable. Before evacuating the workshops the Syndicalists will resort to sabotage; all the instruments of labour will be destroyed.

The railways will remain unusable; the ruin of the capital will be complete.[1]

What then? After that frankly the apostles of Syndicalism promise nothing; their conception ceases with this final climax — " a series of atrocious scenes, of burnings, of ruins, of murders, of terror," carried out by " tramps, poachers, marauders, with terror rising from below and ending in a fearful mêlée." [2]

One must read for oneself the work of M. Georges Sorel to realize that this idea, well characterized by Mermeix as " the dream of a neurasthenic negro king," [3] can seriously enter into the calculations of a man outside a lunatic asylum. But to M. Sorel the prospect offers nothing alarming; on the contrary, whilst admitting that the General Strike will be " a catastrophe of which the process baffles description," [4] the leading apostle of Syndicalism regards it as the goal towards which all agitation should tend. " *Syndicalists*," he declares, " *concentrate all Socialism in the drama of the General Strike.*" [5]

It is, in fact, as a drama, as a spectacle, that M. Sorel looks upon the final cataclysm, or rather as a gigantic cock-fight of such sanguinariness and of such dimensions that one can die happily after witnessing it. For what is to happen afterwards — the *lendemain de la révolution* — one must take no thought; it will be enough to have lived to see " a tidal wave passing over the old civilization."

It will thus be seen, not as a matter of surmise but of fact, that the General Strike as now advocated by the extremist leaders is simply the prelude to the Great Expropriation.[6]

By allying the latter plan with the workers' idea of a corporative General Strike the Syndicalists have evolved the scheme of " The Day " which is to overthrow civiliza-

---

[1] Mermeix, pp. 153-156.   [2] *Ibid.* p. 159.   [3] *Ibid.* p. 232.
[4] *Réflexions sur la violence*, p. 202.   [5] *Ibid.* p. 161.

[6] See the pamphlet called *The Social General Strike* by the British Syndicalist Jack Tanner, which admits this design. "Expropriation," which is to be brought about by the General Strike, means " taking back what belongs to the working-class," and the author goes on to say: " The need for food and the necessaries of life would force the people to help themselves. Hunger forces even the most timid to take what they are entitled to." From the point of view of the people themselves it is appalling to imagine what this sytem of food distribution would lead to.

tion. Of course the workers themselves have no conception of the real design, and each time that a General Strike is attempted doubtless imagine it to be a brilliant inspiration on the part of their leaders in view of a sudden emergency. " The miners are striking for a higher wage. Let us stand by them! Happy thought — let all workers present a solid front to the oppression of Capitalism! One — two — three — all together — strike! "

Thus playing on the simple *camaraderie* of the workers, and urging them to solidarity in the interests of Labour, the Syndicalists hope to drive them onwards into the mêlée which is to end in no amelioration of the workers' lot, but simply in the destruction of the existing social order.

What is to avert the catastrophe? Only greater knowledge on the part of Labour. The first thing, then, is to dispel the illusion that the General Strike is a modern and progressive measure. The workers should be told not only its real purpose but its history; they should be shown that, instead of being the outcome of any present emergency, it is an old scheme that has been going on for at least fifty years and has been turned down as impracticable by all intelligent groups of workers. Let us now follow the vicissitudes of the idea throughout the last half-century.

As a revolutionary method Mermeix suggests that the idea of the General Strike may be traced to the phrase of Mirabeau: " This people whose mere immobility would be formidable."

Now Mirabeau, as we know, was an Illuminatus. Had then even the plan of the General Strike as the weapon wherewith " to deal the deathblow to civilization " entered into the " gigantic conception " of Weishaupt? In a vague sense this is possible, but in its details the General Strike is, as I have shown, essentially a measure adapted to modern conditions.

The plan was first definitely proposed at the Congress of the Internationale in Brussels in 1868, when the declaration was made that " if production were arrested for a certain time the social body could not exist, and that it was only necessary for producers to cease to produce in order to make the personal and despotic enterprises of

Government impossible." [1] From this date the idea of the General Strike was current, and in 1873 the Belgian section of the Internationale invited the other sections of the association to prepare for the attempt to bring it off, but the Congress of Geneva declared it to be at present impracticable.

In 1884 the Government attempted to arrest class warfare by founding " Bourses du Travail," or Labour Exchanges, which should not only provide work but maintain harmony between employers and employed. But the Bourses, like the Chambres Syndicales, soon became hotbeds of revolutionary intrigue, and in 1888 the plan of the General Strike was pressed with renewed vigour by the Anarchist carpenter Tortelier.

After achieving some success in the faubourgs of Paris, Tortelier this same year came to London, where he preached his gospel before a Labour Congress. But " the apostle of the General Strike," with his thick-set figure, bull's neck, hoarse voice, and slovenly attire, whose aspect suggested that of a satellite of Marat, was not taken seriously by British working-men and met with scant success.

In France, however, the cherished scheme of Tortelier found increasing favour. " The idea of the General Strike," says Mermeix, " charms the working masses because it is so simple." And in France there are always the anarchic elements who crave to *faire sauter le bazar*. Thus at a congress of members of the Syndicates and of the Bourses held at Nantes in 1894 the policy of the General Strike was definitely adopted by 65 votes against 37. In the following year the formidable association known as the Confédération Générale du Travail was founded by the extremists with the General Strike as the principal plank in its platform. From this date, 1895, onwards a seven years' war was waged between the C.G.T. and the Bourses, until in 1902 the Bourses were finally extinguished and Syndicalism was left in triumphant possession of the field.

Several attempts have already been made to bring about the revolutionary General Strike — in Spain in 1874, in Belgium in 1902, in Sweden in 1909, in South

---

[1] Mermeix, p. 131.

Africa in 1911, in France in 1920, but so far the firmness of governments and the resistance of the community at large have averted the climax of the " Grand Soir " dreamt of by the Syndicalists, and the principal sufferers have been the strikers themselves. But this fact in no way deters the advocates of the General Strike from pursuing their purpose, which has now become the accepted policy of the C.G.T. At the same time other revolutionary measures have been adopted with a view to fretting away the foundations of Capital. Thus after 1889, when the dockers of Glasgow enforced their demands for higher pay by "going slow," the policy of Ca' Canny became a definite part of the Syndicalist programme.[1] In 1897 sabotage, which had hitherto been regarded as a measure of violence to be employed in the open warfare of revolution, was introduced as a method of passive resistance. Railwaymen had discovered that with a pennyworth of a certain ingredient engines could be put out of working, and the bright idea of applying this method to other instruments of labour met with an enthusiastic response at the Congress of Toulouse in 1897. Pouget, one of its most ardent advocates, describes this incident as " the baptism of *sabotage*." [2]

One variety of sabotage known as " Obstructionism," introduced in 1905, consists in following out regulations to the letter — " accomplishment of duty with excessive care and no less excessive slowness." Pouget gleefully describes the inconvenience to which railway travellers may be put by this plan.[3] For it should be remembered that the methods of Syndicalism are directed not merely against the Government or employers but against the whole community. It is therefore perfectly accurate to distinguish between Syndicalism and Socialism, because the policy of Syndicalism is avowedly anti-social and oligarchic, whilst Socialism at least professes concern for the welfare of the majority.

The plan of the General Strike further emphasized this division between the Socialists and Syndicalists. For although, as we have seen, Socialists are not unwilling to

[1] Émile Pouget, *Le Sabotage*, pp. 6-8.
[2] *Ibid.* p. 17.   [3] *Ibid.* pp. 55-64.

consider the idea of the parliamentary General Strike which will bring them into power, they have always continued to prefer the ballot-box as a method of procedure. As to the revolutionary General Strike, this was opposed throughout even by the followers of Marx, represented in France by the Guesdists. " I only wish some one would explain to me," said Jules Guesde, " how breaking street lamps, disembowelling soldiers, and burning down factories can constitute a means of transforming property. We ought to put an end to all this war of words calling itself revolutionary. No corporative action, however violent, partial strike or general strike, would be able to transform property." [1]

Thus although the Marxians were at one with the Syndicalists in wishing to bring about the grand catastrophe, they differed only in the manner by which it was to be effected. " They (the Syndicalists) said: ' The catastrophe will be caused by the General Strike. It is the General Strike that will be the catastrophe.' This catastrophe is distinguished from that which is awaited by the Marxists, the Socialist politicians, in that it will not be brought about by chance, it will arise when the workmen wish it. Syndicalism disciplines the catastrophe which the Socialists await with the fatalism of *marabouts*." [2]

But according to Georges Sorel the Marxians have entirely misinterpreted their master's meaning, which in reality excluded " any hypothesis constructed on future Utopias " ; in fact, Sorel represents Marx to have actually declared that " *whoever has a programme for the future is a reactionary.*" [3]

Now, of course, if Marx really said this the whole theory of Marxian Socialism is founded on a fallacy and is proved to be a system in which Marx himself never believed. But to do him justice we must recognize that there is some truth in Sorel's contention that Marx never pretended to have devised any definite system for " the organization of the proletariat," that he merely made use

---

[1] Paul Leroy Beaulieu, *Le Collectivisme* (1909), p. 650.
[2] Mermeix, p. 122.
[3] *Réflexions sur la violence*, pp. 185, 191.

of the " enormous mass " of ready-made material which he found in the British Museum for his great work on Capital,[1] and that it was his disciples who read into it ideas for the reconstruction of the social system.

On these grounds Sorel is able to claim Marx as his ally, that is to say, as a pure destructionist — not as a Syndicalist, for nowhere in Marx's writings could one find any hint of the Syndicalist theory of industrial organization; but above all it is as the great promoter of the class war that Sorel finds in Marx his true affinity. To this one point the apostle of Syndicalism is ready to sacrifice all other considerations. " The scission of classes," he declares, " is the basis of all Socialism ";[2] the one thing to be avoided is social peace.

Indeed, Sorel's one fear is that modern nations," stupefied with humanitarianism (*abruties par l'humanitairisme*) "[3] — the phrase might be taken straight from Nietzsche — may prevent the conflict.[4] To guard against this danger every effort must be made to keep up the class war, not only by inciting Labour to attack Capital, but by stiffening the resistance of Capital to the demands of Labour. " The more ardently Capitalistic the *bourgeoisie*, the more will the proletariat be filled with a war-like spirit confident in its revolutionary force, the more will the movement be assured."[5]

It is necessary, therefore, by violence " to force Capitalism to occupy itself solely with its material rôle," so as " to give back to it the warlike qualities it once possessed."[6] Employers of labour must be made to understand " that they have nothing to gain by works of social peace or by democracy."[7] " All then," Sorel concludes hopefully, " can be saved if by violence it (the proletariat) succeeds in consolidating class divisions and in restoring to the *bourgeoisie* something of its energy; that is the great aim towards which must be directed the thought of all

---

[1] *Réflexions sur la violence*, pp. 185, 191.
[2] *Ibid.* p. 257.   [3] *Ibid.* p. 110.
[4] See Sorel's whole chapter on "La Décadence bourgeoise et la violence," *i.e.* the disinclination of employers to fight labour. *Ibid.* pp. 91-121.
[5] *Ibid.* p. 105.   [6] *Ibid.* p. 110.
[7] *Ibid.* p. 109.

men who are not hypnotized by the events of the day but think of the conditions of the morrow." [1]

Such, then, is the aim of Syndicalism as set forth by its chief exponent, Georges Sorel. At first sight the one merit it seems to possess is frankness. Hitherto revolutionary writers, to whichever faction they belonged, had always professed that their system would conduce in some degree to human happiness; even the Anarchists appeared to derive enjoyment from the prospect of their lunatic dreams of the future. But Sorel promises nothing; " Utopias of easy happiness " he openly derides; even on the system of Syndicalism he has practically nothing to say — the only thing that matters is to keep up revolutionary ardour. Yet, after all, we find that Sorel is not much more honest than his predecessors, for whilst denouncing the visionary Socialists who lead the proletariat towards a mirage, Sorel goes on to admit that the General Strike, which, like *Der Tag* of the Germans, must ever be held before the eyes of the people, is in reality a *myth*. It will probably never come off, but just as the early Christians maintained their religious ardour by looking forward to the second advent, so the people must be taught to centre all their hopes on the coming cataclysm. Thus the idea of the General Strike will serve the purpose of continually unsettling industry and fretting away the foundations of Capital.

To the normal mind the theory of Sorel as set forth in the foregoing pages must of course appear unbelievable; the incredulous should therefore read his book for themselves in order to be convinced that such views can be seriously put forward. Is Sorel, however, sincere, or is he secretly an agent of reaction? The hypothesis is not beyond the bounds of possibility. At any rate if the author of *Réflexions sur la violence* had been put up by the Government to discredit the whole Socialist movement by working it out to a *reductio ad absurdum*, he could not have stated his case more ably or have offered sounder arguments for the defence of the existing order against the encroachments of so-called democracy. " Experience

[1] *Réflexions sur la violence*, p. 120.

shows," says Sorel, " that in all countries where democracy can develop its nature freely the most scandalous corruption is displayed without anyone considering it of use to conceal its rascalities," [1] and after a scathing indictment of democratic government in America and elsewhere he ends with the words: "Democracy is the land of plenty dreamt of by unscrupulous financiers." [2]

But it is for the parliamentary Socialists that Sorel reserves his bitterest scorn. The sole object of these people —" Intellectuals who have embraced the profession of thinking for the proletariat " [3] — is to bring themselves into power. In reasoning on social conflicts " they see in the combatants only instruments. The proletariat is their army, which they love with the love a colonial administrator may feel for the bands which enable him to subject a great many negroes to his caprices; they concern themselves with leading it on because they are in a hurry to win quickly the great battles which are to deliver up the State to them; they keep up the ardour of their men, as the ardour of the troops of mercenaries has always been kept up by exhortations to coming pillage, by appeals to hatred, and also by small favours which already permit them to distribute a few posts." [4] But in reality it will not be the proletariat who will share the spoils, for the prospect on which the leaders' eyes are fixed is " the day when they will have the public treasure at their disposal; they are dazzled by the immense reserve of riches which will be delivered then to pillage; what feastings, what *cocottes*, what satisfactions to vanity! " [5] Then, then, at last " our official Socialists can reasonably hope to achieve the goal of their dreams and sleep in gorgeous mansions." [6] After that " it would be very naïve to suppose that people profiting by demagogic dictatorship would easily give up their advantages." [7]

As to the " dictatorship of the proletariat " advocated by the Socialists but " on which they do not much care to give explanations," [8] Sorel declares that this would be

[1] *Réflexions sur la violence*, p. 320.
[2] *Ibid.* p. 321.
[3] *Ibid.* p. 186.
[4] *Ibid.* p. 233.
[5] *Ibid.* p. 112.
[6] *Ibid.* p. 101.
[7] *Ibid.* p. 236.
[8] *Ibid.* p. 234.

a return to the Old Régime, a plan for feudalizing Capital, and he quotes Bernstein in saying that it would end simply in the dictatorship of club orators and littérateurs.[1] Who, he asks, is to profit by such a government? Certainly not the country, which would be ruined, " but what does the future of the country matter as long as the new régime provides a good time for a few professors who imagine they invented Socialism and *a few Dreyfusard financiers?* "[2]

In the opinion, therefore, of the great Syndicalist, Jewish finance is largely interested in the triumph of State Socialism.

The inconsistency of Jaurès and other French Socialists on the question of Dreyfus is shown up in Sorel's book by a parallel drawn from the first French Revolution, of which he ruthlessly shatters the legends and destroys the prestige of " the great revolutionary days,"[3] and he asks why Danton, of whom Jaurès in his great history of the Revolution had made a hero, but whose conduct during the sad days of September " was not very worthy of admiration,"[4] should be defended on the score of acting in the interests of national defence, when Jaurès himself took part against the anti-Semites who also believed they were acting in the interests of national defence in the matter of the Affaire Dreyfus. The revolutionaries were represented by Jaurès as " sacrificing immediate human tenderness and pity " for the success of the cause, but then Sorel inquires: " Why have written so much on the inhumanity of the tormentors of Dreyfus? They too sacrificed ' immediate human tenderness ' to what seemed to them the salvation of the country."[5]

Not only Jaurès and Clemenceau in France but the Socialists of England become in turn the butt of Sorel's pleasantries:

Sidney Webb enjoys a very exaggerated reputation for competence: he had the merit of compiling uninteresting *dossiers*, and the patience to compose one of the most indigestible compilations on the history of Trade Unionism, but he is one of the most *borné* minds which could only dazzle men little

[1] *Réflexions sur la violence*, pp. 234, 235.
[2] *Ibid.* p. 102.
[3] *Ibid.* pp. 124-130, 238, 239.
[4] *Ibid.* p. 147.
[5] *Ibid.* p. 146.

accustomed to think. The people who introduced his glory into France did not understand a word of Socialism, and if he is really, as his translator asserts, in the first rank of contemporary authors of economic history, the intellectual standard of these historians must be very low.

And Sorel adds that, in the opinion of Tarde, Sidney Webb was simply " a blotter of paper " (*un barbouilleur de papier*).[1]

In order to appreciate the antagonism between the opposing camps of Syndicalism and State Socialism it is only necessary to read Sorel's book in conjunction with Mr. Ramsay MacDonald's little work on Syndicalism, where " the fantastic programme of revolution produced by the Syndicalist " is admirably shown up. " If," the British advocate of Socialism concludes, " the grand programme of Syndicalism is a mere delusion, its immediate action is mischievous. Sabotage, destruction of industrial capital, perpetual strikes injure the workers far more than any other class, and rouse in society reactionary passions and prejudices which defeat the work of every agency making for the emancipation of labour. They put labour in the wrong. The Syndicalist might be an *agent provocateur* of the Capitalist, he certainly is his tool." [2]

But in this feud between Syndicalism and Socialism — the mere continuation of the old conflict between Anarchy and Communism — it would be folly to see any security for society. The rival revolutionary camps may be — and are — bitterly antagonistic in their aims, but both will stand together for the overthrow of the existing social order, and only when the country has been reduced to chaos by revolution, or to bankruptcy and ruin by Socialist administration, will the leaders of the opposing forces take each other by the throat in a life-and-death struggle.

. . . .

Although, as we have seen in the preceding pages, the root idea of Syndicalism — organization and control of industry by independent groups of workers — has somewhat been lost to sight by Syndicalist writers, who have concentrated their attention more on the revolution than

[1] *Réflexions sur la violence*, p. 163.
J. Ramsay MacDonald. *Syndicalism*, p. 167.

on its morrow, a more constructive phase of the same theory has been inaugurated in recent years by the movement known as *Guild Socialism*.

Now Guild Socialism is nothing new. To any one familiar with Socialist literature the task of embarking on the gospel of Guild Socialists, as set forth in the writings of Mr. G. D. H. Cole, must appear something like sitting down to read through a *Dictionary of Famous Quotations*. But this is an experience to which the patient student of Socialism must resign himself, for since by the middle of the last century everything that could be said on the subject had been said already, further exponents of the creed can only dish up the cold remains left by their predecessors. The process is, however, frequently very successful; nothing is easier than to gain a reputation as a brilliant Socialist writer by simply rearranging the same theories, the same phrases, and the same catchwords in a different manner to tempt the jaded palate. Yet never have the chefs of Socialism produced a galantine to compare with that of Mr. G. D. H. Cole! Here a little bit of Louis Blanc, there a scrap from Vidal, but, above all, solid slabs of Marx and Sorel. And all this concealed by a cunning glaze of modernity!

In reality Guild Socialism is simply Syndicalism with the addition of a State. But the State is not to exercise authority, only to act as a municipal body, also as a banker to the workers, and occasionally as umpire in industrial disputes. National finance would be decided by " a Joint Committee representing equally the State and the Guild Congress. The State would own the means of production as trustee for the community: the Guilds would manage them, also as trustees for the community, and would pay to the State a single tax or rent." [1]

The assurance of Guild Socialists that the Guilds would always honourably act up to their part as trustees is based on " confidence in man," although we note that a large portion of the human race, the present employing class, is to be regarded with the blackest suspicion. Apparently the fact of becoming a " Guildsman " miraculously does

[1] *National Guilds, an Appeal to Trade Unionists*, p. 13.

away with all such characteristics as greed and self-interest. All this is pure Buchez, and we have only to turn back to page 109 of this book to see Guilds where " every man is a master " in operation, whilst Louis Blanc's " associations of working-men," financed by the State, demonstrate the precise system of Guild Socialism — and incidentally its failure in the past.

Unhappily it is not in the spirit of Buchez or even of the fanatic Louis Blanc that Guild Socialists set about their task. For all its professions of spirituality and love for humanity, Guild Socialism is avowedly revolutionary. " To Revolutionary Trade Unionism the Guild idea looks," [1] its aim is " the realization of Industrial Unionism, the building up of the whole body of Labour into one fighting force." [2] Borrowing Marx's phraseology on the doctrine of " wage-slavery," it sets out to promote class hatred of the most virulent description and advocates strikes to overthrow the Capitalist system. In its denunciations of State Socialism the influence of Sorel is clearly detected.

The only point, then, in which Guild Socialism shows itself superior to Syndicalism is that, instead of concentrating solely on destruction and the General Strike, it makes some plans for the " morrow of the revolution."

In its conception of guilds of busy workers co-operating in a spirit of fraternity to make a success of their trade, it takes us back to the original idea of Syndicalism — Proudhon's old simile of the hive where we see in imagination the swarms of happy bees flitting through the summer sunshine laden with honey for the comb, full of joy in their labours.

Yet all that is to be said in favour of the industrial system that Guild Socialism advocates can equally be said of Co-operation. Co-operative industry exemplified by such schemes as profit-sharing, co-partnership, etc., is simply Guild Socialism without its economic fallacies — and also without revolution. This is precisely why co-operation finds in Socialists and Syndicalists alike its bitterest opponents.

[1] *The Guild Idea*, p. 14.   [2] *National Guilds*, p. 19.

But there is also a further difference between Co-operation and Guild Socialism. Co-operation is an honest movement, for it has always been willing to put its theories to the test by inaugurating industries on a co-operative basis. Sometimes these experiments have failed, sometimes they have triumphantly succeeded. Co-operation has not been proved a failure.

But it will be noticed that neither Syndicalists nor Guild Socialists ever propose to start industries on the lines they advocate, but always to " expropriate " by violence those already in existence and hand them over to the workers: In this respect their record compares unfavourably with that of Socialists. The earlier Socialists, whose sincerity we cannot doubt, did attempt to carry out their schemes by means of Communists' Settlements; Syndicalism ventures on no such experiments. This is the more significant in that the reason given by Socialists for their failures in the past does not apply to Syndicalism. For if one is tactless enough to question Socialists on these abortive efforts one is inevitably met with the stock reply: " Oh, of course Socialism cannot exist in isolated communities; in order to test its efficacy it must be adopted by the State." Now although we know that it was not through outside opposition or competition but from internal disintegration that these settlements went to pieces, it is nevertheless obvious that *State* Socialism can only be practised by a Socialist State. This condition, however, is quite unnecessary to the existence of Syndicalism, since the system it advocates is to consist of autonomous groups of workers independent of State control. There is therefore no reason why these should not exist under the present régime. What is there to prevent a syndicate of miners from taking over a mine, or of factory workers buying a factory, and running it on Syndicalist lines? The huge funds of the Trade Unions would surely be better spent in an outlay of this kind than in strikes that deplete their exchequer to no purpose. For not only would a successful experiment on these lines satisfy the aspirations of all the workers who took part in it, but would proclaim to the world the efficacy of the Syndicalist theory. Henceforth only Syndicalist industries would attract workers, and employers who continued to maintain the old system of wage payment would find themselves denuded of employees. Thus without any violence, without the shedding of a drop of blood, the whole industrial system could be revolutionized.

Why is this not done? Simply because the leaders of Syndicalism know that it could not succeed. They are well aware that an industry which adopted the principle of control by all the workers would come to grief as surely as a ship that adopted the plan of navigation by all the crew. In a word, they do not believe in the theories they teach.

One experiment founded to a certain extent on Syndicalism may, however, be quoted. This was the settlement inaugurated by William Lane in Paraguay at the end of the last century. Lane, an English journalist who had settled in Australia, appears to have been a perfectly honest man who had become deeply imbued with the doctrines both of Karl Marx and of Syndicalism. Hence he believed that " the factory-hand was the rightful owner of the factory, that the sheep-shearer was entitled to the full profits of the shearing industry, that the legal owners of all forms of property were robbing the manual workers of their dues." [1] Lane, therefore, entered whole-heartedly into the great Syndicalist strikes which at this date of 1890 were paralysing the trade of the country. But perceiving the futility of this method of warfare — which had the effect of reducing the high wages of Australian workers to the level of forty-five years earlier — Lane decided to found a workers' paradise in another land. Accordingly at the end of 1892 he set sail with 250 faithful followers for Paraguay, where he started a colony under the name of " the New Australia " a few miles from Asuncion.

The subsequent adventures of the settlers have been vividly described by Mr. Stewart Grahame in a narrative which is much more amusing than *Three Men in a Boat*, and has the additional merit of being true. It should be

[1] *Where Socialism failed*, by G. Stewart Grahame (John Murray, 1913), p. 5. In view of the above quotation it would perhaps have been more accurate to name the book *Where Syndicalism failed*. But the generic term of Socialism is frequently used to include Syndicalism.

read by every one interested in Socialistic ventures, for only a brief résumé can be given here.

At first everything promised well; the colonists entered into possession of 350,000 acres of the very finest land in Paraguay, with pasturage sufficient to keep at least 70,000 head of cattle, and since all were filled with " communal ardour," and also with the warmest confidence in their leader, there seemed no reason why a flourishing settlement should not result. But precisely the same experiences befell William Lane as had befallen Étienne Cabet forty-four years earlier. The colonists before long took turns in quarrelling amongst themselves and in accusing Lane of tyrannizing over them. " The man who worked arduously for eight hours in the vegetable garden envied the more fortunate fellow who spent his day riding about the pastures herding cattle. The cowboy, on the other hand, considered that the schoolmaster had a considerably easier job, and he was perhaps moved to compare his lot with that of the colonist whose principal duty appeared to be to blow the dinner horn."

Inevitably " bitter charges of favouritism were levelled at the head of Lane and at the heads of the foremen in charge of every industry." " We have surrendered all civil rights and become mere cogs in the wheel," wrote one of the colonists who had come to New Australia to find joy in " work by all for all." " In fact a man is practically a slave. Lane does the thinking and the colonists do the work. Result, barbarism."

At the end of fourteen months Lane found nimself obliged to expel a number of malcontents; in the following year (1894) no less than a third of the colony seceded of their own accord. " We came," said one, " to found Utopia and we have succeeded in creating a Hell upon Earth." But on the arrival at this juncture of 190 new-comers, who had been attracted to the New Australia by delusive reports, Lane was himself deposed, and started off at the head of a few followers to found another settlement, which he named Cosme.

For a few years the two colonies struggled on in misery, but finally in 1899 Lane abandoned his experiment at

Cosme and returned to Australia. By dint of employing native labour on the hated wage system they had set out to destroy, the Cosmians partly succeeded in restoring their shattered fortunes; but before long the Socialist principle was recognized as a failure and abandoned by both settlements in favour of Individualism.

From this moment the energy of the colonists revived. " In an incredibly short space of time houses shot up surrounded by well-tilled kitchen gardens. . . . Very soon the grass lands were once more dotted with cattle . . ." ; in a word, New Australia became " an average community of sane, sober, hard-working, self-respecting farmers, living at peace with one another and taking for their motto: ' What we have we hold ! ' "

The experiment of New Australia offers an interesting demonstration of Proudhon's theory of the hive and the bees when carried out to its ultimate conclusion. For in New Australia, as in all other communal settlements, the principal difficulties encountered were the lack of public spirit and the inclination to " slack." " There is absolutely no regard for common property," one member of the colony wrote to the *Pall Mall Gazette*. Moreover, " it was freely alleged by almost every colonist against some other that the latter was working less vigorously for the benefit of ' all ' than he would have done in his own interest." Mr. Stewart Grahame goes on to show us how this lack of energy would be overcome in a Socialist State, and by a curious coincidence he illustrates the fate of " won't works " under Socialist administration by the same simile as Proudhon in a description of the massacre of the drones, quoted from Maeterlinck's *La Vie de l'abeille;*

' One morning the long-expected word of command goes through the hive, and the peaceful workers turn into judges and executioners. . . . Each one is assailed by three or four envoys of justice. . . . Many will reach the door and escape into space . . . but towards evening, impelled by hunger and cold, they return in crowds to the entrance of the hive to beg for shelter. But there they encounter another pitiless guard. The next morning, before setting forth on their journey, the workers will clear the threshold, strewn with the corpses of the useless giants.

On closer inspection the industrial system of the hive is thus seen to be less peaceful than it had been represented by the Father of Syndicalism — Proudhon. Yet all the more it demonstrates the manner in which alone Socialist or Syndicalist administration can be carried out on a large scale.

In isolated settlements of the kind, idlers or objectors can be banished, but once the system has been made universal the refusal to do the share of work allotted to one can only be punishable by death. The text adopted by militant Socialists as their battle-cry, " If a man will not work neither shall he eat!" must be literally carried out by a Socialist State, and the proletarian disciples of Ca' Canny, no less than the " idle rich," as also those workers for whom no employment can be found, will find that the law of the hive can be even more ferocious than the hated government of " Capitalism."

Mr. Stewart Grahame has well said that " few, even amongst Socialists, realize the ferocity of Socialism." They imagine that " that classic pattern of Socialist administration, the Reign of Terror," was an accident that need not recur if the experiment of Socialism is repeated. But we have only to examine the writings of Socialists to recognize that the Reign of Terror was simply Socialism carried out to its logical conclusion. Thus we find even a Socialist of such reputed moderation as Mr. H. M. Hyndman writing these words:

The whole noble array of barristers, solicitors, accountants, surveyors, agents, and about ninety-nine hundredths of the present distributors would be wholly useless in a properly organized society. They live upon the existing *bourgeois* system . . . They will *disappear* with the huckster arrangements on which they thrive.[1]

Since there is at present no way of making human beings " disappear " it is obvious that they must be killed off, for, as Robespierre perceived, they cannot all be absorbed by " work of essential utility," and can therefore only be left to die of starvation. So all Socialist roads lead back to the old system of depopulation, and it is question-

---

[1] H. M. Hyndman, *The Historical Basis of Socialism* (1883), p. 461.

able whether the guillotine was not the humaner method.

Syndicalism at any rate does not conceal its intentions in this matter. The massacre of the drones — and of those whom overcrowding of the hive forces to become drones — forms an essential part of the programme that Mermeix has well described as " a Neronic dream."

In the exultations of Georges Sorel over the coming death struggle between Capital and Labour, we seem to hear a Roman Emperor rejoicing in anticipation over the collision between two racing chariots that is to strew the arena with the mangled remains of men and horses and drench its sand in blood.

Syndicalism as formulated by George Sorel is the plan of the World Revolution stripped of its illusory wrappings and revealed in all its naked deformity. It is avowedly anti-patriotic, anti-religious, anti-democratic; it is, in the words of one of its own advocates, Pouget, " the negation of the system of majorities," and its sole aim is rule by force and violence. Far more than Socialism, it is the direct continuation of the programme of the Illuminati. Can we not see Weishaupt smiling in his grave as we read the words of Sorel: " It is impossible not to see that a sort of irresistible wave will pass over the old civilization "?

(Since writing the above chapter I have been informed on good authority that M. Georges Sorel has definitely gone over to the Royalists. I wonder how many youthful Syndicalists are told of this incident in the life of their prophet. — AUTHOR'S NOTE.)

CHAPTER X

THE REVOLUTION OF 1917

The Great War — Rôle of British Socialists — Rôle of German Social Democrats — The Russian Revolution — Bolshevism — Rôle of the Jews — The Protocols of Nilus — German Organisation.

WHEN the Great War broke out in 1914 it was on International Socialism that Germany counted to break the resistance of her enemies.

Everywhere the ground had been carefully prepared. In England, from the founding of the First International onwards, German intrigue had never ceased to play a leading part in the succeeding Socialist organizations, each of which in turn had been diverted from its original course in the direction of pan-German interests.

Although the influence of Marx amongst the British working-men was practically *nil* during his lifetime, the Marxian tradition had been carried on by his colleague Engels and his British middle-class disciples who formed the Socialist associations in this country.

Thus the Second Internationale, founded in 1882, became Germanized by 1893, and remained so until the outbreak of war, when it was suspended and did not reconstruct itself until the Geneva Congress of 1920. The Fabian Society, inaugurated in 1883, fell almost immediately under the control of Mr. G. Bernard Shaw who has made no secret of his international sympathies. In the same year the Social Democratic Federation was founded by Mr. H. M. Hyndman, with *Justice* as its organ, and in the following year of 1884 produced an offshoot in the Socialist League founded by William Morris with the co-operation of Mr. Belfort Bax, an Austrian semi-

Anarchist named Andrea Scheu, several English Anarchists, and Dr. Aveling, the " husband " of Marx's daughter, as editor of its organ *The Commonweal*.

This ceased to exist in 1892. The original S.D.F. meanwhile continued its course, but in 1911 changed its name to the British Socialist party.

The alien influence in all these associations is thus plainly visible, but it was not sufficient to content Friedrich Engels, who therefore set to work on another enterprise, the " Independent Labour Party," which, with the collaboration of Mr. Keir Hardie, he afterwards boasted that he helped to create. Engels then instructed Dr. Aveling, who had formed a " free union " with Marx's daughter,[1] to join the Executive Committee of the I.L.P., whilst Eleanor herself " was told off to work for the Gas Workers' and General Labourers' Union."

Engels now imagined that, with the aid of the Independent Labour Party, he would obliterate the Social Democratic Federation and the Fabians, as a punishment for not showing sufficient subservience to German leadership. He evidently believed that he was eminently successful in these efforts. On July 20, 1889, Engels wrote to Sorge: " I think that we are going to make great progress here." Then he goes on to explain that as the Anglo-Saxons are slow and dull of comprehension, it was quite natural that English workmen should be "bossed" (*gebosst*) by Germans.

In a subsequent letter Engels boasts that the gas workers of London " were led by Tussy," the diminutive name of Marx's youngest daughter (Eleanor). Finally, in 1892, Engels repeats triumphantly:

We are making great progress here in England. Affairs advance splendidly. Next year there will be seen marching behind Germany, not only Austria and France, but also England.[2]

These hopes found their fulfilment on the declaration of war in 1914. What part did the Socialists play? The true meaning of Internationalism was then revealed. Although the war on the part of Germany was one of pure aggression, and on the part of England one of urgent national defence, *the whole German Social Democratic Party*

---

[1] How admirably Marx was fitted to direct the affairs of the human race is shown by the way he managed his own family. Eleanor Marx, her " husband," Dr. Aveling, and her sister all committed suicide.

[2] Adolphe Smith, *The Pan-German Internationale*, p. 6.

in a body went over to the German war-party,[1] whilst all the Socialist organizations in this country — the Independent Labour Party, the British Socialist Party, and the Socialist Labour Party—opposed England's participation in the war.[2]

Not content with this Pacifist attitude before the outbreak of hostilities, certain Socialists — notably the members of the I.L.P. — continued, after the war had begun, to give active encouragement to the enemy. Mr. Ramsay Macdonald, who had published a violent indictment of the British Government on August 13, 1914, was mentioned on several occasions with the warmest approbation in the German press. At a congress of the I.L.P. in Norwich in April 1915, a resolution was passed by a huge majority opposing recruiting. Worse still, industrial troubles were stirred up amongst the workers, delaying the supply of war materials to the troops, so that the *Referee* declared that " German Socialists and their English allies were responsible for the death of thousands of Englishmen on the battle-front."[3]

It is only just to add that the question of the war brought about a split in the British Socialist Party, and though the name was retained by the anti-war party — a party largely composed from 1916 onwards of Russian-Jews and foreign Anarchists, with *The Call* for their organ — a group of British Socialists, under the leadership of Mr. Hyndman, stood out for national defence, and in 1916 reorganized themselves under the name of the " National Socialist Party." In 1920 this society resumed the original name of the Social Democratic Federation, whilst at the same date the British Socialist Party, now affiliated to the Third (Moscow) Internationale, became the British Communist Party and changed the name of its organ from *The Call* to *The Communist*. The fact then remains that at the outbreak of war British Socialism was represented by no national and patriotic party. The work of Germany had been well and truly done.

[1] On this point see Laskine's admirable pamphlet, *Les Socialistes du Kaiser, la fin d'un mensonge* (Floury, 1915).
[2] *The Two Internationals*, by R. Palme Dutt (Labour Research Department, 34 Eccleston Square), 1920, p. 3.
[3] Laskine, *L'Internationale et le pan-Germanisme*, pp. 377-382.

Unless these preliminaries are clearly recognized, the attitude of the Socialists must appear only as the most extraordinary paradox. Why should the so-called champions of democracy have accorded their sympathy to Imperial Germany, the most monarchic and the most autocratic country in the world, rather than to Republican France, the home of the revolutionary tradition? It is true that the Government of Germany under Wilhelm II. was probably the best in Europe from the point of view of the working-classes, but this was precisely because it repudiated the Socialistic theory of the dictatorship of the proletariat, and owed its success to the fact that it treated the people like children, cared for them like children, punished them like children, and never allowed them to dictate.

The pro-German sympathies of British Socialists are therefore incomprehensible unless we realize that all their ideas had been instilled into their minds by German agents. " I am anti-French, but I am none the less anti-English," Marx, their prophet, had declared,[1] and the " anti-Allies " attitude of " International " Socialists in this country was the natural result of these influences.

In France German propaganda had been less successful. Although there were a few notorious pro-Germans in the Socialist and Radical camps the French Socialist party stood solidly for national defence. Even Jaurès, whose illusions on Germany had excited suspicions of complicity with the enemy, warned his countrymen that they must " beware of the *Illuminati*, who seek to organize the proletariat on a non-national basis."[2] Anti-patriotism is a sentiment not easily aroused in France, and inspires little admiration there when professed by foreigners. In this connection it is amusing to observe the attitude of Georges Sorel — Syndicalist, and therefore International, as he might profess to be — towards our British pacifists.

" Arbitration," he remarks, " always gives results disastrous to England; but these good people (the English Liberals) prefer

[1] *Briefwechsel zwischen Marx und Engels*, iv. 335, date of September 12, 1870.
[2] Quoted in speech of M. Brunet, Socialist deputy for Charleroi, August 2, 1920.

to pay or even to compromise the future of their country rather than affront the horrors of war. . . . Many Englishmen think that by humiliating their country they will become more *sympathiques* — this is not clearly proved." [1]

But it was by pacificism that the great conspiracy gained its end in Russia. This is not the place to recount the story of the Russian Revolution, which is still too fresh in the minds of the public to need repeating; all that concerns us here is to trace the course of the World Revolution throughout the movement and to controvert the purblind declarations of certain leading politicians in this country, who persisted in regarding the Russian upheaval as something quite new in the history of the world. Thus in the House of Lords on February 10, 1920, Lord Curzon observed:

When we look at Russia, who can regard that spectacle without consternation and dismay? — a country at this moment prey to a revolution of a character unprecedented in history. Because, although every one is always drawing analogies with what happened in France 140 or 150 (*sic!*) years ago there is no analogy whatever. Everybody knows that the circumstances of what is happening in Russia at the present time are wholly without parallel in the history of the world, and you can imagine how in what are called the inner circles of statecraft at every moment we are confronted with this appalling spectacle outside our door, upsetting us, perplexing our resolution, and confounding our calculations at every turn.

What wonder that our foreign policy is frequently at fault and that our statesmen find themselves perplexed and confounded at every turn if this is the extent of their historical knowledge? Not only is there an exact analogy between the revolutions of France and Russia, but as every one who has studied the latter movement knows, the Russian Revolution from November 1917 onwards was a *direct continuation of the French*. This was admitted by the Bolsheviks themselves, who repeatedly declared that the first French Revolution must be copied in every detail, and who from the outset took Marat and Robespierre as their models.[2]

[1] *Réflexions sur la violence*, p. 89.

[2] Sir Paul Dukes informed me that at a meeting of the Bolsheviks he attended in Russia at the beginning of the Revolution, Marat was held up as the great example to be followed. In June 1919 an article in the

It has been objected that in two important points the Russian Revolution differs from the French, firstly, that whilst the French Revolution was National, the Russian was International; secondly, that the French Revolution was directed against the aristocracy, but the Russian Revolution aimed particularly at the destruction of the *bourgeoisie*. Both these statements are inaccurate. The French Revolution, like the Russian Revolution, contained both National and International elements. In its declaration " all men are brothers " the French Constituent Assembly gave expression to the purest Internationalism, and Clootz, the apostle of this doctrine, received as we have seen, the loudest acclamations from the Convention. It was only when the Jacobins' declaration of world anarchy met with opposition from foreign countries and also ran counter to the innate patriotism of the French people that the Convention found itself forced into an attitude of Nationalism it had never intended to assume, and under the domination of Robespierre, the greatest opponent of Internationalism, Clootz and the " parti de l'étranger " were condemned to death. In Russia, on the other hand, the Revolution did not bear at the outset an entirely International character: amongst the Social Revolutionaries who brought about the rising of March 1917 were several national groups; the Mensheviks likewise comprised a national party, led by Plechanov. It was not until the Bolsheviks seized the reins of power that the Revolution became frankly International, and this was facilitated by the fact that the Russian people were less patriotic than the French, and also that whilst the Jacobins of France could count on no support from abroad the Bolsheviks depended almost entirely on foreign co-operation and founded all their hopes on the prospect of a world revolution.

Daily Herald described the closing down by the Bolshevik authorities of a play entitled *The Death of Danton,* for fear it might be offensive to the memory of Robespierre. A Russian who had been imprisoned under the Bolsheviks wrote to me after reading my *French Revolution:* " Your book . . . seems to be the diary of our own revolution, so thoroughly well have our apes learnt their rôles . . . everybody in Russia knew by heart that bloody era, though many of the actors hardly knew how to sign their names! "

In the matter of the class war the Bolsheviks of Russia pursued precisely the same course as the revolutionaries of France. In both countries the monarchy and aristocracy were the first to suffer; in both the turn of the *bourgeoisie* came next. In the summer of 1793, as we have seen, war on the *bourgeoisie* was declared by the Convention, and the battle-cries of that period have been adopted verbatim by the Bolsheviks. Let us follow the same process, as carried out by Lenin, in his own words:

What is the first stage? It is the transfer of power to the capitalist class (bourgeoisie). Up to the March revolution of 1917 power in Russia was in the hands of one ancient class, namely the feudalist-aristocratic-landowning class headed by Nicholas Romanov. After that revolution power has been in the hands of a different, a new class, namely the capitalist class (the bourgeoisie). The shifting of power from one class to another is the first, the main, fundamental symptom of a revolution, both in the strictly scientific and the practical political sense of the word. To this extent, the capitalist or bourgeois-democratic revolution in Russia is at an end. [1]

In Russia as in France war on the *bourgeoisie* was only the second stage of the movement, and in both the complete subjection of the people formed the next point on the programme.

The Bolshevik revolution was, from the very beginning, avowedly anti-democratic and in no sense the outcome of the Russian revolutionary movement. Until the end of the last century the subversive forces in Russia had been mainly anarchic, resulting from the doctrines of Bakunin and Kropotkine; but with the formation of the Russian Social Democratic Party a definite Marxian school was inaugurated and found further support in the Jewish Bund of Social Democrats. It was at a congress of the Russian Social Democratic Party in London in 1907 that the split took place, resulting in division into the two groups of Bolsheviks under Lenin and Mensheviks under Martoff, the former signifying the majority, the latter the minority, but since then the terms have come to denote the extreme and the less extreme party.

At the outbreak of the March revolution of 1917 the

---

[1] *The Soviets at Work*, p. 8.

Bolsheviks were, however, completely in the minority amongst the various revolutionary groups — a fact frankly admitted by the Bolsheviks themselves [1] — and it was only by a course of systematic deception, and finally by force of arms, that the party which might be described in Bakunin's words, " the German-Jew Company," the " red bureaucracy," succeeded in establishing its domination. Such popularity as it had achieved had been won by the old method of the conspiracy — promising one thing and doing precisely the opposite. Thus according to the word of command of the Secret Societies — " Constitution " — the Bolsheviks had clamoured for a Constituent Assembly, and their first act was to dissolve the assembly elected by universal suffrage; exploiting the war-weariness of the troops they had promised the people immediate peace, and having by these means created disaffection first in the navy, then in the First army, and finally throughout all the troops, they inaugurated a régime that could only exist on warfare and of which the whole policy is aggressive militarism; they had promised the peasants the land they coveted, and then denied them the right to own the crops they grew on it.

From the outset, however, the Bolsheviks had never succeeded in obtaining a following amongst the peasants, of which the revolutionary elements looked to the Social Revolutionaries for salvation, and it was on the workmen of the towns that they counted for support. But here again their promises proved delusive, and the workers who imagined that they were to run the industries in which they were engaged found themselves bitterly disillusioned. Great efforts have been made by the Bolsheviks to persuade Syndicalists that their plans are identical, as we see in the overture made by Zinovieff in the name of the Third Internationale to the I.W.W. of America (date of January 1920), where soothing assurances are given on the subject

---

[1] " At the beginning of the Revolution, the Socialist Revolutionary Party became by far the strongest in the whole political field. The peasants, soldiers, and even the masses of the workers voted for the Socialist Revolutionaries " (Trotzky, *The History of the Russian Revolution to Brest-Litovsk* (Allen and Unwin), p. 62). A report in the White Paper on Bolshevism asserts that 90 per cent of the population were in favour of the monarchy (date of October 14, 1918).

of the State. " Our aim is the same as yours — a commonwealth without State, without Government, without classes, in which the workers shall administer the means of production and distribution for the common benefit of all." But the appeal goes on to explain that this cannot be done all at once, and the old process of the " withering away of the State," originating with Louis Blanc, is to take place. In the face of Lenin's views on control by the workers the hypocrisy of this protestation is, however, apparent.

" Socialism," Lenin wrote in May 1918, " can only be reached by the development of State Capitalism, the careful organization of finance, control, and discipline amongst the workers. Without this there is no Socialism. . . . To every deputation of workers which has come to me complaining that a factory was stopping work, I have said: ' If you desire the confiscation of your factory, the decree forms are ready, and I can sign a decree at once. But tell me: can you take over the management of the concern? Have you calculated what you can produce? Do you know the relations of your works with Russian and foreign markets? " Then it has appeared that they are inexperienced in these matters; that there is nothing about them in the Bolshevik literature, nor in the Menshevik either. The workers who base their activities on State Socialism are the most successful." [1]

Bolshevism then is not Syndicalism, it is State Socialism, it is Marxism, it is Communism, in a word it is *Babouvisme*.

It is therefore no figure of speech to describe it as the most reactionary school of thought now in existence, for it does not even carry on the traditions of 1848 or 1871, but goes right back to the century before last — the Bolshevik revolution of 1917 began where the French Revolution left off in 1797. Is it possible to conceive anything more retrogressive?

Let us now follow the programme of Bolshevism as set forth by its own advocates in order to realize its exact resemblance to that of Babeuf. We shall find it most clearly propounded in the pamphlet of Bucharin, the right hand of Lenin, from which the following passages are taken:

[1] *The Chief Task of our Times*, by Vladimir Oulianoff (Lenin), published by the Workers' Socialist Federation, p. 12.

We already know that the root of the evil of all plundering wars, of oppression of the working-classes and of all the atrocities of capitalism, is that the wealth of the world has been enslaved by a few State-organized capitalist bands, who own all the wealth of the earth as their private *property*. . . . To deprive the rich of their power by depriving them of their wealth by force, that is the paramount duty of the working-class, of the Labour Party, the party of Communists. . . . In a Communist order all the wealth belongs not to individuals or classes, but to society as a whole; no one man is master over it. All are equal comrades. . . . The work is carried out jointly, according to a pre-arranged labour plan. A central bureau of statistics calculates how much it is required to manufacture in a year: such and such a number of boots, trousers, sausages, blacking, wheat, cloth, and so on. It will also calculate that for this purpose such and such a number of men must work on the fields and in the sausage work respectively, and such and such a number in the large communal tailoring workshops, etc., and working-hands will be distributed accordingly. The whole of production is conducted on a strictly calculated and adjusted plan, on the basis of an exact estimate of all the machines, apparatus, all raw material, and all the labour power in the community.[1]

Compare this with Babeuf: " A simple affair of numbering things and people, a simple operation of calculations and combinations." [2]

All this, Bucharin goes on to inform us, " can be attained only by working to a single plan and by organizing the whole community into *one vast labour commune*." [3]

This process, which is to begin with the *bourgeoisie*, is to be carried out

by means of introducing labour record books and labour service. Every one of the above-named class should receive a special book in which an account is kept of his work, that is to say of his compulsory service. Fixed entries in his book entitle him to buy or to receive certain food products, bread in the first place. . . . If such an individual refuses to work there is no corresponding entry in his book. He goes to the store but is told, " There is nothing for you. Please to show an entry confirming your work." [4]

This may be very pleasing to the proletarian who sees in imagination the " idle rich " being forced to shoulder

[1] N. Bucharin, *The Programme of the World Revolution* (Socialist Labour Press, Glasgow, 1920), pp. 16, 17.
[2] P. 63 of this book.
[3] *Programme of the World Revolution*, p. 17.   [4] *Ibid.* p. 55.

spade or pickaxe in order to secure a meal, but the proletarian smile fades away as the end of the page is reached
and these ominous words appear: " Of course labour
service for the rich should only be a transitory stage
towards general labour service."

If we turn to *The Russian Code of Labour Laws* (published by the People's Russian Information Bureau in
1920) we shall find that " *all* citizens of the Russian Socialist Federal Soviet Republic over 16 and under 50 years of
age " — with certain exemptions in case of illness — " are
subject to compulsory labour " of eight hours a day.[1]

In fact a great part of Lenin's writings are devoted to
the problem of enforcing this system, to " the higher discipline of the toilers," [2] " iron discipline during work with
absolute submission to the will of one person," [3] for which
purpose " a merciless dictatorship[4] must be exercised."
Moreover, we find that after all " wage-slavery " still
exists, for a whole section of the Russian Code relates to
the " transfer and discharge of wage-earners." But in
time the wages though not the slavery are to disappear, for
Bucharin explains that sale and purchase will by degrees
give way to barter:

An " exchange " of goods must then begin between town and
country, without the agency of money; municipal industrial
organizations send out textile, iron, and other goods into the
country, while the village district organizations send bread to
the towns in exchange . . . when production and distribution
are thoroughly organized money will play no part whatever,
and as a matter of course no kind of money dues will be demanded from any one. Money will have generally become
unnecessary. Finance will become extinct.[5]

In order to attain this ideal condition of things the
working-class must engage in a " bloody, painful, heroic
struggle."

We have only to turn back to the earlier pages of this
book to see that this is identically and in every detail the
plan of the Babouvistes; the Third International in its
" New Communist Manifesto " in fact admits its direct

[1] Pp. 6 and 16.
[2] *The Soviets at Work*, p. 25.
[3] *Ibid*, p. 35.
[4] *Ibid.* p. 40.
[5] *Programme of the World Revolution*, p. 69.

descent from Babeuf. How are we to explain the continuity of idea? Simply by the fact that both systems are founded on the same doctrines — those of Illuminism, and that the plan now at work in Russia has been handed down through the secret societies to the present day.

The Bolshevik revolution has in fact followed out the code of Weishaupt in every point — the abolition of monarchy, abolition of patriotism, abolition of private property and of inheritance, abolition of marriage and morality, and abolition of all religion.

On the last two points queries will be raised. Has the Bolshevik Government *officially* abolished marriage? No; simply because it has not dared to do so, but its intentions in this respect are made quite clear in the pamphlet of Madame Kolontay, the friend of Lenin, *Communism and the Family*,[1] in which it is explained that the old form of " indissoluble marriage " is to give place to " the free and honest union of men and women who are lovers and comrades " — that is to say simply to "free love." Does this imply then " the community of women " ? Much discussion has been devoted to this question, heated controversies have taken place as to whether the mandate of Ekaterinodar ordering the " socialization " of women was a part of the Bolshevik programme or merely the act of an individual commissar. Yet all the time the answer is quite simple. Bolshevism is avowedly Marxism; to follow the precepts of Marx in every detail is the supreme aim of the leaders. And the " *official and open community of women* " *is laid down in Marx's Communist Manifesto.*[2] If, therefore, the Bolshevists have not established it in Russia it is because public opinion was evidently too strong for them. The mandate of Ekaterinodar, never intended for publication in Western Europe, gave away the plan and prevented its execution. But Madame Kolontay's pamphlet leaves no doubt as to the ultimate design. For " free love " must inevitably lead to the same conclusion — the removal of all protection from women. The hypocritical pretension

[1] Published by " The Workers' Socialist Federation," 152 Fleet Street.
[2] Manifesto of the Communist Party published in pamphlet form by the Socialist Labour Party, p. 19.

put forward by Marx and the Bolsheviks of wishing to abolish prostitution can deceive no one — Communism would simply replace voluntary prostitution by forcible rape.

In this matter the Bolsheviks go much further than Babeuf, who does not touch on the community of women, although he is no less insistent on the necessity for the break-up of the family by taking away the children from their parents; and his further stipulation that they should not be allowed to bear their father's name " unless he had distinguished himself by great virtues," certainly seems to indicate abolition of the present marriage system. But in their plan of the communal education of children the Bolsheviks have followed Babeuf to the letter. The English Communist, Mr. Bertrand Russell, has described the idea formulated by Madame Kolontay more or less vaguely — so as not to alarm Western mothers — as he saw it in operation during his stay in Russia, and it is curious to notice that Babeuf's plan of teaching the children dancing has been carefully followed — an irony which even Mr. Russell could not fail to perceive, since the education of these " Eurythmic " dancers contrasted pathetically with " the long hours of painful toil " to which they were " soon to be subject in the workshop or factory." [1] The exact resemblance between the Bolshevik system with that of Babeuf is further shown by this passage from Mr. Russell's book:

It is necessary first to admit that children should be delivered up almost entirely to the State. Nominally, the mother still comes to see her child in these schools, but in actual fact, the drafting of children to the country must intervene, and the whole temper of the authorities seemed to be directed towards *breaking the link between mother and child.* [2]

In the matter of religion the Bolsheviks seem to have been unable to carry out their programme entirely, for, although churches have been desecrated and destroyed, ikons torn down and spat upon, and countless priests murdered, religious worship has not been officially pro-

[1] Bertrand Russell, *The Practice and Theory of Bolshevism* (Allen and Unwin), 1920, p. 69.
[2] *Ibid.* p. 66. Cf. with p. 59 of this book.

hibited as under the French Terror. But the intentions of the Soviet Government on this question admit of no misunderstanding. Turning again to Bucharin we find the following principles laid down:

One of the agencies in achieving this object (dulling the minds of the people) was the belief in God and the Devil. A great number of people have grown accustomed to believe in all this, whilst if we analyse these ideas and try to understand the origin of religion and why it is so strongly supported by the *bourgeoisie*, it will become clear that the real significance of religion is that it is a *poison* which is still being instilled into the people. It will also become clear why the party of the Communists is a strong antagonist of religion. [1]

Adopting the aphorism of Marx that " religion is opium to the people," Bucharin goes on to show the mental degeneracy that results from any religious beliefs, and emphasizes his conclusions with these words in large black lettering: " *Religion must be fought, if not by violence, at all events by argument.*" [2]

All religions, moreover, fall under the ban, for after describing the follies of fasting and penance, Bucharin adds:

Equally foolish things are done by the religious Jew, the Moslem Turk, the Buddhist Chinese, in a word, by every one who believes in God. . . . Religion . . . not only leaves people in a state of barbarism, but helps to leave them in a state of slavery. [3]

In these words we seem to hear again the voice of Anarcharsis Clootz, " the personal enemy of Jesus Christ," uttering his declamations on " the nullity of all religions."

What is all this indeed but Illuminism, of which the anti-religious fury had blazed out successively in Weishaupt, Clootz, the chiefs of the Alta Vendita, in Proudhon, and in Bakunin? Indeed the final aim of the Illuminati, the destruction of Christian civilization, has been frankly admitted by the Bolsheviks of Russia. " Wherever I went in Russia," the Rev. Courtier Forster said on his return from that unhappy country, " the Bolsheviks assured me that ' civilization was all wrong ' and must be done away with. An important follower of Lenin observed: ' We have

[1] *Programme of the World Revolution*, p. 73.
[2] *Ibid.* p. 77.   [3] *Ibid.* p. 76.

now been at work for two years and you see what we have already done, but it will take us twelve years to destroy the civilization of the world.' " And Mr. Lansbury, that obedient pupil of Lenin's, after his visit to Russia echoed the same sentiment in the columns of the *Daily Herald*: " We believe that man has been on the wrong road ever since the dawn of that thing we call civilization." [1] The very words employed by Robert Owen under the influence of Illuminism nearly 100 years earlier!

Yet another witness to the persistence of this theory is Mr. H. G. Wells, whose visions of the future expounded in the concluding chapters of his *Outlines of History* and articles on Russia are simply a compound of Rousseau, Weishaupt, Clootz, and Babeuf. Thus at the end of the former work we find Mr. Wells anticipating a partial return to the " nomadic life " — the identical expression employed by Barruel in describing Weishaupt's theory, — whilst the same writer's views on Internationalism are pure Clootz. What else is the " World State " now being advocated by Mr. Wells in the *Sunday Times* but Clootz's "Universal Republic," or his idea of union between all peoples regardless of nationality but Clootz's " solidarity of the human race " ? The following genealogy of an extraordinary remark by Mr. Wells on the subject of cities will show how curiously he has been impregnated with "illuminated" thought, and incidentally illustrates the method by which one can acquire the reputation of being an " advanced thinker " today:

Barruel explained that the plan of Weishaupt had been to do away with fixed abodes so that man should return to the nomadic life,[2] and that this had been the influence at work behind the French Jacobins when they set out to destroy the manufacturing towns of France.[3] " Be free and equal," he quotes from the original writings of Weishaupt, " and you will be Cosmopolitans and citizens of the world. Know how to appreciate equality and liberty and you will not fear to see Rome, Vienna, Paris, London, Constanti-

---

[1] *Daily Herald* for June 30, 1920.

[2] *Mémoires sur le Jacobinisme*, iii. 127, 130, and 198, quoting *Originalschriften*, Part II., letter No. 10 to Cato.

[3] *Ibid.* pp. 141, 142, 178.

nople burning. . . ."[1] This plan, as we have seen, was put into execution during the Commune of 1871, and still forms an important part of the programme of World Revolution.

In 1796 Babeuf, Illuminatus, expressed the hope that in time all the large towns of France would disappear, as it was in towns that wage slavery flourished and that Capitalists were able to surround themselves with luxury and display.[2]

Seventy years later the Nihilists under the influence of German Illuminism declared: " We must burn down the towns. . . . What is the good of these towns? They only serve to engender servitude ! "[3]

And in 1920 Mr. H. G. Wells excuses the ruin of the towns of Russia under Bolshevism by saying: " It was not Communism which built up *these great impossible cities, but Capitalism.*"[4]

Now this is an argument too silly to have been invented by any one of Mr. Wells's intelligence, and we can only conclude that in putting it forward he is simply repeating a phrase that he has heard from his Russian friends, to whom the idea of the necessity for doing away with towns has descended direct from Weishaupt through the Secret Societies.

It is obvious that ideas such as these in no way correspond to the desires of the " people " in any country. Even the peasants of Russia do not want a return to savagery, whilst to the proletariats of Western Europe nothing would be more abhorrent than the destruction of cities. They love the busy life of towns and all the amenities of civilization; they ask for better homes, a higher standard of living, for modern conveniences that will lighten the burden of the working-woman, for the devices of science, for cinemas and music to beguile their hours of leisure. They do not wish to solve the housing question by becoming nomads. The cure for social evils — slums, sweating, unemployment, exploitation — is not less civilization but *more*. The

[1] *Mémoires sur le Jacobinisme,* iii. 197.
[2] Buonarotti, *Conspiration pour l'égalite dite de Babeuf,* i. 221.
[3] Fribourg, *Association Internationale des Travailleurs,* p. 184.
[4] *Sunday Express* for Oct. 31, 1920.

" people " understand this very well, and thus the programme of the revolutionary leaders is still, as it has been throughout, in direct opposition to the wishes of the people.

If any doubt on this point still remains, if the history of the World Revolution related in this book does not prove that the revolutionary movement for the last 140 years has been the work of a conspiracy whose aims are entirely unconnected with the interests and demands of the people, how are we to account for the following undeniable facts?

1.   That although the grievances of the people throughout this period have varied according to the changing conditions of our civilization, the programme of the social revolution has never varied. For if the succeeding outbreaks had been made by the people each would have been distinguished by different war-cries, different aims arising from the exigencies of the moment; instead of this each outbreak has been carried on to the same slogans, has repeated the same catch-words, and each has been directly copied from the earliest — and until 1917 the most successful — attempt, the first French Revolution.

2.   That the leaders of the movement have never, in a single instance, been men of the people, but always members of the upper or middle classes who could not by any possibility be regarded as victims of oppression. And if it is objected that these men were disinterested fanatics fighting in a cause that was not their own, then —

3.   That, with rare exceptions such as Louis Blanc, they invariably displayed complete unconcern for the sufferings of the people and a total disregard for human life. No instance has ever been recorded of pity or sympathy displayed by the Terrorists of France towards any individual members of the working-classes; on the contrary, they turned a deaf ear to all complaints. The Marxists and Bakuninists mutually accused each other of regarding the people as " cannon fodder."

4.   That each outbreak has occurred not when the cause of the people was hopeless but on the eve of great reforms.

5.   That each has been followed not by reform but by

a period of reaction. For twenty years after the first French Revolution the very word " reform " could hardly be breathed even in England.

6.   That in spite of the fact that each outbreak has thus thrown back the cause of the people, each has been represented to the people as a step forward and further revolutions have been advocated.

The revolutionary movement of 1776 to the present day is therefore the work of a continuous conspiracy working for its own ends and against the interests of the people.

.   .   .   .

But now we come to the further question — who are the modern Illuminati, the authors of the plot? What is their ultimate object in wishing to destroy civilization? What do they hope to gain by it? It is this apparent absence of motive, this seemingly aimless campaign · of destruction carried on by the Bolsheviks of Russia, that has led many people to believe in the theory of a Jewish conspiracy to destroy Christianity. And indeed, if one examines the present régime of Russia apart from the revolutionary movement of the last 140 years, this provides a very conclusive solution to the problem. To the unprejudiced observer Bolshevism in Russia may well appear to be a wholly Jewish movement.

For many years before the present revolution the Jews had played a leading part in the forces of disruption in that country. The correspondent of *The Times* at Odessa in 1905 described the riots that took place there at the end of October when " excited Jewish factory girls donned red blouses and ribbons and openly flaunted them in the faces of the Cossacks." Out of a population of 430,000 inhabitants over one-third were Jews, and about 15,000 took part in the rioting. " The main part of these demonstrators were students and Jews; . . . excited Jews unblushingly exhibited Republican emblems," red flags were unfurled, the Russian national flag was dishonoured by having all colour except the strip of red torn from it, the Emperor's portrait was mutilated. In the fight that ensued over 400 Jews and 500 Christians were killed.   The writer of this article further showed the demonstration to have been organized at headquarters; " amongst other Socialistic fraternities the Central Jewish organization located in Switzerland sent emissaries from its branches in Warsaw and Poland to Odessa." [1]

Mr. Wickham Steed, in his book *The Hapsburg Monarchy*, quotes a letter written in this same year of 1905 by a semi-Jew on the question of the Jews in Hungary, in which this remarkable passage occurs:

There is a Jewish question and this terrible race means not only to master one of the grandest warrior nations in the world, but it means, and is consciously striving, to enter the lists against the other great race of the north (the Russians), the only one that has hitherto stood between it and its goal of world-power. Am I wrong? Tell me. For already England and France are, if not actually dominated by Jews, very nearly so, while the United States, by the hands of those whose grip they are ignorant of, are slowly but surely yielding to that international and insidious hegemony. Remember that I am half a Jew by blood, but that in all I have power to be I am not.[2]

Twelve years later this prophecy was terribly fulfilled. For, whatever the Jewish Press may say to the contrary, the preponderance of Jews amongst the Bolsheviks of both Hungary and Russia has been too evident to need further proof. The Executive of the Communist Government established in Hungary in March 1919 consisted in a Directorate of Five which included four Jews — Bela Kun, Bela Vago, Sigmund Kunfi, and Joseph Pogany. The Secretary was another Jew — Alpari. Szamuelly, also a Jew, was the head of the Terrorist troops.[3] In Russia Jews have again predominated. An article in *The Times* for March 29, 1919, stated that:

Of the twenty or thirty commissaries or leaders who provide

[1] *The Times* for November 22, 1905, article entitled " The Reign of Terror at Odessa." The Chief Rabbi Gaster wrote in *The Times* of November 25 to contradict these statements, but brought forward no proofs to the contrary.

[2] *The Hapsburg Monarchy* (1913), p. 169. " In Austria-Hungary," the author observes on p. 155, " the spread of Socialism has been largely the result of Jewish propaganda. Dr. Victor Adler, the founder and leader of the Austrian party, is a Jew, as are many of his followers. In Hungary the party was also founded and inspired by the Jews."

[3] See the pamphlet, *In the Grip of the Terror*, by Lumen, printed by Jordan Gaskell. Agents, W. H. Smith & Son, 186 Strand.

the central machinery of the Bolshevist movement not less than 75 per cent are Jews. . . . If Lenin is the brains of the movement, the Jews provide the executive officers. Of the leading commissaries, Trotsky, Zinoviev, Kameneff, Stekloff, Sverdloff, Uritsky, Joffe, Rakovsky, Radek, Menjinsky, Larin, Bronski, Zaalkind, Volodarsky, Petroff, Litvinoff,[1] Smirdovitch, and Vovrowsky are all of the Jewish race, while among the minor Soviet officials the number is legion.[2]

In fact the Jewish Press has on occasions admitted this influence in Bolshevism. Thus in *The Communist*, a newspaper published in Kharkoff (number for April 12, 1919), we find Mr. M. Cohan boasting that,

. . . without exaggeration, it may be said that the great Russian social revolution was indeed accomplished by the hands of the Jews. . . . It is true that there are no Jews in the ranks of the Red Army as far as privates are concerned, but in the committees and in Soviet organizations, as Commissars, the Jews are gallantly leading the masses of the Russian proletariat to victory. . . . The symbol of Jewry, which for centuries has struggled against capitalism, has become also the symbol of the Russian proletariat, which can be seen even in the face of the adoption of the Red five-pointed star, which in former times, as it is well known, was the symbol of Zionism and Jewry.[3]

This star from the beginning of the Bolshevik revolution has decorated the caps of Lenin's guards.

Even in England the activities of Jews are clearly evident in the Bolshevik camp; the audiences at " red flag meetings " have been observed to contain a very large Jewish element, Jewish interrupters have been sent to shout down speakers at patriotic meetings, Jewish agitators have taken part in every riot and urged young British hooligans to violence, and, according to the admission of the *Daily Herald*, a very large number of its readers are Jews.[4] The *Jewish Chronicle* has in fact frankly declared that " there is much in the fact of Bolshevism itself, in the fact that so many Jews are Bolsheviks, in the

---

[1] A prominent member of the Jewish Bund in 1907 and Bolshevist " ambassador " to England.

[2] On this point see the remarkable pamphlet, *Who rules Russia?* published by the Association Unity of Russia, 121 East 7th Street, New York (1920), where the exact names and number of Jews in the different departments of the present Russian Government are given.

[3] Quoted in American edition of *The Protocols*, p. 88.

[4] Letter to the *Morning Post* from George P. Mudge, Aug. 31, 1920.

fact that the ideals of Bolshevism at many points are consonant with the finest ideals of Judaism." [1]

In the face of all this overwhelming evidence on the rôle of the Jews in the revolutionary movement, what wonder that the amazing *Protocols of the Elders of Zion*, first published in Russian by Sergye Nilus in 1902 [2] and in English under the title of *The Jewish Peril* in 1920, came as a revelation and appeared to provide the clue to the otherwise insoluble problem of Bolshevism? Here was the whole explanation — a conspiracy of the Jewish race that began perhaps at Golgotha, that hid itself behind the ritual of Freemasonry, that provided the driving force behind the succeeding revolutionary upheavals, that inspired the sombre hatred of Marx, the malignant fury of Trotzky, and all this with the fixed and unalterable purpose of destroying that Christianity which is hateful to it. Is this theory true? Possibly. But in the opinion of the present writer it has not been proved — it does *not* provide the whole key to the mystery.

The only way in which the truth can be reached is by scientific investigation. And the first step in the process of establishing the authenticity or non-authenticity of the famous Protocols is to endeavour to trace their origin. Now to any one familiar with the language of Secret Societies the ideas set forth in the Protocols are not new; on the contrary, many passages have a strange ring of familiarity. To the present writer the thought that recurred at every page was: " Where have I read that before?" and by degrees the conviction grew: " But this is simply Illuminism!" So striking, indeed, are certain analogies not only between the code of Weishaupt and the Protocols, but between the Protocols and later Secret Societies, continuations of the Illuminati, that a continuity of idea throughout the movement becomes apparent. The following parallels may prove of interest as evidence of the theory that the Protocols are founded on much earlier models:

[1] Article entitled " Peace, War, and Bolshevism," April 4, 1919.
[2] The copy in the British Museum is dated 1905, but there is said to have been an earlier edition in 1902.

PROTOCOLS	ILLUMINISM (Weishaupt, 1776-1786)
He who wants to rule must have recourse to cunning and hypocrisy (p. 3).	Apply yourselves to the art of counterfeit, to hiding and masking yourselves in observing others (Barruel, iii. 27, *Originalschriften*, p. 40).
We must not stop short before bribery, deceit, and treachery, if these are to serve the achievement of our cause (p. 6.).	
The end justifies the means. In making our plans we must pay attention not so much to what is good and moral, as to what is necessary and profitable (p. 4).	The end sanctifies the means. The good of the Order justifies calumnies, poisonings, murders, perjuries, treasons, rebellions; briefly, all that the prejudices of men call crimes (Barruel, iv. 182, 189, quoting evidence of Cossandey, Utzshcneider, and Grunberger).
With the Press we will deal in the following manner. . . . We will harness it and will guide it with firm reins; we will also have to gain control of all other publishing firms . . . (p. 40).	We must take care that our writers be well puffed and that the reviewers do not depreciate them; therefore we must endeavour by every means to gain over the reviewers and journalists; and we must also try to gain the booksellers, who in time will see it is their interest to side with us (Robison, p. 191).
All news is received by a few agencies, in which it is centralized from all parts of the world. When we attain power these agencies will belong to us entirely and will only publish such news as we allow . . . (p. 40).	If a writer publishes anything that attracts notice, and is in itself just, but does not accord with our plan, we must endeavour to win him over or decry him (Robison, p. 194).
No one desirous of attacking us with his pen would find a publisher . . . (p. 42).	
Our programme will induce a third part of the populace to watch the remainder from a pure sense of duty and from the principle of voluntary government service. Then it will not be considered dishonourable to be a spy; on the contrary, it will be regarded as praiseworthy (p. 65).	Every person shall be made a spy on another and on all around him (Spartacus to Cato; Robison. p. 135).
We will transform the universities and reconstruct them according to our own plans. The	We must acquire the direction of education — of church management — of the professorial chair

PROTOCOLS	ILLUMINISM
heads of the universities and their professors will be specially prepared by means of elaborate secret programmes of action. . . . They will be very carefully nominated, etc. (p. 60).	and of the pulpit . . . (Robison, p. 191).
We intend to appear as though we were the liberators of the labouring man. . . . We shall suggest to him to join the ranks of our armies of Socialists, Anarchists, and Communists. The latter we always patronize, pretending to help them out of fraternal principle and the general interest of humanity evoked by our socialistic masonry (p. 12).	' We must preach the warmest concern for humanity and make people indifferent to all other relations (Robison, p. 191). We must win the common people in every corner (Robison p. 194).
In the so-considered leading countries we have circulated an insane, dirty, and disgusting literature (p. 49).	We must try to obtain an influence . . . in the printing-houses, booksellers' shops. . . . Painting and engraving are highly worth our care (Robison, p. 196. Note adds: " They were strongly suspected of having published some scandalous caricatures and some very immoral prints. They scrupled at no means, however base, for corrupting the nation.")
Our Sovereign must be irreproachable (p. 86).	An Illuminated Regent shall be one of the most perfect of men. He shall be prudent, foreseeing, astute, irreproachable (Instruction B. for the grade of Regent).
In the place of existing governments we will place a monster, which will be called the Administration of the Super-government. Its hands will be outstretched like far-reaching pincers, and it will have such an organization at its disposal that it will not possibly be able to fail in subduing all countries (p. 22). Our International Super-government (p. 28).	It is necessary to establish a universal régime of domination, a form of government that will spread out over the whole world . . . (Barruel, iii. 97).

We will destroy the family life of the Gentiles . . . (p. 31).

We will also distract them by various kinds of amusement, games, pastimes, passions, public houses, etc. (p. 47).

The essential thing is to isolate a man from his family, to make him lose his morals. . . . He loves the long conversations of the cafés and the idleness of shows. . . . After having shown him how painful are his duties you will excite in him the idea of another existence (Piccolo Tigre to the Vente Piemontaise; Crétineau-Joly, ii, 120).

The people of the Christians, bewildered by alcohol, their youths turned crazy by classics and early debauchery, to which they have been instigated by our agents, . . . by our women in places of amusement—to the latter I add the so-called "society women"—their voluntary followers in corruption and luxury (p. 5).

Let us . . . never cease to corrupt . . . but let us popularize vice amongst the multitude. Let us cause them to draw it in by their five senses, to drink it in, to be saturated with it. . . . It is corruption *en masse* that we have undertaken . . . (Vindex to Nubius; Crétineau-Joly, ii. 147).

The masonic lodge throughout the world unconsciously acts as a mask for our purpose (p. 16).

It is upon the lodges that we count to double our ranks. They form, without knowing it, our preparatory novitiate (Piccolo Tigre to the Vente Supreme; Crétineau-Joly, ii. 120).

Most people who enter secret societies are adventurers, who want somehow to make their way in life, and who are not seriously minded. With such people it will be easy for us to pursue our object, and we will make them set our machinery in motion (p. 52).

This vanity of the citizen or of the *bourgeois* for being enrolled in Freemasonry is something so *banal* and so universal that I am always full of admiration for human stupidity. . . . (The lodges) launch amidst their feastings thundering anathemas against intolerance and persecution. This is positively more than we require to make adepts (Piccolo Tigre to Nubius).

We employ in our service people of all opinions and all parties; men desiring to re-

Princes of a sovereign house and those who have not the legitimate hope of being kings

PROTOCOLS

establish monarchies, Socialists, etc. (p. 28).

We have taken great care to discredit the clergy of the Gentiles in the eyes of the people, and thus have succeeded in injuring their mission, which could have been very much in our way. The influence of the clergy on the people is diminishing daily. To-day freedom of religion prevails everywhere, but the time is only a few years off when Christianity will fall to pieces altogether (p. 64).

We must extract the very conception of God from the minds of the Christians . . . (p. 17).

We must destroy all professions of faith (p. 48).

PROTOCOLS

We persuaded the Gentiles that Liberalism would bring them to a kingdom of reason (p. 14).

We injected the poison of Liberalism into the organism of the State . . . (p. 33).

We preach Liberalism to the Gentiles . . . (p. 55).

HAUTE VENTE ROMAINE

by the grace of God, all wish to be kings by the grace of a Revolution. The Duke of Orleans is a Freemason. A prince who has not a kingdom to expect is a good fortune for us (Piccolo Tigre to Nubius).

There is a certain portion of the clergy that nibbles at the bait of our doctrines with a marvellous vivacity . . . (Nubius to Volpe; Crétineau - Joly, ii. 130).

It is corruption *en masse* that we have undertaken: the corruption of the people by the clergy and the corruption of the clergy by themselves, the corruption that ought to enable us one day to put the Church in her tomb (Vindex to Nubius; Crétineau-Joly, ii, 147).

Our final end is . . . the destruction for ever of Catholicism and even of the Christian idea (Dillon, *The War of Antichrist*, etc., p. 64).

In order to kill the old world surely we have held that we must stifle the Catholic and Christian germ (Piccolo Tigre to Nubius; Crétineau-Joly, ii. 387).

ALLIANCE SOCIALE DÉMOCRATIQUE
(Bakunin's Secret Society, 1864–1869)

The fourth category of people to be employed thus described by Bakunin: " Various ambitious men in the service of the State and Liberals of different shades. With them one can conspire according to their own programme, pretending to follow them blindly."

PROTOCOLS

We will entrust these important posts (government posts) to people whose record and characters are so bad as to form a gulf between the nation and themselves, and to such people who, in case they disobey our orders, may expect judgment and imprisonment. And all this is with the object that they should defend our interests until the last breath has passed out of their bodies (p. 26).. ·· ·¯· · ..·ºº·ºº·

We will pre-arrange for the election of . . . presidents whose past record is marked with some " Panama Scandal " or other shady hidden transaction (p. 34).

Out of governments we made arenas on which party wars are fought out. . . . Insuppressible babblers transformed parliamentary and administrative meetings into debating meetings. Audacious journalists and impudent pamphleteers are continually attacking the administrative powers (p. 11).

We will create a universal economical crisis. . . .[1] Simultaneously we will throw on to the streets huge crowds of workmen throughout Europe. These masses will then gladly throw themselves upon and shed the blood of those of whom, in their ignorance, they have been jealous

ALLIANCE SOCIALE
DÉMOCRATIQUE

The third category of Bakunin thus described: " A great number of highly placed animals who can be exploited in all possible ways. We must circumvent them, outwit them, and by getting hold of their dirty secrets make of them our slaves. By this means their power, their connections, their influence, and their riches will become an inexhaustible treasure and a precious help in various enterprises. . . "

In the same way with the fourth category: " We must take them in our hands, get hold of their secrets, compromise them completely in such a way that retreat will be impossible to them."

The fifth category of Bakunin consists of: " Doctrinaires, conspirators, revolutionaries, all those who babble at meetings and on paper. We must push them and draw them on unceasingly into practical and perilous manifestations which will have the result of making the majority of them disappear whilst making a few amongst them real revolutionaries."

The Association will employ all its means and all its power to increase and augment evils and misfortunes which must at last wear out the patience of the people and excite them to an insurrection *en masse.*

---

[1] Marx was evidently in this secret. In *Réflexions sur la violence* (P. 183) Georges Sorel says: " Marx thought the great catastrophe would be preceded by an enormous economic crisis."

PROTOCOLS

from childhood, and whose belongings they will then be able to plunder (p. 14).

We will make merciless use of executions with regard to all who may take up arms against the establishment of our power (p. 50).

We must take no account of the numerous victims who will have to be sacrificed in order to obtain future prosperity (p. 51).

The masonic lodge throughout the world unconsciously acts as a mask for our purpose (p. 16).

ALLIANCE SOCIALE DÉMOCRATIQUE

In the first place must be destroyed the men who are most pernicious to revolutionary organization and whose violence and sudden death may most frighten the government.

My friends, abandon that absurd idea that I have been won over to Freemasonry. But perhaps Freemasonry would serve as a mask or as a passport . . . (Letter to Herzen and Ogareff, *Correspondance de Bakounine*, 209).

Through all these parallels the plan of World Revolution runs like a "*complot suivi*," and when we further compare them with the utterances of the modern Bolsheviks we see the plan carried right up to the present moment. Let us now consider how the Protocols of the Elders of Zion tally with the Bolshevist programme:

PROTOCOLS

It is expedient for the welfare of the country that the government of the same should be in the hands of one responsible person (p. 5).

The system of government must be the work of one head.

The despotism of capital which is entirely in our hands will hold out to it (the State) a straw, to which the State will be unavoidably compelled to cling . . . (p. 2.)

On the ruins of natural and hereditary aristocracy we built

BOLSHEVISM

How can we secure strict unity of will? By subjecting the will of thousands to the will of one (Lenin, *The Soviets at Work*, p. 35).

What is the first stage? It is the transfer of power to the capitalist class. Up to the March Revolution of 1917 power in Russia was in the hands of one ancient class, the feudalist-aristocratic - landowning class, headed by Nicholas Romanov

PROTOCOLS	BOLSHEVISM
an aristocracy of our own on a plutocratic basis. We established this new aristocracy on wealth, of which we had control . . . (p. 8).	After that revolution, power has been in the hands of a different, a new class, namely, the capitalist class (the *bourgeoisie*) (Lenin, *Towards Soviets*, p. 8).
Soon we will start organizing great monopolies — reservoirs of colossal wealth . . . (p. 22).	We must improve and regulate the State monopolies . . . which we have already established, and thereby prepare for State monopolization of the foreign trade (Lenin, *The Soviets at Work*, p. 20).
Our government is in so exceedingly strong a position in the sight of the law that we may almost describe it by the powerful expression of dictatorship (p. 27).	We advocate a merciless dictatorship (Lenin, *The Soviets at Work*, p. 40).
When we accomplish our *coup d'Etat*, we will say to the people: "Everything has been going very badly; all of you have suffered; now we are destroying the cause of your sufferings — that is to say, nationalities, frontiers, and national currencies. Certainly you will be free to condemn us, but can your judgment be fair if you pronounce it before you have had experience of what we can do for your good ?." (p. 31).	We must study the peculiarities of the highly difficult and new road to Socialism without concealing our mistakes and weaknesses. We must try to overcome our deficiencies in time (*The Soviets at Work*, p. 18).
	What we have already decreed is yet far from adequate realization, and the main problem of today consists precisely in concentrating all efforts upon the actual, practical realization of the reforms which have already become the law, but have not yet become a reality (*ibid*. p. 20).
Our laws will be short, clear, and concise, requiring no interpretation, so that everybody will be able to know them inside out. The main feature in them will be the obedience required towards authority, and this respect for authority will be carried to a very high pitch.	Economic improvement depends on higher discipline of the toilers. . . . To learn how to work — this problem the Soviet authority should present to the people in all its comprehensiveness (*The Soviets at Work*, p. 26).
Then all kinds of abuse will cease, because everybody will	The revolution . . . demands the absolute submission of the

PROTOCOLS	BOLSHEVISM
be responsible before the one supreme power, namely, that of the sovereign (p. 56).	masses to the single will of those who direct the labour process (*The Soviets at Work*, p. 35).
We will make it clear to every one that freedom does not consist in dissoluteness or in the right of doing whatever people please. . . . We will teach the world that true freedom consists only in the inviolability of a man's person and of his property, who honestly adheres to all the laws of social life (p. 83).	It mustt take some time before the ordinary representative of the masses will not only see . . . but come to feel that he must not just simply seize, grab, snatch — and that leads to greater disorganization (*The Soviets at Work*, p. 36).
In order to demonstrate our enslavement of the Gentile governments in Europe we will show our power to one of them by means of crimes of violence, that is to say, by a reign of terror (p. 25).	We will turn our hearts into steel, which we will temper in the fire of suffering and the blood of the fighters for freedom. We will make our hearts cruel, hard, and immovable, so that no mercy will enter into them, and so that they will not quiver at the sight of a sea of enemy blood, etc. (*Krasnaya Gazette*, the official organ of the Petrograd Soviet of Workers, Red Army, and peasants' deputies, presided over by Zinovieff, *alias* Apfelbaum, a Jew. Date of August 31, 1918).[1]
We must destroy all professions of faith (p. 48).	Religion must be fought, if not by violence, at all events by argument (Bucharin, *Programme of the World Revolution*, p. 77).
When the time comes for us to take special police measures by putting the present Russian system of the Okhrana in force . . . (p 67).	A highly organized intelligence department, or rather the renewed Okhrana of the old autocracy, is a necessary part of . . . this régime. Lenin was perfectly right to emphasize this before the last Soviet conference in Moscow (Dec. 1919) (Miliukov in *The New Russia* for February 12, 1920).

[1] Quoted in American edition of the *Protocols*, p. 89. Nine years earlier M. Copin Albancelli, in his *Conjuration juive contre le monde chrétien* (p. 452), had written: " France has known — and she has forgotten! — the régime of the Masonic Terror. She will know, and the world will know with her, the régime of the Jewish Terror."

The foregoing parallels prove, therefore, a clear connection between the Protocols and former Secret Societies working for World Revolution, and also between the Protocols and Bolshevism. But they do not necessarily establish their authenticity. One possibility immediately suggests itself. Might they not be a forgery compounded by some one versed in the lore of Secret Societies? Supposing Nilus to have been a student of this subject and also, as he was known to be, a pronounced anti-Semite, it would not have been difficult for him to reconstruct the programme of World Revolution from earlier models, weaving into them at the same time the idea of a Jewish conspiracy. Why, then, was this very obvious explanation not put forward by the Jews? Why, on the contrary, when it was suggested by the present writer in a newspaper article, did it meet merely with resentment? Here was a loophole indeed! But instead of using it the advocates of Jewry contented themselves with angry expostulations, or fell back on absurd explanations, as that the Protocols were invented by the Russian police or by the " Tzarist reactionaries " in London, or that they were copied from a notorious forgery by Goedsche — why choose a forgery when such admirable authentic models were at hand? — or again, the attempt was made to draw a red herring across the track by dwelling on Nilus's personality and his own literary work, which had no bearing whatever on the question. The point was to prove whether the document which he purported to have discovered was genuine or not.

The truth is, then, that the Protocols have never been refuted, and the futility of the so-called refutations published, as also the fact of their temporary suppression, have done more to convince the public of their authenticity than all the anti-Semite writings on the subject put together.

The only line of defence, namely, that this document was the work of illuminized Freemasonry, and not of a purely Jewish association, has been rejected by the advocates of the Jews themselves, and the only conclusion that we can draw is either that the Protocols are genuine and what they pretend to be, or that these advocates put iorward by the Jews have some interest in concealing the activities of Secret Societies in the past.

The question then arises: Were the Jews concerned in the organization of Illuminism and its subsequent developments? At present this is not clearly proved. It is true that Cagliostro was probably a Jew, that Kölmer who partly indoctrinated Weishaupt may have been a Jew, that a certain Simonini wrote to the Abbé Barruel in 1806 declaring that " the freemasons and the *illuminés* were founded by two Jews " — whose names the author has forgotten [1] — that the Jewish financiers of Frankfurt may have contributed to the funds of the Illuminati or of the Duc d'Orléans, but all this rests so far on no contemporary documentary evidence. The " *illuminés* " referred to by Simonini may well have been the Martinistes founded, as it is known, by the Jew Paschalis and frequently referred to under this name. We should require more than such vague assertions to refute the evidence of men who, like Barruel and Robison, devoted exhaustive study to the subject and attributed the whole plan of the Illuminati and its fulfilment in the French Revolution to German brains. Neither Weishaupt, Knigge, nor any of the ostensible founders of Illuminism were Jews; moreover, as we have seen, Jews were excluded from the association except by special permission.[2] None of the leading revolutionaries of France were Jews, nor were the members of the conspiracy of Babeuf.

The claim of the " Elders of Zion " to have inspired all revolutionary outbreaks since 1789 is not therefore at present substantiated by history, and it is not until the Alta Vendita from 1820 onwards that they can be proved to have taken an active part in the movement. Yet Monsignor Dillon, who clearly recognizes their importance as agents of this secret society, nevertheless attributes its efficient organization to " Italian genius." From this date

[1] Deschamps, *Les Sociétés secrètes*, iii. 659.

[2] Since these words were written, and at the moment of this book going to press, a number of *La Veille France* has appeared (date of March 31-April 6, 1921) in which it is stated that five Jews were concerned in the organization and inspiration of the Illuminati — Wessely, Moses Mendelssohn, and the bankers Itzig, Friedlander, and Meyer. But the contemporary authority for this statement is not given.

onward their rôle is, however, more apparent. In Germany before 1848 Disraeli himself declared them to be taking the lead in the revolutionary movement, and with the First Internationale they come forward into a blaze of light. Henceforth along the line of State Socialism their influence is no longer doubtful.

But whilst the question of Jewish organization from the beginning of the World Revolution remains obscure, the workings of illuminized Freemasonry are clearly visible. It is strange that in the controversy that has raged over the Protocols so little attention has been paid to the fact that the so-called " Elders of Zion " were admittedly masons of the 33rd degree of the Grand Orient. Considered from this point of view, all their statements regarding the past history of the Revolution are substantiated by facts. For if by " we " is meant " illuminized Freemasons," then the assertion that " it is we who were the first to cry out to the people ' Liberty, Equality, and Fraternity ' " is clearly accurate. Nothing can be truer than that since the French Revolution " the nations have been led from one disappointment to another," and that " the secrets of its preparatory organization were the work of our hands " — the hands of the Freemasons and Illuminati. If, then, the Protocols are genuine, *they are the revised programme of illuminized Freemasonry formulated by a Jewish lodge of the Order*.

But whilst the influence of the Jews cannot be proved throughout the early history of the society, German inspiration and organization is apparent from the very beginning. It was the German Weishaupt who founded the Illuminati with the aid of his German colleagues, it was the German Knigge who effected its alliance with French Freemasonry, German emissaries who introduced it to the lodges of the Grand Orient; it was this German Illuminism that inspired the campaign of universal corruption waged by the Alta Vendita and the anarchic fury of Bakunin; and again it was pan-Germanism, working by the methods of the Illuminati, that assured the success of Marx and Engels and secured control of all Socialist organizations up to the present day.

This revolutionary machine that threatens the peace of the world today, though manipulated in the past by men of all nationalities — French, Italian, Jewish, Russian, and in a few instances English — is primarily the work of German hands and is still mainly controlled by Germans with the aid of their Jewish allies. The German military authorities sent Lenin and the Jew Radek in a special train to Russia, German officers organized the Bolshevik armies, and German poison gas contributed to the final defeat of Wrangel.

It was also Germany who fanned the flames of civil war now raging in Ireland. Sinn Fein, which in its origins was largely a national and religious movement, is now being exploited by the International Atheist movement, whose "dark directory," as in 1884, "laughs at Ireland and her wrongs." For the plan of the conspiracy has always been to adopt a *protégé* and enlist its aid as an ally. Hitherto the two *protégés* invariably selected have been Ireland and Poland. But now that Poland has dared to assert its independence Poland has been thrown to the wolves, and when the day comes, as it must come if the World Revolution triumphs, for Ireland to resist the tide of Bolshevism, then Ireland with all her national and religious aspirations will be thrown to the wolves likewise. The organization of the revolutionary movement is even now less in the hands of Sinn Fein than of the Irish Republican Brotherhood, modelled like its predecessors, the Fenians and the United Irishmen, on the Illuminati of Weishaupt.[1] The same organization is at work in India, and both are directed, not by Moscow, but by the invisible council which holds in its hands the threads of the whole conspiracy.

Bolshevist propaganda all over the world has been carried out by German organization and financed by German as well as by Jewish gold. " I affirm," wrote Bourtzeff, the Russian refugee, " that since August 1914, and in a relatively short lapse of time, the Germans handed over personally to Lenin more than 70,000,000 marks for the organization of Bolshevist agitation in the Allied Coun-

---

[1] For this reason Sinn Fein will not be found marked in the chart accompanying this book. It is not a part of the World Revolution.

tries." Bernstein, a member of the German Social Democratic Party, has declared in the official organ of the party, *Vorwärts*, that he knew as far back as December 1917 that Lenin was in the pay of Germany. More recently, Bernstein has learnt from " a responsible person " that the sum given to Lenin was more than 50,000,000 gold marks, or £2,500,000.[1] The Jewish Bolshevik emissaries to the recent Tours Congress, Abramovitch and Clara Zetkin, were discovered by the French authorities to have received money from Germany for the expenses of propaganda in France. The Jewish agitator is the tsetse fly carrying the poison germ of Bolshevism from the breeding-ground of Germany.

As long as England retains any belief in Carlyle's theory of " noble, patient, deep, pious, and solid Germany," the true cause of the evils now afflicting Europe will never be understood. Doubtless there are noble and pious elements in Germany, but let it not be forgotten that Germany holds within her a poison centre which has become a source of moral infection for the whole world. The campaign of militant atheism and moral corruption that is now being carried out systematically in our own country, in France, and in America, is of German devising. Weishaupt in his apology for Illuminism said that "Deism, Infidelity, and Atheism were more prevalent in Bavaria than in any country he was acquainted with." [2] Seventy years later, in 1846, Lord Shaftesbury, travelling in Germany, remarked: " Here is a peculiarity among the German *literati*; professorial chairs are held and public lectures given by men of open, acknowledged, and boastful Atheism " ; and if we are reminded that Disraeli had declared most of these professorial chairs at this date to be monopolized by Jews, let us note that Lord Shaftesbury goes on to say: " Nor does opinion frown them down. We have bad people in England, but few dare to parade their make-beliefs with ostentation and joy." [3] German Athe-

[1] Article by Mr. Adolphe Smith, "Lenin: Russian Traitor and German Agent," in the *National Review* for April 1921. The whole of this important article, from which the above quotations are taken, should be read carefully.
[2] Robison's *Proofs of a Conspiracy*, p. 102.
[3] Edwin Hodder, *Life of Lord Shaftesbury*, p. 362.

ism and Jewish antagonism to Christianity have combined
to form the great anti-religious force that is making itself
felt in the world today.

Again, Internationalism, the policy of national suicide
advocated by the modern revolutionaries, has been frequently attributed to the Jews, and it is obvious that a
race without a country of its own must see in the propagation of Internationalism much to commend it; but the
originator of Internationalist doctrines as they are
preached today was not a Jew but a German — Anacharsis
Clootz. The so-called " International Jew " is not in
reality International at all; he is first a Jew and then a
German — sometimes indeed he is a German first.[1] Internationalism, then, is simply another word for pan-Germanism, and it will always be noticed that advocates of Internationalism in this country betray a peculiar *tendresse* for
Germany. As Mr. Adolphe Smith has well expressed it:
" The Socialist and revolutionary doctrines . . . taught
under the mantle of Marxism spread the idea that a
Socialist has no country unless, of course, he has the good
fortune to be a German." And again: " The doctrines of
the older Socialists, the Socialists at whom Bismarck
aimed by his anti-Socialist law, were now reserved for
foreign exportation . . . abroad they were just what was
wanted to disintegrate communities, to weaken the sense
of nationality, and lessen the desire for strong armies of
defence. . . . In all fields of action *the German as an
Internationalist* needs to be studied with far greater care
than as yet has been bestowed on him." [2] The International doctrines of Weishaupt and of his disciple Clootz
have served the cause of Germany well.

It will be urged, " But why should Germany encourage
Illuminism, since she herself is now a victim of World
Revolution? " True, the Spartacists of Germany today
are undoubtedly the direct descendants of Spartacus

[1] On March 29, 1913, an influential German-Jewish Association, the
" Central Society of German Citizens of Jewish Faith," in a strongly anti-
Zionist resolution, declared: " On the soil of the German Fatherland we
wish, as Germans, to co-operate in German civilization and to remain
true to a partnership that has been hallowed by religion and history "
(Wickham Steed, *The Hapsburg Monarchy*, p. 177).

[2] Adolphe Smith, *The Pan-German International*, pp. 4, 9, 12.

Weishaupt from whom they take their name; [1] Liebknecht and Rosa Luxembourg were both leading members of the Order. Inevitably those who handle poison gas are liable at moments to inhale its fumes. But Germany has Sparticism well under control — meanwhile it can be used as a bogey to prevent her disarmament by the Allies. Between Berlin and Moscow the understanding is complete. Nicholas Lenin is not the controlling brain of the gigantic conspiracy. Great pains have been taken to represent the present dictator of Russia as a " Superman " of vast conceptions. Lenin's own writings refute this theory. Where in all his numerous pamphlets do we find a hint of genius or even of original thought? The writings of Robespierre bear at least the stamp of his personality. Babeuf, Illuminatus though he was, brought some native inspiration to bear on his diatribes, but from the days of Marx onwards revolutionary Socialism has always borne the same " machine-made " character and Lenin's pamphlets resemble nothing so much as the instructions of a bogus company promoter directing other would-be bogus company promoters how to " do the trick." Mr. Wells has hastened to assure us that Lenin's writings are not representative of himself, that the great man must be seen to be appreciated; yet how is it that the many ardent pilgrims to the shrine of the deity at Moscow have never been able to bring back a single phrase uttered by the oracle that gives evidence of the slightest gleam of inspiration or of concern for the people of Russia? The one point that appears to occupy him is how to make the system work in spite of the opposition of the people.

Lenin, then, is neither a demagogue nor a superman, but the agent of the great German-Jewish company that hopes to rule the world.

How do the Germans and the Jews come to be allied in this design? Are not their aims mutually antagonistic. If we regard the Jewish plan as a racial conspiracy — yes. But there is no evidence to show that the whole Jewish race is concerned in it; on the contrary, many Jews in our

---

[1] On this point see *Weltfreimaurerei, Weltrevolution, Weltrepublik,* by Dr. Wichtl (Munich, 1921), p. 262.

own country, as in France, have shown themselves fearless opponents both of Germany and Bolshevism. Nor does religious fanaticism appear to enter into the question. The insistence on the idea of a Jewish Messiah is the least convincing part of the Protocols. It is not religious Jews, even Talmudic Jews, but apostate Jews who have thrown themselves into the revolutionary movement. In the diatribe of Bucharin against religion quoted above, the Jewish faith is derided equally with that of the Christian or the Buddhist. Yet if we examine the plan of Bolshevism we shall see the motive for a certain section of the Jews to take part in it. Now the avowed plan of the Bolshevists is to do away with the right of private property and establish universal *Communism*. But the ruse of the conspiracy has always been to use words with a double meaning, and not only this, but with meanings diametrically opposed to each other. Thus when they proclaim the " dictatorship of the proletariat " their real intention is to bring about the complete enslavement of the proletariat; when they talk of the " equality of sexes " what they really mean is to reduce women to a position lower than the rank of squaws. The word " constitution," as we have seen, has been employed throughout as the signal for crushing an attempt to introduce constitutional government or for overthrowing it when it has been established. In the same way the word " Communism " has a double meaning.

To the simple proletarian Communism conveys a very alluring idea, namely, that of " having everything in common." Of the real theory of Communism he has no conception, but the propagandist who tries to win him over to Communism knows very well. He knows, moreover, that Communism is a system which has been tried and in every instance found wanting, and that, on the lines which he advocates, can never succeed.

For the only form of Communism which it has ever been possible to carry out successfully is that practised by religious communities. Monasteries and nunneries are, of course, Communist, but the fact which makes this possible is that they are composed of people who have renounced all interest in earthly things and centre all their thoughts and desires on the Kingdom of Heaven. Secular Communism, by its insistence on materialism, eliminates the only factor that makes the system feasible — belief in God and the Hereafter. It is inconceivable that leading Communists should be unaware of this fundamental error in their teaching, or of the failure that has attended every attempt to put it into practice in the past — above all, of its colossal failure in Russia.

If, then, Communism or State Socialism has been proved impracticable, if, moreover, it is a system that no one who understands it can possibly want, who is to profit by establishing it? Sorel answered the question long ago — " A few professors who imagine they invented Socialism and a few Dreyfusard financiers." In other words, the Intellectuals who cherish the hope of being given official posts in the Socialist State which will give them an advantage over their fellow-men, and a few Jewish financiers. Werner Sombart, summing up the system of the latter, says: " Their aim was to seize upon all commerce and all production; they had an overpowering desire to expand in every direction." The system of free trade was all part of this plan and can be traced back as far as Anacharsis Clootz, who was doubtless considering the interests of his friends the Jews when in his *Universal Republic* he advocated " all the peoples forming one nation, *all the trades forming only one trade*, all interests forming only one interest." It is easy to see that State Socialism may be merely the prelude to this scheme, and here M. Sorel and M. Copin Albancelli are curiously in accord.

" One formula," the latter wrote in 1909, " sums up the whole Collectivist propaganda: All for the State. All for the State! The people imagine that this means: All for All! and they march forward, intoxicated with hope, towards the conquest of this fallacious idea, not dreaming that the State being henceforth in the hands of the Jews ' all for the State ' . . . will be ' all for the Jews!' . . . The dictatorship imposed by the Jewish race will be a financial, industrial, and commercial dictatorship." [1]

What could better describe the government of Russia

[1] *La Conjuration juive contre le monde chrétien*, pp. 448, 450.

today? The plan of wresting all capital out of private hands and placing it in the hands of the State, as under Communism, or in the hands of industrial syndicates as under Syndicalism, may well be the prelude to State Capitalism or to gigantic trusts controlled by international financiers. In this case the so-called war on capitalism is simply a war in favour of capitalism, of ruining all small holders of wealth or property in order to enrich a ring of multi-millionaries. A passage in Mr. Wells's articles on Russia lends colour to this theory:

> Big business is by no means antipathetic to Communism. The larger big business grows the more it approximates to Collectivism. It is the upper road of the few instead of the lower road of the masses to Collectivism.[1]

Conversely, then, may not Communism be the lower road which the masses are being invited to follow leading to " big business," that is to say, to super-Capitalism? Once embarked on this road there can be no turning back. The present Capitalist system — that is to say, the system that aims at the distribution of capital amongst as large a number of hands as possible — having been destroyed by the workers' own folly in favour of concentration of capital in the hands of the State, they will be obliged to work or starve. Their new masters will have them completely at their mercy.

It will be urged: " But the workers will never stand this; they will rise against their tyrants and overthrow them! What government of this kind could maintain itself in power? "

But this is where the rôle of the German armies comes in. It is quite true that a group of international financiers could not of its own strength maintain itself in power against an enraged industrial proletariat, but if we imagine this financial power backed by a superb military system, if, in a word, we picture *an alliance between Prussian militarism and international finance*, the plan no longer appears impracticable.

It is this alliance that today menaces civilization, and it is an alliance of long standing, as we have seen in the

[1] *Sunday Express* for November 28, 1920.

earlier chapters of this book. The present campaign of anti-Semitism raging in Germany is largely a strategic manœuvre with the object of reinstating Germany in the eyes of the world and throwing all the blame for both the war and the revolution on the Jews. Germany will not relinquish her Jews as long as they can help her towards the attainment of her dream of world-power. Nor will the International Jew forsake Germany as long as by her military strength she remains the horse to back.

Yet, formidable as this coalition may be, does it provide the whole force of Bolshevism? The organization — yes; but the force — no. In following the history of World Revolution one other factor, an immense factor, must be taken into consideration — the power of anarchy. All Bolshevists are not Jews or Germans; all are not inspired by Jews or Germans. *The importance of the constitutional destructionist cannot be over-estimated.* It is essential to recognize that there are men and women in the world who will throw themselves into any subversive movement for sheer love of violence — it is idle to seek with them a motive. This has been so all through the revolutionary movement. For although down the line of State Socialism the influence of the Germans and the Jews is clearly evident, down the line of Anarchy, except for the original inspiration of Weishaupt and the agitations of Most and Hartmann, it is hardly to be found at all. Bakunin was the author of a *polémique* against the Jews; Sorel was an ardent anti-Dreyfusard; Lev Chorny, the Russian Anarchist, at the beginning of the present revolution warned the Russian people against the Jewish leaders of Bolshevism. If modern Communism, that is to say, Marxian Socialism, is German and Jewish, Syndicalism and Anarchy are peculiar to the Latin and Slavonic races. It was this fearful element that contributed largely to the ferocity of Bolshevism, and, exploiting the native tendency of the Russian people towards violence, could inaugurate an orgy of blood and terror.

Bolshevism uses Syndicalism, like Anarchy, to establish its power, it encourages the General Strike, which enters in no way into its own programme, but the spirit of

Syndicalism exists apart from Bolshevism and is as much to be feared. If revolution breaks out in this country it will be a Syndicalist revolution — the General Strike with its fearful programme of *sabotage* and violence, its carnival of rioting and destruction. But it is not Syndicalism that will win the day. The lessons of history prove that anarchy, ephemeral in its essence, must always give way before organization. And if this organization is not supplied by the forces of law and order, it will be the iron bureaucracy of the German armies and the international financiers which will establish its domination over a ruined country and a helpless people.

CONCLUSION

Bolshevism in England—Our Illuminati—Danger now threatening
civilization—Methods of defence.

In the course of this book I have endeavoured to trace the
workings of the great conspiracy throughout the history
of the last hundred and forty years; a few concluding
words are now necessary in order to indicate the manner
in which it is being carried on in our country at the present
moment and the means by which it may be defeated.

It is extraordinary how in the light of Illuminism many
things that are happening today which appear at first
inexplicable become clear as daylight; for not only do the
six points of Weishaupt form the exact programme of the
revolutionary party in England, but it would hardly be an
exaggeration to say that every device now employed by it
can be traced back to the code of the Illuminati.

Now it will be remembered that the precept most
emphasized by Weishaupt was that the Illuminati should
not be known as such, and after their suppression in
Bavaria every effort was made by the conspirators to persuade the world that their Order had ceased to exist. As
the instructions for the degree of Regent expressed it:
" The great strength of our Order lies in its concealment; let it never appear in any place in its own name,
but always covered by another name, and another
occupation." [1]

This device has alway been exactly carried out; Freemasonry, Carbonarism, Socialism, the Internationale,
have all in turn served as covers to the designs of the conspiracy, and the same method is being followed today.
Every effort is made to persuade the public that no con-

[1] Robison's *Proofs of a Conspiracy*, p. 195.

318

spiracy exists, for once its existence is generally recognized its defeat is certain. Its whole success depends on secrecy. This much, however, is known.

The Order of the Illuminati exists in England; its statutes are those of the head lodge in Germany, reorganized in 1880. At the same time an association called Co-masonry, which has its headquarters in Paris and derives from the Grand Orient, is also active. By way of winning the confidence of the women it is hoped to enlist, they are frequently told that the Order has the approval of the Grand Lodge of England. This is absolutely untrue. British Masonry has repudiated the Grand Orient and *recognizes no form of masonry that admits women as members.*

But, according to the plan of Weishaupt, the principal activities of the conspiracy are conducted " under other names and other occupations." The instructions to the Regents go on to explain the different guises under which one may work. Next to Freemasonry " the form of a learned or literary society is best suited to our purpose, and had Freemasonry not existed, this cover would have been employed; and it may be much more than a cover, it may be a powerful engine in our hands. By establishing reading societies, and subscription libraries, and taking these under our direction, and supplying them through our labours, we may turn the public mind which way we will." The way in which the necessary literature is to be forced on the attention of the public is described in the passage already quoted in the parallels to the Protocols:

> We must take care our writers be well puffed and that the reviewers do not depreciate them; therefore we must endeavour by every means to gain over the reviewers and journalists; and we must also try to gain the booksellers, who in time will see that it is their interest to side with us.

This is exactly what we see happening today. Not only have the modern Illuminati succeeded in organizing such avowedly subversive " literary societies " as the Fabian Society, and other minor associations, but also in gaining control over ordinary circulating libraries and bookshops, by placing at their head men or women who are definitely working for the propagation of revolutionary doctrines. At the same time journalists, even in the employ of the so-called "Capitalist Press," devote long and important notices to every book that is calculated to serve the cause — works ranging from heavy treatises on intellectual Socialism to the lowest form of demoralizing fiction. No book subversive of order or morality ever passes unnoticed in the press.

Of course the greater part of this organization is carried out by the power of gold — not necessarily by bribery but simply by making agitation a "paying job," or by offering the most lucrative posts to adepts or at least agents of the conspiracy. But apart from these material advantages subtler methods are employed. Of these the two which prove the most effectual were thus laid down by Weishaupt:

1. *Exploiting grievances.* — Amongst the people to enrol are "above all those who have experienced misfortune, not by mere accidents, but through some kind of injustice, that is to say, those that one can most certainly count amongst malcontents: those are the men that we must call into the bosom of Illuminism as into their asylum." [1]

2. But by far the most potent inducement offered was the *promise of power.* "The pupils are convinced that the Order *will* rule the world. Every member therefore becomes a ruler." Robison quoting this passage adds: "We all think ourselves qualified to rule. The difficult task is to obey with propriety; but we are honestly generous in our prospects of future command. It is therefore an alluring thought, both to good and bad men. *By this lure the Order will spread.*" [2]

How truly has Robison's prophecy been fulfilled! Nothing indeed could better describe the mentality of the converts to what is now called "Bolshevism" than these two passages. Nearly all the promoters of disorder today will be found to be either people suffering from some real or imaginary injustice or those with an inordinate desire to rule over their fellow-men. They are convinced that if only

---

[1] Barruel, iii. 35.   [2] Robison's *Proofs*, p. 213.

the reins of power were once confided to their hands the whole social system would be miraculously transformed; they are further convinced that this day must come, for all have been taught to believe that " their Order will one day rule the world." It is this that gives them their immense confidence, for young Oxford Intellectual and Trade Union Leader alike has been assured of the important post he is to occupy under the coming régime. Neither, of course, has been admitted into the real plan of the conspiracy; neither probably suspects that any such conspiracy exists, for, according to the pyramidical scale of Weishaupt, each is acquainted only with the directors immediately above him and knows nothing of the higher adepts who are really controlling the movement.

Another motive that undoubtedly drives many people into the revolutionary camp is *fear*. They think that if a revolution is to take place in this country they will ensure their safety by throwing in their lot with the subversive party. Mirabeau, Illuminatus, voiced precisely this policy when he said to his followers: " You have nothing to fear from the aristocrats; those people do not pillage, they do not burn, they do not assassinate — what harm can they do you?" On the policy, therefore, of propitiating a malignant deity, numbers of timorous people become apologists for Bolshevism, imagining that all such utterances will be counted to them for righteousness when the " day of conflagration " arrives. Revolutionary violence has been carefully designed to produce this effect, for the method of the conspiracy is the same today as it was a hundred and forty years ago — " calumny, corruption, and *terror*."

But a little knowledge of the history of World Revolution would dispel the illusions of those who hope to save their heads by cowardly compromise; it would teach them that in times of revolution *no one's life is safe*, that men have never yet been spared on the score of past professions of sympathy with subversive doctrines, that on the contrary it has invariably been the less extreme revolutionaries who have fared the worst. Demagogues once in power need the co-operation of bold and despotic men, and these are not to be found amongst the timorous and time-servers but amongst the agents of reaction. The French Revolution employed the Marquis de Sade but killed off the Girondins, and in Russia Social Revolutionaries and Mensheviks have perished by the score whilst Tzarist officials and members of the Okhrana have occupied official posts under the Soviet Government.

There is nothing, then, to be gained by cowardice, and there is much to be lost. A man who dies for his convictions can mount the scaffold with serenity, but what must be the bitter remorse of those who have sold their souls and profited nothing?

This form of " terrorism," of frightening people into siding with one, is peculiarly German. " Sabre-rattling " undoubtedly proved a highly effectual method of overcoming opposition amongst neutrals during the recent war. And the German psychology in the so-called Labour movement is everywhere apparent today. It is curious to notice the organization of illuminized Freemasonry during industrial crises. " All modern revolutions," wrote Eckert in 1857, " prove that the Order is divided into two distinct parties: one pacific, the other warlike," or, as Monsignor Dillon describes them, " the party of direction " and " the party of action." At moments of tumult the war party descends into the arena whilst the peace party retires into the back-ground. " The Pacific lodges hasten by every means to protect the brothers of the belligerent division by representing them as over-ardent patriots who have allowed themselves to be drawn on by the current beyond the limits of order and prudence."

This process is repeated every time a revolutionary strike is now threatened, and the so-called moderate Labour leaders, whilst dissociating themselves from the actual preparation of revolution, give it all the support in their power by representing the Extremists as " hotheaded " enthusiasts whom it is impossible to restrain but whose cause nevertheless is just. The public, always deceived by this manœuvre, falls on the necks of the " moderates," trusting to them to save the situation and bring the hot-heads to reason, the truth being that the very moderation of the former immensely aids the work of revolution by reconciling those who would be alienated by the violence of the Extremists.

Trade Unionism, in its origins a wholly pacific system for the protection of the workers, has thus been captured by the conspirators, and the industrial disputes which form the ostensible purpose of each succeeding crisis are merely pretexts covering the real design of World Revolution.

Revolution by the General Strike is not the only danger to be feared; State Socialism by the ballot-box will ruin us more slowly but none the less surely. For State Socialism, with its crushing of all individual enterprise, must inevitably destroy our commerce, bring about vast unemployment and finally bankruptcy and starvation, whilst the pro-German sympathies of its leaders will lead to the rupture of our alliance with France, on which the security of both countries depends. At the same time, all measures of military and naval defence will be abandoned, national traditions will be swept away, Socialist teachers will inculcate anti-patriotism and materialism into the minds of the rising generation, and Germany will be able to take over the British Empire without an effort.

The manner in which the women of this country have been enlisted in the service of the conspiracy can also be traced to illuminized Freemasonry. Just as in the first French Revolution the advocates of " Women's Rights " were persuaded to throw themselves into the movement, so the conspiracy today has succeeded in capturing a large proportion of the " Feminist " movement for its purpose of general demoralization. The female missionaries who recently visited England for the purpose of preaching " The Right to Motherhood " — a theory which was of course given wide publicity in the Press — were not solitary enthusiasts who had evolved this theory out of their own inner consciousness, but mouthpieces repeating a phrase that has long been current in the language of illuminized Freemasonry and forms a part of the plan for the break up of family life. [1]

[1] M. Copin Albancelli, writing in 1910, described the campaign being carried out by " the Occult Power " for the demoralization of French women and children: " All facilities of corruption . . . are offered to mothers of families — the family, they go so far as to say, must be destroyed

Nothing is more extraordinary than the way apparently intelligent women have allowed themselves to be drawn into a plot of which they will be the chief victims. Women have obviously far more to lose than men by the destruction or even by a decrease of civilization, whilst the Suffragist has everything to lose by the abolition of the Parliamentary system which accords her the vote she has so long demanded, but the modern Illuminati, following Weishaupt's precepts by " flattering their vanity " and giving them " hints of emancipation," have succeeded in persuading numbers of women to assist in digging their own graves. These words of warning written 123 years ago might well be laid to heart by the women of our country and of America today:

There is nothing in the whole constitution of the Illuminati that strikes me with more horror than the proposals of Hercules and Minos to enlist the women in this shocking warfare with all that " is good and pure, and lovely, and of good report." They could not have fallen on any expedient that will be more effectual and fatal. If any of my countrywomen shall honour these pages with a reading, I would call on them, in the most earnest manner, to consider this as an affair of the utmost importance to themselves. I would conjure them, by the regard they have for their own dignity and for their rank in society, to join against these enemies of human nature and profligate degraders of their sex; and I would assure them that the present state of things almost puts it in their power to be the saviours of the world. But if they are remiss, and yield to the seduction, they will fall from that high state to which they have arisen in Christian Europe and again sink into that insignificancy or slavery in which the sex is found in all ages and countries out of the hearing of Christianity.

For as Robison truly adds:

Woman is indebted to Christianity alone for the high rank she holds in society. . . . It is undoubtedly Christianity that has set woman on her throne. . . .

If not only Christianity but all religion is to be destroyed, then indeed women will sink to a condition which Robison describes as lower than a " Mahomedan paradise."

. . . prostitution is honoured . . . conferences are held in its temples (of the Grand Orient) on free maternity (*la libre maternité*) " (*Le Pouvoir occulte contre la France*, pp. 417, 418).

But even more horrible than the degradation of women is the systematic demoralization of children which is now being carried out by the conspiracy. The plan of Weishaupt for obtaining influence in the schools has been followed by the establishment of Socialist Sunday Schools, attended, it is said, by no less than 10,000 children in the United Kingdom, where the poison of class-hatred, of greed, and of materialism is sedulously instilled into the child-mind.

At the same time, still following faithfully in the footsteps of Weishaupt, our Illuminati are careful to win the sympathy of " those who have a hankering for religion," by telling off a few of their number to profess the doctrines of Christian Socialism. Thus Mr. Lansbury, returning from the land whose Government has adopted as its motto, " Religion is opium to the people," where the churches have been desecrated and Christians crucified for their faith, proclaims in the same breath his allegiance to Christ and Lenin. Bebel, the German Socialist, was more honest when he declared: " Christianity and Socialism stand towards each other as fire and water." Yet in the face of such declarations we find a dignitary of the Church of England proclaiming that " if Christ came to earth today He would be a Bolshevik." Can we not hear again the exulting tones of Weishaupt saying, " The most admirable thing of all is that great Protestant and reformed theologians who belong to our Order really believe they see in it the true and genuine mind of the Christian religion. Oh! man, what cannot you be brought to believe! "

Not amongst the Protestant clergy alone is this strange delusion to be found; Catholics likewise have allowed themselves to be blinded to the real forces at work behind the troubles in Ireland. Have they forgotten the warnings of their eloquent predecessor the Abbé Barruel? Do they forget the prophecy of Cardinal Manning, now so terribly fulfilled: " On the day when all the armies of Europe will be engaged in an immense conflict, then, that day, the revolution which until now has been working secretly underground will have found the favourable moment to show itself in the light of day " ?

Cardinal Manning repeatedly warned his generation of the danger of Secret Societies; Monsignor Dillon still more clearly indicated the nature of the formidable sect that was to bring about this consummation, and also the occult force behind it:

" We only want a knowledge of the evil to avoid it . . . all secret societies aiming at bad and irreligious ends are no other than *deadly illuminated Freemasonry.* Let them be called by whatever name, they are a part of the system of revolutionary fraud, invented and cast upon earth by Satan to compass the ruin of souls and the destruction of the reign of Jesus Christ." The final end is " to form, and that before very many years, the vast kingdom of anti-Christ, which already spreads its ramifications over the whole earth." Only by a realization of this truth can the true meaning of the World Revolution be understood. Neither greed of gold nor power, neither political nor social theories, however subversive, could alone have produced the unspeakable horrors, the moral perversion, the far more than bestial cruelties that have marked its course. The description of " bloody baboonery " applied to Bolshevist atrocities is unjust to apes. Beasts may wound and kill — they do not torture, do not gloat over the sufferings of their victims; savages may do these things, but even they content themselves with torturing the body, they do not set out to destroy the soul. The spirit of evil that finds expression in the defilement and desecration of sacred things, in the systematic destruction of all nobility, all decency of thought and life, above all, in the poisoning of the child-mind, can be explained by no natural laws or mere human passions.

Let us not forget that the cult of Satan which flourished in Bavaria at the same time as Illuminism, and was in all probability connected with it, is practised today in our own country. The powers exercised by the modern Illuminati are occult powers and range from hypnotism to black magic, which, since the days of the magician Cagliostro, have always formed part of the stock-in-trade of the sect. It is therefore no fantastic theory but the literal truth to say that the present world crisis is a conflict between the powers of good and evil. Christianity is a beleaguered citadel surrounded by the dark forces which have mustered for the supreme onslaught. Only in one way can it be withstood. The words of Joseph de Maistre, who, like Barruel, regarded the French Revolution merely as the first stage in the campaign, must be taken as the battle-cry of the White Army today: " The French Revolution is Satanic in its principle and can be only really killed, exterminated, and finished by the contrary principle." (" La Révolution française est satanique dans son principe et ne peut être vraiment tuée, exterminée, finie que par le principe contraire.") The Christian principle — that is the force that must be opposed to the Satanic power of the World Revolution.

It is because England, with all her shortcomings, in spite of the recent betrayal of her traditions in the compact entered into with the Bolsheviks by her politicians, in spite of the attempts to poison the life-blood of her people with alien germs of corruption, yet remains the stronghold of Christian civilization, that the conspiracy has made her the principal point of attack. If England goes the whole world goes with her. Marx knew this when he said: " Every revolution that does not spread to England is a storm in a tea-cup." And it was also Marx who uttered the cry of despair: " England is the rock on which revolutionary waves are broken! " Is that rock at last to be overwhelmed? Not if we hold fast to the same principle that has saved us in the past. It is recorded that the Comte de Provence when in England during the French Revolution " said to one of the gentlemen about him, that ' if this country was to escape the general wreck of nations, it would owe its preservation to religion.' " After the revolution of 1848 a Frenchman observed to Lord Shaftesbury: " You have been saved by the religion of your people." And today Lenin has declared the greatest obstacle to the success of Bolshevism in England to be the fact that the English working-man founds his ideas upon the Bible.

If the people of our country will but realize the diabolical nature of the conspiracy at work amongst them, the powers of Hell cannot prevail against us. In ignorance and indifference lie our principal danger. Every outbreak of the World Revolution that has so far occurred has been rendered possible by the apathy of the nation in general. Let the words of Barruel, uttered in the face of the same peril a hundred and twenty-five years ago, ring in our ears today:

Cease to flatter yourselves. The danger is certain, it is continual, it is terrible, it threatens you all without exception. Keep yourselves, however, from giving way to that kind of terror which is only cowardice and discouragement; for, with all the certainty of the danger, I say to you none the less: " Will to be saved and you will be saved. . . . *One cannot triumph over a nation that resolves to defend itself.* Know how to will as they do and you will have nothing more to fear from them."

Illuminism is mustering all its forces for a supreme onslaught in our own country at the present moment. But the nation at heart is sound and has resolved to defend itself. Is it possible that this little island of ours is finally to stem the tide of World Revolution and save not only herself but Christian civilization?

THE END

Made in the USA
Columbia, SC
18 April 2024

34576014R00187